HOWARD BARKER

For Kenny Ireland

HOWARD BARKER

COLLECTED PLAYS

VOLUME TWO

THE LOVE OF A GOOD MAN
THE POSSIBILITIES
BRUTOPIA
ROME
UNCLE VANYA
TEN DILEMMAS

CALDER PUBLICATIONS · RIVERRUN PRESS
Montreuil London New York

This edition first published in Great Britain in 1993 by
Calder Publications Limited
9–15 Neal Street, London WC2H 9TU

and in the U.S.A. in 1993 by
Riverrun Press Inc
1170 Broadway, New York, NY 10001

Copyright © Howard Barker 1980, 1987, 1993

All performing rights in these plays are strictly reserved and application
for performance should be made to:

Judy Daish Associates Limited, 83 Eastbourne Mews, London W2 6LQ

ALL RIGHTS RESERVED

British Library Cataloguing-in-Publication Data
Barker, Howard
    Collected Plays. – Vol.2: "Love of a Good
    Man", "The Possibilities", "Brutopia",
    "Rome", "Uncle Vanya", "Ten Dilemmas"
    I. Title
    822.914

ISBN 0-7145-4182-6

Library of Congress Cataloging-in-Publication Data
    Barker, Howard
      Collected Plays.
      (A Calderbook CB448)
      Contents: v. 2. Love of a good man; The possibilities;
    Brutopia; Rome; Uncle Vanya; Ten dilemmas. I. Title.
    PR6052.A6485A19 1993   822'.914   88-36769
    ISBN 0-7145-4182-6

The right of Howard Barker to be identified as the author of this work has been
asserted by him in accordance with the Copyright Design and Patents Act 1988.

Any paperback editions of this book whether published simultaneously with, or
subquent to, the hardback edition is sold subject to the condition that it shall not,
by way of trade or otherwise, be lent, resold, hired out, or otherwise disposed of
without the publisher's prior consent in any form of binding or cover other than
that in which it is published and without a similar condition being imposed on the
subsequent purchaser.

Apart from any fair dealing for the purposes of research or private study, or
criticism or review, as permitted under the Copyright, Designs and Patents Act,
1988, this publication may not be reproduced, stored or transmitted, in any form
or by any means, without the prior consent of the publishers, or in the case of
reprographic reproduction in accordance with the terms of licences issued by the
Copyright Licensing Agency, London. Inquiries concerning reproduction outside
those terms should be sent to the publishers.

Typeset in 9/10pt Times by Pure Tech Corporation, Pondicherry, India.
Printed in Great Britain by Loader Jackson Printers, Arlesey, Bedfordshire.

CONTENTS

	page
The Love of a Good Man	6
The Possibilities	75
Brutopia	129
Rome	197
Uncle Vanya	291
Ten Dilemmas	343

THE LOVE OF A GOOD MAN

CHARACTERS

PRINCE OF WALES	Heir to the English Throne
GENTLEMAN	His Equerry
FLOWERS	An Army Sergeant
HACKER	An Undertaker
CLOUT	His Assistant
RIDDLE	A Soldier
BASS	A Soldier
TROD	A Soldier
MRS TOYNBEE	A Bereaved Parent
LALAGE	Her Daughter
BRIDE	A Commissioner for Graves
COLONEL HARD	A Recruiter
BISHOP	

ACT ONE

Scene One

A part of Passchendaele in 1920. Looking over a scene of desolation, the PRINCE OF WALES. *He wears a bowler hat and clasps a pair of gloves behind his back. Pause.*

PRINCE: Feel sick. (*Pause*) Somebody. (*Pause*) **Feel sick!** (*A* GENTLEMAN OF THE HOUSEHOLD *hurries in and assists the* PRINCE *into a stooping posture. Pause. The* PRINCE *straightens.*) Want to say something. Want to be apt and truthful. Do you understand? Feel the need for it.

GENTLEMAN: Sir.

PRINCE: For lovely words.

GENTLEMAN: Sir.

PRINCE: Can make it better, if you find the proper words. (*Pause*) Sorry, for example.

GENTLEMAN: Sorry?

PRINCE: Yes. Good word. Cheapened by over-use, that's all. But in this context, perfect. In this context, pure poetry. (*He points to the horizon.*) Get it up there, d'ye see? In hundred foot high letters. Spanning Flanders. **Sorry.** Coloured lights on it at night!

GENTLEMAN: Yes. (*Pause*)

PRINCE: Wish I spoke better. Wish I had an education. Didn't like Sandhurst at all. There is a man down there. Digging.

GENTLEMAN: Oh, yes. So there is.

PRINCE: Fetch him, will you?

GENTLEMAN: Fetch him?

PRINCE: Up here, please. (*Reluctantly, the* GENTLEMAN *beckons.*)

GENTLEMAN: Can't see me.

PRINCE: Shout, then. Please. (*Pause while the* GENTLEMAN *clears his throat.*)

GENTLEMAN: Hey.

10 *Howard Barker*

PRINCE: No. Shout. (GENTLEMAN *looks at him.*) You know. Shout.

GENTLEMAN: **Hey!**

PRINCE: Seen us. (GENTLEMAN *beckons wildly.*) I shall be King of England soon. When Daddy's cancer gets the better of him.

GENTLEMAN: Yes, indeed.

PRINCE: Very funny thing to be.

GENTLEMAN: I don't see why.

PRINCE: Unusual.

GENTLEMAN: Possibly.

PRINCE: Like to be good at it. Like to make a decent go of it. Win the people's hearts and so on.

GENTLEMAN: You already have.

PRINCE: And do things, too. (*Pause*)

GENTLEMAN: What things?

PRINCE: They do have such a lot of power, don't they? Kings? Daddy chose the generals.

GENTLEMAN: Yes.

PRINCE: Rather badly, I believe . . . (*A MAN in a leather garment enters, holding a spade.*)

FLOWERS: Guv? (*Pause. They examine him.*)

PRINCE: T–t–tell me, w–w–were you a soldier of the war?

FLOWERS: I was.

PRINCE: Please may I k–k–kiss your hand?

GENTLEMAN: **Kiss his hand?**

PRINCE: Please? (FLOWERS *extends a muddy hand. The* PRINCE *kneels and takes his hand to his lips.*)

GENTLEMAN: **He is a commoner!**

PRINCE: Do you know who I am?

FLOWERS: I 'ave a rough idea, guv.

PRINCE: I am Edward, Prince of Wales.

FLOWERS: Tha's what I reckoned. (*Pause*)

PRINCE: I wish you to know that I am sorry.

FLOWERS: What for?

GENTLEMAN: You see, there isn't really any point in this.

PRINCE: Now ask me to rise, will you?

GENTLEMAN: Ask you to **what!**

PRINCE: Will you, please? The ground is rather wet.

FLOWERS: Rise, please. (*The* PRINCE *gets up, brushes his coat.*)

PRINCE: Stained the new coat Mummy gave me.

GENTLEMAN: Dear, oh, dear! Look at it! (*He begins rubbing it with a handkerchief.*)

PRINCE: She can always get another one.

THE LOVE OF A GOOD MAN
11

GENTLEMAN: That's all very well, but coats cost money!

PRINCE: His hand had mud on it . . .

GENTLEMAN: Better let it dry, I think.

PRINCE: Did it get onto my lips?

GENTLEMAN (*stands up, looks at the* PRINCE's *mouth*): No.

PRINCE: The ground here is alive with tetanus. Suppose I had a small cut on my lip?

GENTLEMAN (*looking closely*): Can't see one . . .

PRINCE: I might have died from it . . . (*He muses on the idea.* FLOWERS *goes out unobserved.*) This will get around, won't it? That I knelt to a common soldier?

GENTLEMAN: Their Majesties will splutter. I shall feel the Royal saliva.

PRINCE: It will get in the papers, though?

GENTLEMAN: I imagine he is heading for the nearest journalist.

PRINCE: What was he doing here? All the troops went home, surely?

GENTLEMAN: Some were kept back. To re-inter the corpses. Shall we go? (*He starts to move off. The* PRINCE *is frozen. Pause.*)

PRINCE: Feel sick. (*Pause*) Somebody! (*Pause*) **Feel sick!**

Scene Two

THREE MEN, *dressed in Wellington boots and heavy coats, come in, carrying dividers, plans, maps, etc.*

HACKER: I took on more labour. I don't like taking labour but there was this contract going begging and I would 'ave been an idiot to pass it up. Silly, I know, but I am timid about labour. I would say there is a ratio between workers and bother. The more workers the more bother. I tried to take the sons of my existing masons but most of 'em were dead, so I 'ave been obliged to take on strangers. I expect wage demands. I expect all kinds of nonsense, but I will deliver. No question of that. Won't I, Clout? I will deliver.

CLOUT: Your strong point, Mr 'acker, is delivery.

HACKER: Loyal, ain't he? Fuckin' parrot. Always says the right thing. No, I love him, I do. Now, what's the situation?

BRIDE: Before I go into that. I wonder if I might ask you something?

12 *Howard Barker*

HACKER: Fire away.

BRIDE: That you are careful not to swear. (*Pause*)

HACKER: Swear? Did I swear?

BRIDE: Yes.

HACKER: Oh. Beg pardon.

BRIDE: I wasn't thinking of myself. I was referring to our situation. You see, I don't expect you swear in church. (*Pause*)

HACKER: Not often.

BRIDE: And this is a church. I think we have to regard this whole enterprise as the building of a church.

HACKER: A church.

BRIDE: Yes.

HACKER: Right. (*Pause*) That cuts out the swearing, then.

BRIDE: There are a million dead men here.

HACKER: Yup.

BRIDE: A million Englishmen.

HACKER: And as many monuments, of which five thousand will be mine. 'and chiselled in my Peckham factory. It will be time and 'alf on Sundays for a year, but they will be a credit to the Empire, Mr Bride, I promise yer.

BRIDE: This is not so much a contract with the government. It is a contract with our dead people.

HACKER: Mr Bride, I am a rough character, perhaps, but if you scratch me I do bleed. Clout 'ere will tell you I am not impervious to grief. I am 'ere to make money, I make no bones about it. I am in business. But I 'ave a soul. The idea got around during the war that businessmen do not 'ave souls. But did we not lose our boys as well? Not me personally, but the business people did. Money was made on the one 'and, but sons were slain on the other. Now either we are animals or the system's buggered. Take yer pick, I 'ave no answers, do I, Clout? I am not a provider of answers any more than you.

CLOUT: What's the stake-out, Mr Bride?

BRIDE: This ridge we are standing on is about a thousand yards in length. It changed hands many times during the war. They do not know how often, but it got very bloody, being so exposed, you see. And as a consequence, it is very deep in bodies. I do not want to dramatize, but where we are standing is not ground so much as flesh. (*Pause*. HACKER *clears his throat.*)

HACKER: Nasty business.

CLOUT: When we got out the taxi, I said to Mr Hacker, isn't there a smell?

HACKER: All right, Clout.

THE LOVE OF A GOOD MAN 13

CLOUT: I know we're in a church, but definitely there is a smell.

HACKER: **All right.**

BRIDE: This ridge is designated No. 14 Cemetery. It will be according to the Commission's specifications. At least there is no drainage problem here. If you want me, I shall be here. I am recording everything.

HACKER: A lifetime's work, Mr Bride.

BRIDE: It must be written and recorded. Every death and every maiming. There is no truth in war except this truth.

HACKER: I wonder if it isn't best forgotten? All that. A decent veil drawn over it.

BRIDE: I am presenting the bill, Mr Hacker. It is my mission. Ignore the dead and you will cheat the living.

HACKER: Cheat, Mr Bride?

BRIDE: This place has been the scene of awful lies. Such lies as nearly swamped humanity. We must not cheat the people of their consciences. We must name names. All million of them! Till we are dizzy with the lists!

HACKER: Yes. Right.

BRIDE: Dazzle them with suffering!

HACKER: Right.

BRIDE: Christ, man, would you draw a veil across all this?

HACKER: No. (*Pause*) No, of course, I wouldn't. Just a suggestion. A silly one, I see that now.

BRIDE: I am against all veils. Give the dead their voice!

HACKER: Absolutely.

BRIDE: Which is your task, Hacker. You will orchestrate their suffering. (*He looks into* HACKER's *eyes.*)

HACKER: Yup. (*Pause, then* BRIDE *turns and goes out. They watch him disappear.*)

HACKER: Bananas. Fuckin' bananas.

CLOUT: Swearing.

HACKER: Fuck swearing!

CLOUT (*shrugs*): All right.

HACKER: I don't want lecturing. I didn't come to Belgium for a lecturing. I 'ave respect. My own respect. Let me do it my way. Not bananas fashion, thank you very much.

CLOUT: Funny. Funny though.

HACKER: What?

CLOUT: Standing on — a million dead Englishmen — did he say?

HACKER: Something like that.

CLOUT: Not so much ground, he said, more 'uman flesh . . .

14 *Howard Barker*

HACKER: Give over, Clout.

CLOUT: Creepy, Mr 'acker.

HACKER: Yeah, well, it will be if you give into it.

CLOUT: It's getting dark, Mr 'acker. Shall we get back to the lodging 'ouse?

HACKER: Yeah, why not? Fleas are getting 'ungry, I expect. (*They go a few yards. HACKER stops.*) Yer know, Clout, this is easy money. Let's be honest for a minute, this is cream and fucking jam. I can't see myself going back to ordinary funerals after this. All the whispering and decorum. Stuff it. It's wars for me in future. Someone's got to benefit.

CLOUT: Mr 'acker, I'm sorry, I'm getting the creeps.

HACKER: Got to get used to it, ol' son. Going to be 'ere bloody months.

CLOUT: I know, Mr 'acker, but — **Whass that!** (*He grabs HACKER's arm impulsively.*)

HACKER: **Shuddup!** (*Pause. They are holding each other's arms.*) Git. Look at me. Made me jump, yer git. (*He shakes off CLOUT's hand, prepares to move on.*)

CLOUT: **There it is!** (*He grabs HACKER again.*)

HACKER: What! Fuck it! What?

CLOUT: 'eard it.

HACKER. 'eard what? (*There is a faint sound of singing.*) Oh, bloody 'ell, what do they have to fight wars 'ere for? In the middle of a bleedin' swamp . . . ?

CLOUT (*pointing*): **It's dead men!**

HACKER: Clout. Come 'ere, will yer?

CLOUT (*starting to run*): Sorry, Mr 'acker, I can't —

HACKER: **Clout!** (*CLOUT disappears. HACKER hesitates. The singing gets louder.*) It's only — **Clout!** (*He tears after him in a panic.*)

The singing grows louder. FOUR MEN *enter, dressed in leather garments which virtually conceal soiled army uniforms beneath. They carry shovels and each holds the corner of a large canvas bag. They sing to the tune of* 'She was a Bird in a Gilded Cage'.

FLOWERS: It was only a corpse in a canvas bag,
BASS: A wonderful sight to see,
TROD: With no bollocks or legs,
  With no arse and no 'ead,
  Why is it so fucking 'eavy?

THE LOVE OF A GOOD MAN 15

They dump the bag unceremoniously.

FLOWERS: Our picturesque language. Our funny songs that kept us faithful in the midst of death. Us cockney sparrers. Us criminals and layabouts made decent for a royal kiss. (*He rolls a cigarette.*)

BASS: Still in Flanders. Two years after the armistice. While Vickers, Krupp and Schneider get their scrap metal back, slightly imperfect owing to its passage through the human body, and Belgian whores we fucked in cellars buy up the farms as soon as we have cleared the corpses of their clients out of it.

FLOWERS: If someone 'as to do this job, why not the chinks and wogs? What is the Empire for if this degrading labour ain't given over to the chinks and wogs? (*He lights his cigarette.*)

RIDDLE: Are we ready? I would like to be pissed in time for bed, and twilight's dirty fingers are creeping into our moist crevices.

FLOWERS: Mr Riddle has spoken. We may shove on.

BASS: Before the war I never met a type like Riddle. Then suddenly, there were hundreds of 'em. It opens whole perspectives up, a war. The longer they go on, the more you see. A couple more years and England's innards would have been hanging out, all red and twitching. It would have been a bloody great dissecting room.

FLOWERS: Compared with clearing battlefields, fighting was 'ealthy. It is clearing battlefields that's made young lads like Trod 'ere go mysterious. That is why I urged the use of chinks and wogs. I wrote this to *The Times*, and Riddle 'ere, with 'is command of English, phrased it for me. But widows and vicars were outraged. It made ex-majors' noses bleed. The general opinion was the English soldiers' flesh would shrink from the touch of blacks. I said we could 'ave issued 'em with gloves. In any case, whoever 'eard a corpse protest?

TROD: You have no ears to hear them. I hear them.

FLOWERS: You see what I say about Trod?

TROD: You are frightened of death. Because I understand death you mock me.

FLOWERS: I don't mock you, son, I pity you.

RIDDLE: It is rather damp here and I am thin. I have reason to believe I have rudimentary TB. Shall we push on?

BASS: Silly to die at this stage, Riddle. After what you've been through. You would look a silly bugger to your friends.

RIDDLE: I have no friends.

16   *Howard Barker*

FLOWERS: Did you not 'ave a mate killed, Mr Riddle? A painter or a poet or something?

RIDDLE: They talk about the friendships of the war, but they were not friendships. They were the whimperings of shared discomforts. None has survived the peace. The mania for bonhommie is the most disgusting fetishism of war. I could fight for twenty years if it were not for the singing.

TROD: I had a friend —

FLOWERS: So you did, son, but we don't wanna go into that now, do we?

BASS: We don't. Shove on. (*They bend to the canvas bag, each taking a corner.*)

FLOWERS:⎫ It looked like a body, but it was all shit,
BASS: ⎬ It was no grave that was marked with a cross,
TROD: ⎭ We shovelled away,
             At this fucking French clay,
             While the turds giggled in piss, blood and toss!

Scene Three

Morning. Two English women are staring over the battlefield. Pause.

MRS TOYNBEE: Do you feel anything yet?

LALAGE: No.

MRS TOYNBEE: I do.

LALAGE: I expected you to.

MRS TOYNBEE: In my womb.

LALAGE: But of course.

MRS TOYNBEE: It goes hot. (*Pause*) Yes! There! (*She takes* LALAGE's *hand.*) Feel it! (*She places* LALAGE's *hand on her belly.*) Convulses!

LALAGE: Can't find it . . .

MRS TOYNBEE: Yes, there! Oh!

LALAGE (*turning away, walking from her*): I suppose this is Hill 60? We have got it right? (*She looks at a map.*) Not that there are many hills. If you can so dignify these miserable humps . . . (*She turns back.*) Have you finished, mother, please? (*Pause.* MRS TOYNBEE *opens her eyes.*)

MRS TOYNBEE: I have never known that before. I will put it in my diary.

THE LOVE OF A GOOD MAN

LALAGE: What about Mahler's Fifth?

MRS TOYNBEE: What about it?

LALAGE: Look in your diary. It got to your womb.

MRS TOYNBEE: Don't remember.

LALAGE: Everything seems to get to your womb. I suppose you are that kind of woman.

MRS TOYNBEE: Well, I am a woman, most certainly.

LALAGE: Me too.

MRS TOYNBEE: I'm glad. I'm glad we are women. Bereaved men are a pitiful sight.

LALAGE: Can't cope, you mean? Poor, silly dears?

MRS TOYNBEE: Compared to us, yes. They are poor, silly dears.

LALAGE: I don't have that view of men. Not at all.

MRS TOYNBEE: You don't know them.

LALAGE: Well, of course not. Not like you.

MRS TOYNBEE: They are not used to expressing real feelings.

LALAGE: They have no wombs.

MRS TOYNBEE (*patiently*): It is not sex that draws them towards us. It is the sheer luxury of being sincere.

LALAGE: Well, you seem to know all about them.

MRS TOYNBEE: I've had the opportunity to form an opinion. You have not.

LALAGE: No. And I don't want to. I hate the idea there are things called men. Things which experience will teach you to handle. Like ponies or dogs.

MRS TOYNBEE: We are standing among them. They are lying under our feet. They are lying as far as the eye can see. Ranks deep . . . (*Pause*) No two women have ever been surrounded by so much male flesh . . . When they find Billy they want to put him in the official, standard grave. There is even a uniform headstone. I am not having that for him.

LALAGE: They may not find him.

MRS TOYNBEE: Oh yes, he will come back. And when he does, I am claiming him.

LALAGE: They won't like that.

MRS TOYNBEE: Of course not. But two women can do a great deal. We will take him back to England and bury him under the tree.

LALAGE: Is that what he wanted? I never knew.

MRS TOYNBEE: He worshipped the tree.

LALAGE: He was fond of it, I know.

MRS TOYNBEE: Hills and trees. You knew Billy. Look at his poems. All hills and trees.

LALAGE: Yes, but did he actually say —

MRS TOYNBEE: Lalage, I am bringing my son home! (*Pause*)

LALAGE: A million corpses coming home. That would be grotesque . . .

MRS TOYNBEE: I am not bringing a million. Everything is repulsive that everybody does. Every moving gesture, every beautiful thought, is hideous in proportion to its popularity. This is between Billy and us. (BRIDE *comes in, accompanied by* FLOWERS *and* TROD, *carrying plans and ledger.*)

BRIDE: Are you ladies off the Cook's Battlefields tour?

MRS TOYNBEE: Certainly not.

BRIDE: There are unexploded things round here.

MRS TOYNBEE: We aren't afraid.

BRIDE: We have quite enough dead.

MRS TOYNBEE: My son among them. (BRIDE *stops.*)

BRIDE. Hill 60?

MRS TOYNBEE: Toynbee. Second Lieutenant.

BRIDE (*aroused*): P. Toynbee? Scots Guards?

MRS TOYNBEE: No. W. Hussars. (BRIDE *cogitates.*)

FLOWERS: 'e 'as a million names jammed in 'is 'ead. Ask 'im who's prime minister, who won the Derby, when 'e last 'ad a piss, 'e couldn't tell yer, but who died by bayonet and who by bomb —

BRIDE: August the eighth.

MRS TOYNBEE: Correct.

BRIDE: Missing, presumed dead. Aged twenty-eight.

MRS TOYNBEE. Twenty.

BRIDE (*shocked*): Twenty? Are you sure?

MRS TOYNBEE: Of course I'm sure. (BRIDE *concentrates his memory, starts to go out.*) Where do we look?

BRIDE (*stops*): Look? He is missing, isn't he? There is everywhere to look. Or nowhere. (*He goes out.*)

MRS TOYNBEE (*to* FLOWERS): But he will show up? His body must eventually show up?

FLOWERS: They don't just kill yer. They destroy yer. Where a geezer might have been standing, there is just a black hole in the mud, and a trickling as the water drains back into it. You could argue that somewhere 'e still exists. Matter, I 'ave 'eard, is indestructible. But not impossible to separate, alas. (*He follows* BRIDE *out.* TROD *hangs back. Pause.*)

TROD: The dead do not die. (*Pause. The* WOMEN *look at him.*)

LALAGE: What do they do, then?

TROD: Transhabilitate. (*They look at him.*)

THE LOVE OF A GOOD MAN

LALAGE: And what is that? (*Pause.* TROD *looks to see that* FLOWERS *is out of sight and sound.*)

TROD: I had a friend. Have you got time?

MRS TOYNBEE: All the time in the world.

TROD: He was beautiful. He was holy. I never looked at him without thinking I stood in a fountain of pure light. He had been a shepherd and it had brought him near to God. Not God. Not the God. But another God. Also called God.

MRS TOYNBEE: Yes . . .

TROD (*looking over his shoulder for* FLOWERS): During his shepherding, the secret of Transhabilitation had been revealed to him by a saintly sheep. The sheep was known as Trotters. Have you got time?

MRS TOYNBEE (*cooling*): I think we have, yes . . .

TROD: During a trance this holy ewe revealed that England was a segment of the moon, broken off and crashed near Europe aeons ago. The inhabitants of the moon had been herbivorous quadrupeds.

FLOWERS (*appearing left*): Come on, Trod!

TROD: Damn. Bloody damn.

MRS TOYNBEE: They seem to want you.

TROD: To keep it brief, the lunar quadrupeds, breathing the terrestrial aether —

FLOWERS: **Fuck it! Come on!**

LALAGE: Perhaps we could hear a bit more later.

TROD: He meant there is no death, only re-ordering of spirit —

FLOWERS: **Trod.** (TROD *turns to go, then stops, looks at* MRS TOYNBEE.)

TROD: You are very beautiful. I don't know what you looked like before, but it has touched you with beauty. (*He hurries away. Pause.*)

MRS TOYNBEE: Has it?

LALAGE: Billy's death?

MRS TOYNBEE: Put a little shadow in my face?

LALAGE: Max Factor's Stricken Mum . . .

MRS TOYNBEE *turns on her, just as* CLOUT *appears carrying a wooden peg and a mallet. He hammers the peg into the ground, and begins measuring from it with a linen tape. At the requisite distance, he hammers in a second peg.* HACKER *comes in, reading from the official plan.*

HACKER (*quoting*): Footpaths will traverse the cemetery at angles

20   *Howard Barker*

corresponding to the pattern of the Union Jack . . . fuck . . . did
we bring a Union Jack? I think we can assume we didn't . . . (*He
reads on.*) With the cross of sacrifice placed at the confluence . . .
the confluence . . . **The confluence?** Bugger this. (*He reads on.*)
Each section thus delineated will contain sufficient area for one
hundred graves, the surface of each grave to be eight foot by four.
Got that, Clout?

CLOUT: Eight foot by four.

HACKER: Correct. And not an inch more. 'ave 'em spilling over,
otherwise. Did yer bring the flask with yer?

CLOUT (*measuring*): In the bag, Mr 'acker.

HACKER: Got to keep the sodding damp out, 'aven't we? (*He sees
the women.*) Morning, ladies. Cheerful business, ain't it? (*He
removes the flask from* CLOUT's *bag.*) Note the Frogs 'ave
scarcely bothered. Just chuck the spare bits in a bonery. Mind
you, it's their crops stand to benefit. Fertilizing on this scale 'as
no precedent. 'ave you an interest in this?

MRS TOYNBEE: A dead boy.

HACKER: Well, no doubt you are thoroughly nauseated with official sympathy, so we won't add our little voices to the chorus,
will we, Clout?

CLOUT: Sir.

HACKER: There is so much 'ypocrisy about yer could launch a
ship on it. (*He indicates the string line.*) This 'ere will be the
central road of the cemetery, north–south.

CLOUT: West–east, Mr 'acker.

HACKER: West–east, is it? Got ears all over 'im. Good job I
wasn't making an improper suggestion to the lady, Clout
would 'ave been a party to it. No, 'e's a good lad. I love 'im,
don't I, Clout? (*Silence*) Now pretends 'e can't 'ear. Bloody 'ell,
this coffee's disgusting, Clout. It is the drippings of the stable
gutters, son. (*He casts it away, screws the lid on the flask.*)

LALAGE: Shall we move on?

MRS TOYNBEE (*to* HACKER): Are you —

HACKER: 'acker.

MRS TOYNBEE: Hacker. And you are — burying the dead?

HACKER: Building a Garden of the Fallen, actually.

MRS TOYNBEE: I see.

HACKER: I am the contractor for No. 81. I put in my estimate
and got it. Rock bottom, practically a loss, but a beginning. A
man with a government contract shall not starve. I 'ave also
tendered for Gallipoli. They say the sunsets over Lesbos are
remarkable.

THE LOVE OF A GOOD MAN

MRS TOYNBEE: All the dead, then, come to you?

HACKER: Funny way of putting it. Sounds like the Day of Judgement.

MRS TOYNBEE: All right. Pass through your hands?

HACKER: I suppose so, yeah. (*He looks at her, closely.*)

MRS TOYNBEE: I see. Mr Hacker. (*Pause. He cannot take his eyes away.*)

HACKER: Ronald, if you like.

MRS TOYNBEE: We are staying in the village.

HACKER: So are we. Getting fed on Christ knows what at Monte Carlo prices. Bitten by the Belgian flea.

MRS TOYNBEE: I expect we'll see a lot of one another.

HACKER: Every morning, should you wish. Squelching about. Though the Passchendaele mud doesn't seem to stick to you. You are very neat and spotless. (*Pause*)

MRS TOYNBEE: Well, good-morning.

HACKER: Good-morning, Madam. (*The* WOMEN *start to go.* MRS TOYNBEE *turns.*)

MRS TOYNBEE: I am Sylvia Toynbee. (HACKER *nods, smiles, the* WOMEN *go out. He watches them disappear.*)

HACKER: Oh, God our 'elp in ages past . . . (*Pause*) I could use 'er shit as toothpaste . . . (*Pause*) I could crawl across three fields of broken glass just for a piss in 'er bathwater . . .

CLOUT: Got the plan, please, Mr 'acker?

HACKER: Ronald, you are buggered for concentration now . . .

CLOUT: Plan, Mr 'acker?

HACKER: Fuck it, Clout! The plan, the plan! Did you see that?

CLOUT: Sir.

HACKER: Well, what does that do to yer measurements?

CLOUT: Very pleasant lady. sir.

HACKER (*looking down at* CLOUT): Oh, the little urges of the little man. Never mind, Clout, 'ere's yer plan. (*He drops the plan on the ground.*) Out of all this — filth and squalor — comes forth sweetness. I shall never feel disgusted by a corpse again.

Scene Four

The same place, late at night. Someone is smoking a cigarette. Pause.

22   *Howard Barker*

LALAGE (*coming in*): Is that you? (*The cigarette does not reply.*)
Is it? (*Pause*) **Please, is that you?**

RIDDLE: Yes.

LALAGE: Why don't you answer?

RIDDLE: I like the shake in your voice.

LALAGE: I've cut myself. My leg is bleeding.

RIDDLE: There is a lot of old iron up here.

LALAGE: Will you take my hand please? I've come such a long
way. My knees are shaking. Take my hand, **please.** (*He stands,
gives her his hand. They sit. Pause.*) Did you fight here?

RIDDLE: No.

LALAGE: Did you shoot anyone?

RIDDLE: I don't talk about the war.

LALAGE: What do you talk about?

RIDDLE: You want to talk, not me.

LALAGE: Yes, I do. I have to talk. I'm nervous and I have to talk.
I haven't been with many men. (*Brief pause.*) What do you think
will happen to England now?

RIDDLE: I don't care.

LALAGE: It's bound to change, isn't it, though? There are women
doing men's jobs, for example. And more questions being asked.
I think it's very good that people ask more questions now. You
may kiss me if you want. (*Pause*) My mother organizes seances.
She invites other mothers to our house. They try to reach their
sons. They cry and have hysterics. I don't think we should give
in to it, do you? The war was superstition, we should —

RIDDLE: Place my hand there. (*Pause*)

LALAGE: Where?

RIDDLE: You place it there. (*Pause*)

LALAGE: Do you not really care about England? When you have
given such —

RIDDLE: Shh.

LALAGE: I must talk, really I have to —

RIDDLE: **Shh.** (*Pause*) There's someone here.

*BRIDE is standing looking over the battlefield. He has no trousers
on.*

BRIDE: Abbey. Abbey. Abbott. Abbott. Abbott. Abel. Abercrom-
bie. Abernathy. Abraham. Abraham. Ackerley. Ackerley. Ackerley. Ackerley. Ackock. Ackroyd. Ackroyd. Ackroyd. Ackroyd.
Ackroyd. Ackroyd. Ackroyd. Acland. Acland. Acton. Acton. Adcock. Adcock. Adcock. Addison. Addison. Adey. Adkin.

THE LOVE OF A GOOD MAN

RIDDLE *stands up as* BRIDE, *gathering momentum, removes a revolver from his jacket pocket and puts the barrel to his head.*

RIDDLE: Put it down, Bride. (*Silence, for some seconds.*)

BRIDE: Fuck. (*Pause*) Oh, fuck.

RIDDLE: They go off, you know. When you don't mean them to.

BRIDE (*his back still towards him*): Who is it?

RIDDLE: Riddle.

BRIDE: I thought I knew the voice.

RIDDLE: Please put it away, old boy. (*The revolver is lowered.*)

BRIDE: Resent this. Interference. Very much. (*He turns on him.*) I have a rank! My acting rank! (*Pause*) God . . . I forgot to put my trousers on . . .

RIDDLE: Never mind.

BRIDE: Oh, Christ . . .

RIDDLE: Nothing really matters. Ranks or trousers. Go home, now. (BRIDE *starts to go out, stops.*)

BRIDE: It was you last time, wasn't it?

RIDDLE: Yes, I spend a lot of time up here. (BRIDE *goes out. Pause.*) There are no bullets in his gun. But it's best to humour him. Everyone to his own agony. (*He looks at her.*)

LALAGE: What do you mean by saying nothing matters?

RIDDLE: Bride thinks the dead matter. I don't. But I don't think the living matter, either. England is having her recurring nightmare, isn't she? Crackerjacks and bangers. Mounted policemen in Trafalgar Square. A lot of angry soldiers asking what happened to their acre and their cow, clinging to some punctured lie. No one will lie to me. Rot England. I will make love to as many women as will have me. That way there is no lie. Will you have me? I have talked too much. (*Pause*)

LALAGE: You have not said a loving word to me. Or even called me by my name.

RIDDLE: No.

LALAGE: I don't know you.

RIDDLE: No. (*Pause*)

LALAGE: Good.

24   *Howard Barker*

Scene Five

Early next morning. LALAGE *is straightening her clothes after a night in the open.* MRS TOYNBEE *appears, looks at her.*

MRS TOYNBEE: You haven't slept in your bed.

LALAGE: No.

MRS TOYNBEE: You weren't at breakfast.

LALAGE: No. (*Pause*)

MRS TOYNBEE: Well, you must please yourself. What's the matter with your leg?

LALAGE: Barbed wire.

MRS TOYNBEE: You know there is tetanus round here?

HACKER *and* CLOUT *come in, followed by* FLOWERS, TROD *and* BASS.

FLOWERS: We're one short this morning. Mr Riddle is in bed with a cold, or 'is TB is nagging 'im, or 'is ulcers, or 'is varicose veins.

HACKER: Good morning, Mrs Sylvia Toynbee.

MRS TOYNBEE: Good morning, Mr Hacker.

HACKER: A nice one. A nice pink tinge in the sky. Do you like skies, Mrs Sylvia? I do. I have a set of lantern slides on skies. My favourite is 'Stratocumulus over the Pentland Firth'. (*He gazes up.*) I don't think there is a great deal to be said about these Belgian skies. When you think of Belgium you don't think of skies.

LALAGE: What do you think of?

HACKER: Getting skinned by the inhabitants, Miss.

FLOWERS: Poppies. (*They turn to him.*) Supposed to say poppies, aren't yer? Springing out of dead men's eyes? (*He turns to his men.*) Shall we move along, gents?

HACKER (*as they pass*): I 'ope you won't be getting under my feet, Flowers.

FLOWERS: We're raising bodies, guv'nor. The longer you leave it, the 'arder it gets.

HACKER: That may well be.

FLOWERS: Earth to earth is a very true saying.

HACKER: Is it? Go on.

FLOWERS: The human substance 'as a tendency to imitate the soil in which it's placed. In Palestine, our dead blokes are made of sand, while 'ere, unluckily, they absorb their weight in water and

THE LOVE OF A GOOD MAN   25

turn into mud. (*Categorically*) We are moving west to east. You'll 'ave to lump it.

HACKER: Discuss it with Bride. Bride is Graves Commissioner.

BASS (*stopping*): Mr 'acker. Bride will bend down for a finger. He would put an eyeball in 'is 'andkerchief. (MRS TOYNBEE *lets out a pathetic sob*. HACKER *turns in alarm*.)

HACKER: Clumsy idiot! (*He hurries to her side*.) Sylvia, love, I — (*He sees the* SOLDIERS *watching*.) Don't bloody gawp! Christ, everything is witnessed! (*He shakes out a handkerchief*.) 'ere, use this . . . (*He looks at* LALAGE.) Is she gonna faint?

MRS TOYNBEE: I may just . . . (*Pause*) No, I shan't faint . . . (*The* SOLDIERS *drift away*.)

HACKER: She isn't.

MRS TOYNBEE: I'm all right . . .

HACKER: She's all right.

LALAGE: When my mother was a girl to faint was sexual provocation. Now it's taken as a sign of malnutrition, but the habit's very difficult to break.

MRS TOYNBEE (*in full possession of herself again*): It gave men the opportunity to fulfil a need. A need to be powerful. Isn't that right, Mr Hacker? (*He clears his throat nervously*.) It was when I fainted that my husband fell in love with me. He wasn't a strong man, but I made him feel it. Naturally he was full of gratitude. When you look at me, Mr Hacker, don't you feel strong? (*He shifts uncomfortably*.)

HACKER: Clout, do you need to work under my feet?

CLOUT: Mr 'acker?

HACKER (*waving him away*): More that way, eh? (CLOUT *removes himself*. HACKER *turns back to* MRS TOYNBEE.) Where were we?

MRS TOYNBEE: I said when you look at me, don't you feel strong?

HACKER: Yes — I — I suppose I — (*Then, desperately*.) What happened to your 'usband, Mrs Toynbee? (*Pause. She turns away a little*.)

MRS TOYNBEE: When the Eastern Front collapsed he switched all our money into Russian tea. Buying in depressed markets was his speciality. We acquired the entire crop until 1960. Then, six months later, while we were at breakfast, I heard this funny little thud from behind the newspaper. It was his forehead on the tablecloth. The Bolsheviks had seized our tea. Coming on top of Billy's death, he became possessed by the idea we were a cursed family. He died insane, two days before the Armistice. I have

26   *Howard Barker*

tried to reach him through mediums, but they say he is trapped
in the aether . . . somewhere above Siberia.

HACKER: What a tragedy . . .

MRS TOYNBEE: Ronald, I want my Billy's body. I want to take
him home. (*Pause. HACKER is confused.*)

HACKER: Your boy Billy — you want —

MRS TOYNBEE: Help me.

HACKER: Well, I —

MRS TOYNBEE: Look into my eyes. (*He looks. Pause.*) Will you?

HACKER: Er . . .

MRS TOYNBEE: Answer my eyes.

HACKER: Er . . .

MRS TOYNBEE: Say yes. Say yes to my eyes.

HACKER: Sylvia . . .

MRS TOYNBEE: Say yes, I beg you.

HACKER: Yes. (*Pause*)

MRS TOYNBEE: Thank you.

HACKER: Yes what? What have I said yes to?

MRS TOYNBEE: Me. (*Pause. CLOUT is tapping in a peg.*)

HACKER: I think it's illegal, in fact, I know it is. (*She looks at
him, he shrugs.*) So what? It's illegal.

MRS TOYNBEE: Will you take my hand?

HACKER: If it's all right with you. (*She extends a hand, he takes
it, is about to kiss it, when she withdraws it. She gives him a slip
of paper.*)

MRS TOYNBEE: This is his name and number.

HACKER (*deeply aroused*): Christ, Sylvia, you do — (*There is a
sudden shout of despair from CLOUT.*)

CLOUT. **Oh, God 'elp us!** (*He flings down his shovel and runs to
HACKER.*)

HACKER: Control yerself, Clout!

CLOUT: I can't do this! I can't do this!

HACKER: Can't do what?

CLOUT: Dig 'ere! I can't dig 'ere, I won't!

HACKER. If yer want payin', yer will.

CLOUT. **Just put me spade through someone's 'ead!** (*Pause*)

HACKER: Clout. That is the sort of language that makes a lady faint.

MRS TOYNBEE: I am perfectly all right.

HACKER: You're in luck. She is perfectly all right. Now go and
fetch Mr Bride and tell 'im you 'ave uncovered somebody. 'e'll
know who it is, I expect. (*Pause*) Get along, son! (CLOUT *goes
out.*)

MRS TOYNBEE: It could be Billy.

THE LOVE OF A GOOD MAN

HACKER: Oh, I don't think so.

MRS TOYNBEE: Why ever not? He must be here somewhere, mustn't he?

HACKER: If you say so.

MRS TOYNBEE: I don't say so. It is the War Office who says so.

LALAGE (*who has wandered to the place*): It's a German.

MRS TOYNBEE (*turning*): Darling, do you have to look? (LALAGE *shrugs, walks back.*)

HACKER: Fine people, the Germans. In many ways. Got to admire 'em, 'aven't you?

MRS TOYNBEE: No, actually you haven't. (*Pause. He shrugs.*)

HACKER: Maybe not.

LALAGE: What do you mean, 'maybe not'?

HACKER: I've forgotten where I was now.

LALAGE: Why not admire them if you want? (*He shrugs.*) I admire them. As much as I admire anyone.

MRS TOYNBEE: They are not like other people.

LALAGE: It was only his uniform that marked him out.

MRS TOYNBEE: That is shallow. It is so easy to say everyone is just the same as everybody else. It is all the craze now. But because it is easy it does not make it true.

HACKER: Hear, hear.

MRS TOYNBEE: I hate the Germans because they don't know when to stop.

CLOUT *comes in, with* BRIDE. CLOUT *points at the place,* BRIDE *looks. Pause.*

BRIDE: Unfortunately, I haven't been able to compile a comprehensive German list. They have a different attitude to us. Mass graves and tiny granite tablets. As if there was something to be ashamed of in being dead . . . (*He comes to the others.*) Of course, they haven't been allowed to raise great monuments.

LALAGE: They can't afford it, can they? They've gone bust.

BRIDE: Is that so? I rarely see a newspaper.

LALAGE: I wonder if we wouldn't have done better by sending them something to eat. Instead of all these endless English cemeteries.

MRS TOYNBEE: No. Let's have the cemeteries.

LALAGE: The dead before the living?

BRIDE: Yes, oh, yes. (*Pause. He is about to go, stops.*) The most repulsive aspect of humanity is the ease with which it reproduces. If conception were more difficult, we would be less

28   *Howard Barker*

contemptuous of our lives. Were we pandas, should we have
fought the Battle of the Somme? (*He looks at* HACKER.) Mr
Hacker's stones will tell no lies. Count them. Each one had lips
to kiss. I loathe oblivion. I loathe the word forget.

LALAGE: They will forget. They will eat sandwiches here, and
bring their dogs to shit. (FLOWERS, BASS *and* TROD *come in,
carrying a canvas shelter.*)

BRIDE. It's a German. I will tell their people. (*He goes out, as the*
SOLDIERS *erect the shelter round the place.* CLOUT *is just
watching.*)

HACKER: Perhaps you could start that end, Clout? Rather than
'ang about?

CLOUT: Sorry, Mr 'acker. It was a shock.

HACKER: The first one always is, isn't that right, lads? Your first
corpse shakes yer, then it's like 'aving a fag? (RIDDLE *arrives
for work. He joins the soldiers.*)

BASS: 'ello, look who's 'ere.

RIDDLE: I overslept.

FLOWERS: 'ave to report it, Riddle.

RIDDLE: War's over two years, Mr Flowers. Report what you like.
(MRS TOYNBEE *and* LALAGE *start to go out.* LALAGE *hangs
back, speaks boldly to* RIDDLE.)

LALAGE: It was a beautiful night. (*They stop working, all look at
her, pause.*)

RIDDLE. Was it? (*She goes out, behind her mother.* TROD *watches
them.*)

TROD: I could not desire a woman who had not known death.

HACKER (*seeing to whom he refers*): Desire? What's desire got
to do with you?

BASS: Trod ain't in a fit condition to desire anyone.

FLOWERS: Six months in the 'ighlands 's what 'e wants. It's shell
shock with you, ain't it, Trod?

TROD (*still looking after the women*): A woman like that moves
you, turns your bowels . . .

FLOWERS (*looking at* BASS): Want to see the M.O. Get some
medicine for that.

HACKER: They are arresting blokes in London for that sort of
trench filth, Trod.

BASS: They would not arrest me, the bastards.

HACKER: No, well, you don't talk filth, do you?

BASS: They will not arrest me, I say.

HACKER: In fact, you 'ardly talk at all.

FLOWERS (*as he digs*): Is that the daughter? The trembling one?

THE LOVE OF A GOOD MAN

HACKER: It is Miss Toynbee, yes.

FLOWERS: She's over-ripe. Someone should pluck 'er or she's gonna drip.

HACKER: **You can't talk about people the way you do!**

BASS (*having thrust his spade*): Gone through the leg.

FLOWERS: Fuck the leg.

BASS: No. Get it up. Don't leave the leg.

FLOWERS: 's' a German.

BASS: Do it proper.

FLOWERS: Please yerself. (*He leans on his spade while* BASS *digs.*) So what about the daughter? On the subject of legs?

HACKER: 'er bum crack you couldn't slip a five pound note in.

FLOWERS: While the mother 'as an arse to swallow a donkey's cock.

HACKER (*seething*): Stick to the daughter, shall we? Stick to one.

BASS: Right. Ready. Are we ready? (*They place their spades under the remains.*) and **Hup!** (*Staggering, they transport their burden to a canvas stretcher, withdraw their spades.*)

FLOWERS: Mr Riddle, do your stuff. (RIDDLE *puts on a pair of rubber gloves and kneels beside the remains.*)

HACKER: That's it, then, is it?

FLOWERS: As soon as Mr Riddle's 'ad 'is delve. 'is nimble fingers 'ave explored vast numbers of 'uman cavities. Some 'ot and female, which 'ave no doubt benefitted from 'is tenderness, but more often the rigor-mortised guts of soldiers, accidentally penetrated in the search for valuables.

RIDDLE: Nothing. (*He stands up.*)

BASS: No disc?

FLOWERS: Fuck the disc. Let 'im join the missing.

RIDDLE (*feeling again*): No disc.

TROD: Herr Nichtmann.

FLOWERS (*pulling a cover over*): Mr Nobody it is, then.

HACKER: Is this delving really necessary? I can't see it is myself.

RIDDLE: Eight wristwatches yesterday. Two in good order. A cigarette case. A hall-marked whisky flask.

FLOWERS: In future wars all combatants will be requested to bring valuables into battle. As tips for the poor bastards who will have to dig 'em up.

RIDDLE: We aren't getting the officers, that's the pity.

HACKER: Must be an easier way of earning a few bob.

FLOWERS: No doubt you'll tell us if there is. There is no work at 'ome. The factory I worked for has closed. They switched from

30   *Howard Barker*

bicycles to howitzers, but the market for howitzers has dropped
off.

BASS: We will go home, and if there is no work we will demand
it.

FLOWERS: Just like that.

BASS: Exactly.

FLOWERS: You will be put inside.

BASS: I will not.

FLOWERS: 'ow will you not?

BASS: I will refuse.

FLOWERS: 'e will refuse.

BASS: It is that simple, we are the soldiers.

RIDDLE: Bass, they have already got your rifle back. They have
swopped your weapon for a spade.

FLOWERS: Come on, let's move. (*They bend to the stretcher.*)

HACKER: Gents, one moment, gents. Can I whisper a little some-
thing in your ears? Something related to the ladies we discussed?
(*They stand upright again.*) You see, they're looking for a body.
Mrs Toynbee is looking for 'er son. (*He looks over his shoulder.*)
This particular youth is listed missing. Round 'ere.

TROD: She is brought here by his astral body. He calls her and she
has to come . . .

HACKER: Something like that. So if you could make a special
effort I, for one, would be prepared to make my appreciation very
clear.

TROD: She bears his wound in her. She weeps his blood.

FLOWERS: **Stuff it, Trod!**

HACKER: Thank you. What I'm saying is, this particular corpse
would earn you more than a nickel fag-case. (*Pause*) To put it
another way, can you get 'im this week?

RIDDLE (*indicating two points on the horizon*): There are tens of
thousands between here and there . . .

HACKER: I never said it was easy. (*He reaches for his wallet,
removes a note.*) I wonder if you could find 'im in a week? (*He
holds the money out.*)

FLOWERS: We can do it.

HACKER: William, he is, William Toynbee. That's 'is number and
'is regiment. (*He hands* FLOWERS *a scrap of paper, turns to go
out.*) Means a lot of work, of course. But there's more money
where that came from. I'm not made of money but I admit I'm
bloody keen.

FLOWERS: To knob the lady, would 'e mean?

HACKER (*stopping*): I heard that, Flowers. Vile insinuation, vile.

THE LOVE OF A GOOD MAN   31

Four years of squalor 'as made you cynical, I suppose. (*He walks away, past* CLOUT, *who is working.*)

Scene Six

CLOUT *is still working here next day.* BRIDE *comes in, with a copy of* The Times. *He reads it out to* CLOUT.

BRIDE: Ferocious argument in the House. Copies of *Hansard* employed as missiles following the Government's decision to enforce the standard model headstone for officers and all other ranks. Described as creeping socialism. As lowering downwards. As further evidence of the persistent erosion of individual choice. Desperate parents have become the body-snatchers of our time. One body only is to be returned, for interment in the place of kings. The Prince of Wales will choose the Unknown Warrior, being blindfold and using a pin. (*He folds the paper and tucks it under his arm.*) There is something gone in my head. If I jerk it quickly, something moves. Have you ever had that?

CLOUT: No, sir.

BRIDE: I'm not married, are you?

CLOUT: No, sir.

BRIDE: Which is difficult, because what happens if I'm ill? Someone has to wipe your bum. I should have thought of this, but I've been racked with work here — (*He moves his head.*) There it goes! **Who will wipe my shit away!** (*He goes out as* LALAGE *appears.* CLOUT *gets up, is about to go out.*)

LALAGE: They don't abuse my mother, do they? (*He stops.*) Please tell me she is not the subject of their filthy talk. (*Pause.*) I see. (*He goes out.* LALAGE *stares over the country.* RIDDLE *comes in, looks at her.*)

LALAGE: Why didn't you come for me? I was here all night.

RIDDLE: I didn't want you.

LALAGE: All night here. I was so cold.

RIDDLE: What would have been the point in coming? As I didn't want you?

LALAGE: To tell me. That would have been the reasonable thing to do.

RIDDLE: I don't do the reasonable. That's why you like me.

LALAGE: I thought you might be ill. I thought anything.

32   *Howard Barker*

RIDDLE: Desperate.

LALAGE: Yes.

RIDDLE: In the freezing night. Hot and clamouring in the womb.

LALAGE: No. Sneezing and bloody uncomfortable.

RIDDLE: Quivering from knee to belly.

LALAGE: Look, we must have a talk some time. (*Pause*) Mustn't
    we? Get to know each other?

RIDDLE: Ah. So it begins.

LALAGE: I feel like having a conversation. I love your darkness
    but I am finding it too quiet.

RIDDLE: Nothing you can say will be worth saying.

LALAGE: Try it, shall we?

RIDDLE: Not with me.

LALAGE: I love you, but I cannot go on if we don't learn to
    speak!

RIDDLE: Go on? **Go on?** (CLOUT *appears pushing a wheel-
    barrow full of gravel. He takes a rake off the top.*)

LALAGE: If you want to fuck me. (CLOUT *does not react.*) If you
    want to go on doing it. (*Pause, then she goes out.* CLOUT *tips
    out the gravel into a heap.*)

RIDDLE: I know her. Through and through I know her. I read what
    is engraved on every vertebra along her spine. It says I am clean,
    and I do good.

CLOUT (*spreading the gravel*): Someone 'as to.

RIDDLE: Her good is all to do with ventilation. Ventilated villas
    in suburbia. Ventilated underwear. She is throbbing with con-
    viviality. (HACKER *comes in with a Union Jack.*)

HACKER: 'ere we are, son. 'ere at last. Two years after a world war
    and a million rotting Englishmen, yer can't lay yer 'ands on a
    Union Jack. Grateful bleeding Belgians turn 'em into shopping
    bags. It's this way up, is it? (*Spreading the flag on the ground.*)
    Or is it? (*He points to the pathway.*) This 'ere's the 'orizontal, am
    I right?

CLOUT: Er . . .

HACKER (*waving his hand*): This 'ere.

CLOUT: Er . . .

HACKER: What you're laying, come on, son!

CLOUT: This is the diagonal.

HACKER: What? 'ere?

CLOUT: Sir.

HACKER: Diagonals is four foot wide.

CLOUT: Er . . .

HACKER: Whatcha mean er? Whatcha mean, er, er? Give us the

THE LOVE OF A GOOD MAN   33

measure. (*He gets up, takes* CLOUT's *rule.*) Bollock this up at
your peril, Clout. (*He tests the width of the path.*) Well, so it is.
Why didn't yer say? This is the diagonal. (*He gives him the rule
back.*) Well, I can see I am a burden on your ingenuity. (*He turns
to* RIDDLE.) How's things going, Riddle?

RIDDLE: We have him.

HACKER: You what?

RIDDLE: Young Toynbee.

HACKER: You 'ave 'im? You — 'ang on.

RIDDLE: Oddly enough.

HACKER: Oddly enough. **Come on.**

RIDDLE: War is like that, Mr Hacker.

HACKER: War is like that. **Come on.**

RIDDLE: Do you have to repeat everything I say? We have him. I
can't compel you to believe it, obviously.

HACKER: You can't. You damn well can't.

RIDDLE: Shall we bring him? Or will you collect?

HACKER: Yesterday I ask you, keep an eye open for certain remains. Today, remains arrive, on the doorstep like a loaf. Come
on, it stinks.

RIDDLE: You have to give some credit to coincidence. The war has
made us all so sceptical. If we were working one on you, Mr
Hacker, wouldn't we have left a few days' grace? That would be
cleverer, you must admit. Our spades upturned him within an
hour of you leaving us. (*Pause, while* HACKER *looks at him
searchingly.*)

HACKER: You're a cool one, Riddle. All right, bring him 'ere.
(RIDDLE *starts to go, stops.*)

RIDDLE (*turning*): There isn't all that much to see.

HACKER: No, of course, there wouldn't be. (RIDDLE *goes out.*)
Smart bastard. Smart bastard, don't yer think? (CLOUT *pretends
not to hear.*) Still, it has its advantages. Bona fide or non bona
fide, I can't complain. I wonder where you take a woman 'ere?
Pity they 'ad to knock the coast about. Yer can't take a lady like
that to an allotment shed. (*Pause*) Or maybe you can. Christ
knows what the gentility conceals. Christ knows what itch . . .
(*The* SOLDIERS *come in bearing a stretcher draped in tarpaulin. They dump it down, stand back.*) I would be right in
thinking, wouldn't I, there can't be much left of 'is 'ead?
(FLOWERS *shakes his head.*) Is there an 'ead? (FLOWERS
shakes his head.) Unlucky. Nor nothing in 'is pockets neither?
(FLOWERS *shakes it.*) No pocket? (FLOWERS *shakes it.*) Well,
what is there, then? (*Pause.*) I can't sell 'er a bag of peat! (*They*

Howard Barker

just gawp. He goes over to the stretcher, lifts the tarpaulin.) Very funny. Fifteen quid for that. I love your sense of 'umour. Come on, lads, you're dealing with a businessman.

FLOWERS: Yer wouldn't be accusing us of cheating?

HACKER: You said the word, not me.

BASS: British Soldiers of the Great War for Civilization? **Heroes of Armageddon?**

HACKER: Very good, Bass, but can we be serious for just a minute? (*Pause*) It is not so much a matter of convincing me. I am 'appy with a pound of sausage meat. It is Mrs Toynbee, isn't it? It's 'er feelings I 'ave to consider.

RIDDLE: Look at his disc. Round what was once a neck there hangs a disc. Otherwise we should not have bothered you. (*HACKER goes to the remains, looks at an army disc.*)

HACKER: 1127161 Toynbee. Royal Hussars. (*He looks up.*) Well, I'll be buggered. (*Pause. He gets up.*) Well, I regard that as conclusive.

RIDDLE: She will be satisfied. We have watched widows weep on horsemeat supplied by less scrupulous squads. (*HACKER gazes at the remains.*)

HACKER: To think that — muck — down there came out between 'er lovely limbs . . . (*He bites his lip. The SOLDIERS look puzzled.*) That is the measure of war, I think . . . (*He turns, stops.*) Christ, that shakes me . . . (*He walks a little, staggers, stops.*) Bloody 'ell . . . Clout . . . **Clout!** (*CLOUT drops his rake, hurries over.*) Bloody 'ell, man, I've come over sick . . .

CLOUT: Bend over, Mr 'acker.

HACKER: Ridiculous . . . (*He retches.*) Cor . . . silly, ain't it, but I . . . (*He retches again, dabs his mouth with a handkerchief.*) What are they gawping at?

BASS: The money, guv. (*HACKER takes out his wallet, gives CLOUT two notes, which he hands over. The men withdraw.*)

HACKER: Clout, I 'ave 'ad a vision of death. I saw beyond the grave. I saw Alpha and Omega. Are you listening?

CLOUT: Mr 'acker.

HACKER: I saw a thin 'ole to the bottom of the world . . .

CLOUT: Sir.

HACKER (*with sense of horror and discovery*): **I shan't be 'ere long!** (*He holds CLOUT by the shoulders.*) Fuck it, I am scared of death! All these years gone and I never noticed 'em! I got to 'ave a child, Clout! Somebody must give me a kid!

CLOUT: Mrs 'acker, sir?

HACKER: Mrs Hacker? Mrs Hacker? Are you barmy? Mrs Hacker

THE LOVE OF A GOOD MAN

is forty-three and sterile as a collar stud. It's been like shooting into concrete these last twenty years! What's gonna 'appen suddenly? Use yer 'ead!

CLOUT: Sorry.

HACKER: This 'as touched me. This 'as touched me very deep. Who's gonna remember me? What'll 'appen when I'm gone? (*He strides about in despair.*) Shakespeare was a lucky sod. Day and night they're stuffing 'im down schoolkids' gobs. Won't forget 'im, will they? What about me?

CLOUT: The name 'acker, Mr 'acker. Over the shop.

HACKER: Next geezer who takes over the business will 'ave my sign down in the dust.

CLOUT: It's on all the memorials, ain't it? Hacker fecit, it says. In little letters on the back.

HACKER: You said it. Little letters on the back. First bit of moss obliterates it. No, I shall 'ave to 'ave a kid. The common man's immortality, such as it is. You 'ave been busy working, so you won't 'ave noticed an interest I've developed in a certain lady —

CLOUT: Shit as toothpaste.

HACKER: Wha'?

CLOUT: Shit as toothpaste. (*Pause.* HACKER *glares at him.*)

HACKER: Clout, I urge you to eradicate that particular phrase from your mind. I most earnestly encourage you to be a tabula rasa as far as Mrs Toynbee is concerned. I do urge you. (*Pause*)

CLOUT: Get on with the pathway, Mr 'acker. (*He goes off, starts working, stops, looks at* HACKER.)

Scene Seven

The remains on the stretcher are mid-stage. MRS TOYNBEE *and* LALAGE *stand together,* MRS TOYNBEE *in a pure white dress. Pause.*

MRS TOYNBEE: I shall kiss him. Will you want to?

LALAGE: No, I shan't.

MRS TOYNBEE: Sometimes I wonder if you loved him. (*Pause*) I mean really loved him.

LALAGE: Really loved him. Loved him. What's the point of qualifying it?

36   *Howard Barker*

MRS TOYNBEE: Then kiss him.
LALAGE: No. I said.
MRS TOYNBEE: Why?
LALAGE: Because it won't be him, will it?
MRS TOYNBEE: Who will it be, then?
LALAGE: It's two years since he died. Imagine that.
MRS TOYNBEE: Love does not die at the grave. I shall kiss him.
  In my white dress.
LALAGE: You must do exactly what you want.
MRS TOYNBEE: You think I'm making too much of this? Making
  a banquet of my grief?
LALAGE: That's about it, yes.
MRS TOYNBEE: I am. You're right. I am drinking it to the dregs.
  (*She walks towards the body, stands looking down.*)
LALAGE: I think you are making a fool of yourself.
MRS TOYNBEE: Or you, is it? You think I am making a fool of
  you? There is nothing quite so embarrassing as a parent who
  can't keep her feelings checked. Especially when your own are
  so trapped and strangled. Isn't that it?
LALAGE: No.
MRS TOYNBEE: You oppress your spirit too much. Everyone
  does. And the world is an uglier place for it. I loathe dourness
  and grinding teeth. So did Billy. He wrote to me that if people
  hadn't been so stiff-lipped with their grief the war would have
  finished two years earlier.
LALAGE: I didn't mean that. I meant — (*At this moment
  HACKER appears, discreet in a dark suit. He watches from a
  proper distance.*) I meant how do we know that is him?

*MRS TOYNBEE ignores this. She kneels beside the stretcher. At
this moment, the SOLDIERS come in bearing a number of empty
coffins. HACKER, trying to preserve decorum, waves them away.
They do not notice him.*

FLOWERS: These are getting lighter, or I'm getting stronger.
RIDDLE: They are using thinner wood. Out of consideration for
  our backs.
BASS: Or the maker's profits, could it be?

*Seeing HACKER, they stop, look at MRS TOYNBEE, who, in an
ecstasy of emotion, leans forward and places her lips on the remains. TROD, with a groan, collapses in a faint, and the coffins
clatter to the ground as the SOLDIERS struggle to hold them.*

THE LOVE OF A GOOD MAN

FLOWERS: Hold it!

BASS: Jesus Christ!

FLOWERS: Hold it!

HACKER: You clumsy buggers! Oh, you clumsy sods!

BASS: Trod's fainted!

HACKER: Sod Trod.

FLOWERS: Who are you abusing, guvnor?

HACKER: There is a woman 'ere, paying 'er respects . . . Christ, what is England coming to? What did we fight the war for? Women, wasn't it? Women and their feelings?

BASS: I love the 'we'.

HACKER: Christ, appealing to Englishmen to 'ave an 'eart. I never thought I'd see the day.

FLOWERS: Come on. Shove off. (*He leads off.*)

BASS: What about Trod?

RIDDLE: He'll recover there as well as anywhere. (*They go out, leaving* TROD *on the ground. After a pause* MRS TOYNBEE *gets up.*)

MRS TOYNBEE: Oh . . . ! There is mud on my dress . . . !

LALAGE: Oh, really, you are so — (*She turns on her.*) **What is it for?**

HACKER (*hurrying forward with a handkerchief*): I wonder if I might brush it off? This is a brand new handkerchief — (*He kneels at her feet.*)

MRS TOYNBEE: No.

HACKER: No?

MRS TOYNBEE: It is there forever.

LALAGE (*mockingly*): Surely you realized that?

HACKER: I'm afraid I didn't. But I understand it. I don't think I 'ave ever been so moved. I think if someone made a painting of it, it would sell. You might call it 'The Patriot's Farewell'. I think it would hang in bedrooms all over England. (LALAGE *walks out smartly. Pause.*) I 'ope everything is satisfactory, then? (*Pause*) Took a bit of doing, obviously. Finding one person in all this — I think you're so beautiful — so one way and another we were lucky, I suppose they — I would give my life to kiss your arse . . . (*Pause*)

HACKER: Did you 'ear me, Sylvia?

MRS TOYNBEE (*her back still to him*): Yes.

HACKER: No doubt others 'ave said similar things.

MRS TOYNBEE: Yes.

HACKER: Naturally. Well. (*Pause*) Can I? (*Pause*) What more can I say? I'm not a poet. (*Pause*) Can I? (*Pause. Then, nervously*

38 *Howard Barker*

he extends a hand, at last touching her, running his hand over her. Then with a groan, falling to his knees and burying his face in her clothes.) I am so 'appy! Isn't it easy to make a man 'appy?

MRS TOYNBEE: Yes. It is. (*Pause*) Now I think you should get up. (*Obediently, he rises, brushing his knees.*)

HACKER: May I book a room, Sylvia? Sorry — a suite? There's this place called Blankenberghe. I 'ave the brochure — (*He goes to take it from his pocket.*)

MRS TOYNBEE: Yes. Why don't you? (*Pause*)

MRS HACKER: Why don't I? Yes . . . (*He looks at her, then hurries out. MRS TOYNBEE remains motionless for some time. There is a groan behind her, then TROD sits up.*)

TROD: Blood . . . (*She turns. He indicates her dress.*) Blood on your dress . . .

MRS TOYNBEE: Blood?

TROD: I am going to be killed.

MRS TOYNBEE: Oh, no. Not now the war is over, surely?

TROD: Yes. It's the meaning of that blood.

MRS TOYNBEE: It isn't, though. As a matter of fact. It's mud.

TROD: I'm not afraid. You carry death in you but I'm not afraid. Bride and I, we are going to cross over soon . . . (*Pause*)

MRS TOYNBEE: Really. It's mud. (*She goes out. The SOLDIERS reappear.*)

BASS (*to TROD*): Come on, son. Up on yer feet.

FLOWERS: Herr Nichtmann is done with, then, is 'e?

BASS: What number do we paint on this?

FLOWERS (*looks in a book*): Missing No. 1127161. Then put it with the others in the shed.

BASS (*with a paint can*): 1127161.

TROD: We should not have done it . . .

FLOWERS: Done what, son, exactly?

TROD: She kissed it. With her lips . . .

BASS: Yeah, well, she is a performer, ain't she?

TROD: We have mocked her pity! We have sinned against the ordinance of death!

RIDDLE: It doesn't matter, Trod. All your conscience. All your guilt. From the right distance all the thundering of bishops is drowned by a rat's squeak.

BASS: Only the rich come 'ere, yer notice.

RIDDLE: They are not rich. It is all appearance with them.

BASS: The poor rich, then. My mother could not come 'ere. My missus could not.

THE LOVE OF A GOOD MAN 39

RIDDLE: Why should they want to? As you're not dead?

BASS: The rich can filch some bastard's body. The poor make do with telegrams.

RIDDLE: She got nothing for her privilege. For all we know the corpse she kissed had killed her son. (*He gets up.*) Are we ready, then? (*They lift the remains into the coffin, and start hammering down the lid.*)

FLOWERS: Mr Riddle, what plans 'ave you got when it's our turn to enjoy the peace? I can swallow ten pints at a sitting, but I 'ave a feeling no one's employing men for that.

RIDDLE: Why don't you emigrate? You like the Empire, don't you?

FLOWERS: I should like it. I 'ave two brothers killed for it. One in Palestine shot by the Turks, the other lost 'is footing racing an Australian down a pyramid. The Australians lose 'alf their men through dares, did you know that? (*He hammers in the final nail.*) Yes, I like the Empire. Where do you suggest? (*They look up, suddenly aware of a stranger in their presence. The man wears khaki riding breeches and boots and a police jacket. He taps a small riding whip against his leg.*)

HARD: Good men. (*Pause. He stares at them.*) Oh, good men. (*He wanders around them, feasting his eyes.*) Oh, very good!

ACT TWO

Scene One

The cemetery is partly built. The gravel path is laid, there are headstones lining the back of the stage, but a sense of disorder prevails. CLOUT *is unloading turfs from a wheelbarrow.* HACKER *is blowing into his cupped palms and sniffing earnestly.*

HACKER: Is it my breath? (*Pause. He blows and sniffs.*) You can say. I won't 'old it against yer. (CLOUT *works on.*) Two bookings, both cancelled. I'm the laughing stock of Blankenberghe. (*He sniffs again.*) I've got this idea it's my breath, yer see. Last night I cleaned my teeth so hard I was bleeding. Sink 'ad gone pink. (*Pause*) She lets me fondle 'er clothes, but I 'aven't actually kissed her. Not 'er lips . . . (*Pause*) Clout.

CLOUT: **Can I just get on with this!** (*Pause.* HACKER *is astonished.*)

HACKER: What? What did you say? Come again?

CLOUT: I'm sorry, Mr 'acker. Can I just get on with this? (BRIDE *comes in.*)

BRIDE: Mr Hacker.

HACKER: Mr Bride.

BRIDE: If you can finish by the end of this week there is every chance the Prince of Wales will perform the dedication. He is in Paris on a social visit and would like to fit it in. The other cemeteries have drainage problems. What do you think? Can you finish?

HACKER (*wide-eyed*): Yes.

BRIDE: You're certain?

HACKER: I'll swear to it.

BRIDE: How many graves have still to be placed?

HACKER: Forget it. No problem.

BRIDE: I ask because —

HACKER: Easy.

BRIDE: Yes, but —

THE LOVE OF A GOOD MAN   41

HACKER: Say a hundred —

BRIDE: **A hundred?**

HACKER: Less. Definitely less. Say fifty.

BRIDE: You just said a hundred.

HACKER: Dunno why I said that. Wasn't thinking. Fifty at the outside.

BRIDE: That is still a lot of work.

HACKER: I can do it.

BRIDE: Yes, but properly?

HACKER: Obviously properly.

BRIDE: You have the staff?

HACKER: No problem.

BRIDE: And proper turfing?

HACKER: I said yes, didn't I! (*Pause*) Sorry. Yes.

BRIDE: If he selects this one it must be right.

HACKER: Work through the night if it comes to it. (*Pause*)

BRIDE: Good. All right. (*He starts to go out.*) I want to be laid here myself.

HACKER: Well, why not?

BRIDE: I am not war dead, am I?

HACKER: No, I suppose you're not. (BRIDE *goes out.* HACKER *turns to* CLOUT.) Did you 'ear that? Did you cop that, Clout? Hacker, by appointment to the Prince of Wales! Oh, the way of the world! You can be shit one mouthful and sugar the next!

CLOUT (*dourly*): Two 'undred, Mr 'acker. (*Pause*)

HACKER: Two 'undred, is it? Is it? Two 'undred?

CLOUT: Sir.

HACKER: As much as that . . .

CLOUT: Never do it.

HACKER: Shut up.

CLOUT: Not in a month. Not in three.

HACKER: If you keep on about bloody months, Clout, I will do something I might regret. The word month is not permitted 'ere! (*Pause*)

CLOUT: Twelve weeks.

HACKER: All right, clever. Now listen. It is a fact that nothing is impossible. They said the war was impossible but it still 'appened. I say we can do it. All we need to know is 'ow. So let's forget the when and stick with the 'ow. 'ow do we get two 'undred cadavers in their 'oles and two 'undred slabs of Portland laid on top of 'em. In seven days? 'ow? 'ow? (*Pause. He walks up and down.*) Christ, this is a bugger . . . (*Pause*) All this battlefield clearance yer can't get staff . . .

42   *Howard Barker*

CLOUT: I could tell yer.

HACKER: Fire away, then. (*Pause*. CLOUT *just looks at him*.) Well, let's 'ave it. (*Pause*) Clout? (CLOUT *just stares at him, very coolly*.) Oh, blimey . . . the worm is contemplating turning, I do believe . . . (*Pause*)

CLOUT: 'alf the profits. (*Pause*)

HACKER: Comedian. (CLOUT *shrugs his shoulders, goes back to his shovel*.) You're wasted 'ere. They're looking for you at the Palladium. (CLOUT *digs on*.) I knew you 'ad something. I knew something 'ad to go on in that peculiar 'ead of yours. But a stand-up comic? Never dreamed of it. (*Pause*. CLOUT *begins unloading turfs*. HACKER *watches him some time*.) Under the law of the land, all your ideas are my property.

CLOUT: What land?

HACKER: England, of course.

CLOUT: This ain't England, Mr 'acker.

HACKER: Oh, but it is. Ceded to H.M. Government in perpetuity. From the grateful Belgians. Corner of a foreign field, etcetera. I wouldn't 'esitate to sue, I warn yer.

CLOUT: My 'ead's my 'ead.

HACKER: Look, I pay yer, so I own yer. Put it bluntly 'cos yer make me.

CLOUT (*picking up the wheelbarrow*): Get more turfs —

HACKER: **'ang about.** (CLOUT *stops*.) Up yer wages. (*He starts going again*.) **Fuck me, where is your loyalty!** (*He stops again*.) Not just to me. Not just to me who 'as provided you with work and wages when work and wages can't be 'ad, but to these dead Englishmen. They died for us. It makes yer blush to 'ave to mention it! (CLOUT *starts off again*. HACKER *watches him to the edge of the stage*.) 'alf the profits in what?

CLOUT (*stopping*): Gallipoli.

HACKER: Never mind the little jobs, eh? Kindly overlooks the bread and butter funerals. Decent of yer. **Fucking 'ell!**

CLOUT: Mr 'acker, look at the papers. From now on there is gonna be a world war every week. This is an expanding business like no other. If you're appointment to 'is 'ighness, you can't miss. 'alf the profits will be 'undred times what you 'ave 'ad —

HACKER: And a million times what you 'ave!

CLOUT: I'm not asking for my name on the factory gates. But if we miss this it could be Peckham for good. (*Pause*)

HACKER. 'e looks a silly bugger but 'e's cunning as a —

CLOUT: **'ow about it?** (*Pause*. HACKER *smiles, but thinly*.)

THE LOVE OF A GOOD MAN   43

HACKER: All right. What's the idea?

CLOUT (*taking a dirty paper from his pocket*): Appreciate it if you'd sign 'ere, sir.

HACKER: Christ, 'e doesn't miss a trick. (*He takes it, examines it.*) 'ow long's this been 'anging about?

CLOUT: Fair number of years, sir.

HACKER: I can see. Waiting till yer got me in a corner, eh?

CLOUT: Sign there, Mr 'acker . . .

HACKER (*perusing it*): You've 'ad a lawyer on it.

CLOUT: It's proper, sir, down to the stamp. (HACKER *reads it, then takes a pen and signs it, but as* CLOUT *goes to take it, holds on to one side.*)

HACKER: This 'ad better be good, ol' son. God in 'eaven, it 'ad. (*Pause*)

CLOUT: Yer put four in one 'ole. (*Pause*)

HACKER: Come again.

CLOUT: You 'eard me.

HACKER: Yes, I think I did.

CLOUT: It reduces labour by four 'undred per cent. (*Pause.* HACKER *is still holding on to his end of the paper.*)

HACKER: Disgraceful. Bleeding disgraceful.

CLOUT (*significantly*): Prince of Wales.

HACKER: Repulsive, unpatriotic, fucking disgrace.

CLOUT: **Prince—of—Wales.** (*Long pause. Suddenly,* HACKER *releases the paper, walks away, turns again.*)

HACKER: If Bride sees it — **I don't agree with it.** (*Pause. Then with decision.*) After this is over I will commission a fucking great big sculpture called the 'Agony of War'. For Peckham churchyard. I will 'ave a chapel built for war widows. To make amends.

CLOUT: Least we can do.

HACKER: All right, then. That I swear. Now let's get on with it. Be working nights, of course. I imagine you won't be putting in a claim for time and 'alf?

CLOUT (*putting away the contract*): 'sir.

HACKER: **Sir?** Bit redundant, ain't it? **Sir?**

CLOUT: Prefer it, Mr 'acker, if you don't mind.

HACKER: Why should I mind? Grovelling's an 'abit like any other, I suppose. (*He follows* CLOUT, *who is pushing a wheelbarrow.*)

MRS TOYNBEE *and* LALAGE *come in.*

MRS TOYNBEE: They've put Billy in the long shed with the

44   *Howard Barker*

others. In a coffin with a number on. I am suggesting to Hacker
he is brought home labelled tools. I originally thought we could
manage this ourselves, but not now there are military policemen
everywhere. We aren't the only people forced to steal our loved
ones from the government. We loaned our sons for the duration
but they are hanging on to them till Judgement Day.
LALAGE: You're going on a bit . . .
MRS TOYNBEE: I want him in England!
LALAGE: This is, apparently . . .
MRS TOYNBEE: England? How can it be? England is an island.
LALAGE: Because it's full of English dead.
MRS TOYNBEE: That doesn't make it England.
LALAGE: Well, what does? This is more England than Knights-
    bridge is. (*Pause*)
MRS TOYNBEE: I don't think you want him brought home. I
    don't think you want Billy underneath our tree. (*Pause*)
LALAGE: No. I don't think I do. (*Pause*)
MRS TOYNBEE: I see. So I can't rely on you?
LALAGE: I don't think so . . .
MRS TOYNBEE: You don't think so.
LALAGE: I mean no. (*Pause*) I think we are creating a new world
    now. A new world of equality and justice. This is 1920, isn't it?
    And the way we treat the dead will show our intentions about all
    the rest. They have decided to abolish all distinctions in the
    graveyards. The same style for everyone. I accept it. If we cannot
    even manage that, what will happen to the rest of it?
MRS TOYNBEE: You are a socialist.
LALAGE: Is that what it is?
MRS TOYNBEE: Yes.
LALAGE: Probably I am, then.
MRS TOYNBEE: You are for this regulation. This monotonous
    equality.
LALAGE: Yes.
MRS TOYNBEE: This greyness. This sameness.
LALAGE: Yes, I am. (*Pause*) I am. (*Pause*)
MRS TOYNBEE: You'll note, I'm sure, how this equality has to
    be enforced. How they've had to send in the police. To terrorize
    us. To arrest and imprison people like me. You'll notice how this
    urge for sameness causes misery and grief!
LALAGE: I'm afraid I think you should conform. Of your own
    free will.
MRS TOYNBEE: I will not! They do not own my son, I do.
    (*Pause*) I take it you won't hinder me?

THE LOVE OF A GOOD MAN 45

LALAGE: They're taking one dead soldier home. To shake their plumes over in the Abbey.

MRS TOYNBEE: You haven't answered. Will you hinder me?

LALAGE: I don't know! (*Pause.* MRS TOYNBEE *stares at her.*)

MRS TOYNBEE: This is your socialism. This. You will have me taken by the police.

LALAGE: Please, don't be emotional.

MRS TOYNBEE: It is not emotional, it is a fact. Will you see me taken by the police?

LALAGE: I can't answer.

MRS TOYNBEE: You have answered. (*Pause*) We are enemies, then. (*Pause*) Of course I shall not disclose anything more to you. That is the price of socialism. Sealed lips. (*She starts to go, stops, turns.*) I must tell you, I haven't said one quarter of what I might have said. Not one tenth.

LALAGE: No, of course. (MRS TOYNBEE *goes out, passing* RIDDLE, *who is on his way to work, carrying a spade.*) You're late again.

RIDDLE: Dead men are very patient. Very good employers on the whole.

LALAGE: Will you help me?

RIDDLE: I do. Every night.

LALAGE: Tell her it isn't Billy. (*Pause*) Because it isn't, is it? Anyone can see that.

RIDDLE: On the contrary, no one can see anything.

LALAGE: Precisely. Disabuse her, please. (*Pause. He just looks at her.*) If you love me. (*Pause*) Or desire me, or what.

RIDDLE: I would forfeit three pounds seventeen and sixpence.

LALAGE: I will make it up to you.

RIDDLE: No. Let her believe. I would not steal her orgasm from her. It is too divine a thing. (*He starts to move away.*)

LALAGE: Why do you attack me all the time?

RIDDLE (*stops*): Attack you?

LALAGE: Orgasm.

RIDDLE: Did I say orgasm?

LALAGE: God Almighty. I wish I knew what I had done to you.

RIDDLE (*significantly*): Nothing. You've done nothing to me.

LALAGE: I'm sorry I can't do what you expect. I've tried, and I will go on trying.

RIDDLE: You would say that. That's so typical of you. You will try. You will improve. What you will never see, you English women in your laundered lingerie, is that effort never altered

46   *Howard Barker*

anything. For all your trying, I've known better from army
whores though I was the ninety-ninth man in the queue. (*Pause*)

LALAGE: Well, there seems no point in discussing what effort
cannot influence, does there? You will have to take us as we are.

RIDDLE: Nothing will ever wake you.

LALAGE: And what will wake you?

RIDDLE: I'm finishing with Europe. I'm finishing with dead con-
tinents and dead women. I'm going to a place where there is
desire in the hips of the women and a slow look in their eyes,
where flesh is flesh and as old as sex itself, where men do not
come chattering from books.

LALAGE: Mexico? Peru? (*He looks at her, full of contempt.*)

RIDDLE: You mimicking, unloved, female thing.

LALAGE: I'm sorry, but that is a lie. However I have disappointed
you, out of ignorance or shame, I know that is nonsense and a
lie. You have suffered four years of one lie and now, out of pain,
you've given yourself to another. The lie of submissive, dark-
skinned women. I know it is a nonsense. I know it like I know
nothing else. It makes me pity you.

RIDDLE: Well, that ends it, then. I will not lie with a woman who
scorns the man.

LALAGE: You see, you will keep on using these phrases like 'to
lie with' and 'Woman' and 'Man'. It is meant to put mystery into
it but all it does is fuddle things. I would have expected the war
to make men desperate for truth, but it's made you bow down.

RIDDLE: Nothing will ever move your womb. (*She turns away, in
frustration and despair.*) You should be sodomized. It's all you're
fit for, jellies, creams and second rate hotels . . . (*He waits to see
if he has provoked her, then turns to leave.*)

LALAGE: Marry me. (*Pause. He stares at her.*) I will help you.
Marry me. (*He looks at her, blankly, then goes out.*)

Scene Two

*Night. Some hurricane lamps indicate work is still going on. Voices
off calling a dog.*

PRINCE: } **Passchendaele! Here, boy!**
GENTLEMAN: } **Passchendaele!**

THE LOVE OF A GOOD MAN   47

There is a bout of whistling.

PRINCE (*clattering against some old iron*): F–F–Fuck! Banged my knee!

GENTLEMAN (*entering with a dog's lead*): **Pass–chen–daele!**

PRINCE (*hobbling in and sitting*): F–F–Fuck the dog! (*He rubs his knee.*)

GENTLEMAN: Spaniels cost money.

PRINCE: Get another one.

GENTLEMAN: Silly. (*He walks up and down whistling. The* PRINCE OF WALES *looks around, takes out a map.*)

PRINCE: This must be Hill 60. We've walked f–f–fucking miles . . . (*He leans back, staring at the night sky.*) The sky was all lit up at night.

GENTLEMAN: Really?

PRINCE: A firework party lasting four years. Green flares for artillery. Red for gas. Starshells trickling through the air . . . obviously lovely. Lovely as only proper evil can be . . . (*Suddenly he dives flat in mock battle.*) **German attack!**

GENTLEMAN (*crouching unconvincingly*): Oh, not again . . .

PRINCE (*being a machine gun*): Rat-tat-tat-tat-tat-tat-tat! You're hit!

GENTLEMAN: Naturally. (*He gracefully lays back.*)

PRINCE: But I'm all right. I stand up, to help you. I'm a captain, you're a private, but I help you — (*He stands.*) **Then I'm hit too!**

GENTLEMAN: Same as last time . . .

PRINCE (*collapsing*): Stretcher-bearers! Help my men!

GENTLEMAN: 'Oh, our beloved captain's dead, who we would have followed to the gates of Hell . . .'

PRINCE: Where's the f–f–fucking dog? It should be licking me.

GENTLEMAN: Got fed up, I expect. This is the third time tonight, you know . . .

PRINCE (*dying*): They gather round me —

GENTLEMAN (*tugging at a shoe*): My shoes are soddened . . .

PRINCE: **Gather round me.**

GENTLEMAN (*scrambling over to a suitable pose*): Sorry.

PRINCE: Gather round me, eyes moist in the star shell's eerie glare . . . (*They are a tableau for some seconds, then the* PRINCE OF WALES *sits up.*) I wish they'd let me fight here, George. I think if I'd died national unity would be secure. Sometimes princes have to be sacrificed. I hate seeing England cracked up as she is. We are good people, aren't we?

48   *Howard Barker*

GENTLEMAN: I wish I could see the dog.
PRINCE: As a king in the making, I feel I should know what's
    making 'em beef. As soon as we've done the battlefields I intend
    to do the slums. I will go to them at their cottage doors, and
    pulling aside the rambling roses I will say tell me what is wrong.
    Do not be frightened. I am only a king. (GENTLEMAN *walks to
    the edge of the stage and whistles again.*) Of course the risk is
    they won't tell the truth. They will hand me a cup of tea and say
    everything is lovely. That is their way. They mistake that for
    loyalty. But I will say, no, that is false loyalty. Give me the facts
    and I will act on them.
GENTLEMAN: Can't do more than that, can you?
PRINCE: I can't think why no one thought of it before . . .
    (CLOUT *comes in with a wheelbarrow.*)
GENTLEMAN: Excusez-moi, avez-vous vu un petit chien?
CLOUT: Sorry, guv?
GENTLEMAN: Ah. English.
PRINCE: We're looking for a little dog. Answers to the name of
    Passchendaele.
GENTLEMAN: When it feels like it.
CLOUT: No, sir. (*He carries on working.* PRINCE OF WALES
    watches him.)
PRINCE: Working damn late.
CLOUT: If I could, sir. (*Pause*)
PRINCE: You are an English workman, aren't you? An ordinary
    English workman? (CLOUT *ignores this.*) So let me ask a simple
    question. What is wrong? (CLOUT *lays a turf.*) Nothing? **Noth-
    ing** is wrong? (*Pause*) I don't believe that, because you see I live
    in London. I have a house there and when I look out of my
    window the streets are full of people. Rather angry people, fall-
    ing down, and fellows on horses being rather rough with them.
    (*Pause.* CLOUT *ignores all this.*) Please help me. I want to be
    good. (CLOUT *ignores him.*)
GENTLEMAN: It isn't on, you know. Every flag-waver is an as-
    sassin in his darker blood. A proper king knows that. He never
    stoops. (PRINCE OF WALES *looks at him, resentfully.* MRS
    TOYNBEE *appears, clasping a spaniel.*)
MRS TOYNBEE: Clout, I'm looking for Mr Hacker.
CLOUT: 'e's laying 'eadstones, Mrs T.
MRS TOYNBEE: Would you mind telling him I'm here? (*Grudg-
    ingly, flinging down his spade,* CLOUT *goes out. Pause.*)
PRINCE: Excuse me, but I think that m–m–may be my dog . . .
MRS TOYNBEE: Ah . . .

THE LOVE OF A GOOD MAN

PRINCE: Yes, it definitely is m–m–my dog . . .

MRS TOYNBEE: I heard him whining and I picked him up. I was afraid he'd fall into a shell-hole. What's he called?

PRINCE: P–P–Passchendaele. Out of respect . . . (*He gazes at her, captivated.*) I w–w–wish I could think of something else to say . . .

MRS TOYNBEE: Let me give him back to you.

PRINCE: Would you like it?

GENTLEMAN: Can't possibly.

PRINCE: W–w–would you?

GENTLEMAN: **You can't.**

PRINCE: I think it would be very nice to be your d–d–dog . . . (*In a sudden rush of embarrassment, he flees. The* GENTLEMAN *looks at* MRS TOYNBEE, *then hurries after him.* HACKER *comes in, muddy.*)

HACKER: God, Sylvia, you look wonderful . . .

MRS TOYNBEE (*going to him*): Shhh.

HACKER: Why shh?

MRS TOYNBEE: Because we've got enemies.

HACKER: Who 'as?

MRS TOYNBEE: You and I.

HACKER: Enemies? I've never 'ad enemies.

MRS TOYNBEE: Well, you have now.

HACKER: Who?

MRS TOYNBEE: Someone who would frustrate a cherished scheme. Why else do you think I'm creeping round here at night?

HACKER: I can't think with your health — (*He goes to stroke her collar.*) **Christ, it's a dog!**

MRS TOYNBEE: Will you listen?

HACKER: Thought it was a fur, sorry.

MRS TOYNBEE: About Billy. About my boy.

HACKER: Yep.

MRS TOYNBEE: About taking him home.

HACKER: Yep.

MRS TOYNBEE: My idea is that we —

HACKER: **Taking 'im 'ome?**

MRS TOYNBEE: Will you be quiet!

HACKER: Sorry. (*Pause*) Taking 'im 'ome? Did we say that? Did we? (*Pause*) Bugger. I never — I forgot we said that.

MRS TOYNBEE: Are you helping me, or are you not?

HACKER: Sylvia, my love —

MRS TOYNBEE: I am so cold, hold me.

HACKER (*holding up his hands*): Muddy —

50   *Howard Barker*

MRS TOYNBEE: Hold me! (*He puts his arms round her.*) Don't
    abandon me.
HACKER: Abandon you?
MRS TOYNBEE: I'm sorry that we haven't — haven't —
HACKER: Blankenberghed?
MRS TOYNBEE: Yes.
HACKER: You ain't been well.
MRS TOYNBEE: No. And I shan't be until this is done. (*She
    separates from him.*) In England we will. After his funeral. I
    promise you. (*Pause.* HACKER *is diffident.*)
HACKER: Sylvia . . . I 'ave never 'ad one like this in my life . . .
    (*Pause*) I wonder if . . . forgive a bloke for asking . . . I wonder
    if . . . down there . . . you feel the same as me . . . (*Pause*)
MRS TOYNBEE: Yes. I promise you.
HACKER: Thank God. I thought it might be all on my side. (*He
    turns away, modestly.*) Thank God . . .
MRS TOYNBEE: I thought we might hide Billy in a tool-box.
    Does that seem sensible?
HACKER (*turning to face her again*): Yes. I'll arrange it.
MRS TOYNBEE: Thank you. (*She turns to go.*) I pretend to no
    equality. I put my hand on my heart and thank God for a man.
    (*She goes out.* HACKER *watches her.* CLOUT *is making up for
    lost time, heaving a headstone across the stage.*)
HACKER: An English funeral, Clout . . . rooks in the tree tops . . .
    the smell of dew . . . 'er in 'er stiff black dress, aching for me
    underneath . . .
CLOUT: **Shall we just get on with it!**

Scene Three

In the pale dawn light, the figure of COLONEL HARD *is seen
silhouetted. Voices off, and shovels clanging. The* SOLDIERS *come
in.*

RIDDLE: It has occurred to me, these last few mornings, there is
    no singing any more. Now this says something.
BASS: It says we're workers again. You don't 'ear workers sing-
    ing. Not in England.
RIDDLE: Singing is the slaves' consolation. When you hear it, kill it.

THE LOVE OF A GOOD MAN   51

FLOWERS: Riddle would shut down the music halls.

RIDDLE: Had I the slightest wish to change the world, Mr Flowers, it would be the first thing I should think of. (*They are moving offstage when* HARD *speaks.*)

HARD: Gentlemen. (*They drift to a standstill.*) Give me five minutes of your time. The corpses will not grudge it. (*They examine him.*) I have watched you, and read you. I read men like others read horses or books. And in your strong backs I read a certain privilege, the privilege of making history. I am inviting you to write with me what children will pore over in their history books. What do you say? (*Pause*)

FLOWERS (*sarcastically*): You're keeping the best part back, guvnor. Who is it you want to kill?

HARD: The task is Ireland. Screwing the lid down on the Gaelic beast. We have our own uniform, and the money is ten shillings a week. (*He walks round them, tapping his stock on his boot.*) This is not men's work. Give your oath and I will whisk you away within the week. (*Pause*)

RIDDLE: Is there singing?

HARD: Singing?

RIDDLE: Yes. Do they sing?

HARD: It is not obligatory.

BASS: I like the money. What's the oath?

HARD: To the Crown.

BASS: I can take or leave the Crown.

HARD (*shrugs*): The Crown's a word, sir.

FLOWERS: I thought you were waiting for the revolution, Bass? The great up'eaval and what not?

BASS: In the meantime I 'ave a family wants to eat.

TROD: I had a sister died in Cork. She said all the girls are named Colleen . . .

FLOWERS: This man is mentally ill.

HARD: We wouldn't discriminate against him for that.

FLOWERS (*to* TROD): You need an 'ospital, son. Not a Black and Tan camp.

HARD: You may not dissuade a volunteer. It is sedition. (*Pause.* FLOWERS *stares at him.*)

FLOWERS: You should not come 'ere, guvnor. Of all places, not 'ere.

HARD: The Empire commands us.

FLOWERS: We 'ave served the Empire. I 'ave two brothers dead for it.

HARD: No amount of sacrifice can be enough. I am a speaker for the Empire. I have had Chinese rebels stand on their benches to cheer me while their wrists bled from the chaffing of their chains. I have been kissed on both cheeks by great black mutineers before we hanged them. And do you know why? Because I reminded them of Duty, which is the purest essence the man-animal can extract from himself. Duty, which smoulders as a tiny flame in every drug-blinded Calcutta tramp, and which Empire fans into a blaze that none can stop. All men long to serve. Service to the Empire lifts us from our secret cess.

FLOWERS: It put me in it, mister. Four sucking years of it. I'm not against yer Empire. Good luck to it. I fancy a farm in Africa myself. Black men running about while I sit on my arse. But you 'ave a neck to come 'ere after what we've seen and done. I am 'uman, and I take offence. (*Pause*)

HARD: There can be no African farm for you. Not without this. What happens in the Irish bog will silence tremors in the Bush. These gentlemen will hold the Empire together if you will not. (*He turns to* TROD, *taking out a card and a Bible*.) I swear to serve . . .

TROD (*placing a hand on the Bible*): I swear to serve . . .

HARD: My King and Country . . .

TROD: My King and Country . . .

HARD: To the best of my endeavour . . . (FLOWERS *walks forward to the edge of the stage as* BASS *waits his turn.* RIDDLE *joins him*.)

RIDDLE: Do we disappoint you, Mr Flowers?

FLOWERS: It's not a mistake to make a mistake. It's a crime not to profit by it.

RIDDLE: It's not true that the war was not enjoyed. It was, by some of us. It has got around how terrible it was. Because of the poets. But some of them enjoyed it too. I am against sentiment and pacifism. We must live in the blood.

FLOWERS: Killing Irish, Riddle?

RIDDLE: One day. And making love to their widows the next. (FLOWERS *stares at him*.) You do not understand me, do you?

FLOWERS: No. I do fucking not. (RIDDLE *goes back to* HARD *for the oath, as* TROD *comes down*.)

TROD: I had a vision, then, as I was speaking. We were in Connemara, in a truck. I saw green fields, and a winding road. I saw us on it, singing, and three men standing behind a hedge. Why were they behind a hedge?

FLOWERS: Pissing, no doubt. Though the Irish aren't usually so

THE LOVE OF A GOOD MAN   53

modest . . . (MRS TOYNBEE *comes in as* RIDDLE *finishes the oath. The* MEN *pick up their shovels and go out.*)

MRS TOYNBEE: Colonel Hard?

HARD (*turning*): Yes, I am Colonel Hard.

MRS TOYNBEE: *Cult of Empire?*

HARD: I am the author of that book.

MRS TOYNBEE: At Tonbridge I asked you a question once. About the place of women.

HARD: Women?

MRS TOYNBEE: Yes. Service, you said.

HARD: Really? I may well have done.

MRS TOYNBEE: Then I bought a copy of your book.

HARD: I am flattered.

MRS TOYNBEE: And you signed it.

HARD: Yes, I do that, after the meetings I hold a stall. (*Pause*)

MRS TOYNBEE: Lies. (*Pause*) Your book. (*Pause*) Lies upon lies.

HARD: I'm sorry you felt that. Empire is a difficult subject.

MRS TOYNBEE: My son read it. He believed you. Now he's dead.

HARD: I'm sorry. We lost a lot of people.

MRS TOYNBEE: Give me my money back. (*He gawps.*) My five shillings. Give it back. (*He smiles uncomfortably. Suddenly,* BRIDE *bursts in.*)

BRIDE (*to* HARD): **You cannot take them! Give them back!**

HARD: Everybody seems to want something from me.

BRIDE: I am desperately short-handed, you have no right to take my men!

HARD: Hire civilians.

BRIDE: The fallen are to be buried by their comrades! It is the usage of war, it's written in the articles, how dare you subvert the articles?

HARD: I hold the King's Commission. I come from London.

BRIDE: Shit on London! London killed them! Piss on it!

MRS TOYNBEE: Mr Bride . . .

BRIDE: Oh, Abbey, Abbey, Abbey, Abbott, Abbott, Ackroyd, Ackroyd, Ackroyd, Ackroyd —

MRS TOYNBEE: Mr Bride —

BRIDE: **I'm all right!** (*She recoils. He turns on* HARD.) Release them from their oath.

HARD: The war is over now. It must take second place.

BRIDE: I am an acting colonel! I hold rank!

HARD (*moving suavely away*): Very good luck. (*He stops, feels in his pocket.*) I don't have five shillings. Will three and ninepence do instead? (*He holds out the money to* MRS TOYNBEE. *She*

54   *Howard Barker*

ignores him. He goes out, passing HACKER *who charges in distraught.*)

HACKER (*to* BRIDE): They're quitting! The buggers are quitting at the end of the week!

BRIDE: You said you would finish by the end of the week.

HACKER: I 'ad every intention, but 'ow can I. The buggers are standing about. Once a man's given notice 'e's a burden on yer.

BRIDE: My poor boys . . . my unfinished cathedral . . .

HACKER: Clout and I are up to our eyeballs and all we get is backchat and cheek.

BRIDE: How far are you?

HACKER: Nowhere near it.

BRIDE: It is for the fallen, Hacker . . . !

HACKER: That's all very well, Bride, but they don't shift marble, do they?

BRIDE (*decisively*): I'll help you myself.

HACKER (*horrified*): No call for that.

BRIDE: If things are going badly, we must —

HACKER (*blocking his way*): No, they're not. (*Pause*) Badly, yes, but there are degrees of badness. This is quite good as badness goes . . . (*Pause. In desperation.*) You'd only get under our feet. There's eight 'undred cemeteries, ain't there? Give them a look.

BRIDE (*drifting away, stops*): I had a practice in Bermondsey before the war. It was all rickets and TB. The same dirty infants kept on coming back. The smell! Piss and infestation! I had a vision of the perfect world. Trim grass, rose trees, clean homes, square and brilliant white. My silent city. My just society . . . (*He goes out.*)

HACKER: Bride's mad.

MRS TOYNBEE: Yes. He is.

HACKER: Well, I suppose I 'ad better get back. Threaten the labourers. Oh, look who it is. (LALAGE *comes in.*) Good morning, Lalage. I do like the name. I 'ad Clout look it up. It's Greek for wild and awkward isn't it?

LALAGE: I've made up my mind.

HACKER: About what?

LALAGE: If you try getting my brother home. In a toolbox or whatever. I will go running to the police. (*Long, awful pause.* HACKER *looks at* MRS TOYNBEE.)

HACKER: Sylvia? What police?

MRS TOYNBEE (*to* HACKER): Go back to what you're doing.

HACKER: **What police!**

THE LOVE OF A GOOD MAN   55

MRS TOYNBEE: Tell you later.

LALAGE: Tell him now.

MRS TOYNBEE (*she turns to* HACKER): There will be no funeral in England, if she can stop it.

LALAGE: I could apologize, but I'm not going to. Once you apologize for something you know to be right, you may as well pack up. I shall have to accept that doing the right thing nearly always upsets people. It's one of the defining characteristics. Nothing that ever changed the world was very welcome. But that's the way of progress. The best of us are spoilsports.

HACKER: You've been talking to Riddle. Riddle's got at you.

LALAGE: Got at me, yes. Talked to me, never. (*She starts to go out, then stops. To* HACKER.) I want you to be certain what the consequences are going to be. If you persist. There are military police here and the penalties are considered rather excessive for this kind of thing. (*She goes out.*)

HACKER: Christ, Sylvia, right now this is something I could do without. (CLOUT *comes in with his wheelbarrow, drops it noisily to remind* HACKER *of their tasks.*) All right, Clout.

MRS TOYNBEE: Are you capitulating to that threat?

HACKER: I don't think so . . .

MRS TOYNBEE: You don't **think** so?

HACKER: Of course I'm not, I — (*He sees* CLOUT *is standing impatiently.*) I'm coming, Clout! (*He turns back to* MRS TOYNBEE.) Only I'm buggered if I see a way round — (CLOUT *drops his spade noisily into the empty wheelbarrow.*) Someone wants to make a point.

MRS TOYNBEE: Do this for me. I am yours for this. But not without it. (*Pause.* HACKER *looks injured.*) Does that hurt you?

HACKER: A little bit . . . I thought you might have wanted me for myself . . .

MRS TOYNBEE: I promise you I will be all you want. To the limit of my ability.

HACKER: Sounds like athletics. (CLOUT *is watching, arms folded. She takes his hand, kisses it.*) I mean, what sort of kiss is that? Is it pity or respect? (*She releases it.*) I wish it was just a bit of common or garden lust. I'm sorry, but I do. (*She goes out. He watches her.*)

HACKER: Ol' son, you could do it to 'er if she was a corpse . . . (*He shakes his head, then remembers* CLOUT.) I'm not pulling my weight, Clout, I admit that. There are things on my mind preventing me from giving my all to this . . . (CLOUT *just looks at him.*) I 'ave to get a body back to England. (*Pause. He looks*

56 *Howard Barker*

in despair to his employee.) Clout, will you 'elp me, please?
(*Pause*)

CLOUT (*coldly*): Sixty-six and two thirds.

HACKER: What?

CLOUT: **Per cent.** (*Pause. The full import sinks in.*)

HACKER: **This is supposed to be a partnership!** (CLOUT *bends,
picks up the handles of the barrow.*) 'old it! (*Pause.* CLOUT
waits.) Give us the fuckin' paper, I'll sign it.

ACT THREE

Scene One

The 'Dead March' *is played by a Military Band, offstage. In the middle, on the turf stands a dais, draped in a Union Jack. Other Union Jacks are massed along the rear. Either side of the dais, the* SOLDIERS *in crisp uniform. Grouped around,* MRS TOYNBEE *and* LALAGE, BRIDE, *clasping his ledger, and a* BISHOP *in ceremonial scarlet.* HACKER *and* CLOUT *stand modestly to one side. The Royal* GENTLEMAN *attends the* PRINCE OF WALES. *At last the music stops. The* BISHOP *climbs up.*

BISHOP: Why God likes pain. (*Pause*) Always being asked that one, why God is so very fond of pain. (*Pause*) Because He is. Wriggle round it as we might, it's inescapable He must like pain. His own and other people's. He must approve of it. And this is as good an occasion to mention pain as any. Better than most, in fact. Because we are situated in a sea of it. An Atlantic of stilled agony. (*Pause. He examines his fingers a moment.*) Well, I will not apologize for Him. I am always apologizing for Him. It's getting a bit much.

GENTLEMAN (*standing underneath, arms folded*): **Not — the — speech.**

BISHOP: It is, in fact, becoming something of an outrage.

GENTLEMAN: **Wrong — speech.**

BISHOP: This mission — this so-called calling — (*he plucks his robes*) which consists in making the vile palatable, and finding symmetry in the hideous, it is becoming an impertinence. (*The* GENTLEMAN *begins coughing.*) Fear not. I do not deny the existence of the person God. I merely ask what sort of character He has.

GENTLEMAN: **No.**

BISHOP: I ask you, would you let Him near your child? Because, quite frankly, I would not!

58   *Howard Barker*

GENTLEMAN (*coughing*): **No. No. No.**
BISHOP: I look around me at His works — (*He waves an arm over
   the graves.*) And I must answer, let Him touch me not!
GENTLEMAN: **Finish.**
BISHOP: However —
GENTLEMAN (*declaring publicly*): **The Prince of Wales!** (*There
   is a fanfare.*)
BISHOP: I consecrate this cemetery, therefore —
GENTLEMAN: **The Prince of Wales!**
BISHOP: All right, I consecrate it!

The fanfare sounds again as the BISHOP *is bundled down by the*
GENTLEMAN. *The* GENTLEMAN *urges the* PRINCE OF WALES
to go up with jerks of his head. Reluctantly, he does so. An awful pause.

PRINCE (*paralyzed by shyness*): I — I — I — (*He stops.*) Our —
   Our — Our — (*He stops again.*) This is torture to me . . . (*He
   hangs his head. Suddenly,* MRS TOYNBEE *steps forward.*)
MRS TOYNBEE: You are very good. Believe me, you are very
   good. (*He looks at her. He is charged.*)
PRINCE: I — I — I am the head of what they call the British
   Establishment.
GENTLEMAN: **No.**
PRINCE: The g–g–great British Establishment that sends young
   soldiers to their deaths.
GENTLEMAN: **Wrong speech.**
PRINCE: No more of that. No more deaths. I am King Edward and
   I won't have deaths! Finish with that. Altogether better estab-
   lishment from now on. Promise.
MRS TOYNBEE: God save the Prince of Wales!
PRINCE (*joyously*): I declare this cemetery open!

Clapping, and the SOLDIERS *raise their caps three times, with
cheers. Grinning, the* PRINCE OF WALES *starts to come off the
dais, but is stopped.*

GENTLEMAN: Stay there. You stay there. Christ, what is going
   on today! (*He goes back up. The* GENTLEMAN *takes a slip of
   paper and gives it to the* PRINCE OF WALES *to read.*)
PRINCE (*reading*): It is now my solemn duty, on behalf of King
   and Empire, to choose from all our missing the Unknown Warrior. (*He clears his throat.* BRIDE *steps forward with his ledger.*

THE LOVE OF A GOOD MAN   59

The GENTLEMAN *takes it from him and hands it up to the*
PRINCE OF WALES.)

GENTLEMAN: Book. (*He removes a pin from his lapel, hands this
up.*) Pin. (*He shakes out a white handkerchief.*) Blindfold. (*He
goes behind the* PRINCE OF WALES *and covers his eyes, then
holds the book for the* PRINCE OF WALES *to flick through the
pages. The* PRINCE OF WALES *stops at a page and jabs with
the pin. The* GENTLEMAN *looks down.*) No. 1127161. (*The*
PRINCE OF WALES *starts to descend.*)

FLOWERS: 'Shun! (*The* SOLDIERS *stamp to attention. As he
comes down the* PRINCE OF WALES *stops by* FLOWERS.)

PRINCE: I remember you.

FLOWERS: Me, sir?

PRINCE: Why didn't you tell them that I kissed your hand?

FLOWERS: Tell who, sir?

PRINCE: The newspapers. It was a cameo of m–m–modern
history. Like Sir W–W–Walter Raleigh laying down his cloak.

FLOWERS: Thought we should keep it to ourselves, sir.

PRINCE: It was meant to be symbolical.

FLOWERS: Sym — what, sir?

PRINCE: Don't d–d–damned well keep it to yourself, that's what
symbolical means!

GENTLEMAN (*administering the formalities*): The Contractor,
your Highness, (*he looks at a list*) **Mr Ronald Hacker.**

HACKER (*attempting to bow*): Pleased to —

PRINCE: Jolly pretty. Lovely. Everything. (*He walks past* HAC-
KER). Want to meet the woman.

GENTLEMAN: As you wish. (*He beckons* MRS TOYNBEE *with
a finger, as she comes forward he leans towards her inquiringly.*)
Who are you?

MRS TOYNBEE: Sylvia Toynbee.

GENTLEMAN: Mrs or Miss?

MRS TOYNBEE: Mrs.

GENTLEMAN (*turning back to the* PRINCE OF WALES): Your
Highness, **Mrs Sylvia Toynbee!** (*The* PRINCE OF WALES *shyly
takes her hand. The* GENTLEMAN *picks out* BRIDE *next.*) Next!

PRINCE: Tongue-tied.

MRS TOYNBEE: Like last time.

PRINCE: Yes. Yes. (*With sudden inspiration.*) The dog! The dog!

MRS TOYNBEE: He's very well, thank you. (*Pause. The* PRINCE
OF WALES *looks down, ashamed.*)

PRINCE: God, I have simply nothing in my head . . . ! (*The* GEN-
TLEMAN *coughs, waiting with* BRIDE.)

60   *Howard Barker*

MRS TOYNBEE (*smoothly*): I am holding a seance here tonight.
   Would you care to join us?
PRINCE: Yes, oh, yes! (*She turns away.*)
GENTLEMAN: Your Highness, Chief Graves Commissioner, **Mr
   Hector Bride!** (*The* PRINCE OF WALES *shakes his hand. There
   is a silence.*)
PRINCE: Nothing to say. Nothing to say to this man.
GENTLEMAN (*to* BRIDE): You may withdraw. (*He steps back.*)
PRINCE: That's it, then, is it?
GENTLEMAN: You must be polite to the officials!
PRINCE: George, she wants to meet me here tonight.
GENTLEMAN: Will you listen! You have got to be decent to
   officials. Sans them, sans everything! Do you follow me?
PRINCE: I'm sorry, yes. (*He is suddenly cast down.*) Oh fuck, I've
   ballsed-up everything!
GENTLEMAN: Don't say that.
PRINCE: Yes, I have.
GENTLEMAN: Keep your head up, please. (*He nods to stage left.
   The band strikes up. They leave sedately. After a few bars, the
   band stops. The* SOLDIERS *break rank, tearing off their caps
   and belts.*)
BASS (*to* FLOWERS): Kissed your 'and? 'e kissed your 'and?
RIDDLE: Never told us, Mr Flowers. That a prince had genu-
   flected to your cunt-crazed paw.
FLOWERS: Five years of my life. I won't be used. (*He stalks out.*
   TROD *and* BASS *hurry out after him.*)
BISHOP: I meant to say that God is merciful to those who perish
   in a just cause . . . that's what I meant to say . . .
RIDDLE: Is there a God? What is a just cause? Did they even perish?
BISHOP: Precisely the objections that occurred to me . . . (*He goes
   out.*)
HACKER: Well, Clout, they 'ave the Unknown Warrior.
CLOUT: Sir.
HACKER: Mr Billy Toynbee. In Westminster Abbey before a
   massive concourse of the nation. Buried among kings and poets.
   Ramsay MacDonald, Mr Asquith, and assembled upper-class
   tarts weeping. I feel quite envious.
CLOUT: Unknown, though, Mr 'acker.
HACKER: Yeah, but what a spot! Fuck it, I wouldn't say no to
   obscurity like that. (*He claps* CLOUT *on the shoulder.*) Your
   triumph, Clout. Your credit, son.
CLOUT (*with a yell*): Don't squeeze me arm, please, Mr 'acker!
HACKER: Why what's the matter with it?

THE LOVE OF A GOOD MAN   61

CLOUT: Got fluid on the elbow, copying that number out three 'undred thousand times.

HACKER: Not used to writing, are yer, son? Brute strength 's more your forte.

CLOUT (*moving off*): Better get after Bride. Switch these ledgers back ... (*He removes a ledger from his jacket. It is the one* BRIDE *always carries.*)

Scene Two

Night. Hurricane lamps are burning. HACKER *and* CLOUT *carry on a table, on which are balanced some chairs.*

HACKER: Don't geddit. Sensible woman. Don't geddit. What's she after?

MRS TOYNBEE (*carrying a chair*): We'll have four more chairs and cushions, Mr Clout, please, if you can manage it. (*He goes out, ill-temperedly.* HACKER *sets them out.*) The Bishop is swallowing his theological inhibitions, which will bring us up to eight. Eight is a good number. It is mystical, being a figure formed from two noughts.

HACKER: I must say, Sylvia, I dunno if I go for this.

MRS TOYNBEE: Go for it?

HACKER: Black magic.

MRS TOYNBEE: It's not black magic.

HACKER: Whatever it is, then.

MRS TOYNBEE: It's not the seance you object to, is it? It's the Prince. (*He shrugs.*) He is a lonely young man.

HACKER: So am I, Sylvia.

MRS TOYNBEE: You are married.

HACKER: No. I'm not. (*Pause. He recollects.*) Oh, yes, I am ...

MRS TOYNBEE: You told me so yourself.

HACKER: All right, I am, I'm married, but I'm lonelier than 'im. You can be lonely in a double bed. You can 'ave a body next to yer and it can be as 'ostile as lead ripped off a prison roof. (*He looks at her, as she plumps a cushion.*) Christ, Sylvia ... take my 'and ... take it ... (*She looks round quickly, then takes it, across the table.*)

MRS TOYNBEE: You've been drinking.

62 *Howard Barker*

HACKER: Yep . . . (*She withdraws her hand.*) This new arrange-
ment. 'im being put in Westminster Abbey . . . it's not the funeral
I 'ad 'oped for . . .
MRS TOYNBEE: We will sneak in. Watch from the back.
HACKER: Promise me you'll wear the dress.
MRS TOYNBEE: I promise.
HACKER: Oh, Christ, my love, my 'ands will be all over it —
MRS TOYNBEE: **I hope to God you are not drunk.** (CLOUT
comes in, with chairs. HACKER *sinks into a chair, as* CLOUT
and MRS TOYNBEE *organize them round the table.* BRIDE
appears, in coat and scarf.) Good evening, Mr Bride.
BRIDE: They have just taken him. The Unknown Warrior. They
are all unknown except to me!
MRS TOYNBEE: Would you care to take a seat?
BRIDE: This monstrous funeral in obscene London, London that
killed them, one practised parade for dignitaries to weep! There
should be a million! A million wailing funerals clogging every
street, a million caskets lumbered through the traffic, tumbling
and bursting, a million bodies spilling off of carts in Piccadilly
and a howling of relatives to shake their palaces! (*Pause*) Instead,
it is an exhibition of their dignity, civilized and ordered as befits
a governing race, an occasion to make Sikhs and Bantus wet-
eyed with respect . . . (*He looks at* HACKER.) Did I tell you, I'm
not proper in my head?
HACKER: I think you mentioned it.
BRIDE (*sitting*): When he returned the book to me, after pricking
with his pin, all the numbers seemed the same. Page after page.
1127161.
CLOUT: Not possible.
BRIDE: No. Something's happened in my head . . . (*The* BISHOP
comes in.)
BISHOP: Good-evening, Mrs Toynbee.
MRS TOYNBEE: I'm very glad you've come.
BISHOP: I brought a half bottle of Black and White. In case it
turns any colder. The spirits have nothing against alcohol, have
they? Might help them a bit.
MRS TOYNBEE (*indicating a place*): Sit there, would you? Lal-
age has generously offered to read. It is the fate of sceptics to
record the ecstasies of others.
HACKER (*as the* BISHOP *sits*): Get something in the glass, won't
we, yer worship? Liquid spirits is better than none.
BISHOP: I am a clergyman, not a judge. I am a doctor.
HACKER: Doctor, is it? Might need a doctor when we've done

THE LOVE OF A GOOD MAN   63

with this. If it turns any colder. Look! See yer breath! (*He stands up, breathes out.*)

MRS TOYNBEE: Please, don't persist about the weather.

HACKER: No, I was only saying — (*He moves up two places to sit next to her.*)

MRS TOYNBEE (*indicating his original place*): Sit there, would you?

HACKER: No cushion on that seat.

MRS TOYNBEE: Does that matter? Take one off another seat.

HACKER: I really mean, it's not next to you. That's what I really mean.

MRS TOYNBEE: No. It isn't.

HACKER: Who's next to you, then?

MRS TOYNBEE: Ah, there's someone coming . . .

HACKER: If I'm not next to you, who is, then?

MRS TOYNBEE: Would you lay out the cards, please, Bishop?

BISHOP: Willingly.

MRS TOYNBEE: In a circle, reading inwards.

HACKER (*persisting*): Sorry, I'm not getting through, who is, then?

MRS TOYNBEE (*looking off*): It's Lalage . . .

HACKER: All right. Don't answer. (*He goes back to his place. CLOUT moves to be beside him.*) Not next to me, Clout!

CLOUT: Sorry, Mr 'acker.

HACKER: See enough of you all day.

CLOUT: Sorry.

HACKER: No, I'm sorry. Spooks are getting at me. Sorry, son. (*He helps himself to the* BISHOP's *whisky.*)

LALAGE (*coming in*): I can't believe that soldiers who died for one superstition are likely to come flocking to another.

MRS TOYNBEE: All we ask is for you to write. No one wants you to participate. (LALAGE *sits.*)

HACKER: Look out, Bishop, there's a thing on yer back!

BISHOP (*turning*): What —

HACKER: 's 'all right. Flown off. Looked like a bat with 'airy legs . . . (*He laughs, drinks.*)

LALAGE: I think it's time we scrapped beliefs, don't you? Made them illegal or something.

BISHOP: This is an entertainment, surely. We wouldn't want to be governed by the supernatural, would we, Mr Bride?

HACKER (*acting sudden strangulation*): Ahhhhrrrr! Something's got me round the neck!

BISHOP: It has as much truth as the Communion. And as little.

HACKER (*sinking down, hands to his throat*): Aghhh . . . Agh . . .

64   *Howard Barker*

LALAGE: Who are we waiting for?

MRS TOYNBEE: The Prince of Wales.

LALAGE: The Prince of Wales?

HACKER (*on the ground now*): **Get . . . it . . . off . . .**

MRS TOYNBEE: He had nothing to do, so I asked him along.

LALAGE (*sitting*): Funny. Princes having empty evenings.

MRS TOYNBEE: He's only human.

HACKER (*getting up*): Only? Nearly human, she means. (*He brushes off his knees, sits again.*) Spirits got me. All right now.

MRS TOYNBEE: Mr Hacker has been drinking.

HACKER: **Mr** Hacker? **Mr** Hacker? As a point of fact I 'ave barely touched it. Clout will bear me out. I 'ave 'ardly touched it, 'ave I, Clout?

BISHOP: You have knocked the cards off.

HACKER: Clout, what 'ave I drunk this evening? I am not a drinking man, am I? This is purely to keep the Belgian damp out of my gizzard.

BISHOP: You have knocked the cards off.

HACKER: Yes, and I will pick 'em up. (TROD *appears as* HACKER *bends down.*)

TROD: Excuse me. (*They look at him.*) I hear you're planning to establish contact here tonight.

HACKER: **Establish contact?** That's good. **Establish contact.** I like that.

MRS TOYNBEE: That is correct.

HACKER: Establish contact with what, I wonder? Who would you want to make contact with? **Don't tell me!**

MRS TOYNBEE (*turning angrily on him*): Why don't you go home if you won't take this seriously?

BISHOP: Hear, hear! (*Pause.* HACKER *is stunned.*)

HACKER: Me? Is that supposed to be for —

MRS TOYNBEE: Yes. You. (*Pause*) I'm not sure there is a seat.

TROD: I can find a box.

MRS TOYNBEE: All right. Get a box. (*He goes out again. Uncomfortable pause.*)

LALAGE: How long do we have to wait?

BISHOP: Royalty are late on principle. I've stood in many freezing places for a duke or duchess and never got a thank you. Why don't we start? There is nothing so good for the soul as the discovery you are dispensable.

BRIDE: We are sitting above men who knew that fact above all other things. Their souls were near to perfect by that reckoning . . .

PRINCE (*off*): **Coo-eee!**

THE LOVE OF A GOOD MAN 65

LALAGE: Would that be him?

HACKER: That's 'im, I know 'is voice, such as it is. Needs a tannoy to be 'eard across a dinner table.

PRINCE (*coming in, followed by the* GENTLEMAN): Good evening, Mrs Toynbee . . . (*He removes his cap. He is wearing matching cap and plus fours.*)

MRS TOYNBEE: Your Highness . . .

PRINCE: Brought George. Hope you don't mind. Got to bring George. George is an equerry.

GENTLEMAN: Good evening, madam, gentlemen.

PRINCE: Want to do away with him, don't I, George? Will do, in fact. Have a very modern monarchy. Where do I sit?

MRS TOYNBEE: There is a seat here.

HACKER: Next to Sylvia.

PRINCE (*sitting, as the* GENTLEMAN *takes the remaining seat*): Thrilled about this. Absolutely.

MRS TOYNBEE: You must believe.

PRINCE: Oh, yes.

MRS TOYNBEE: It's futile if you don't believe.

PRINCE: Believe anything you say.

MRS TOYNBEE: No, it has to be a positive belief.

PRINCE: Yes . . .

MRS TOYNBEE: Must trust.

PRINCE: W–w–will do, yes.

MRS TOYNBEE: Very well, then, place your fingers on the glass.

HACKER: Trod 'asn't come back yet.

PRINCE: Oh, let's begin! Please let's begin!

MRS TOYNBEE: Place your index fingers on the glass.

HACKER: Clout, I 'ope you're properly manicured for this.

MRS TOYNBEE (*as they reach out*): No talking. Everyone to close his eyes, and concentrate every ounce of mental energy upon the glass. Think. Just think. (*Long pause.*)

LALAGE: Nothing.

MRS TOYNBEE: Shh. (*Pause*)

HACKER: Christ, my arm. (*Pause*)

BRIDE: They will not speak to us. They will not demean themselves.

MRS TOYNBEE: Is there a spirit present?

PRINCE: Must be. This is Passchendaele!

BRIDE: They are present but they will not speak to us.

HACKER: Is it just me? My arm's like a — (*Suddenly* MRS TOYNBEE *lets out a strange little cry.*) What? (*She shudders, breathing deep.*) Sylvia.

PRINCE: I feel it!

66 *Howard Barker*

HACKER (*eyes wide open*): What? **Feel what?**

MRS TOYNBEE: Oh . . . oh . . . !

PRINCE: Oh, yes, I feel it!

LALAGE: The glass is perfectly stationary.

HACKER (*on his feet now*): **Feel what exactly?**

PRINCE: **Oh!** (*He suddenly leaves the table, wanders a little way, clasping his face. The* GENTLEMAN *rises.*)

MRS TOYNBEE (*opening her eyes*): My God . . .

HACKER: What in Christ's name is all this?

MRS TOYNBEE (*going to the* PRINCE OF WALES): It's all right . . . it's perfectly all right. This does happen. This is a phenomenon known as the surge.

HACKER (*to the* GENTLEMAN): Shouldn't you be seeing to 'im? Mr Equerry?

GENTLEMAN (*ineffectually*): I think . . . I . . .

HACKER: Seeing as 'e's so 'orribly affected?

GENTLEMAN: I think . . . I . . .

HACKER: Seeing as being so near to Mrs Toynbee 'as spiritually buggered 'im?

MRS TOYNBEE: Would everybody just keep quiet?

HACKER (*helping himself*): Whisky for you, Bishop? Doctor, or whatever. Keep the evil out of yer?

BISHOP (*taking it*): I had no feeling. I had no feeling at all.

HACKER: No, well you wouldn't 'ave done. Nor did Clout 'ere. Nor anybody else, I think. But then look where we are sitting.

BISHOP: Too far from the source of —

HACKER: Much too far from the source, I'd say.

PRINCE (*returning to his seat*): Extraordinary. Q–q–quite extraordinary.

LALAGE: It's awfully dull down here.

HACKER: 'ear, 'ear!

MRS TOYNBEE: Yes, well, perhaps you aren't good at giving yourself, dear.

LALAGE: That must be it.

PRINCE: Try again, shall we?

BRIDE: They will not speak with us. What can they tell us we could ever understand?

MRS TOYNBEE: Mr Bride, all over the world mothers and widows are seeking contact with their loved ones. They are doing this from Texas to the Urals.

BRIDE: We mock them with our curiosity.

MRS TOYNBEE: It is not curiosity! I have lost my son.

THE LOVE OF A GOOD MAN

BRIDE: Lost, yes. There is no compromise with lost.

HACKER: Might I suggest we all change seats? Shuffle round a bit? Give the spirits a bit of variety?

MRS TOYNBEE: We are all talking too much. Close your eyes and —

HACKER (*jokingly*): Clout, you bugger, you're asleep! (TROD *comes in, holding an ammunition box.*)

TROD: You've started.

BRIDE: Here is a soldier. Here is a man who has seen the very bottom of the earth. If they will not talk to their brother, they will not talk to anyone. (*He shifts along.* TROD *puts his box between him and the* BISHOP.)

MRS TOYNBEE (*to* TROD): Will you ask, then? Ask for a spirit?

TROD: If you desire me . . .

PRINCE: We do desire you. I m–m–must tell you, I have not enjoyed an evening more in my whole life.

HACKER: I dread to contemplate your evenings, Mr Wales.

GENTLEMAN: He is not to be titled Mr Wales.

HACKER: Mr Prince, then, is it?

GENTLEMAN: It is nothing, or your Highness.

HACKER: Nothing or your Highness?

GENTLEMAN: I mean, no title, or —

PRINCE: Teddy.

GENTLEMAN: Yes.

MRS TOYNBEE: Can we get on?

TROD (*closing his eyes*): Contemplate the dead. They are with us. Welcome them into your thoughts . . .

PRINCE: It's moving! Already, it's moving!

BRIDE (*appalled*): **They all want to get through!**

MRS TOYNBEE: Somebody read!

BRIDE: **Oh, God!**

LALAGE (*reading as the glass darts about*): **Fritz Immelmann** . . .

BRIDE: German!

LALAGE: **Wur–tem–burg . . . Reg–iment . . .**

BRIDE: **Oh, God!**

LALAGE: **Cor . . . poral . . . Age . . . 19 . . .**

TROD: Have you a message for us, Corporal Immelmann?

LALAGE: Yes . . . **Syl–via . . .**

MRS TOYNBEE: Oh, God, it's the man who murdered my son! I'm going to faint . . . Teddy! (*The* PRINCE OF WALES *puts an arm round her.*)

68   *Howard Barker*

HACKER: Bloody 'ell . . . !
LALAGE: **Would . . . like . . . to . . . kiss . . . your . . . arse.** (*The glass stops.*)
HACKER (*getting up*): Trod, you dirty little bleeder!
BRIDE: Sit down! Will you sit down!
PRINCE: Bit thick. Bit thick. I think . . .
HACKER (*to* TROD, *who is shuddering in his seat*): Murky young devil.
BRIDE: They revile us! We have offended them!
LALAGE: Perhaps we could break off now?
HACKER: Why not? My fingers are like ice. But then, I keep 'em to myself, yer see. (*Suddenly the glass shoots away again.*) I'm not on it!
PRINCE: Shut your eyes!
TROD: Read! Read!
LALAGE: **Bride . . . Hector . . . Bride . . .**
BRIDE: I hear you! I hear you!
LALAGE: **Wait–ing . . . for . . . you . . . Come . . . Come . . .** keeps saying come . . . (*Suddenly the glass flies off the table.*)
HACKER: Woke you up, Clout!
LALAGE: Oh, the glass is broken . . .
PRINCE (*disappointed*): No message for me, then . . .
HACKER: Not impressed by titles, are they? Probably Bolshevik spirits, fruit. (BRIDE *gets up, and unnoticed, drifts out.*)
BISHOP (*getting up*): I think we should call it a night, don't you?
LALAGE (*tying up her scarf*): A silly ending to a silly day.
HACKER: Sylvia. I would like a word with you. In private. Please.
MRS TOYNBEE: Would somebody collect the cards?
HACKER: Sylvia, please? (*There is a pistol shot. Everyone freezes. Then there comes a terrible dejected moan.*)
LALAGE: Somebody! (*No one moves, all horror-struck.*) Isn't anyone going to look? (*As no one moves, she hurries off.*)
PRINCE: I'm sorry, I — I never look at people who are hurt . . . (MRS TOYNBEE *hurries off after* LALAGE.) The war cripples . . . I could never visit them . . .
TROD (*still seated, gathering the cards*): No more for tonight, I take it . . .
HACKER (*staggered*): Christ, someone's dead! (TROD *just carries on.*) You khaki bloody maniacs. What 'ave you been up to out 'ere? Don't come 'ome. We don't want you. (*The* WOMEN *enter, supporting* BRIDE *between them. His head is draped in* LALAGE's *scarf.*) Oh, Christ . . .

THE LOVE OF A GOOD MAN 69

MRS TOYNBEE: He seems to have missed. And got his eye.

HACKER: Oh, Bride, poor bloody Bride . . . (*They help him to a chair.*) Poor bloody Bride . . .

MRS TOYNBEE: It isn't helping, saying that.

HACKER: I 'ave to say it.

GENTLEMAN: Not exactly helping though, is it?

HACKER: **It's 'elping me!**

LALAGE: Somebody's got to go for help. (*She looks at the GENTLEMAN.*) Will you?

GENTLEMAN: I am an Equerry.

LALAGE: All right, you are an Equerry!

GENTLEMAN: I'm not permitted to —

PRINCE: George has got to stay with me.

BISHOP: I'll go. (*He moves off, stops.*) If someone else went in the opposite direction —

LALAGE: Mr Hacker —

HACKER: Trod, you go.

LALAGE (*puzzled*): Why don't you?

HACKER: 'e knows it round 'ere. It's 'is battlefield. (TROD *doesn't move.*)

LALAGE (*exasperated*): I'll go.

HACKER: No need for that.

LALAGE: Evidently there is. (*She goes out, left, the BISHOP right.*)

MRS TOYNBEE (*to HACKER*): Go with her, please.

HACKER: I'd rather not.

MRS TOYNBEE: **Why ever won't you help this man!**

HACKER: Why me? Why don't they go? (*He indicates the PRINCE OF WALES and the GENTLEMAN.*) If I've gotta go, why not them? Why can they stay 'ere and not me? (*Pause. She looks at him.*) All right! (*He goes out, followed by CLOUT. The GENTLEMAN sits down again. TROD holds the cards.*)

TROD: My friend did that. The night before we broke their line. He didn't even say goodbye to me. He said if ever he went I was to expect him to appear to me, in the body of a sheep. (*Pause*) When we got into their line I got lost. In the Hindenburg line. I was completely lost. I went down all these concrete steps. There was electric light on. It smelt damp. Down and down, I went, past all these sausages and pairs of boots. Millions of sausages. Millions of boots. I walked for half an hour, underground. Then I saw a mattress, and I fell asleep. When I woke up I was being nuzzled by a sheep. They kept animals down there, for fresh meat . . . (*Pause, then he buttons up his greatcoat. Turns to go. He*

70   *Howard Barker*

looks at MRS TOYNBEE *a moment.*) Your white widow's arse
. . . (*Pause, then he goes out.*)

PRINCE: I wish I had been in the war. Then I might have said that.
If you haven't been in the war, you cannot get away with that . . .
(*He looks at* MRS TOYNBEE.) The number of times I have
wanted to speak crudely to a woman . . . the crude things that
have lingered on my lips . . . (*Pause*) I w–w–would like you to
be my mistress, please.

MRS TOYNBEE: There are times I don't think one discusses that
sort of thing.

PRINCE: Such as?

MRS TOYNBEE: Such as Mr Bride is very ill . . .

PRINCE: It m–m–makes me more impatient. Can you understand
that?

MRS TOYNBEE: Yes.

PRINCE: I have twelve castles. Say which one you want.

MRS TOYNBEE: I don't want a castle.

PRINCE: No, no. S–s–sorry. Some people do, though.

MRS TOYNBEE: Not me.

PRINCE: No. (*The* GENTLEMAN *lights a cigarette.*)

MRS TOYNBEE (*looking at* BRIDE): I do think we should —

PRINCE: Can we settle this! (*Pause*) S–s–sorry . . . (*She turns,
looks at him for some time.*)

MRS TOYNBEE: All right. Yes.

PRINCE: Swear you love me.

MRS TOYNBEE: I said yes.

PRINCE: Say you wanted me from the day we met.

MRS TOYNBEE: Really, you're a little bit too forward.

PRINCE: **Got to! Got to!** (*She looks coolly at him.*)

MRS TOYNBEE: You are very childish, and very weak . . . I don't
think you will make much of a king.

PRINCE: Poor old England. Rotten luck. (*Pause, then with desperation.*) **I want to f–f–f** — (*he shuts his eyes in despair*) **fuck your
cunt!** (*He turns away, ashamed.* MRS TOYNBEE *goes to him,
takes his hands.*)

MRS TOYNBEE: Don't be afraid, I desire you . . . (*She releases
them, just as* HACKER *appears from the darkness. To*
HACKER.) Have you found someone? (*Pause. He just looks at
her.*) You never went.

HACKER: Why is it, I wonder, in this world, muck comes up tops?
Why is it that the narky, dirty little corners of yer character are
the places the truth chooses for its nest? When you look in the
mirror of a bedtime and say, Hacker, you 'ave so much in you

THE LOVE OF A GOOD MAN   71

that I blush to recognize, and the mirror says, yes, but without it
you would be the fool of the universe . . . (*Pause*) I didn't get to
any 'ouse. Nor a telephone. I went a 'undred yards, and doubled
back. I felt filth lying there behind them 'eadstones. Then I heard
yer, and the 'ole bleeding world was the same filth. (*Pause*)

PRINCE: If you will lie around eavesdropping —

HACKER: Shuddup.

PRINCE: No, I shan't shut up —

HACKER: **Shuddup!** (*He looks at him, for the first time.*) You
thing. Pick a castle. Jesus Christ.

PRINCE: If you love someone you want to give them all you have.
I happen to have Cornwall.

HACKER: Shut up. You will 'ave me in prison.

GENTLEMAN: Do bear that in mind. *Lèse majesté* and so on.

HACKER: Majesty? 'im? I would serve twenty years in Dartmoor
before I took my 'at off to it. To think I bust my back, getting
this finished, for you to mince in . . .

GENTLEMAN: This will be reported.

HACKER: Let it!

GENTLEMAN: Lose your contract, I'm afraid . . .

HACKER: **Riddance to it!** (*Pause*) England . . . what I would not
'ave done for that place once . . . (*Pause*) No. Be honest, Hacker.
Don't exaggerate. With Bride there, in that condition, must be
honest, 'ard as it is. England, what I would not 'ave done for it
on condition I wasn't out of pocket. You people turn patriots into
spivs. (*He turns to* GENTLEMAN.) Is that sedition? Stick it
down. (*He looks at* MRS TOYNBEE.) And for you . . . to think
I would 'ave given two arms for a sniff of your knicker . . .
(*Pause*) And to be 'onest — as Bride is 'ere — **I still would!** All
the tricks I worked for you, and I could still treasure one of your
muff 'airs in a tin!

MRS TOYNBEE: I promised I'd make love to you. If you insist
on it, I'll stand by that. (*Pause.* HACKER *is winded.*)

HACKER (*sarcastically*): Well, there is honour for yer. There is
cricket as ever was. She tips a fuck to me like dropping a porter
'alf a crown. (*Pause*) I don't believe you 'ave a body. You 'ave
a ready-reckoner bound in skin.

MRS TOYNBEE: We live as we must, don't we!

HACKER: I'm sorry, but I can't stand 'ere and not 'it back. I am
no bloody gentleman, all 'andshakes and treachery. Give a bloke
'is dignity!

PRINCE: My fault. All this.

GENTLEMAN: Nonsense.

72   *Howard Barker*

PRINCE: Mine entirely.

GENTLEMAN (*turning to him*): Nothing can be your fault. It says so in the constitution.

PRINCE: **It is my fault!** (*The* GENTLEMAN *shrugs, turns back.*)

MRS TOYNBEE (*to* PRINCE OF WALES): I think it would be better if you went.

PRINCE: Never.

MRS TOYNBEE: Please. I'm asking you. (*Pause. Then the* PRINCE OF WALES *kisses her hand, and starts to leave. He turns to* HACKER.)

PRINCE: I don't think you should turn on England . . . because of me . . . it's the hereditary system . . . spewed up me . . . (*He goes out, followed by the* GENTLEMAN. HACKER *has not taken his eyes off* MRS TOYNBEE.)

HACKER: If I was a gent, Mrs, I couldn't bring myself to do this. But they don't polish us in Peckham. I want you to know what hurt is, just like me. (*Eyes fixed firmly on* MRS TOYNBEE.) Billy ain't the corpse rattling on the royal train. So there. Under the drapes, behind the colour party's back, there lies the trunk of some obscure Kraut. Your boy never did show up. And never will.

MRS TOYNBEE: I fully understand your bitterness. I've hurt you, and I suppose we shall always have to live with this dismal passion for revenge. You want to hurt me where I'll bleed the most. But there was a disc around his neck. (*She takes it from her bosom.*) I wear it here.

HACKER (*appalled at her innocence*): All right, you 'ave a disc! **They just got 'old of some ol' disc!** (*Pause*)

MRS TOYNBEE: I am eternally grateful to you. In spite of everything.

HACKER: **Grateful? I 'ave made a berk of you!** (*He shakes his head in amazement.*) You people . . . yer gobs are clamped so tight on the tits of privilege, yer can't stop sucking even when the dugs are dry . . .

MRS TOYNBEE: That was my son. I knew it, the moment I knelt down to him. I knew it in my womb. (*She goes out, watched by* HACKER.)

THE LOVE OF A GOOD MAN

Scene Three

Bright early morning. HACKER *is discovered. He has not moved.*
CLOUT *with two suitcases and* HACKER's *hat and coat.*

CLOUT: Mr 'acker, we are gonna miss the boat.
HACKER: Coming, Clout.

SOLDIERS *enter whistling* 'When Irish Eyes'. *They cross the back of the stage.* CLOUT *assists* HACKER *into his coat and hat.*

RIDDLE (*stopping*): Scuttling back to London with the profits, gentlemen?
HACKER: Well, at least we leave something behind us, don't we? Something to feast your eyes on. More than you lot did.
CLOUT: Mr 'acker!
HACKER: Coming! (CLOUT *leaves.*) I hear they've blown a lorry load of Tans to buggery. Enjoy your trip.

Exit RIDDLE *whistling* 'When Irish Eyes'. HACKER's *gaze falls on* MRS TOYNBEE's *chair. Surreptitiously, with a glance over his shoulder, he examines the chair, then picking it up, he kisses the seat.*

HACKER. Fuck it . . . I have the moral fibre of a rat . . . (*He exits.*)

THE POSSIBILITIES

1 The Weaver's Ecstasy at the Discovery of New Colour
2 Kiss My Hands
3 The Necessity for Prostitution in Advanced Societies
4 Reasons for the Fall of Emperors
5 Only Some Can Take the Strain
6 The Dumb Woman's Ecstasy
7 She Sees the Argument But
8 The Unforeseen Consequences of a Patriotic Act
9 The Philosophical Lieutenant and the Three Village Women
10 Not Him

The Weaver's Ecstasy at the Discovery of New Colour

CHARACTERS

THE WOMAN
THE MAN
THE GIRL
THE BOY
FIRST SOLDIER
SECOND SOLDIER

THE POSSIBILITIES

A FAMILY OF TURKS *are weaving a rug. The noise of a bombardment. They concentrate.*

THE WOMAN: My nerves . . . ! I try, but my nerves . . . !

THE MAN: I am ahead of you now . . . Now, because of your nerves, I must wait.

THE WOMAN: The needle goes all —

THE MAN: The needle goes where you command it. (*A shell lands.*)

THE WOMAN (*throwing down the needle*): **You see, my nerves!**

THE GIRL: It's God's will where the shell falls, and our nerves can neither encourage nor deflect it.

THE WOMAN: I know . . . I know . . .

THE MAN: Pick up the needle.

THE GIRL: If we stop for the shells, when the siege is over and trade picks up, we shall be short of stock.

THE WOMAN: These are all things I know.

THE GIRL: I know you do. I am not lecturing you.

THE MAN: There are many terrible things, but the worst thing of all is to be short of stock.

THE WOMAN: I know. Even my death would not be worse.

THE BOY: Nor mine.

THE WOMAN: Nor yours, either. But I cannot hold the needle when these —

THE BOY (*looking*): Our army is retreating!

THE MAN: God has His reasons.

THE BOY: But the Christians will enter the city!

THE MAN: Then it was obviously God's intention. (*A shell falls. There is a cry near. Pause.*) You have stopped. Why have you stopped?

THE BOY: I should take a rifle from a dead man and I should —

THE MAN: **You should finish the rug.**

THE BOY: And if the Christians hang us?

THE GIRL: They won't hang us. They will look at the rug and say, as they always do, what a weave you put in your rugs!

THE BOY: They will tip you on your front and pull up your skirt, on the rug or off it!

THE GIRL: How can I weave if he says that! **How can I weave!**
THE MAN: You have lost a row of stitches.
THE BOY: **And you they'll disembowel for Jesus!**
THE MAN: And another row. We are allowing the winds of
    passing struggles to break our family down. Look, I still work,
    my fingers are as rapid as ever, or as slow as ever, but I persist,
    I have not dropped one stitch for fear or history.
THE GIRL: I will make up my lost row.
THE MAN: She knows! She knows all pain will be smothered in
    the rug. The rug is the rug my father taught me, and his taught
    him, back to the beginning. All Christians, and all Tartars, and
    all Kurds, and neither Genghis nor the Tsar have changed its
    features. In you, boy thirsting for a rifle, the people live, you see
    the message in the threads.
THE BOY: I know.
THE MAN: You say you know but you still prefer the rifle.
THE BOY: Because without the rifle there's no rug! I don't know
    why, but the rug and rifle are the same. (*A shell falls near.* THE
    WOMAN *rises to her feet, shocked, and lets out a cry which does
    not distract* THE MAN.)
THE WOMAN: Don't stop — don't take any notice of me — (*An-
    other shell. She screeches again.*) It's all right, you carry on, I —
THE GIRL: Just sit. If you stand you will be hit by flying splinters.
THE BOY: A horse is hit! (*A flood of blood swiftly spreads across
    the stage.*)
THE MAN: Perhaps the siege is nearly over. Then we shall eat
    again, but to eat costs money, and we shall have nothing to trade
    if we do not have stock. Stock is all. Stock is life.
THE GIRL: My fingers go more quickly when I think of food!
THE WOMAN: Forgive me, my nerves threaten us all. Forgive me
    and my nerves . . .
THE GIRL: We understand, you aren't as young as you were.
THE WOMAN: I was always delicate . . .
THE MAN: But your fingers worked like ants! Impeccable, relent-
    less fingers which I saw and admired —
THE WOMAN: I was the fastest in the city!
THE MAN: She was, and I did not hesitate, I said, this woman
    must be my wife . . . !
THE WOMAN: It is only shells that spoil my concentration. (*A
    shell falls near.*)
THE BOY: **A man is dead in the garden!** (*A flood of blood swiftly
    spreads over the stage.*) I should take his place . . . !
THE MAN: If you abandon the fringes we will never do the rug —

THE POSSIBILITIES

THE BOY: The Christians will take the city!

THE MAN: They have taken it before.

THE BOY: That is the attitude, if I might say, the very attitude that allows them back. I do not criticize, I am doing the fringes.

THE MAN: More wool. You see, I am through my skein. More wool. (THE GIRL *gets up to fetch wool*.) I admit, this assault has unsettled even me, or I should have had it by me. (THE GIRL *returns with a skein. A shell explodes. She slips in the blood and falls*.)

THE BOY: Are you all right?

THE GIRL: I'm all right! Don't stop working, I'm all right. But I have fallen in the horse's blood.

THE BOY: Or the man's blood, is it?

THE GIRL: Don't stand up! The flying splinters . . . ! (*She crawls to them*.) I'm sorry, I slipped.

THE MAN: We are working to eat. We are weaving not only for the rug, but for what the rug will buy us. Give me the wool.

THE GIRL: I'm sorry, the wool is ruined. When I slipped it fell in the horse's blood.

THE BOY: The man's blood, surely?

THE GIRL: I must go back.

THE WOMAN: Mind the flying splinters!

THE MAN: Show me . . . (*Pause*) Look, the colour! The wool was pale, but the paleness has been coloured by the blood . . .

THE GIRL: I'll fetch another —

THE MAN: Wait. Look, as soon as this is dry, we shall have a different red. I feel certain this is a different red.

THE GIRL: Bring more, shall I?

THE MAN: Bring more, and soak it in the blood!

THE BOY: But it's man's blood!

THE MAN: Yes . . . So when this is gone, run to the hospital!

THE GIRL: The hospital?

THE MAN: Ask to take a bucket from the wounds —

THE BOY: The wounds?

THE MAN: From those who haemorrhage! You see, it has a tone which is not the same as ox's blood.

THE WOMAN: It is a beautiful and unusual red . . .

THE MAN: And it will bring us customers. They will gasp and say no other weaver has such reds!

THE BOY: But that is —

THE MAN: **You quarrel with a gift from God.** You quibble at His miracles. Go, if you want, and be shot by the Christians. Die in the trenches and let their cannons grind your face —

THE WOMAN: Shh, shh —

THE MAN: I tell you, in the great cities of the world, they will bid and bicker for this stock . . .

THE BOY: It is not even Christian blood . . .

THE MAN: Would that improve its colour?

THE GIRL: My brother does not know how to take a gift . . .

THE BOY: I do, but —

THE MAN: It will end, this war, because they always do, and then we shall have no more of this colour.

THE BOY: Cut a throat, why don't you?

THE MAN: **What use are you with your indignations and your lip all out at me?** You have not done a stitch.

THE WOMAN: The guns have stopped . . .

THE BOY: The crescent flag is coming down . . . !

THE MAN: Needle, quick . . .

THE WOMAN: The guns have stopped . . .

THE BOY: We've lost!

THE MAN: Some have.

THE GIRL: The Christians, will they give us bread?

THE WOMAN: Give? Give bread? Their own soldiers are half-starving.

THE MAN (*to* THE BOY): Hurry, to the hospital! (*He goes out. Pause. The weavers work.* TWO SOLDIERS *appear. They stare at the weavers.*)

FIRST SOLDIER: We took the city. And we found our soldiers crucified. Some with no eyes. Some castrated and with their pieces in their mouths.

SECOND SOLDIER: So now all bestiality is okay. All looting. And all opening of girls also okay.

FIRST SOLDIER: I'll take that rug. (THE MAN *grasps it defensively.*)

SECOND SOLDIER: Don't be an idiot.

THE MAN: My stock!

SECOND SOLDIER: What's that? An insult in his lingo? Oi! (*He proceeds to stab* THE MAN, *who dies.* THE WOMEN *watch transfixed.*)

FIRST SOLDIER (*to* THE GIRL): You — with me — I am looking for a servant to wash my things — etcetera — (THE GIRL *gets up.* THE SECOND SOLDIER *rolls up the rug.*) Don't look so scared. I am relatively kind, which is more than you lot manage . . . (*They go off.* THE WOMAN *tries to scream, but is dumb and only her mouth opens.* THE BOY *returns with the bucket, looks.*)

THE BOY: The rug . . . (*He looks.*) **The rug!**

Kiss My Hands

CHARACTERS

WOMAN
VOICE
FIRST TERRORIST
SECOND TERRORIST
THIRD TERRORIST
HUSBAND
CHILD

A knocking on a door at night, repeated. A WOMAN in night clothes appears from a room.

WOMAN: We never open the door at night!

VOICE: We have been ambushed and a friend is shot!

WOMAN: Ambushed by whom?

VOICE: The terrorists!

WOMAN: Which terrorists?

VOICE: Trust us!

WOMAN: How can I?

VOICE: Because you are a human being and not a dog.

WOMAN: I am not a dog, but you might be.

VOICE: Then we have to find another house and our friend will die . . . !

WOMAN: All right.

VOICE: God praise your humanity!

WOMAN: I hope so. (*She unbolts the door.* TERRORISTS *burst in.*)

FIRST TERRORIST: Where is he!

SECOND TERRORIST: Bedrooms!

THIRD TERRORIST: Kitchen!

WOMAN: Oh, Christ make me deaf and you speechless ever more, you have murdered every decent impulse, you have killed all language, you are the terrorists!

FIRST TERRORIST: We are, and it's a pity to have to work this way but your husband and his ilk must be cut out of our lives like warts, and then we shall bring back good neighbours, then you'll need no bolts I promise you! (THE TERRORISTS *drag her* HUSBAND *in, naked and roped.*)

HUSBAND: You let them in . . . .

WOMAN: Forgive me, I only —

HUSBAND: You helped our enemies to murder me . . .

WOMAN: I was not — I had not killed the instinct of a neighbour — I apologize —

HUSBAND: Now I will die because you were so ordinary . . .

WOMAN: Let him go. You cheated me!

THE POSSIBILITIES

83

SECOND TERRORIST: One day, all normal again, and when the door is knocked on, open it . . .

WOMAN: **Never open a door again.**

THIRD TERRORIST: But then the genuine will suffer.

FIRST TERRORIST: Take him to the wood and shoot him there.

WOMAN: **Never open a door again.**

HUSBAND: You have made me hate my wife . . . in my last minutes, feel terrible anger for my wife . . .

SECOND TERRORIST: Good. You should suffer everything for your sins. I hope your child spits on your grave.

FIRST TERRORIST: When we have gone, shut the door.

WOMAN: Leave us alone . . . give us a minute on our own . . .

FIRST TERRORIST: If we did that, you would deceive us.

WOMAN: I swear not.

FIRST TERRORIST: How can I believe your oath? Because we cruelly cheated you, you would be justified in betraying us. This struggle wrecks the old relations! Outside with him.

WOMAN: Forgive me!

HUSBAND: I want to — I want to, but — I am dying for your error! And I had such work to do, who will replace me in the village? I might have served so many, and I perish for your error . . .

SECOND TERRORIST: I love this. I had never reckoned this.

WOMAN: Struggle! Struggle to forgive!

HUSBAND: **I want to!**

WOMAN: Struggle, then . . .

HUSBAND: Don't move me yet! (*They stare at him.*) To survive, we must learn everything we had forgotten, and unlearn everything we were taught, and being inhuman, overcome inhumanity. Now, kiss my hands . . . (*He holds out his roped hands. She kisses them.*) All's well between us, then . . . (*They take him out. She is still, then she kneels on the floor, in a ball. Pause. A child's voice.*)

CHILD (*offstage*): Mummy . . . (*Pause.* THE CHILD *enters.*) What was that noise? (THE WOMAN *stares at* THE CHILD.)

WOMAN: Killers.

CHILD: Mummy, don't be —

WOMAN: Fetch the pillow from your bed. (*He goes off, returns with the pillow.*) Give me the pillow. (*He gives her the pillow. She puts it over his face. He struggles. They grapple, as if endlessly. Suddenly she casts away the pillow and takes him in her arms.*) I will open the door . . . **I will open the door . . . !**

The Necessity for Prostitution in Advanced Societies

CHARACTERS

THE OLD WOMAN
THE YOUNG WOMAN
THE YOUNG MAN

THE POSSIBILITIES

AN OLD WOMAN *in a chair*. A YOUNG WOMAN *dressing*.

THE OLD WOMAN: I thought, treading through the broken glass of rich men's houses, how simple this is . . . ! Picking through the bonfires of their letters and waving their corsetry on sticks, how simple, why has it never happened before . . . ! And standing in the soft rain of burning records from the police house, how clean, how swift . . . ! And then I saw, hurrying from the back door, our men, struggling with cardboard boxes, rescuing the police files from the flames, and it came vaguely to me, this would perhaps be less swift after all . . .

THE YOUNG WOMAN: Don't tell me what I never lived through.

THE OLD WOMAN: I have to tell! Why don't you want to know?

THE YOUNG WOMAN: In all the books, the same old thing. In all the films, the same old thing.

THE OLD WOMAN: We have to tell!

THE YOUNG WOMAN: The heroes and the heroines. The red sashes and the rifles waving in the air.

THE OLD WOMAN: It was like that!

THE YOUNG WOMAN: The grinning face of the dirty worker. Grinning and grinning.

THE OLD WOMAN: And you, with your stockings, tugging at the seams. And your heels, you cannot sit without pointing your heels!

THE YOUNG WOMAN: I don't ask you to admire my legs. The party executives do that.

THE OLD WOMAN: You would travel half Europe for your underwear!

THE YOUNG WOMAN: The party chiefs complain if in the bedroom I am dated by my clothes. They say, don't I deserve the best dressed whores? Am I not a son of the people? You should hear! They talk of fifty years of struggle, and putting their noses to my groin they mutter how my pants redeem all sacrifice . . . (*Pause*) Something like that. I am a graduate and I make it witty.

THE OLD WOMAN: We were happy. Happier than you . . .

THE YOUNG WOMAN: No, I am happier because I don't believe.

THE OLD WOMAN: It is happiness to believe!

THE YOUNG WOMAN: You must justify your life. Your terrible life.

THE OLD WOMAN: Mistakes were made —

THE YOUNG WOMAN: **Errors.** (*Pause*)

THE OLD WOMAN: You call them errors, I —

THE YOUNG WOMAN: **The word is errors. Errors is the word.** (*Pause*) I'm sorry. (*Pause*) Shouting at an old woman. Sorry. The young are vile. But I watched the General Secretary on the television and he said, it is a sign of our greatness that we apologize to the people. These are our errors, the people must judge. What errors, too! **The bigger the error the more we must forgive.** Excellent. Sometimes I think the spirits of the executed gather round my bed and whisper as I fornicate, how miniature your errors are, your little errors barely leave a stain! (*Pause*) Of course, I am jealous of you also. Jealous of your passions. But I hate you for being alive. You should have perished with the others. By your constant alterations you avoided the bullet. You wallow in error.

THE OLD WOMAN: History advances, not as I believed at your age, in straight lines, but in —

THE YOUNG WOMAN: **Zigzags like the seam of a falling stocking.** (*Pause*) I am dining with a foreign diplomat. I, the daughter of the revolution, lend my body to the corrupt. He will be half-inebriated from the casino and may not penetrate. **Thus our purity may yet be saved.** (*Pause*) I might have been the director of an enterprise, but I saw the whores waiting for the foreigners and my pity ran out to them and I wanted to know their happiness . . .

THE OLD WOMAN: Happiness . . . ?

THE YOUNG WOMAN: It must be happiness! If it is not happiness, why should the daughters of a free society submit? It is happiness, or there has been another error.

THE OLD WOMAN: I don't know . . .

THE YOUNG WOMAN: You don't know . . . (*She finishes her dressing.*) How beautiful I am. My teeth. My skin. The revolution has manufactured perfect girls. (*She goes out.* THE OLD WOMAN *stares.* A YOUNG MAN *enters.*)

THE YOUNG MAN: Is Magda here? Are you — Is Magda here? Gone to the brothel? Why do you —

THE OLD WOMAN: She hurt me . . .

THE YOUNG WOMAN: Yes, she is a bitch, and with a tongue that — well, she has a tongue to lap a man to ecstasy and lash a

THE POSSIBILITIES

woman into shame! She does. I admire Magda, I love Magda, but she is a bitch.

THE OLD WOMAN: I won't be —

THE YOUNG MAN: No —

THE OLD WOMAN: Made to —

THE YOUNG MAN: The young are vile, we are so vile!

THE OLD WOMAN: **Apologize for my life!**

THE YOUNG MAN: Indeed!

THE OLD WOMAN: No!

THE YOUNG MAN: History doesn't advance in straight lines, but —

THE OLD WOMAN: Who told you that?

THE YOUNG MAN: Well —

THE OLD WOMAN: Who told you that?

THE YOUNG MAN: Everybody knows that —

THE OLD WOMAN: Everybody?

THE YOUNG MAN: It's in all the schoolbooks. Have a brandy and —

THE OLD WOMAN: No!

THE YOUNG MAN: All right, don't have a brandy, I wasn't stopping anyway.

THE OLD WOMAN: How can she — how can she choose to —

THE YOUNG MAN: It's honest work —

THE OLD WOMAN: Neither work nor honest —

THE YOUNG MAN: It is work. Service for reward. That's work.

THE OLD WOMAN: But the body . . . ! How I wanted to say to her, except she frightens me, how I wanted to say — the body!

THE YOUNG MAN: The labourer also has a body.

THE OLD WOMAN: **Yes, but the act of love!** (*She stares at him.*) I think I half went to the barricades for love. I think I threw grenades for genuine desire. And once I cut a policeman's throat for it, when he might have known desire more than me . . .

THE YOUNG MAN: She knows desire. When she does it with me, then it's desire. You make an icon of her fundament, rather as her clients do. Is this the rationalism of the party?

THE OLD WOMAN: You have no souls!

THE YOUNG MAN: **I have a soul!**

THE OLD WOMAN: You murder love, then!

THE YOUNG MAN: **We murder love?** (*Pause*) You, with your eliminations and your liquidations, your rationalisations and your proscriptions, your prohibitions, your revocations, your knifing of the old and slicing of the mystical, your hacking of the incompatible and choking of the incomprehensible, the slaughter of the unnecessary, the suffocation of prejudice and the notional, the extirpation of the ideal and the fanciful, the terrible scorching of all dissonance, and you say you did it in the name of desire, you talk of souls and love — the mystical of the mystical — **To the cellars with this ancient bitch and one shot in the neck . . . !** (*A gulf of silence separates them.*) Forgive me, you insulted my girl friend. Or it seemed so, anyway. (*Pause*) Forgive me. The young are vile. (*He hesitates, goes out.* THE OLD WOMAN *is still. She gets up at last, and bending, picks up the discarded garments* THE YOUNG WOMAN *left. She shakes them out, puts them on hangers.*)

Reasons for the Fall of Emperors

CHARACTERS

ALEXANDER OF RUSSIA
OFFICER
PEASANT

The Emperor ALEXANDER *in his tent at night. A camp bed. An* OFFICER *in attendance. Terrible sounds distantly at intervals.*

ALEXANDER: Listen, the enemy are cutting my soldiers' throats.

OFFICER: It's wolves.

ALEXANDER: No, the enemy are cutting my soldiers' throats. (*Pause*)

OFFICER: Yes, they are. Go to bed, now.

ALEXANDER: I must listen.

OFFICER: Why?

ALEXANDER: I must. (*Pause*)

OFFICER: They do that. They will not collect the wounded. They are not like us.

ALEXANDER: I watched the battle. You were with me. Did I tremble?

OFFICER: No, not so very —

ALEXANDER: Not tremble?

OFFICER: You trembled, but not —

ALEXANDER: With fear?

OFFICER: Not with fear, no. Pity, rather, and at one point you seemed to have gone deaf.

ALEXANDER: I heard everything.

OFFICER: At one point you kicked the brandy over, a little wave over the generals' feet, and the brandy glasses rolled across the wooden deck of the observation point, splintering as they dropped . . . go to bed now . . . tomorrow they will begin a new attack . . .

ALEXANDER: They die willingly . . .

OFFICER: Yes, they shout your name.

ALEXANDER: They shout it, and they die. I heard them, shouting and dying **I cannot stand that sound** can't we send out patrols?

OFFICER: No, it is too near their lines.

ALEXANDER: It is a terrible sound.

OFFICER: They plead.

ALEXANDER: It is the worst sound in the world.

THE POSSIBILITIES

OFFICER: They plead, but still the enemy cut their throats, such is their hatred for us. I can fetch some wax for your ears.

ALEXANDER: No.

OFFICER: The officers have distributed wax to the sentries. But there is not enough for all the troops. In any case there is some disagreement as to the virtue of this wax. On the one hand it may enrage our soldiers to hear this torture of their comrades, which is good. On the other, it may make their blood run cold and tomorrow they may falter. We have sent to the capital for more wax, but the roads are bad.

ALEXANDER: Leave me now.

OFFICER: As you wish. But if I may advise you, sleep, so you look refreshed and then the troops will think, how confident the Emperor is, we must win! Whereas if you seemed tired or full of grief, they will attack despondently.

ALEXANDER: So it is in their interest I do not listen to their cries?

OFFICER: Yes. Are you sure you won't have the wax?

ALEXANDER: Good night. (*The* OFFICER *withdraws. The* EMPEROR *lies down. The sound of a boot brush, incessantly. Suddenly he sits up.*) Who's there! (*Pause*) Come in, who's there! (*Pause. A* PEASANT *enters, holding the Emperor's boots.*)

PEASANT: Excellency?

ALEXANDER: Who are you?

PEASANT: I am a peasant. I am polishing the Emperor's boots. If the sound of the brushes offends him I will go behind the horse lines, perhaps he will not hear it there, but you can't be sure.

ALEXANDER: You are a peasant?

PEASANT: I am. Doing six years' service with the regiment.

ALEXANDER: How does a peasant sleep?

PEASANT: He sleeps better than the Emperor.

ALEXANDER: Why, do the sounds of his brothers dying not disturb his rest?

PEASANT: They were born in pain. They slit the throats of oxen. They beat and sometimes kill their wives. They die of famine in filthy huts and fall into machinery. The Turk is swift with the knife, though not as swift as the Bulgarian. As for the cry, it's brief. The ox protests as well. Who hears him?

ALEXANDER: I think of this. I think of the grief in distant villages, the orphans who scour the long white lane . . .

PEASANT: They say the Emperor is a sensitive man. Some say they've seen him weep in hospitals.

ALEXANDER: He does.

PEASANT: But the war must go on, at least until it stops. (*Pause*)

92 *Howard Barker*

ALEXANDER: When I hear you, little brother, I know I must build more schools. Do you read?

PEASANT: Read what?

ALEXANDER: The Bible.

PEASANT: No, but I listen, and agree with every word of it.

ALEXANDER: Is it not often contradictory?

PEASANT: I agree with all the contradictions, too. As for schools, if I could read the gentlemen's books, I should only lose sleep, and then the battle would certainly be lost and the Turks would slit not only our throats but the Emperor's too, and that would surely be the end of the world.

ALEXANDER: Do you love the Emperor?

PEASANT: It is impossible not to love him!

ALEXANDER: But he weeps so much!

PEASANT: I forgive him for that. I had an aunt who wept continually but could not say why. She just wept.

ALEXANDER: He weeps for you.

PEASANT: And we for him! We do! Shall I get on with the boots? He will need them in the morning. (*He goes to pick them up.*)

ALEXANDER: **I think that's wrong.**

PEASANT (*stopping*): I apologize to His Excellency. I am a boot polisher and unable to follow arguments —

ALEXANDER: **Liar.**

PEASANT: I am sure we all lie but only by accident —

ALEXANDER: **You are not so wooden as —**

PEASANT: No, obviously not —

ALEXANDER: **As you pretend.** (*Pause. They stare at one another.*) Oh, little brother, I could kiss you on the mouth . . .

PEASANT: My mouth, as all my flesh, is at Your Excellency's service . . . (*The* EMPEROR *sits on the bed and weeps silently. The* PEASANT *watches. Pause.*) My brother died today. So when I get home I shall have twice as many children. Life . . . ! He was a good father and drank so much he punched their eyes black, one after another! Still, they'll weep! And if I die . . . !

ALEXANDER: Don't go on . . .

PEASANT: Then it's the orphanage, but the orphanages are chock-a-block after this war, so they'll end up roaming and probably criminals —

ALEXANDER: Don't go on . . .

PEASANT: There's a murderer in all of us, God says so, so a couple will be hanged and a couple flogged, and a stranger hacked to pieces in his drawing-room, but then the war has

THE POSSIBILITIES 93

little wars inside it like one of His Excellency's decorated eggs —

ALEXANDER: **I said I —**

PEASANT: I only meant — it is not good for an emperor to weep in front of a peasant.

ALEXANDER: On the contrary, what is your love worth if it attaches itself only to a dummy? **That sound!**

PEASANT: It is a good sound, believe me! It is the sound of sacrifice, you should hear it as another hymn to your house, different in tone but not in quality, from the crowd's gasp at your coronation. The Emperor should know the people will go on dying until the villages are dry sticks and the cattle skeletons. The dead only encourage further sacrifice. Along a road of skulls he might dance if he chose to . . . ! (*Pause*)

ALEXANDER: I will put an end to slavery. I will abolish feudalism. I will place teachers in every hamlet. I will break the stooping habit and the ingrained servility of serfs. I will run electricity to every hut and create a corps of critics who will yell at every inhumanity! (*Pause*)

PEASANT: I must finish the boots. It will be dawn and they need all hands at the batteries.

ALEXANDER: Undress me. (*Pause. The* PEASANT *puts down the boots. He goes to the* EMPEROR *and unbuttons his tunic. He removes it.*) Your fingers do not tremble . . .

PEASANT: Why should they? If they trembled it could only be because I was disloyal or entertained some thought of treason, or even that I felt my position shameful in some way, which I do not. How much clothing should I remove?

ALEXANDER: The Emperor will be naked.

PEASANT: He will be cold. (*A cry in the distance.*)

ALEXANDER: Then it will be him who trembles. (*The* PEASANT *proceeds.*) Oh, there is shit in my pants!

PEASANT: Yes. Has His Excellency a chill on the bowel?

ALEXANDER: He was seized by terror during the attack . . .

PEASANT: It was a terrible battle. Our soldiers climbed each other to the Turkish trench.

ALEXANDER: I wept, and I shat . . .

PEASANT (*folding the clothes*): The error was the lack of high explosive shell. The trenches were undamaged.

ALEXANDER: And I pleaded, blow the retreat!

PEASANT: Yes, I heard the bugle! Which was I think, unfortunate, because the retreating men collided with the second wave and more died in the confusion than if the attack had been pressed —

94   *Howard Barker*

ALEXANDER: That was me — and only me —
PEASANT: It is the Emperor's right to have bugles blown at his
  whim —
ALEXANDER: They died, and yet more died . . .
PEASANT: Better luck tomorrow. Shall you keep your socks on?
  The earth is damp.
ALEXANDER: **No socks.**
PEASANT: The Emperor is goose-fleshed, shall I massage his
  limb?
ALEXANDER: **No massage.** (*He stands naked, shivering. A dis-
  tant cry.*) You are dressed and I am naked. You are strong and I
  am weak. You are fine and I am stunted.
PEASANT: Yes.
ALEXANDER: Justify your failure to assassinate me, then.
PEASANT: Justify . . . ?
ALEXANDER: Yes, justify it.
PEASANT: The Emperor takes me for a wolf. I am offended he
  should think I am a wolf. But let him offend where he wishes.
  He is the Emperor. (*A Pause.* ALEXANDER *looks into him.
  Suddenly he shouts.*)
ALEXANDER: **Flog this man! Hey! Flog this man!** (*The* OF-
  FICER *enters.*)
PEASANT: What for . . . ?
ALEXANDER: **Flog and flog this man!**
PEASANT: In Jesus's name, what for . . . ? (*The* OFFICER *takes
  the man by the shoulder.*)
ALEXANDER: What for? No reason. Flog him for no reason. (*He
  is taken out.* ALEXANDER *sits. A cry in the distance. The*
  OFFICER *enters.*)
OFFICER: You want him flogged? You're sure?
ALEXANDER: Yes. And do it now. (*The* OFFICER *goes out.
  Pause. A cry in the distance. He stands. The sound of flogging
  begins, monotonous.* ALEXANDER *listens. A cry in the distance.*) **The boots!** (*The* OFFICER *enters.*) No one is buffing the
  boots. (*The* OFFICER *picks up the boots, goes out. To the other
  sounds, the brushing of boots.* ALEXANDER *stares into the
  dark. He is engulfed by sound, the sound fills him.*)

Only Some Can Take the Strain

CHARACTERS

BOOKSELLER
THE MAN
THE WOMAN

An AGEING MAN *appears with a handcart. The handcart is laden with books.*

BOOKSELLER: Usual wind on the embankment. Usual unkind wind. (*Pause*) Usual bird shit on the volumes. Usual unkind birds. (*Pause. He wipes the books.*) I railed at the birds. I railed at the wind. But I was young, then. Now I say, shit on! Blow on! (*Pause*) Usual fumes from the motor cars. The ever-increasing torrent of motor cars. Our arteries are clogged with anxiety, our lungs are corroded with fumes. **What a conspiracy and nobody knows except me.** We are out of control, oh, so out of control. (*He shuffles the books.*) Yesterday I sold a book. To be precise, I took money and surrendered a book. This was certainly what is commonly known as a sale. Unfortunately, or fortunately, since not every setback appears so on reflection, hardly had the customer left the stall when for some obscure reason I shall never understand, he turned on his heel and replacing the book, asked for his money back. I said, you do this to torture me! But thinking this over during the night, I have concluded that this peculiar action was, in the most general sense, beneficial, since I have the book still in my stock and consequently the knowledge it contains remains in safe hands. I regard it as a bookseller's mission to be cautious regarding who might get his hands on stock. (*Pause. He fusses.*) Of course this cannot last. This will not be allowed to last. **They will act.** Both I and the books will be **eliminated.** I have lived with this for years. I knew, as if by intuition, that time was short. I knew we would be burned. The books burned, and the booksellers also. You think the stake was something of the Middle Ages? No, they shall be my pyre, and I, their pyre. **Oh, something has shit on the books!** (*He pulls out a dirty cloth, rubs a volume.*) Oh, we are out of control, so out of control . . . ! (*A figure has appeared who stares at the* BOOKSELLER. *The* BOOKSELLER *is aware.*) Police. (*He rubs on.*) I act dishevelled. I act the tramp. This way I avoid the attention of both criminals and police. This way the cart appears to be a cart of junk and not, as it is, a pantechnicon of truth which might lever up the world.

THE POSSIBILITIES   97

THE MAN (*tentatively*): All right if I —

BOOKSELLER: Browse, yes, do browse. (THE MAN *examines the books*.) They are closing in on me. They no longer bother to disguise their intentions. I can almost, if I try, I can almost smell the charring of leaves and flesh. But though elimination awaits me with its twisted eye I struggle on.

THE MAN (*with a title*): I have been looking for this everywhere!

BOOKSELLER: Ah.

THE MAN: Everywhere!

BOOKSELLER: You see, it exists.

THE MAN: It does, it does indeed.

BOOKSELLER: Oh, yes, it exists.

THE MAN: How much? It has no price.

BOOKSELLER: It has a price.

THE MAN: Where? (*He turns the book round.*) Is that the price? Is that seriously the price?

BOOKSELLER: The price is perfectly serious, but are you?

THE MAN (*amazed*): But that is . . . !

BOOKSELLER: **Do you want everybody reading it?**

THE MAN: But —

BOOKSELLER: Its price is merely the reflection of its power.

THE MAN: That may be so, but —

BOOKSELLER: Anyway, I don't want to let it go.

THE MAN: You don't want to sell the book?

BOOKSELLER: No.

THE MAN: But it's on the counter and it's priced —

BOOKSELLER: And you think that's evidence I wish to sell it? It proves nothing. Any day I might regret selling it, and then I should have to track you down. God knows where you might take refuge. In any case, how do I know you will understand it? It may be beyond your comprehension. The book will therefore be wasted. The efforts of the author, the printer and the publisher, all wasted. Criminal. No, I have to be sure.

THE MAN: I can't find this book anywhere. I must have it, even though the price is —

BOOKSELLER: Not absurd —

THE MAN: Not absurd, perhaps —

BOOKSELLER: No, in fact, given its scarcity and my reluctance to sell, it is oddly cheap.

THE MAN: Given that you don't want to sell —

BOOKSELLER: It is dirt cheap **and you are the police.**

THE MAN (*pause*): I am the police?

BOOKSELLER: Yes. And that explains your hunger for the title.

Only the police show such persistence in the tracking down of literature.

THE MAN: I assure you I —

BOOKSELLER: Never mind your assurances —

THE MAN: I wanted the book —

BOOKSELLER: To burn. And then, late in the night, you will return to burn me. I shan't be here, however. I shall be on the road. I shan't say which. And those who want the truth will say, he's not here today, he's on the road. We must tramp the streets of every city. Probably he is in Zurich.

THE MAN: Listen, I am honourable and want the knowledge I believe this title might contain.

BOOKSELLER: Or Frankfurt. He is in Frankfurt, they will say. (THE MAN *shakes his head, starts to move off.*) Damn all oppressors! (THE MAN *goes.*) I hate to swear but I think, to fend off his type, it is permitted occasionally to swear. **Shit! The pigeon also hates my trade!** (*He wipes the counter with a filthy cloth.*) Understandable. Look how populous and base the pigeon is. The more it shits the more certain I become that I am the last disseminator of knowledge. No doubt the oppressor is returning to his station to collect a squad. This squad will beat me to death here on the embankment, and no one will look. And he pretended, most convincingly, to want the book. (*He polishes it.*) I have had this by me twenty years. I have saved it from unscrupulous buyers at least five times. It is a struggle, a terrible struggle not to sell and I am tired. I honestly believe he would have paid **three times the price.** That is the measure of how unscrupulous he was. How long can I keep this up? This lonely life? In certain states of light I smell my pyre . . . (*A WOMAN appears.*) I am shutting. I have been open long enough today. (*He starts to pull the canvas over.*)

THE WOMAN: Are you the bookseller?

BOOKSELLER: No.

THE WOMAN: Then what's —

BOOKSELLER: Beetroot.

THE WOMAN: Then why aren't your hands red?

BOOKSELLER: You know everything. Why are you pestering me? I am an old man and they have wanted to eliminate me all these years. God alone knows how I have evaded them.

THE WOMAN: I will help you.

BOOKSELLER: Help?

THE WOMAN: Yes.

BOOKSELLER: Help how, exactly? I need no help. You are a

THE POSSIBILITIES   99

murderer. It is a well-known characteristic of murderers to offer
help. I have a whistle here which I will blow until the last breath
leaves my body. And though they will not stir from their cars but
only watch me through the windows still I will whistle.

THE WOMAN: Your lonely struggle . . .

BOOKSELLER: I have been married, thank you.

THE WOMAN: Your imminent death . . .

BOOKSELLER: What is this? Death is always imminent. It was
imminent when I first lay screaming in the scales. Are you a
philosopher? Not a very good philosopher and thank you I have
been married.

THE WOMAN: The truth . . .

BOOKSELLER: What do you know about the truth?

THE WOMAN: In the cart.

BOOKSELLER: I have to go. I am meeting a man who runs a
theatre.

THE WOMAN: And what have you ever done for the common man?

BOOKSELLER: I have never seen one. Now if you will be so —

THE WOMAN: I am impounding the books. I am Miss Leishman
from the Ministry of Education.

BOOKSELLER: There's no such thing —

THE WOMAN: Put down the handles of your cart, I am officially
sealing your stock. (*She takes a roll of sticky tape from her bag.*)

BOOKSELLER: I was expecting you! All these years I was expecting you!

THE WOMAN: This is an Official Seal. (*She winds it round the
cart.*)

BOOKSELLER: **My speech from the pyre!**

THE WOMAN: Later, someone will give you an inventory.

BOOKSELLER: The cars go by! The truth is sealed and the cars
go by!

THE WOMAN: And the pigeons shit.

BOOKSELLER: They would do, nothing stops their cloaca. I once
saw pigeons shit on a tramp as she gave birth, and the fall of the
Bastille did not change their habits.

THE WOMAN: There, sealed up . . .

BOOKSELLER: **Never to see the light again.**

THE WOMAN: Policies change. Yesterday's shocker is tomorrow's standard text.

BOOKSELLER: More philosophy, where are you trained?

THE WOMAN: You are not to break the seals, all right?

BOOKSELLER: I am tired and I ache for the stake . . .

THE WOMAN: A van will be along —

100   *Howard Barker*

BOOKSELLER: Driven by them . . .

THE WOMAN: By Brian and Gary, I expect . . . (*She leaves.*)

BOOKSELLER: They hunted us, and with such human expression. We are out of control when the oppressor has a human face, so out of control . . . (THE MAN *appears again.*)

THE MAN: Your rudeness almost dissuaded me. I walked four streets and then I thought, I need the knowledge, why be put off? Knowledge only comes to the one who perseveres. I also called at the bank.

BOOKSELLER: Too late.

THE MAN: **It's sold?**

BOOKSELLER: Not sold, but too late.

THE MAN: You are maddeningly obscure and I will have the book if I have to fight you for it. Take off your glasses.

BOOKSELLER: The seals of the State are on my stock. (*Pause*)

THE MAN: Idiot.

BOOKSELLER: Idiot, yes. All my life I struggled. That is the mark of an idiot.

THE MAN: Then where is the author?

BOOKSELLER: The author? Dead, or he became a postman. I forget. Anyway, he could tell you nothing.

THE MAN: Very well. Open the box.

BOOKSELLER: **Open the box?**

THE MAN: Why ever not?

BOOKSELLER: It's gaol and I am seventy.

THE MAN: This is gaol and I am twenty.

BOOKSELLER: The van will be here.

THE MAN: But look, the traffic's heavy, they will be stuck and the engine will overheat. We have hours.

BOOKSELLER: What is this reckless thirst that masters you?

THE MAN: It is the only copy.

BOOKSELLER: How many did you want?

THE MAN: I am breaking the seals.

BOOKSELLER: You are going to disseminate it! I knew when I saw you, he is either a policeman or a disseminator! You will copy it on machines and leave the pages in launderettes.

THE MAN: Yes.

BOOKSELLER: I knew! What do you think knowledge is? Sherbert? (THE MAN *is cutting the seals with a knife.*) Enticer! What are you trying to do, wreck people's lives? **Only some can take the strain!** (THE MAN *covers the* BOOKSELLER's *mouth.*)

THE MAN: Speak and you die. (*Pause. He frees him, finishes*

THE POSSIBILITIES

cutting the seals, and removes the book. He conceals it under his coat. The BOOKSELLER *is still.* THE MAN *turns to go.*)
BOOKSELLER: Zurich. (THE MAN *stops.*) Down by the river. (THE MAN *leaves.*) Under the trees.

The Dumb Woman's Ecstasy

CHARACTERS

THE TORTURER
THE WOMAN
THE YOUTH

THE POSSIBILITIES

103

A widow's house. A MAN *arrives with a bag of tools.* THE WOMAN *is seated.*

THE TORTURER: They said if I came here you would have a room. Have you a room? (*She looks at him.*) You have a room? You have a room but you don't know if you like me? Understandable. I am not local and the accent's odd. Perhaps I'm dirty from the road? I'll pay in advance. Or rather, as I have no money yet, I will give you the toolbag as a pledge. (*He puts the bag down.*) They say they pay on Fridays. What do you say? I am a foreigner, but though I am in many ways unlike you, in others I am identical, so we might progress from there. (*She just looks.*) I don't know what your silence means. I have come across many silent people, but in the end, they spoke. Perhaps that is how it will be with you. I am a skilled man and eat a light breakfast. Also, I sleep soundly and bring no friends back to my lodgings. I am not solitary, but neither am I convivial. What do you say? I won't plead for a room. I would rather lie in a ditch than plead. I am proud, which is perhaps my single fault. (*Pause. He picks up the bag.*) All right, I haven't satisfied you. (*He starts to go, then stops.*) Ah, now I remember. You are deaf and dumb! They told me at the castle, she lets rooms but she is deaf and dumb. Now I have made us both feel foolish! (*He laughs. Pause.*) I am the torturer from Poland and I have been offered a post at the castle. The new lord said there could be no more torture it was against his conscience and dismissed the old one, who, like me, set off across the country in search of a new post. But after six months, the necessity for torture made itself apparent, as it always does, and execution also could not be done without for long, so it was my luck to knock at his gate when the vacancy existed and the need was obvious to all. I have references from previous employers, all of whom were sorry to see me go, but I am a wanderer, I love to travel and I know my trade is never low for long, now shall I go up you unpleasant hag I detest the sight of you and one interview in a day is quite enough. Your eye is fixed on mine like a crow on dying vermin and I know your

104 *Howard Barker*

rooms all stink. (*He picks up the bag, and goes up to his room.
A* YOUTH *creeps in.*)

THE YOUTH: He's here? He's taken the room? I'll wait. (*Pause*)
Listen, he bangs about! He kicks the furniture! And stamping on
the boards! Dust falls from the ceiling! (*Pause*) And now he
dreams . . . Bring him some soup! Poles love their dinner! (THE
WOMAN *goes out.* THE TORTURER *appears.*)

THE TORTURER: A stinking crevice of a room.

THE YOUTH: It is a cheap and dirty hovel for a man like you.

THE TORTURER: It is a gutter of a room, a sewer of a room which
my body shrinks to lie in, and the sheet is steeped in dead men's
vomit. However, I am here now.

THE YOUTH: It is a scandal that a man like you should —

THE TORTURER: Yes —

THE YOUTH: Whose skills deserve the highest respect and the
appropriate accommodation.

THE TORTURER: You flatter brilliantly but I do not take appren-
tices. All I do I do myself.

THE YOUTH: I admire that. The single-minded craftsman who
leaves behind him only —

THE TORTURER: Pain —

THE YOUTH: Or truth? Just as the cabinet maker, with his tools
on his back, leaves in a string of villages the mended doors and
little boxes of his craft, so you —

THE TORTURER: Burst thumbs and leave eye sockets dark as
pits.

THE YOUTH: You are so clear and unambiguous, I do admire you,
I have no craft —

THE TORTURER: You flatter brilliantly.

THE YOUTH: Do I?

THE TORTURER: Perhaps there is employment for you there.

THE YOUTH: As a flatterer?

THE TORTURER: Yes, have you never thought of that?

THE YOUTH: As a profession? No . . .

THE TORTURER: I never thought of pain, either, as a profession,
yet I have never gone without food, women, or a bed. These
discoveries are like lightning flashes, they can illuminate your
life.

THE YOUTH: I will give it some thought. (THE WOMAN *enters
with a bowl.* THE TORTURER *sits and eats.*)

THE TORTURER: What I despise is bad workmanship.

THE YOUTH: Oh, yes!

THE TORTURER: Just as a flatterer flatters best when he half-

THE POSSIBILITIES

believes his compliments, so a man in my trade must concentrate on one thing only — the confession, and not indulge in pain for pain's sake. I have sometimes achieved my ends not by the infliction of pain, but merely by the description. Punishment is another matter. Punishment I never thought of as a work for life. But others do, obviously. This soup is the very sediment of drains. Why is she dumb? Because she's deaf?

THE YOUTH: She has no tongue. And her eardrums burst.

THE TORTURER: Is that so?

THE YOUTH: She is my mother but maternity has limits to its commands, and you're right, she's dirty. I sometimes beat her, and then I think, no, she gave me birth!

THE TORTURER: So rats do their verminous offspring.

THE YOUTH: It is a silly sentiment.

THE TORTURER: Our births result from squalid fornications, we were not thought of then.

THE YOUTH: I never thought of that! You do go — beyond the obvious.

THE TORTURER: Your compliments come naturally.

THE YOUTH: Only out of admiration!

THE TORTURER: There you go again!

THE YOUTH (*laughing*): Oh, yes —

THE TORTURER: You cannot stop yourself!

THE YOUTH: No, no! But who would employ a flatterer?

THE TORTURER: A man in power, obviously.

THE YOUTH: Yes, a man in power.

THE TORTURER: Or alternatively, a recluse.

THE YOUTH: A recluse?

THE TORTURER: Yes, for in renouncing power, he hungers for congratulation.

THE YOUTH: We all love that . . . (*Pause*)

THE TORTURER: She looks at me like a beaten animal, a mongrel half-drowned, this thing you call a mother.

THE YOUTH: I don't know why she cannot be content. Her life is not so bad. She was kept in the castle for less than seven years. Some never leave. No, she is lucky but quite without gratitude.

THE TORTURER: For what offence?

THE YOUTH: Selfishness.

THE TORTURER: Is that an offence?

THE YOUTH: Oh, yes! She claimed to know things others didn't. She spoke in long sentences. (*Suddenly* THE TORTURER *gets up from the table and going to a corner of the room, he thrusts his finger down his throat and vomits.*) What — Are you — Is

106   *Howard Barker*

it — (THE TORTURER *makes a sign of impatience, wipes his mouth, returns to his chair.*) Can I —

THE TORTURER: It is an odd thing, that sometimes, though only in rare cases, those who have suffered lack the dignity that comes with the experience and seek petty revenge. It is possible the soup was poisoned. I don't assert it, I only say it's possible. And the way the hag looked at me, it's clear she hasn't accommodated to the grandeur of spirit pain can bestow. (*Pause*)

THE YOUTH: Amazing man . . .

THE TORTURER: It is easy to be amazing, simply by stating the truth. I have so few enemies, yet I have led people down terrible corridors of pain . . .

THE YOUTH: For truth.

THE TORTURER: Truth? I never ask for truth. Only for confession.

THE YOUTH: I see.

THE TORTURER: Do you?

THE YOUTH: I try.

THE TORTURER: The confession, even if invalid, improves the soul. The victim participates in the act which led to his arrest and in doing so shares, on the one hand, the moral power of the crime, which may have been a crime of freedom, or on the other, the universal evil of mankind, if the crime was only malice. There is no such thing as arbitrary punishment.

THE YOUTH: You mean we all —

THE TORTURER: Deserve our pain. I remember this when my victim cries out in despair, 'But I am innocent!' I think, if she were in the throes of illness she would not cry 'I'm innocent,' would she? (*Pause*)

THE YOUTH: So torture's illness? (*Pause.* THE TORTURER *gets up.*)

THE TORTURER: Does she sleep at all? She has the hollow eyes of an insomniac.

THE YOUTH: But you will one day find your own corpse on the rack!

THE TORTURER (*Pause, he looks at* THE YOUTH *a long time*): I expect it daily. Of course I keep my eyes open, no man willingly exposes himself to a disease. And I frequently move on.

THE YOUTH: You have the right belief for such a craft.

THE TORTURER: I had the good fortune to be trained by a religious man, and after him, a man who had cursed God out of his life. They shared this view, however, that life and pain are inextricable. Is there an inn here? I drink deeply before bed.

THE POSSIBILITIES

THE YOUTH: I think you will find the company dull and their stench noxious, you are so fastidious in mind and body —

THE TORTURER: Remember, when you begin your new career, not to describe yourself as Flatterer, but Truth Teller. Emphasize your cruelty, the harshness of your judgements. Then carry on in your normal way. You will soon be shot of this hovel. (*He goes out.* THE WOMAN *looks at* THE YOUTH.)

THE YOUTH: Yes. I know. I know and I will. **I said I will.** When he returns drunk, or less than drunk, I will. Go up and wait. When you hear it, come down fast, with a swab and a bucket. (THE WOMAN *withdraws.* THE YOUTH *paces uneasily, taking out a pocket knife, which he wipes and clasps again.* THE TORTURER *returns.*)

THE TORTURER: You're right. It stinks and the quality of life is bestial.

THE YOUTH: Did you drink much? You were not long.

THE TORTURER: Much, yes. I find the bestial society brews the best ale.

THE YOUTH: You drank much? And yet you seem — if anything — more vigorous.

THE TORTURER: Would you want me otherwise?

THE YOUTH: Never. Merely that normally our lodgers come back on four legs from there.

THE TORTURER: Perhaps they have no work to go to in the morning.

THE YOUTH: None, most of them.

THE TORTURER: And is the hag asleep?

THE YOUTH: She's gone up.

THE TORTURER: Me, too, then, for the pissy blanket.

THE YOUTH: Good night.

THE TORTURER: Good night — (*Suddenly* THE TORTURER *turns on his heel and seizes* THE YOUTH *in a cruel embrace. He cries out. They struggle.*) Dance!

THE YOUTH: What — I —

THE TORTURER: Dance! (*He spins him round in a mocking dance. A chair crashes over.*)

THE YOUTH: Dance — I —

THE TORTURER: Dance! Dance with me in this —

THE YOUTH: Can't — breathe —

THE TORTURER: — This palace of — hospitality —

THE YOUTH: Can't —

THE TORTURER: Love, oh, love . . . !

THE YOUTH: Oh . . .

Howard Barker

THE TORTURER (*crushing him*): Speak, love . . . ! (*They spin around the floor.*) Oh, speak your heart to me! (THE WOMAN *appears with the mop and bucket.* THE TORTURER *stops the dance, holding* THE YOUTH *fixed and half-conscious.*) She comes, equipped as I do, at the end of a busy day, to swab the stains away . . . **I also love life.** (*Pause.* THE WOMAN *falls on her knees.*) She pleads . . . (*Dumbly, she implores him.*) Silently . . . How good it is . . . her fashion . . . how eloquent her silence is . . . (THE YOUTH *struggles.*) Shh! (*He tightens his grip.*) Oh, this is torture . . . through all her hatred she must plead with me . . .

THE YOUTH: She loves me . . . !

THE TORTURER: Yes . . . she offers herself . . . ! Let me . . . ! Let me . . . ! Who has known pain, know more . . . and all this suffering's for you . . . it is a second birth . . . ! (*As* THE WOMAN *acts her agony*, THE TORTURER *throttles* THE YOUTH, *and lets his body slip to the floor. He goes to the table and sits.* THE WOMAN *is still.* THE TORTURER *breathes deeply.*) Oh, mother . . . I confirm you, mother . . . in your deep fear . . . I'll be your son, now. I will dig the garden. I'll stay.

She Sees the Argument But

CHARACTERS

THE OFFICIAL
WOMAN
MAN

110   *Howard Barker*

A WOMAN OFFICIAL, *seated behind a desk. A* WOMAN *enters, stands before her.*

OFFICIAL: We are so glad you could come.

WOMAN: It was — (*She makes a gesture of casualness.*)

THE OFFICIAL: So glad. (*Pause*) I can see your ankle. (*Pause*) Do you realize that? (*Pause*) You do realize, of course. (*Pause*) And your eyes are outlined in —

WOMAN: Mascara.

OFFICIAL: Mascara, yes. (*Pause*) Very glad you came because we want to understand and I think you do, too. Terribly want to understand! (*Pause*) You see, all this is, we believe, a positive encouragement to criminality. Speak if you want to. (*Pause*) We feel you aid the social enemy. You put yourself at risk, but also, others. The ankle is — your ankle in particular is — immensely stimulating, as I think you know.

WOMAN: I have good ankles.

OFFICIAL: Good? I don't know about good, do you? In what way good? In a sense they are very bad because they stimulate this feeling I am referring to.

WOMAN: I don't like boiler suits.

OFFICIAL: People call them boiler suits! The word boiler suit is meant to — isn't it — prejudice? I don't think we should have called them boiler suits in the first place. In any case we did not succeed with them. For one thing, girls tightened the seats, or undid buttons far below the needs of ventilation. So, indeed, I share your irritation with the boiler suit. But the ankle. What are you trying to do? (*Pause*) You can speak to me, you know. We only want to understand. (*Pause*)

WOMAN: I wish to — this is a difficult question —

OFFICIAL: Is it? You have drawn attention to your ankle, so presumably you must know why. (*Pause*)

WOMAN: Not really, no.

OFFICIAL: You don't know why! How bewildering! You go and buy a length of rather fine wool — many weeks of wages for a typist, I suggest — cut, alter and hem it at this specific point,

THE POSSIBILITIES 111

showing the ankle — without knowing why. Is that honestly the case? (*Pause*) I am so glad you came in. (*Pause*)

WOMAN: I wanted men to suffer for me. (*Pause*)

OFFICIAL: Suffer?

WOMAN: Torment, yes. (*Pause*)

OFFICIAL: I think, don't you, society is so riddled with crisis now, so much healing needs to be done? Crisis after crisis? The food crisis, the health crisis, the newspaper crisis, the suicide epidemic, the lunacy epidemic? So much despair and so much healing to be done? And you say, to all this misery I would add a little more despair, a despair of my own making because it is despair, isn't it? The effect of your ankle on the morning tram, despair?

WOMAN: Yes. Longing and despair.

OFFICIAL: Though of course, among the despairing lurks the criminal. And he, tormented as you wish, will not walk home in silence to his wife, and take his children in his arms with a slightly distant look . . . No, the criminal will own. No city banker has more passion to own. Which is why we stipulated, for a while, the boiler suit. For a long time this damped the criminal statistics. Then they crept up again, thanks to the tightening of the seat and the unnecessary open buttons. You advertise your sexuality.

WOMAN: Yes.

OFFICIAL: I am so glad you came in! (*Pause*) Why don't you marry and show this ankle to your husband?

WOMAN: I am married.

OFFICIAL: You are married! Then why aren't you satisfied to show this ankle in the privacy of your own home?

WOMAN: I don't know.

OFFICIAL: Perhaps you have a secret longing to betray him?

WOMAN: I'm certain of it.

OFFICIAL: You no longer love him?

WOMAN: I love him.

OFFICIAL: You love your husband but you show your ankles to any stranger in the hope of tormenting him, is that correct?

WOMAN: I think so, yes.

OFFICIAL: And where is your responsibility towards the male who cannot contain the lust you stimulate in him?

WOMAN: He should bear his suffering.

OFFICIAL: But you impose it on him!

WOMAN: Yes, and he must bear it. Perhaps I may be seduced. A correct glance or gesture, even a sign of modesty, may do the trick.

112   *Howard Barker*

OFFICIAL: You are a married woman and you say you may be
    seduced —
WOMAN: Yes, I am trying to be honest —
OFFICIAL: Bewildering honesty!
WOMAN: Well, do you want me to be honest or not? (*Pause*) I
    have not yet met this man. But somewhere I have no doubt he
    does exist.
OFFICIAL: And you are seeking him? (*Pause*)
WOMAN: I think so, yes. (*Pause*)
OFFICIAL: The world goes on, crises occur, we struggle towards
    the perfection of democracy, and you, a married woman, dangles
    her ankle on the bus. (*Pause*)
WOMAN: Yes.
OFFICIAL: **You deserve every unwelcome attention that you
    get.**
WOMAN: Ah . . .
OFFICIAL: And I must say, were some monster brought before me
    on a charge of violation I should say half-guilty, only half! (*Pause*)
    My feelings. My real feelings have — soaked through . . .
WOMAN: Good.
OFFICIAL: Don't please, carry your enthusiasm for honesty to
    such inordinate and — (*A MAN has entered and sits at the back.*)
WOMAN: Who's he . . . ?
OFFICIAL: The question is, are you mad?
WOMAN: Who's he?
OFFICIAL: I am married, and I have children also, I am capable
    of love, and have a sexual life, but I do not display myself in
    public, do I? Perhaps you are mad, have you considered —
WOMAN: Who is he?
OFFICIAL: You see, you cannot see a man without —
WOMAN: I just wanted to —
OFFICIAL: The very locality of a man sets off in you some —
WOMAN: How can I continue to be honest when there is a —
OFFICIAL: **He is a human being just like us.** (*Pause*) Such is the
    scale of your obsession you refuse to believe he can observe you
    simply as a person. You think, my ankle will prevent him being
    a **person** and force him to be a **man.** You continually subvert his
    right to be a simple person, you **oppress him.** (*Pause*) But he
    refuses you. He is free. How peaceful he is. He observes you
    with a wonderful and objective comradeship. Your ankle is
    simply an exposed and consequently somewhat absurd piece of
    human flesh. Does he show you his? He also has an ankle.
    (*Pause*)

THE POSSIBILITIES

WOMAN: You are trying to wreck our sanity.

OFFICIAL: Oh, listen, if rational argument is going to be construed as an attempt on your sanity, then your sanity has to be doubted. Is it wrecking your sanity if a man does not suffer your sex?

WOMAN: Perhaps.

OFFICIAL: You define yourself by sexuality?

WOMAN: Yes —

OFFICIAL: You admit your slavery to some arbitrary gendering?

WOMAN: Yes —

OFFICIAL: Bewildering!

WOMAN: I think — this man — this person — frightens me more than a violator would —

OFFICIAL: Oh!

WOMAN: **I am trying to be honest.**

OFFICIAL: **Well, that's not enough!** (*Pause*) That's merely an indulgence. You want us to admire you. But we think you are possibly mad. (*Pause*)

WOMAN: I have to go.

OFFICIAL: The question is, have we the resources to provide a police force whose time and energy are consumed in searching for the violator of women like you? After all, there is a crisis. (*Pause. The* WOMAN *goes to the* MAN.)

WOMAN: You must try to save yourself.

OFFICIAL: Ha!

WOMAN: Yes, you have to try —

OFFICIAL: You look an idiot in those heels —

WOMAN: Look — look at me —

OFFICIAL: He is not moved — he merely suffers the embarrassment any man feels in the presence of a woman who is mad —

WOMAN: Look at me — (*She slaps him around the face.*)

MAN: She hit me! (*Pause. The* WOMAN *goes to the table, leans on it.*)

WOMAN: You want me to be mad, when it is you who is mad.

OFFICIAL: Am I wearing funny heels? Is my clothing so tight I cannot move naturally? Find a mirror, look in it, and ask yourself who's mad. Look in your eyes, which are ringed with soot, and ask yourself who's mad? (*Pause. The* WOMAN *is still.*)

WOMAN: You make me ashamed . . . of things I should not be ashamed of . . .

OFFICIAL: We only want to understand . . . (*Pause. The* WOMAN *leaves the table, goes out. The sound of her heels descending stone stairs.*)

The Unforeseen Consequences
of a Patriotic Act

CHARACTERS

JUDITH
THE SERVANT
THE WOMAN

THE POSSIBILITIES   115

JUDITH, *a year after the slaying of Holofernes, has returned to the country.*

JUDITH: The Israelites could not overcome their enemy, whose resourcefulness was greater than their power. So they sent me to seduce him, being the most beautiful woman of the time, and simple. I went with a servant to his camp, and seduced him. And while he slept, I cut off his head.

THE SERVANT: We put the head in a bag. We carried it past the sentries. What's in the bag, they said. The future of Israel, we replied. A week later Judith lost the power of speech.

JUDITH: For eight months I was dumb.

THE SERVANT: What a blow this was! Because she was the heroine of Israel and looked so sick. What use is a sick hero? So they sent her to the country, and there she gave birth. And with the child, came speech. (*A* WOMAN *from the city enters.*)

THE WOMAN: How happy you seem here . . . !

THE SERVANT: She is!

THE WOMAN: How happy, but no one can place their happiness above all things. Sadly. No one.

THE SERVANT: Why not?

THE WOMAN: Judith, what an example you have set to women everywhere. And on every front our armies drive the enemy beyond the frontier! New frontiers now!

THE SERVANT: And new enemies.

THE WOMAN: None of this was possible but for you. Come back to the city.

JUDITH: I love the quiet.

THE WOMAN: Yes, but just as you owed service to your people, so your people must be allowed to express their gratitude to you!

THE SERVANT: Too bad.

THE WOMAN: It does seem churlish, this exile, this lingering. It curdles the pride they feel in victory. And bring the child! We can accommodate the child. Through the child we show we might be reconciled even with Holofernes's tribes.

THE SERVANT: We haven't packed the olives.

THE WOMAN: Judith, I appeal to you in the name of the people!

THE SERVANT: Oh, don't do that —

THE WOMAN: **Must this person be allowed to speak!** (*Pause*) I'm sorry. I spit. I froth. Forgive me.

JUDITH: I have done enough for the people.

THE WOMAN: Can anyone?

JUDITH: Yes, I have. I have done too much.

THE WOMAN: You made a sacrifice, perhaps the greatest sacrifice a woman can —

JUDITH: I think so, too —

THE WOMAN: To sleep with a man against your will, and you are ashamed —

JUDITH: Oh, no —

THE WOMAN: You feel humiliated and —

JUDITH: No. I often slept with men I did not love, often, I assure you, and never felt ashamed. (*Pause*)

THE WOMAN: That is as maybe.

JUDITH: And acts of violence, I have done them, too. His head admittedly, I had to saw, and hack, it was an ugly act, the sound of it will live with me until I die, but no, that's nothing. (*Pause. THE WOMAN looks at her.*)

THE WOMAN: Then I don't see why —

JUDITH: It was a crime. (*Pause*)

THE WOMAN: A crime? And the war Holofernes made against our infant State? Was that not a crime also? And the extermination of our people which he swore to do, the scattering of our tribe, was that not also, crime? Small crime you did, creeping, insect of a crime. Microbe of a crime. Come to Jerusalem and be worshipped for such a crime. I owe you the lives of all my grandchildren. I kiss you, criminal. (*She kisses her.*)

JUDITH: I spoke desire to him. She heard. Did I not utter such desire that —

THE SERVANT: Even I was —

JUDITH: She was thrilled, and he, too —

THE SERVANT: He looked at her and stood away — when she was naked — stood away —

THE WOMAN: Do I need to know this . . . !

THE SERVANT: They sat naked, and apart. Intolerable, and wonderful! They looked, they drank and ate the sight of one another naked, the air was solid with their stares —

THE WOMAN: I think, enough, don't you?

JUDITH: You see, I did desire him.

THE WOMAN: The ironies! So it was not entirely acting, nor entirely sacrifice . . .

JUDITH: By no means, no.

THE WOMAN: We are human. Or maybe, animal.

JUDITH: And the Israelites, I quite forgot the Israelites.

THE WOMAN: I can imagine . . .

THE SERVANT: No, you can't.

JUDITH: I thrived on him. I was in such a heat.

THE WOMAN: They say he was a handsome man.

JUDITH: Not in the least.

THE WOMAN: No?

JUDITH: Even his breath I longed to breathe. And take him in me, head and shoulders also, if I could. (*Pause*)

THE WOMAN: It seems very satisfactory to have found, on a mission for the State, such private pleasure —

JUDITH: **Oh, I hate this pleasure!**

THE WOMAN: Listen, I come here not to be regaled with —

THE SERVANT: Shut up, she is telling you —

THE WOMAN (*turning on her*): **And you.** (*Pause*)

JUDITH: I could not have cared if he dripped with my father's blood, or had my babies' brains around his boot, or waded through all Israel.

THE WOMAN: You were obsessed. And in my opinion this makes your triumph greater, an epic of will and the supremely patriotic act. Even tragedy. Come to the city and tell this, I'll be by you. (*She smiles.*) Judith . . . (*She extends a hand.*) My dear . . . (*Swiftly,* JUDITH *draws a sword and slices off the proferred hand. A scream.*)

THE SERVANT: Oh, now you've done it!

THE WOMAN: **AAAAAAHHHHHH!**

THE SERVANT: Oh, now you've really done it!

THE WOMAN: **AAAAAHHHHHHH!**

JUDITH: I cut the loving gesture! I hack the trusted gesture! I betray! I betray!

THE WOMAN: Get me to — some hand man — quick! (THE SERVANT *staggers out with* THE WOMAN.) **Hand . . .** (THE SERVANT *rushes back, picks up the hand and puts it in a cloth. She hurries away.*)

The Philosophical Lieutenant and the Three Village Women

CHARACTERS

OFFICER
FIRST WOMAN
SECOND WOMAN
THIRD WOMAN
CORPORAL

THE POSSIBILITIES   119

A hot day. An OFFICER *seated in a canvas chair, his eyes closed.*
THREE WOMEN *enter in peasant costume of the region. They*
abase themselves.

OFFICER (*his eyes unopened*): I see you. You have gone down on
  your knees, and your white foreheads touch the dirty ground. You
  think nothing of your costume, which is grey with dust. This
  morning, you took the garments from your wardrobe, washed and
  ironed them, and picked fresh flowers from the mountain side.
  Not since your wedding day have you been so pristine and immaculate. (*He opens his eyes.*) Is this the national dress? I am not
  acquainted with the peasant costume of this region. Do rise, I am
  the lieutenant of the battery and not a god, though secretly perhaps
  I think I am a god, for reasons you need not concern yourself with.
  (*They rise.*) I have every intention of demolishing the village and
  all the virgins in the continent and all the petticoats however
  perfectly embroidered would not stop me but — (*He gestures with
  his hand.*) Plead. I am not so arrogant as to ban your pleading,
  notwithstanding it could not move me, not a jot.
FIRST WOMAN: My first child was born blind for God knows
  what sin. In the village he has found work among the cattle who
  love his voice. The animals pity him and yield more milk to his
  fingers than any others. If the village is destroyed, he will wan-
  der, fall into ditches, and die.
OFFICER: On the contrary, the destruction of the village will be
  the making of him. You describe a rare gift which any farmer
  would be glad to hire. He is losing precious opportunities in such
  a small place, where he remains only to satisfy your charity. You
  oppress him by your kindness, have you never considered that?
  No, when the battery fires, it will liberate the blind herdsman. If,
  as you say, he has such power over animals, they will help him
  out of any ditch.
SECOND WOMAN: It's obvious you can't be moved by pity, so I
  won't list the cripples or the hours I spent tying in the thatch.
  I won't tell you of the thousand hours we put into the sinking of
  the well, digging the drain to stop the main street flooding, the

labour the women went to embroidering the church, or the carving the men did on the altar, no, nor even the trouble we went to building the little gaol, no, this recitation could not touch you so I only add, if you believe yourself to be a god, and at this moment, we accept you as god, however ugly your face and dirty your uniform, shouldn't gods perfect their souls, polish their consciences and be altogether better than the common infantry whose raping we, whose blinding we, must get accustomed to since our troops are gone?

OFFICER: I am afraid you have a narrow view of deity, which I assert is not to do with virtue but only with truth. I think when I feel myself most superhuman, it is in this way, that I discharge myself of all pity and responsibility and recognize the only laws are those of history, or, to put it very simply, I have a house in the capital and we must win this war or my ability to think in comfort and in peace will be terribly impaired. It was clever of you, and subtle, to seek to persuade me by appealing to my love of my own soul, but gods are by definition, above conscience. It is you mortals who must grapple with that one.

THIRD WOMAN: You can fuck me if you want. (*Pause*. THE OFFICER *gets up and walks around, contemplatively*.)

OFFICER: I think you are only offering me what, on the one hand, I can simply take. And on the other, something my philosophic nature has subdued.

THIRD WOMAN: You can't take my acquiescence, on the one hand, and on the other, I can see from your trembling lip, you haven't subdued anything.

OFFICER: What kind of bargain would it be, between a god and a mortal? I admit your willing submission would make our union qualitatively different from one achieved by force, and I admit too, your observation that even the most stringent mind cannot suppress the cry of future generations who already send my blood pounding, **Don't lift your skirt**, but I have to say I should enjoy you and still wreck the village, what's my bond worth? A god doesn't respect bargains of that sort. (*Her skirt falls*.) So now, by my honesty, I have deprived myself of three satisfactions any normal man would leap at — the satisfaction of showing pity to the weak, the satisfaction of festooning my soul, and the satisfaction of having a child by a woman I shan't see again. You see, I am not corrupted by power! I must be a god! And if you've finished, I will tell the corporal to begin moving the people out. (*Pause*. THE WOMEN *take knives from their skirts*.) Ah, now that is desperation itself! And scarcely an argument.

THE POSSIBILITIES

121

FIRST WOMAN: You have more words than us, you will win all the arguments. We have to save the village and logic's a bastard or we would not be in this war. When we have cut your throat we will go to the corporal and cut his. And having cut his . . . etcetera . . . down to the regimental spaniel. And having buried you and thrown the guns off the cliffs, we'll watch the crops grow thicker round your pit.

OFFICER: May I expose the fallacy in this?

SECOND WOMAN: You are talking for your life and we are deaf.

OFFICER: I have no option. It is the purpose of my life to think, and to express truth, for example, the truth that soldiers are like wasps round jam, in putting one under the knife you only draw others, and instead of losing the village, you also forfeit life.

THIRD WOMAN: We are the village, and the village is us.

FIRST WOMAN: What you say is true, but we still do it.

OFFICER: You possess a truth, and refuse to act on it? This bewilders me.

THIRD WOMAN: For a man like you, to die bewildered can't be a bad thing, and we might have both enjoyed that fuck . . . (*They crowd round him, and murder him.*)

CORPORAL: Hey . . . ! (*They flee.* THE CORPORAL *runs in with a gun.*) Hey . . . ! (*He runs after them. The sound of three shots.*)

Not Him

CHARACTERS

A WOMAN
A SECOND WOMAN
THE MAN

THE POSSIBILITIES 123

A WOMAN *waits for a man. A* SECOND WOMAN *waits with her.*

SECOND WOMAN: Shh!

WOMAN: Not him.

SECOND WOMAN: Could be.

WOMAN: Not him.

SECOND WOMAN: His horse.

WOMAN: But he is not the rider.

SECOND WOMAN: Unless he's changed.

WOMAN: Or I have.

SECOND WOMAN: His step!

WOMAN: He limps . . .

SECOND WOMAN: A wound?

WOMAN: He would not wound . . .

SECOND WOMAN: His knock!

WOMAN: Some other imitates it.

SECOND WOMAN: Oh, this is love! This is hunger! You dare not think, you dare not imagine! All these years and you refused anticipation. Proof itself arouses your suspicion! (*A further knock.*)

WOMAN: Don't go.

SECOND WOMAN: Why?

WOMAN: Something isn't right.

SECOND WOMAN: What?

WOMAN: Either it is not him, or he isn't himself.

SECOND WOMAN: It is his house!

WOMAN: It was, and I was his woman.

SECOND WOMAN: You are so much in love you dread the slightest difference. You have both changed, but only like two skiffs in a river, swung parallel in the current. (*She goes to answer the knock.*)

WOMAN: You will say it's him, but all you will be saying is, it looks like him.

SECOND WOMAN: It has been a long war. Do welcome him. (*She goes. The* WOMAN *covers her face with a veil. The* SECOND WOMAN *returns.*) I think it's him . . . (*The* MAN *enters with a heavy sack. He puts down the sack.*)

MAN: It was a long war, so the sack is heavy.

SECOND WOMAN: You killed many?

MAN (*looking at the* WOMAN): Killed and killed. Sometimes they were brave, sometimes they were reckless, and sometimes they fled! It was never certain. So we sometimes advanced expecting them to flee, and they assaulted us. And other times, in dread of their reputation, we shuddered before the attack, and then they melted away in the darkness, weeping. This was all apparently without reason. But whether they had been stubborn or turned their backs, we still caught them and beheaded them. So in the bag are the heads of heroes and of cowards, which from which is now impossible to distinguish. And now, a chair for me, if I might sit in my own house. (*The* SECOND WOMAN *peers in the bag.*)

SECOND WOMAN: It's true! These are all heads!

MAN: What did you think, I'd cheat you with cabbages? (SECOND WOMAN *goes to fetch a chair.*) You do not raise your veil, quite rightly. You keep your distance, and quite rightly. I have been patient, so what's the delay of a few hours? (SECOND WOMAN *returns. He sits.*) The house is clean. The smell of baking tells me all's well.

WOMAN: And what of their women?

MAN: We raped, of course. And some we murdered, but not often. Their skins were oddly white. As for their villages, they won't forget our visits. Do I babble? I am full of stories and gloat. Say if I bore you, or if I am too loud. Ask her to leave now, I am desperate to talk intimately. (SECOND WOMAN *gets up.*)

WOMAN: Don't go.

MAN: Don't go, she says . . . ! (*He smiles.*) You are as cruel as ever.

WOMAN: What became of him?

MAN: Of who?

WOMAN: I am also desperate to make love, but first, what became of him?

MAN (*to* SECOND WOMAN): There have been no men here?

SECOND WOMAN: No one near! Anyway, who was there?

MAN: Troops passed through, I saw their wheeltracks.

SECOND WOMAN: Some did.

MAN: Some dusty officers, with rose-red epaulettes. Some manly troopers in collapsed boots.

SECOND WOMAN: She hid.

MAN: A woman must.

SECOND WOMAN: Even from her allies.

THE POSSIBILITIES   125

MAN: Well hid! And now she aches for a man.

WOMAN: I do ache. And soon I'll show you how, but what became of my husband?

MAN: I am your husband, and if you raise your veil I'll believe
you are my wife. Though I could love you now, veil or not, here
on the tiles.

WOMAN: The more you talk the more I clamour for your body,
but I still ask —

MAN: **What is this question?**

SECOND WOMAN: She wonders if —

MAN: Is the sack not full enough? The dead not dead enough? (*He
goes to the sack, tips it. Heads spill out.*) I'll hammer bullet cases
through the eyes if she requires it, tell her. I did not maim so
many, look, these still have ears, would she prefer I pruned them?
I come back, not only having saved the village, not only having
defended the frontier but crossed it, over mountain ranges where
the shepherds have strange eyes, and punished the enemy in their
green valleys, burned their churches and their schools, and now
the emperor moves the frontier by a dozen miles, what more can
a husband do? Lie down, and I will give you children, fill your
belly as I tore open others, give you laughing infants as I
skewered others, make you a mother here as I ended maternity
elsewhere. (*Pause. The* WOMAN *raises her veil and kisses his
mouth.*)

SECOND WOMAN: She desires him, as she did not her first husband.

WOMAN: For a long time I did not recognize you. Your voice has
changed, and even your shape. And now you speak long sentences when once you grunted.

SECOND WOMAN: Well, if it's him, I'll leave you.

WOMAN: It's him, though his hair is different and his eyes are
brown, not grey. And look, his fingers are so slender!

SECOND WOMAN: I'll leave you. (*She goes out. The* MAN *goes
to reach for the* WOMAN.)

WOMAN: Put the heads away! I don't want their eyes to see me
naked. (*He thrusts them back in the sack, then goes to undress
her.*) No! Their gore is on your fingers! (*He grabs a cloth and
wipes himself, thrusts it aside and goes to her again.*) Wait . . .
Wait, you smell of death. Quick, to the bath and return as perfect
as I am.

MAN: Did any man require such reservoirs of patience?

WOMAN: Anticipation of this moment kept me whole through
seven years. If we rush through our feelings it will be all over in

126 *Howard Barker*

a second and I shall have no memory to cherish in my widow-hood.

MAN: Widowhood?

WOMAN: To lick and roll around my mind on stagnant even-ings —

MAN: **Widowhood?**

WOMAN: Shh! My neighbour will run in —

MAN: No, explain this widowhood —

WOMAN: Shan't you die? Are you immortal?

MAN: One day. (*Pause*)

WOMAN: Then I'll be your widow. That's all. (*Pause. The* MAN *smiles.*)

MAN: I made widows.

WOMAN: Yes.

MAN: I made them weep so much in places I shall never even see . . .

WOMAN: Good. Let them suffer. Let them weep the sight out of their eyes. Go now, the bath's full. (*The* MAN *turns.*) How beautiful you are. Your hip, and your tense thigh. Nothing is imperfect in you. Nothing offends me, in manner or in speech. (*Pause, The* MAN *goes out. The* SECOND WOMAN *enters.*)

SECOND WOMAN: Is it — has he —

WOMAN: Oh, God, I am sick with desire!

SECOND WOMAN: Oh, wonderful . . . ! And is he — has he —

WOMAN: I sent him to wash —

SECOND WOMAN: I'll go . . . !

WOMAN: No, no, wait with me. I am shaking with wanting him, look at my fingers — and his nakedness!

SECOND WOMAN: I daren't imagine!

WOMAN: His voice —

SECOND WOMAN: Wonderful voice —

WOMAN: His words, his hunger —

SECOND WOMAN: Wonderful words — (*Pause*) But is it him? (*Pause*) It isn't, is it? Not him? (*Pause*) Shh! He's coming! His unbearable haste! (*She goes out. The* MAN *comes in.*)

WOMAN: You were swift.

MAN: I didn't linger —

WOMAN: Swifter than —

MAN: I didn't lie —

WOMAN: Your skin is —

MAN: Damp still — I didn't —

WOMAN: Damp as earth —

MAN: Touch the towel —

THE POSSIBILITIES

WOMAN: Shh! (*Pause*)

MAN: What now? (*Pause*)

WOMAN: Listen, the heads . . .

MAN: The heads?

WOMAN: Mutter.

MAN: Mutter?

WOMAN: Howl!

MAN: I will remove the heads —

WOMAN: No. It's we who must go.

MAN: Go? But —

WOMAN: I know a place —

MAN: **But this is our —**

WOMAN: Not here, though. (*Pause*) I will take you in another place.

MAN: What other place? There is no other. We are peasants not landlords, what place . . . !

WOMAN: I know one. Where I would rather take you. (*Pause*)

MAN: No. Here and now.

WOMAN: No. There and soon.

MAN: **What is this . . . !** (*She looks at him. Pause.*) Very well. The meadow if you want. The barn if you want. The stable by all means. (*They leave. Pause. The* SECOND WOMAN *enters. She sits. She waits. The* WOMAN *returns.*)

WOMAN: I am pregnant.

SECOND WOMAN (*happily*): Yes, I believe you are!

WOMAN: Oh, yes. His desire reached so far, and his splash was such a wave. I have a child or nothing is true.

SECOND WOMAN: And did he yell?

WOMAN: He cried out with the awful cry of disbelief that all men make, and his eyes were searching for their focus . . . (*Pause*)

SECOND WOMAN: You have killed your husband . . .

WOMAN: Shh . . .

SECOND WOMAN: You have —

WOMAN: Shh . . . (*Pause. She sits.*) He thrilled me. Oh, his words of violence, how he thrilled me! And his murders, how they flooded me with desire . . .

SECOND WOMAN: It was him . . .

WOMAN: It was him. Did he think I was fooled?

BRUTOPIA

Secret Life in Old Chelsea

CHARACTERS

SIR THOMAS MORE	An Intellectual
ALICE	His Wife
CECILIA	His Daughter
MEG	His Daughter
ROPER	His Biographer
THE SERVANT	Nurse to Cecilia
HENRY VIII	The Monarch
BERTRAND	A Suitor
BONCHOPE	A Heretic
THE COMMON MAN	An Occupant of the Garden
THE DOCTOR	An Inhabitant of Utopia
THE WORKMAN	
DAKER	A Scholar
FACTOR	Lout to the King
LLOYD	Lout to the King
HOLBEIN	A Court Painter
BOLEYN	A Queen
SERVANTS	
CARTERS	
PRINTERS	
MONKS	
NUNS	
CITIZENS OF BRUTOPIA	

THE SICKNESS

Scene One

The garden at Chelsea. The King of England standing in moonlight. About him, a body of men assemble a massive telescope and its cradle. Others sprawl on the ground.

The Caption

Thomas More published *Utopia* in 1516. It describes the perfect society. His daughter CECILIA composed *Brutopia* in secret. Only now has the text been discovered.

A FIGURE appears pulling on a coat. He kneels before the Monarch.

CECILIA (*aside*): My father did not love me. Therefore I chose to cease loving him. Once I accomplished this, so much confirmed me in the wisdom of my decision. And so it was in Brutopia, that all the reasons one might discover for affection were seen equally to be good reasons for contempt. In Brutopia love was impossible, and anger took its place. This anger was in certain ways, indistinguishable from love.

KING HENRY: I'm here to look at the moon.

MORE: It's late.

KING HENRY: Of course it's late you academic bastard, when else can you look at the moon?

MORE: Forgive me, I'm more than half asleep.

KING HENRY: No, I saw your lamp on, you scholarly bastard, you were in your study.

132   *Howard Barker*

MORE: Sleeping, yes.

KING HENRY: Sleeping in your study? You theological bastard I saw your shadow pass the light or I should not have pestered you. Don't you want to entertain me?

MORE: Want, yes, but —

KING HENRY: That's as I thought, the genius longs to entertain me, so down to Chelsea for a discourse on the moon. Get up now and fix your eye to the lens, you see I come equipped, I come with all astronomy's impedimenta. Gawp. (MORE *is manoeuvred to the eye-piece.* HENRY *speaks quietly into his ear.*) Do you miss me?

CECILIA (*aside*): In Brutopia there was neither lie nor truth. Everyone believed everything.

MORE: Profoundly.

KING HENRY: Profoundly. He misses me profoundly!

MORE: But scholarship abhors society and —

KING HENRY (*squeezing his shoulder*): Look —

MORE: I am looking —

KING HENRY: The moon, the moon . . . !

MORE: Yes —

KING HENRY: Are you looking?

MORE: Yes, of course I'm looking —
          Yes —
          Yes —
          Why do you like the moon so much?

KING HENRY: Don't know. (MORE *leaves the eye-piece.*) Discourse, then.

MORE: I'm no astronomer.

KING HENRY: I have astronomers, I'm here for wit. (*Pause*)

MORE (*returning to the lens*): The moon has long been honoured for its female character — (*a terrible cry is heard*) — a charismatic symbol which in pagan cultures represented —

KING HENRY: What's that?

MORE: What? Charismatic?

KING HENRY: No. The yell.

MORE: Yell . . .

KING HENRY: Yes, I heard one. (*Pause.* MORE *leaves the lens.*)

MORE: You traipse all the way from Westminster in dead of night to —

KING HENRY: Somebody yelled. (*Pause*)

MORE: Bonchope. He preaches heresy.

KING HENRY: The moon has truly entered him.

MORE: I don't know why but regularly this sound issues from

BRUTOPIA   133

him, as if in contempt of speech, I'd say the devil was squatting
in his gob but — (*the cry*) — there it goes again — I don't credit
the devil — shall we proceed, I — (*He returns to the eye-piece.*)

KING HENRY: Where is he?

MORE: In the lock-up.

KING HENRY: Gag him.

MORE (*leaving the lens again*): Gag him? Now?

KING HENRY: His clamour's messing up the moon.

MORE: Gag him?

KING HENRY: Yes, you know, a wad of cloth which inhibits
speech —

MORE: I — I —

KING HENRY (*taking a cloth*): I will. Where do you keep him?

MORE: On the bottom lawn. (HENRY *sets off. The sprawling*
MEN *jump to their feet and follow.*) Should I — do you want
me —

CECILIA (*aside*): And the Brutopians, believing everything, sometimes laughed and sometimes wept at the same spectacle. They
were luckily, bereft of tenderness. This made them perfect
citizens. In Brutopia, you cannot be unkind. So much hypocrisy
is spared by this!

Scene Two

MORE's *garden gaol.* HENRY *addresses its occupant.*

KING HENRY: You explain to me the transmigration of souls and
I will explain to you the paternity of Christ. You first, and re-
member I am a rampant theologian, one slip from orthodoxy and
I hasten your ordeal, speak, I am all monarchic ears. (BON-
CHOPE, *gagged, is seen at the grille of a rustic prison.* MORE
watches.)

BONCHOPE: Mmm . . . mmmmm . . . mmmmm . . .

KING HENRY (*stroking his chin*): Possibly . . .

BONCHOPE: Mmm . . . mmmmmmmm . . . !

KING HENRY (*walking up and down contemplatively*): Possibly
. . . (*The* FOLLOWERS, *propped against trees, laugh.*) Yes . . .

BONCHOPE: Mmm! Mmm! Mmm!

KING HENRY: Steady! Controversial!

BONCHOPE: Mmm! Mmmmm!

KING HENRY: **Heresy! Heresy! We established that at Trent you inveterate liar and manipulator of the doctrine!** (*He goes to the grille.*) Look . . . there is a moon . . . placed in its waters by the Supreme Being . . . do fix your dirty gaze on it, do . . . (BONCHOPE's *eyes rise to the moon.*) Is life not infinitely sweeter than a single thought? For all that got you here is no more than a thought, though you prefer to call it truth, another truth is on its way behind you, shouldering your truth into the truth pit, **look out more truths!** I do assure you, nothing holds, and it hurts to burn, you've seen it . . . (MORE, *unable to contain himself, hurries up to the prison and stares at* BONCHOPE.)

MORE: Oh God, how I do hate him.

KING HENRY: Yes.

MORE: I try to hate his sin, but also I hate him.

KING HENRY: Yes.

MORE: **Hate!** (*Pause*, BONCHOPE's *eyes are full of terror.*)

KING HENRY: Worship the moon, now.

MORE: What?

KING HENRY: Up there.

MORE: You are in a jaunty mood tonight.

KING HENRY: No, no, do it.

MORE: You strain my faith, but I will compose a sonnet.

KING HENRY: Yes, in Latin.

MORE (*after the slightest pause*): Ad lunem, mater et filia —
Lumina et regina stellorum —
Sub canopis aeterna noctum et stabile —

KING HENRY (*holding* MORE *close*): You don't like girls, do you? (*Pause*)

MORE: No. Not in the way you mean. (*Pause.* HENRY *goes to* BONCHOPE.)

KING HENRY (*intimately*): Sir Tom won't jig.

MORE: I think you —

KING HENRY: Your persecutor. Your spiritual whatnot. He won't jig. (BONCHOPE's *eyes move from* HENRY *to* MORE, *and back again.*) Sir Tom wants me to feel the monkey in his presence. He wishes me to feel the ape.

MORE: Not in the least —

KING HENRY: To experience the humiliation of the hungry in the presence of the never-hungry — **hair shirt!** (*He pulls open* MORE's *gown. He wears a hair shirt.*) Hair shirt! I knew it! He

BRUTOPIA 135

mortifies the dirty packet we call skin! He flagellates the sack of gristle we call body, **who can compete with such aversion?** (*Pause. He releases* MORE's *gown.*) No, it's magnificent. It's mastery. He could stare at a woman's belly and think — rot waiting its hour. He could see her hips and think — death's hiding place. Etcetera. No, it's magnificent. Clearly, there is nothing which can stop the mind of More. He is himself a god. (*The moon comes from behind a cloud and floods his face. He turns to* BONCHOPE.) Good night, idiot. Do you know who I am? (BONCHOPE *nods.*) And admire me? (*He nods again.* HENRY *leads the way from the lawn.*) They blinded in Byzantium.

MORE: So I understand.

KING HENRY: Little execution. Much blinding. (*Pause*) More, come to court more often, and show off.

MORE: Show off?

KING HENRY: Yes, you know, show off! (MORE *bows his head.* HENRY *embraces him, holding him tightly.*) Why do you pretend to be a bore?

MORE (*as if puzzled*): I — I —

KING HENRY: Do you want to disenchant me? Do you think a bore is never pestered? Awful error. (HENRY *releases him, strides away, followed by the rest.* MORE *watches them depart.*)

CECILIA (*aside*): In Brutopia, they know no pity. So when hurt, they seek no comfort, but find another to inflict their hurt upon. This eradicates preposterous sympathy! (MORE's *wife appears.*)

ALICE: Are you —

MORE (*turning on her*): **Can't I walk in my own garden! Can't I lurk a little in my plot!** (*Pause*)

ALICE: How powerful the moonbeams are tonight, I —

MORE: **Can't I stroll at any barmy hour without you in flapping slippers —**

ALICE: Yes —

MORE: **Flapping —**

ALICE: Yes —

MORE: **Spy and simperer!**

ALICE: Yes —

MORE (*pointing*): **There is your garden, there!** (*Pause. He swiftly embraces her.*)

ALICE: I understand . . . I do . . . I understand . . .

MORE: Yes . . .

ALICE: I only feared —

MORE: You feared. That is the function of all wives. To fear. Fear on and good night. (*He releases her. She turns to go.*) I am very

136   *Howard Barker*

grateful to you. Thank you. You are perfect and considerate.
Thank you. (*She creates a smile. She starts to go.*) I am writing
a description of the perfect world and consequently cannot sleep
beside you. You understand that, obviously.

ALICE: I understand.

MORE: Good night now and kip well, dear one. (*Again she turns.*)
Hold hands! (*Pause. She returns, takes his hands. Pause. He
closes his eyes.*) Perfect now. The equilibrium of marriage. (*Pause*)

ALICE: Your daughter never sleeps.

MORE (*opening his eyes*): Meg never sleeps?

ALICE: Meg sleeps. I mean the other.

MORE: Other?

ALICE: They are your daughters, both of them.

MORE: Never. (*He laughs.*) How could she, she denies me.

ALICE: Not the paternity.

MORE: No, not that. But the rest. The imitation and the admiration. That she withholds. (ALICE *turns to leave.*) **But I'm not
chagrined!**

Scene Three

Sun in an arbour. CECILIA *sits with* MEG. ROPER, *A young man,
shrugs and grins.*

CECILIA: I dislike you. Shall I tell you why? Because you tell
jokes all the time. I have no sense of humour, so why do you
persist? (*He shakes his head, smiling.*) You want to control me.
That is why you want me to laugh. One day I can see whole
populations laughing, their heads will go back as if on a single
hinge. Laughter! And they will be incapable. They will be en-
slaved! Do stop nodding, you are so — (*He smiles.*) All right,
you have seen my naked arse, do you think that gives you an
authority? (*He shakes his head.*) **Stop smiling you careerist.**
(*Pause*) I wish someone would talk to me who was extraordin-
arily intelligent. Whose eyes. Whose mouth. Radiated like a sun
boiling. But washed. But clean. You seem to think neglecting
yourself is some evidence of moral strengh, to me it is rather —
(ROPER *gets up, walks slowly away,* CECILIA *turns to her
sister.*) How can you love that man, he is a — (MEG *smiles.*)

Shh! His master walks! Shh! His mentor exercises! (*She peers through the foliage.* MORE *is discovered.*)

MORE (*through the trellis*): Do you find nothing funny in the whole wide world? Cecilia?

CECILIA: Nothing.

MORE: Not the absurdity of the posturing prince? Or the monkey's habits?

CECILIA: Neither.

MORE: How hard you are to love.

CECILIA: Impossible, I hope.

MORE: It is a pity we can't talk. It is an indictment of us both, for I can talk to anyone.

CECILIA: I've seen you.

MORE: I have brought workmen crashing off their ladders with an apt remark.

CECILIA: It is an odd talent.

MORE: And left the coarsest labourer choking on my wit.

CECILIA: An extraordinary talent.

MORE: **And you don't giggle.** (*Pause*) My own dear one. My own implacable and adamantine one. My loved, my obdurate. Have you seen spit on a flint? So it is with you. **Girlhood!** Where is it? **Girlhood!** I saw it! There! (*He laughs, turns to go away.*)

CECILIA: Who is in the lock up?

MORE: Nothing.

CECILIA: Nothing? I said who, and you say —

MORE: Nothing. (*He smiles, goes out.*)

Scene Four

A maze. It is raining. CECILIA *enters.*

CECILIA (*calls*): Are you here? (*She goes into the maze, stops.*) You are! I know you are! (*She marches on, to the centre. A* WOMAN *is seated on a bench. She is drenched, but still.*) Mud. Much mud in Brutopia. (*Pause. She sits beside her, embraces her swiftly.*) How cruel are you today? (*Pause*) Oh, bitterly, I can tell. (*She stares at her.*) Warped by resentment, stained by malice, she crouches on her grudges like a hen on eggs . . . ! (*Pause*) Is there war in Brutopia?

THE SERVANT: All the time.

CECILIA: Continuous? The thrashing of the populace in endless struggle! What sort of war?

THE SERVANT: Civil.

CECILIA: Civil war! Yes!

THE SERVANT: The rich against the poor, and the poor are guilty.

CECILIA (*inspired*): The poor are guilty! Yes! Of what, though?

THE SERVANT: Poverty.

CECILIA: Poverty, of course! Their poverty is ugly, and the ugliness of their poverty arouses the indignation of the rich! Yes! The poor rich! The angry rich! So the rich lash the poor, and then? (*Pause*) What? (*Pause*)

THE SERVANT: You don't understand, do you?

CECILIA: I'm trying to.

THE SERVANT: The poor are guilty.

CECILIA: Yes. I said yes.

THE SERVANT: How can you understand Brutopia if you are witty?

CECILIA: I'm sorry.

THE SERVANT: Wit has nothing to do with Brutopia.

CECILIA: No.

THE SERVANT: No wit in Brutopia.

CECILIA: None at all. Forgive me. Anything else? (*Pause*)

THE SERVANT: The poor erupt. They kill the rich. But not only the rich. They kill each other.

CECILIA: Horribly.

THE SERVANT: Horribly. It is their only pleasure.

CECILIA: Yes.

THE SERVANT: This the rich both fear and yet encourage.

CECILIA: They encourage it, why?

THE SERVANT: **Because they need it, obviously!** (*Pause*)

CECILIA: They need it, yes. (*Pause*) Forgive me, why do they? (*Pause*)

THE SERVANT: I can't tell you everything.

CECILIA: No, but —

THE SERVANT: It assures them they are correct. Because in Brutopia nothing is seen to be good unless it is opposed.

CECILIA: Anger is the proof of its correctness! Yes! I'll write this down! (*She goes to move.*) This mud! Everywhere, mud! (*She looks at* THE SERVANT, *who does not move. She stands on the bench, looking over the hedges of the maze. The heads of the Brutopians are seen, plastered by rain, in all the alleys.*) They're not happy. They are sullen. So sullen . . . !

Scene Five

A sunny place. MEG *is reading. Her* FATHER *appears behind her. He leans on her chair.*

MORE: How does my daughter love her husband?

MEG: So admiring is my husband of my father, I might almost say it is my father I have married. Your words ring out in the strangest places, your phrases trickle on our pillow. Peculiar. (*She grabs his hand.*) Promise not to die.

MORE: Never.

MEG: I think to wake and know you cannot be discovered somewhere, in the kitchen or the library, would wreck my —

MORE (*demonstratively*): Thomas More! His tomb! (*Pause. He pretends to contemplate.*) A thing deceptively simple. Severe. A table without embellishment. **More.** His title, in stark and lived letters. **More.** Who dreamed the greatest dream, who overcame the monk, the monarch and the scholar. He dwarfed his peers, and in a cheap time stood a rock of — you finish it —

MEG: I refuse to flatter you, it —

MORE: Indelible and incorruptible —

MEG: No — I said — (MEG *takes his hand playfully. He bites her hand.*) Ow! Ow! (*He laughs.*) Oh, God, you've — ow, you've bitten me! You bite, why do you bite? Look, blood! Why do you bite? (*He laughs.*)

MORE: More's a wolf! (*Pause. He stops laughing.*) I can't apologize.

MEG (*wrapping her hand*): It hurts, it really —

MORE: Yes, but I can't apologize. Don't ask me to apologize . . . (*He walks away, leaving her seated. A wind tugs at the foliage. He walks through covered ways. He stops, seeing a group of figures. He looks at them.*)

Scene Six

A cloaked and hatted FIGURE *is sitting on a low stool staring into a bowl, wide but shallow. Sitting behind him,* THE SERVANT. *A third figure,* THE COMMON MAN, *is squatting behind them.* MORE *approaches them, looks into the bowl.*

140 *Howard Barker*

MORE: What's that?

THE DOCTOR: The solution.

MORE: To what? (*Pause.* THE DOCTOR *does not reply.*) I like the way you keep your hat on it lends you an authority you otherwise might lack, and never meeting my eyes is calculated also, don't forget you are dealing with a genius, where are you from, Spain?

THE SERVANT: I got him in.

MORE: You got him in but where from? He pretends to be a doctor, but suppose he is a murderer?

THE DOCTOR: You have a fever.

MORE: I have a fever, do I? Who told you?

THE SERVANT: I did.

MORE: I am sometimes feverish but that stuff is green. In any case I've never taken medicine. Why doesn't he speak, is he Spanish?

THE DOCTOR: I'm from Utopia.

MORE (*with a laugh*): There are no doctors in Utopia!

THE DOCTOR: Why, is there no sickness?

MORE: How could there be, there is no disharmony.

THE DOCTOR: I promise you, my hands are full.

MORE: With what? Childbirth? And please look in my eyes it is discourteous to stare at the ground, clear evidence to me you never set foot there, it is a society of honest men, without rank, shame or hierarchy. If you think I'm drinking that you are mistaken.

THE DOCTOR: Study the solution.

MORE: Study it? How? What is there to study? (*He kneels.*) All right, I study it. It's opaque. It's odourless. Its colour I have already established.

THE DOCTOR: Nothing else?

MORE: There is a life sized reflection of Sir Thomas More in — (*Pause*) Oh, Jesus, I have put on years . . .

Scene Seven

The rustic prison. BONCHOPE *at the grille.* CECILIA *is looking at him.*

CECILIA: Are you the devil? (*Pause*) Are you, though? Have you got

BRUTOPIA

a **long tongue?** (*He extends it.*) Not long, is it? (*Pause*) I hear you read the Bible in English, why? (*Pause. He retracts his tongue.*)

BONCHOPE: It is God's will His words should —

CECILIA: Do you know God? How do you know His will?

BONCHOPE: It is self-evident God would want His flock to understand —

CECILIA: Nothing is self-evident.

BONCHOPE: You interrupt me when I —

CECILIA: I have to interrupt! I hear such fallacies what can I do but interrupt? (*Pause*)

BONCHOPE: Why don't you cut out my tongue?

CECILIA: Well, of course, that is what they will do, but I am satisfied with interrupting you. (*Pause*) I love the Latin Bible. Latin is music. I don't understand a word of it.

BONCHOPE: Then you are kept from God —

CECILIA: No, I'm nearer —

BONCHOPE: How can you be nearer when you cannot understand the words that —

CECILIA: That's it!

BONCHOPE: When the words are —

CECILIA: That's it! Not understanding. That is it. (*She extends her tongue.*)

BONCHOPE: **Madness!** (*He turns away from the grille.* CECILIA *goes nearer.*)

CECILIA: I think there will come a day you can't hear Latin anywhere. And you will burn the Latin. Because you also are a burner. (*Pause*) Listen! Oh, do come out! Listen! My father sailed to Amsterdam. He went to all the shops and bought up all the Bibles. Your Bibles. The English ones. Hundreds of Bibles! And he went into a field and burned them. Stoke, prod, like the bonfires in the Autumn. But hardly was his back turned and — yes! He didn't understand this thing called printing. Printing really wrecks all discipline! Do you know printing?

BONCHOPE: Yes. It's done with metal.

CECILIA: Metal, is it? Scarcely was he on the boat and they ran off another hundred! (*Pause. She grins.*) So I think it's time to ban paper. (*Pause*)You don't talk more than you have to.

BONCHOPE: I'm horrified.

CECILIA: Horrified? (*A terrible cry comes from the prison.*) Recant, then! Just recant! (*Pause*) Do come up again . . . (*Pause. She looks through the grille. She turns away.*) It's vile in there . . . ! **It's not a dovecote, it's not a dovecote!** (*She hurries away.*)

142   *Howard Barker*

Scene Eight

MORE *is staring into the solution.*

MORE: There is no Utopia. I invented it.
THE DOCTOR: It exists.
MORE: Where, then! Where?
THE DOCTOR: You think you can imagine, and there be no consequences? If a thing is imagined, it is born! I alone escaped Utopia. The place exists.
MORE: You are a Spanish liar and this liquid is a trick, I'm not as old as this!
THE SERVANT: I discovered him outside the gate.
MORE: Yes, well, I'm famous, aren't I? Quacks will queue for me.
THE DOCTOR: I landed at Deptford.
MORE: Deptford, did you? Off what boat?
THE DOCTOR: 'The Angel of Deliverance'.
MORE: I'll check that! I have friends in all the harbours! 'Angel of Deliverance'! Write that down! And then what? Walked?
THE DOCTOR: Exactly.
MORE: Long walk. Deptford to Chelsea. Awful walk. Show me your shoes! (*He peers over the bowl.*) No shoes . . . !
THE DOCTOR: No footwear in Utopia.
MORE: No footwear, why? I never specified the abolition of the cobblers!
THE DOCTOR: No, but it occurred.
MORE: How?
THE DOCTOR: It was a consequence.
MORE: Of what?
THE DOCTOR: Utopia is all consequences.
MORE: You are a Spanish liar! Give its latitudes!
THE DOCTOR: How practical you are, in some respects . . . (CECILIA *appears, breathless.*)
CECILIA: He's standing in shit! (*Pause. She looks at* THE DOCTOR, *then back to* MORE.)
MORE (*standing, brushing his knees*): Well?
CECILIA: That's all right, is it?
MORE: Not only all right, but a good thing. Shit comes from his mouth.
CECILIA: His mouth?
MORE: Therefore he stands in it.
CECILIA: Ah . . . (*Pause*) Thank you . . .
MORE (*to* THE DOCTOR): I shall study the bills of lading, Span-

BRUTOPIA

143

ish doctor, and God help you . . . (*He walks with his arm round* CECILIA, *leaving* THE DOCTOR *seated*.) We must hate evil, we must not extend to evil any tolerance or pity which would stimulate its growth, or even enter into conversation with it, for then it dares assume equality with good, and posturing its legitimacy, corrupts the weaker minds, for some minds are weaker just as some bodies are, it is God's will and we can't dispute it, but to those of us with swift intelligence is lent a natural authority to sort the ideas into heaps, the good and bad heaps, and let the bad heap burn — (*He stops*.) Cecilia, if you withhold your admiration from me is it any wonder I am unkind? Is it? I can embroider what you find hard to speak, but offer up some, do you see, I am being realistic, I am being terribly frank, say you understand me. (*Pause*)

CECILIA: You want — you have to be —

MORE: The focus of your adoration, yes. **Simple enough!** (*Pause*)

CECILIA: Yes. (*Pause*) If only I could be — impulsive.

MORE: Yes. Impulsive, yes. That's what you need. Make Meg your model! (*He smiles at her, squeezes her cheek, goes off. She sees* ROPER *hurrying towards her*.)

ROPER: Sir Tom! (CECILIA *intercepts him*.)

CECILIA: Give us some paper.

ROPER(*who is holding an armful of documents*): Paper, why?

CECILIA: Old stuff. Junk will do.

ROPER: We must account for paper.

CECILIA: Account for it by all means.

ROPER: Four sheets. (*He draws the sheets from his sheaf*.)

CECILIA: Four sheets! You reckless and dissolute man! No, even four's too much, your instinct was correct, I will write it on a **single sheet.**

ROPER: What?

CECILIA: The Fyrste and Most Remarkable Account of the Geography and Society of the Unknowne and Terrible Kyngedom of — Brutopia! Because what is love but emulation? That's love, surely?

ROPER: You should marry.

CECILIA (*sarcastically*): I should have, but you opted for my sister. You married her and not me because she more closely represents my father, isn't that so? He led you to our bedroom and pulled off our covers, and there we were, all arse and breast exposed, and quite honestly, there is not a deal of difference, is there? So it must be —

ROPER: The personality of Meg has always —

144   *Howard Barker*

CECILIA: No, that's codswallop, you thought she was more completely Thomas More. (*Pause*) With necessary adjuncts. Reproductive parts and all female etceteras but him, in essence, whereas I —
ROPER: I think you know so little about love. (*Pause*)
CECILIA: Little? I know nothing.
ROPER (*wryly*): A man will come and steal you. Without your noticing. Steal your whole world. And you will see nothing but him on every page or window. (*Pause*) Hell it will be, I think.
CECILIA: Obviously love's hell, why else would you want it?
ROPER (*slipping away*): Shh! I think he's coming! (*She grins. He disappears. CECILIA turns, and finds a MAN close and staring at her.*)
CECILIA: Who are you?
THE COMMON MAN: The Common Man.
CECILIA: Then go to a common place. This is a private garden.
THE COMMON MAN: Nothing's private any more.
CECILIA: That must depend how many dogs you've got.
THE COMMON MAN: I tame dogs.
CECILIA: How, by suffocating them? You stink and I hate the way you look at me. **Bob!** (*Pause*)
THE COMMON MAN: Bob's my mate. (*Pause. She looks at him a long time. A wind whistles through the garden. Suddenly CECILIA slaps his face violently, time and time again. He staggers backwards, disappears. CECILIA holds her hands in the air.*)
CECILIA: Soap!
         Somebody!
         Soap!

THE SERVANT *appears with a bowl and towel. CECILIA plunges her hands in, washes them, dries them, gives back the towel. She turns, and through the trellis, catches sight of MORE sitting at a table with THE COMMON MAN, talking avidly and laughing. She stares.*

THE SERVANT: Your dad. He loves my class.
CECILIA: Why?
THE SERVANT: My thieves. My criminals.
CECILIA: Why? (*Pause. CECILIA embraces THE SERVANT.*) You are my love. (*THE SERVANT strokes her head.*) Do you hear me? I have no other. (*She frees herself.*)
THE SERVANT: I bathed and dressed you once.

CECILIA: Yes.

THE SERVANT: And slapped and powdered you. And while you slept, skirts up for somebody! (CECILIA *smiles*.)

CECILIA: Good. I trust no one but the two-faced and corruptible. Now say you detested me, even as you spooned my infant mouth.

THE SERVANT: I was near to infanticide.

CECILIA: Oh, nurse, you bitch!

THE SERVANT: Spitefully made pinpricks in you, and hid sharp things underneath your mattress!

CECILIA (*wide-eyed*): You —

THE SERVANT: Sprinkled you with ice-cold water —

CECILIA: Oh, immaculate —

THE SERVANT: Burst paper bags behind your ear —

CECILIA: And no one knew! No one spotted! (*Pause*. THE SERVANT *smiles*.) The world's foul, obviously . . . (*The cry of* BONCHOPE *is heard over the gardens*.) First premise of Brutopia . . . (*She suddenly slaps* THE SERVANT *over the cheek*.) That's for all that, then. Quits. (*She turns away, smartly*.)

Scene Nine

CECILIA *walks through the overhung garden*.

CECILIA (*aside*): Brutopia is a republic, but with a monarch. The population is literate, but there are no books. (*She stops*.) No. (*She continues*.) There are books, but these are written in Brutopic. The rules governing this language are extremely complex! (*Inspired*) Yes! Utterly complex and obscure, and there are no dictionaries! (*She comes to the gate of the maze. The heads of the* BRUTOPIANS *appear among the hedges, complaining*.) No dictionaries, and no grammars, either! (*She goes into the maze*.) Complain away, complaint is the music of Brutopia! (*They mob her. She rebukes them*.) Do you want everybody getting knowledge? What would you do with it? **Upset Brutopia!** Oh, yes, you would, I know you would, it would **unsettle** you. (*She moves on, stops*.) Books can be discovered, yes, they can, but it entails appalling effort. Terrible effort, yes. So those who want must suffer. Knowledge is acquired through pain. (*They groan*.) That's perfectly correct! That's wholly proper!

146   *Howard Barker*

ALICE (*offstage*): Cec — ilia! (*Pause. All is still.*) Cec — ilia!
(*Pause. A* FIGURE *climbs a ladder, stares at her over the hedges.*)
BERTRAND: Is she small? (*Pause*) Is she black? (*Pause. She
   stares back at him.*) I am in the Russia trade. (*Pause.* ALICE
   joins CECILIA.)
ALICE (*sotto voce*): This is a man with a future and good legs.
BERTRAND (*deliberately*): Whalebone. Timber. Fur.
ALICE (*sotto voce*): Twirl a bit.
CECILIA: You twirl.
ALICE: Flick something.
BERTRAND: Leather. Grease. Elkhorn.
ALICE: He has a seat in Parliament. Ask him.
BERTRAND: Resin. Hide. Esparto grass.
ALICE (*nudging* CECILIA): Say something! Don't you want a
   husband?
CECILIA: Welcome to Brutopia.
BERTRAND: Where's that?
CECILIA: Here, of course.
BERTRAND: What happens in it?
CECILIA: Everything.
BERTRAND: And who is the monarch?
CECILIA: The worst swine.
ALICE: His parliamentary seat, ask him.
BERTRAND: And do the people suffer?
CECILIA: Appallingly.
ALICE (*nudging her*): What constituency, say.
BERTRAND: Is there beauty in Brutopia?
CECILIA: Oh, yes. It is an instrument of torture.
BERTRAND: I understand this country. I will be its first explorer.
   I will draw its maps. (*Pause. He climbs off the ladder, disappears
   from sight.*)
ALICE: He's coming!
CECILIA: Yes.
ALICE: He likes you!
CECILIA: Yes.
ALICE (*holding her*): Marriage is a desert. But some find oases.
CECILIA: Yes.
ALICE: And he has wonderful legs! (*She hurries away.* BERT-
   RAND *appears. Pause. A thin wind rattles the foliage.*)
CECILIA (*looking coolly at him*): Brutopia is imperfect, and where
   perfection appears, it is eradicated. (*He looks at her.*) How, did
   you say? (*Pause*) By a committee of eradicators, of course!
   (*Pause. She takes him by the arm and leads him down a walk.*)

BRUTOPIA 147

Well, they call it a committee, but only one member has a vote.
And only one can speak. The same one. The others must applaud,
and the first one to stop applauding — **death!** (*She fixes her
mouth to his, passionately kissing him. She stops, swallows.*) As
for death . . . (*He looks at her. Pause.*) The horror of it is exag-
gerated here. (*Pause*) Do you like women?

BERTRAND: Women? How you generalize!

CECILIA: We do in Brutopia. It's the law.

BERTRAND: I delight in female company.

CECILIA: Do you? Why?

BERTRAND: The female mind is subtle, sensitive, instinctive and —

CECILIA: No, I mean do you like us? Never mind the inventory
of the virtues of the gender, do you like women undressed?
(*Pause. He looks deeply into her.*) I long to marry you, obviously,
but are you coarse enough?

BERTRAND: I try.

CECILIA: You try! Can you try to be coarse? It's a gift, surely?
(*Pause. She looks at him.*) I think you are full of kindness.
(*Pause*) What's called kindness. (*Pause*) Aren't you?

ALICE (*sweeping in*): That's it, then! This way, and mind the
thorns! (BERTRAND *is led away by* ALICE.)

BERTRAND: I love her.

ALICE: Excellent! (*She draws back a bramble.*) Mind your eyes!

BERTRAND: She's ugly. Terribly ugly.

ALICE: Do you think so? I always have, and yet —

BERTRAND: I love her.

ALICE: This all needs trimming back —

BERTRAND: Love her.

ALICE: I heard you —

BERTRAND (*stopping*): **Ugly and I love her.** (*Pause*)

ALICE: Speak to her father, then.

BERTRAND: But what's Brutopia?

ALICE: I wouldn't know.

BERTRAND: She's touched, surely? Be honest, is she touched?

ALICE (*coldly*): Marry and risk it. (*She smiles.*)

148   *Howard Barker*

Scene Ten

MORE *enters the fountain garden at night. He holds up his palm*
to falling snow.

MORE: Are you still here? (*A shadow moves over the snow.*)
Listen, you are a liar and now I can't sleep. (*He discovers* THE
DOCTOR *sitting under a wall.*) Look! (*He points.*) Bare feet!
(*He smiles.*) More the sufferer! (*He stops smiling.*) There is no
boat called 'The Angel of Deliverance', I checked it with my
many friends and the boat's a fiction, there! (*Pause*) A fiction!
(*Pause. Sound of drunken hooliganism in the distance. A broken*
bottle. MORE *stares at* THE DOCTOR.) What's gone wrong in
Utopia?
THE DOCTOR: The flesh.
MORE: Whose?
THE DOCTOR: The body.
MORE: Whose? (*A burst of* LOUTS.)
THE DOCTOR: Erupted.
MORE: Erupted . . . ?
THE DOCTOR: Bodies overflowed the gaols.
MORE: What gaols?
THE DOCTOR: You don't know about the gaols?
MORE: There are no gaols! (*He flings himself down beside* THE
DOCTOR.) You see, you have not been there! Read the book!
No gaols! (*He thrusts a copy of* Utopia *at* THE DOCTOR.)
THE DOCTOR (*coolly*): That is an early edition . . .
MORE: Just off the presses!
THE DOCTOR: No, we have a different binding.
MORE: Oh?
THE DOCTOR: With your profile on the cover.
MORE: Oh?
THE DOCTOR: Every Utopian has one.
MORE: Really? Expensive!
THE DOCTOR: No, cheap and uniform. And inside, a picture of
you seated.
MORE: Really?
THE DOCTOR: Your body in repose stares wisely at the reader.
Your body, for some reason. The only body in Utopia. Officially.
MORE: Only body? What are you — (*A window is broken. Jeers*
and laughter. MORE *bounds to his feet and tears over the snow.*
As he hurtles by, CECILIA, *dark, freezes against a trellis. She*
opens her eyes. Sounds of protest nearby.)

BRUTOPIA   149

THE COMMON MAN (*off*): Oi!

MORE (*off*): Oh, yes!

THE COMMON MAN (*off*): Oi! (MORE *appears again dragging* THE COMMON MAN *with him, fixed in a headlock.*)

MORE: Oh, yes, my eloquent and articulate —

THE COMMON MAN: Oi!

MORE: My monosyllabic deity for whom all alleys are his just imperium —

THE COMMON MAN: Oi! (*They pass* CECILIA, *who follows with her eyes.*)

MORE: To stagger and vomit freely as the whim inspires!

THE COMMON MAN: Oi!

MORE: Yes, yes, my subtle bruiser, my darling criminal spewed from the gob of squalor, luscious delinquent —

THE COMMON MAN: Oi!

MORE: And arch-enemy of silence — there! (*He forces* THE COMMON MAN *to the ground in front of* THE DOCTOR, *retaining his hold.*) You were describing the Utopian. You argued that he had both a body and no body. Do elaborate. Shh! (*He tightens the stifling grip on* THE COMMON MAN.)

THE DOCTOR: In Utopia half are gaoled and half are gaolers.

MORE: How? There are no criminals in Utopia because there is no property.

THE DOCTOR: Is the body not a property?

MORE: They steal bodies? Why?

THE DOCTOR: Is it not the site of all our hopes?

MORE: No, it is the pit of all our instinct! In Utopia all instinct is contained by thought, thought is the civilizer.

THE DOCTOR: And bad thought?

MORE: Bad thought has no place in Utopia! (*A* LOUT's *cry nearby. Breaking glass.* MORE *stops. Bitterly, he thrusts* THE COMMON MAN *into the snow and climbs to his feet.*)

Scene Eleven

A part of the garden. A window is broken. THREE FIGURES *lurch in the darkness. Two are bawling hooligan songs.* CECILIA, *concealed, watches* MORE *hurtle by.*

150   *Howard Barker*

MORE: I claim my peace you —
FACTOR: Oi! (MORE *seizes* FACTOR *by the throat.*)
MORE: Muck-mouth and arse-faced breaker of all contempla-
   tion —
FACTOR: Oi!
MORE: Up my garden, will you, gobflash, I — (*He sees the third
   lout is* HENRY, *who stares at him.* MORE, *holding* FACTOR *in
   a headlock, freezes. Slowly, he releases him, and slowly sinks into
   a posture of obeisance.* FACTOR *sniffs. Pause.*)
KING HENRY: I am no respecter of property. (*Pause*)
MORE: Who is?
KING HENRY: Or chastity. (*Pause*)
MORE: Who is?
KING HENRY: Which also is a property. (*Pause. He looks at*
   MORE. FACTOR *blows his nose. A fine wind scatters snow.*)
MORE: No moon tonight, I was not expecting —
KING HENRY: I love night, when the enemy is drowsing. Down
   I come **The Monarchy!** They shiver in their gowns. Beautiful
   disorder and women trembling. **The Monarchy!** Women in their
   hanging hair and tumbling servants. **The Monarchy!** (*He nods
   in the direction of the others.*) This is Factor. This is Lloyd. (*They
   bow.*) I cannot move without my murderers, but Tom, I must get
   a mob behind me. How can I do this?
MORE: Moral example.
KING HENRY: Tosh, I have to hand out land. (*Pause*)
MORE: What land? (*Pause*)
KING HENRY: I read you my new poem.
MORE: Poem? At two in the night?
KING HENRY: **Why not poems in the night?** (*Pause*) I feel in
   the night. So I write in the night.
MORE: Yes.
KING HENRY: Come, walk.
MORE: Walk?
KING HENRY: Yes, up, while I recite, a poem in three stanzas put
   to music by me obviously, a love whine, a love whimper, a love
   howl — (MORE *climbs to his feet.* LLOYD *tunes his lute.*) —
   dedicated to **I shan't say which bitch** — (*the* LOUTS *laugh*)
   but I paw her glass like a dog in a lather. (*They follow* HENRY
   into the dark.) Oh, English weather I adore you, damp and
   clammy mask of murderers, for without it there could be no
   woman skin such as we long to lap with our insatiable gobs —
   (*He stops.*) That's not the poem — (*The* LOUTS *laugh.*) Play,
   Lloyd — listen, this is my tune —

BRUTOPIA

The tune begins in earnest. The cry of BONCHOPE *echoes across the garden. It is ignored. After an introduction,* HENRY *sings, walking.*

KING HENRY: So shall I dream of her pale breast
                 Half exposed to the eye of swine
                 And her thin mouth so closed and stitched
                 Which grumbles yes to the infant's cry —
(*He explains.*) She has a child you see, which she never wanted — (*He sings.*)
                 Oh, distressed mater — nity,
                 Oh, encumbrance of my life,
                 Oh, maternity in which I walk
                 Like the caged wolf howling.

LLOYD *beats a new intensity.* HENRY *stops walking and turns to* MORE, *delivering the last stanza with a cruel and relentless violence.*

KING HENRY: Oh, fang my back and tear my flesh
                 You hungry and unnourished she,
                 Your thin wrists will struggle with me
                 In the dead light of the mor — ning! (*The music stops. Pause.*)
    The clean version. (*Pause*) You don't understand, do you, Tom? (MORE *shakes his head.*) It is the single flaw in your genius.
MORE: May I sleep now?
KING HENRY: That you do without disturbance, do you?
MORE: So I predict. (MORE *bows, turns and walks.*)
KING HENRY: Obviously, after her, there'll be another! (MORE *stops.*) Which proves nothing.
MORE: The shallowness of your affections, arguably . . .
KING HENRY: No.
MORE: Gratification as a single end is near to comedy, I dare-say —
KING HENRY: No. It is the wordless presence of a god. (*Pause.* MORE *smiles patiently.*)
MORE: What is? (*Snow falls lightly.* HENRY *comes to him.*)
KING HENRY: The clash of unknown parties in desire . . . (*Pause*)
MORE: I don't know . . . (*He looks frankly at* HENRY.) I don't know . . . (*He walks away.*)
KING HENRY: Go to bed, then . . . (*Pause. The cry of* BONCHOPE.)
LLOYD: Sir Tom has never suffered love.

152   *Howard Barker*

FACTOR: He loves God.

KING HENRY: No man loves God who has not suffered women. (FACTOR *laughs*.) I say so! The best priests make a wreck of all their vows. And the best atheists.

LLOYD: Home, James? (HENRY *doesn't move*.)

KING HENRY: More's death is on him like a growth . . .

FACTOR: And ours . . .

KING HENRY: And everyone's, ole! And everyone's, you embroidered disembowellers, and everyone's! (*He walks swiftly, followed by the* LOUTS *past the hidden faces of* CECILIA *and* THE SERVANT, *who follow with their eyes*.)

CECILIA: He grows coarser . . .

THE SERVANT: Yes.

CECILIA: Is that because —

THE SERVANT: Nothing is denied him.

CECILIA: I too shall be coarse. Young and coarse. Brilliant and coarse. Help me. (*She looks at her, kisses her quickly*.) Shall I marry the parliamentary member? He pesters me with notes.

THE SERVANT: Shh! (THE DOCTOR *walks silently through the garden*.)

CECILIA (*aside*): In Brutopia, nothing is what it seems to be. This is universal and a source of comfort. Where nothing is expected, disappointment is unknown, and hope entirely redundant. (*The cry of* BONCHOPE *pierces the night*. THE DOCTOR *stops, listening*.)

CECILIA: Who is he?

THE SERVANT: He is from Utopia.

CECILIA: I long to meet him!

THE SERVANT: Shh! (THE DOCTOR *kneels in the snow, and sobs, noisily*. CECILIA *watches, transfixed. He sobs violently. He ceases, gets up, walks on into the dark*.) His children are dead. His wife is dead. His brother is in prison. (*The sound of mass laughter*. THE SERVANT *disappears in the dark*. CECILIA *looks over her shoulder. The* BRUTOPIANS *are massed in a sunken garden, gazing up at her*.)

CECILIA: Laugh by all means. (*They do*.) The most comic thing in all Brutopia is — yes — the person who believes — (*They laugh*.) The very word — yes — (*They laugh*.) Ridicule — derision — yes — (*They stop*.) In Brutopia all pain is an act. The legless beggar acts discomfort. The orphan performs despair. **How else can you get attention?** (*They begin protesting their individual cases. A cacophony ensues*. CECILIA *watches with bemused satisfaction*.)

BRUTOPIA   153

Scene Twelve

The silence of a thaw. The single sound of THE WORKMAN *tapping at a broken window to remove the glass.* MORE *and* MEG *in the sun.*

MORE (*promenading*): What is the relation between justice and the court?

MEG: None.

MORE: None, for the court merely dispenses punishment. What is the relation between punishment and crime?

MEG: None.

MORE: None, for crime is an effect of property. Without property, crime has no function.

MEG: Does crime need a function? Can't crime exist for itself? (*He looks at her. They are beneath a ladder.*)

MORE (*calling up*): It can't, can it?

THE WORKMAN: Wha'?

MORE: Can't, can it?

THE WORKMAN: Sir?

MORE: Property and crime? Insidiously linked?

THE WORKMAN: Wha'?

MORE: **No stuff no nicking.** Come on, don't ape ignorance, I put a proposition to you, weigh it, test it, the glazier is not without opinion, surely? (*Pause*)

THE WORKMAN: Sir, I —

MORE: **What sir what sir what sir what?** (*Pause. Then with infinite patience.*) If I have, and you don't have, must you have what I have? (*Pause*)

THE WORKMAN: Erm . . .

MORE: Now, don't give me the answer you think I want, give me the answer that accords with your opinion. (*Pause*)

THE WORKMAN: No, sir.

MORE: No, he says, why not?

THE WORKMAN: No, or I would crack your head now, surely?

MORE: And what prevents you? (*Pause*)

THE WORKMAN: Erm . . .

MORE (*sprinting up the ladder he presents his head*): Skull! (*He takes the man's tool.*) Hammer! (*He poses, sacrificially.*) Tension. (*Pause*) Still alive . . .

THE WORKMAN: I do not sufficiently dislike you.

MORE: Liking? Liking's inapplicable, it's fear of punishment! (*Pause*)

154   *Howard Barker*

THE WORKMAN: Could be, I suppose —

MORE: You fear capture —

THE WORKMAN (*thinking*): Could be —

MORE: **The sanction stays your hand.** (*He gives him back the
tool.*) Thank you. Glaze on. (*He rejoins* MEG *at the bottom.*) The
sole protection of all property is fear of violence —

THE WORKMAN: No, not fear of punishment. Sorry, no. (MORE
and MEG *stop. A faint irritation spreads over* MORE's *features.*)

MORE: What, then? Obviously, you want what I have, not having
it yourself.

THE WORKMAN: No.

MORE: Yes. You would rob me of my brain were it not most
securely in a box.

THE WORKMAN: No —

MORE: No? No? It's the best brain in Europe, why don't you want
it? It would be certain proof of your imbecility if, seeing the
special nature of my brain and the — I mean this in all kindness
— relatively mundane nature of your own, you did not covet it —

THE WORKMAN: I don't covet it —

MORE: You do —

THE WORKMAN: Don't covet it, I promise —

MORE: Envy, envy it! (*Pause*)

THE WORKMAN: Forgive me, but I don't want your brain, nor
any other of your property.

MORE (*coolly*): Then you are glazier through and through. (*He
bursts out laughing.*) Through and through! (*He nudges* MEG.)
Through and through!

Scene Thirteen

CECILIA's *breast, the object of* BERTRAND's *fixed stare. A groan
comes from his depths. Swiftly, she lets her garment fall over it.*

CECILIA: Enough, and what did you do today?

BERTRAND (*moved to an ecstasy of frustration*): Oh . . . Cecilia . . .

CECILIA: In the House of Parliament?

BERTRAND: Oh . . .

CECILIA (*perplexed*): You lie. You exaggerate. It is only — (*He*

BRUTOPIA

hides his face in his hands. She watches him. Pause.) Or does it make you really ill? (*Pause*) Does it? (*She goes to him.*) Are you ill with me?

BERTRAND: Mad women always did excite men, though they took them in secret, whereas I —

CECILIA: **I am not mad. I am Thomas More's daughter.** (*The voice of* MORE *laughing with his peculiar tone drifts nearer. The moment he appears,* BERTRAND *releases her hand.*)

CECILIA: The House of Parliament, you said —

BERTRAND (*recovering*): We passed a resolution on the subject of the limitations of continental cloths, silver thread from Nimes and coarse wool from Ravenna, both stuck at seven thousand ells, and went on to discuss apprenticeships, reducing wages and whipping for football, it was a hard debate, some said footballers had their uses, they made good infantry, but I was eloquent, I said in my experience footballers fled at the first sight of a horse . . . (MORE *and* MEG *enter.*)

MORE (*grinning fatuously*): My loves, my loves, my loves, my loves, my loves, my loves, my loves, my loves — (*He turns in a convoluted dance, slowly sinking to the ground, singing to the tune of* 'Greensleeves'.) My loves, my loves, my loves, my loves, my loves, my loves, my loves my lo — oves . . . ! (*He lies on the floor, watched by* BERTRAND, MEG, CECILIA. *Pause. He is rigid.*) And in Utopia, the act of reproduction was perceived as half-distasteful, half-absurd, the necessary but eminently fatuous prelude to the better business of rearing future citizens . . .

BERTRAND (*boldly to* CECILIA): When I meet you again you must submit, and I will submit to you, God help the consequences . . . (*He bows, hurries away.*)

MORE: It's Spring, my season! Spring, I swear! (*A* FIGURE *is seen advancing waving a sheaf of paper.*) Daker!

DAKER: The preface!

MORE (*still turning on the ground from one posture to another*): The preface to *Utopia*! Oh, Daker, I do hope it's kind and complimentary!

DAKER: It is! (*He holds it out.*)

MORE: I hope it honours me immensely!

DAKER: As far as I could honour you without it seeming —

MORE: What?

DAKER: Obsequious and reverential —

MORE: What's wrong with seeming so? Don't you revere me? Are you not obsequious?

156   *Howard Barker*

DAKER: Well, that may be, but —

MORE: Stuff but, if I am worthy, praise me!

DAKER: Read it and see. (*Pause. His hand remains outstretched.*) Do read and judge for yourself. If I offend you, it's only that I — (MORE *takes it, and tears it across.* CECILIA *laughs. Pause.*)

MORE: Are you my ally, and my friend, dear Daker? And have I not educated you?

DAKER: You know it.

MORE: Away, then, to your stool and inscribe this preface without consideration to humility. Only the fullest praise, only the highest compliment, for *Utopia*'s a book commanding reverence and obsequy. Admit its greatness and stop shuddering for fear someone will call you creep, be honourable and praise it to the skies, how else can great work make its mark but by the unreserved devotion of its addicts?

DAKER: Yes. (MORE *smiles, hops up, and clasps him round the shoulder.*)

MORE: Meg! Feed Daker! Meg! (CECILIA *watches the three of them, arm in arm, prance down the arcade.*)

CECILIA (*aside*): The word most common in Brutopia is **we.** I is forbidden. I is severely punished. But **we** is everywhere! **We must. We shall.** This produces such a climate of mutual celebration! Endless mutual celebration until your ears are singing!

Scene Fourteen

A leafy place, intimate. BONCHOPE *is standing before a laden table.* ALICE *is seated. She looks up.*

ALICE: Mr Bonchope! (*She hops up.*) Do have a seat! Or do you find you sit too much? Stand if that suits you better. This is chive, and this is cucumber, they are fresh from the garden, that's shrimp, and that's a little dip I make myself from medlar, do you know medlar? I don't expect someone like you goes in much for medlars! It should be clearer, more a jelly, but in some ways it's better when it's thicker, is it terribly uncomfortable in there? (*He is filthy.*) I haven't seen it but they say it's tiny.

BONCHOPE: Tiny, yes.

BRUTOPIA 157

ALICE: Oh, dear, and that thing there is fish in a glaze, I didn't make it so I'm not responsible — do have a glass, would you like a stem, or do you like the straight ones? People are funny about glasses.

BONCHOPE: A straight one.

ALICE: And do you get plenty of food?

BONCHOPE: Very little food.

ALICE: Oh, goodness, well, tuck in, napkins over there and knives. I never feel hungry myself at lunch times, no matter what I have prepared, I only pick, why do you squawk, by the way? (*Pause*) If it is a squawk? (*Pause*) Perhaps I shouldn't call it a squawk? Is it a signal? (*He sits, stiffly.*) I tell you why I ask, because when you're just getting into bed it can be terribly disconcerting, as I suppose you —

BONCHOPE: I can't help myself.

ALICE: You can't —

BONCHOPE: Can't help myself, no. (*Pause. MORE appears, picks up a plate and helps himself to food.*)

ALICE (*to MORE*): That's hot, that's spicy, that one — (*To BON-CHOPE.*) Let me fill a plate for you, let me pile it up, you must be so — (*She fills a plate.*) You really must — (*MORE is seated and eating.*) How's that? (*She puts a plate in front of him. He looks at the food.*) This is pleasant, isn't it? (*Pause*) This is. (*Pause*) We haven't dared to eat outdoors, this is the first — (*Pause. She closes her eyes.*) Obviously I am your persecutor, too. Obviously you are shit mouth in my estimation. I think the heretic must die. I think the wrong must suffer. (*A long pause. MORE dabs his mouth.*)

MORE: Did you enjoy *Utopia*?

BONCHOPE: It brought Heaven nearer to my mouth.

MORE: How's that?

BONCHOPE: By showing tolerance to be supremely beautiful. Though I stood in my own dung by failing light, it brought tears to my eyes. (*MORE studies him. Pause.*)

MORE: Is that pickle sweet?

ALICE: Which one?

MORE: The yellow one.

ALICE: Yes, the yellow one is sweet.

MORE: She calls it sweet, wherein the sweetness, love?

ALICE (*tasting it*): Well, I — yes, that's surely —

MORE (*to BONCHOPE*): Tolerance appeals to you, then, does it?

BONCHOPE: I think it is the mark of civil society and the glory of all culture.

MORE: You sing its praises, then . . .
BONCHOPE: It is the pinnacle of political society and the highest moment of —
MORE: He hymns! He hymns! (*To* ALICE.) Then what is that one there?
ALICE: That's hot.
MORE: Give me that.
ALICE: It's hot —
MORE: Tolerably, though? Tolerably hot?
ALICE: Well, how do I know what —
MORE (*tasting it*): It's tolerable, certainly. My tongue is quite content . . . but what if it were . . . suppose my tongue were burned? Would that be tolerable, Mr Bonchope? (*Pause*)
BONCHOPE: If your tongue burns, drink some water.
MORE: I am the wit, Mr Bonchope. What are you?
BONCHOPE: A simple preacher.
MORE: No, chuck false modesty, what's your intention?
BONCHOPE: Intention? Must one have intention?
MORE: One must if one goes preaching illegality! One might fake innocence but one has intention!
BONCHOPE: Yes.
         Yes. (*Pause*)
         To make God's word ring clear in every —

MORE *scatters some crockery with his elbow. The noise shocks and shatters. A tin plate rolls over the paving, and stops. Pause.*

MORE: You only love tolerance because it lets your filth flow. (*Pause.* BONCHOPE *stares at him.*) Tolerate me, says the miscreant, that I may come nearer to your throat. You would have me and my family in the gutter, dirt and ash.
ALICE (*to* THE SERVANT *who has appeared*): We've had an accident, would you just — (THE SERVANT *kneels and collects.*)
BONCHOPE: It's not Utopia, this, then?
MORE: Not Utopia, no . . . (*He turns in his chair. Across the lawn he sees* THE DOCTOR, *a distant figure, strolling.*)
ALICE (*to* THE SERVANT): It's too early for a picnic but I thought, risk it, put a shawl on . . .
BONCHOPE: It's death, then, if I —
MORE: Yes.
ALICE (*as* THE SERVANT *sweeps up a broken plate*): Oh, what a pity, I so liked the pattern on that rim!

BRUTOPIA   159

BONCHOPE: I recant.
MORE (*rising*): That's sensible. (BONCHOPE *rises also.*)
ALICE (*to* BONCHOPE): Take a napkin with you, fill it up, here
— (*She stuffs items of food into a napkin.*) Mr Bonchope is going
back to his little den —
MORE: Scripture is a ground, Mr Bonchope, that's all. A ground
of struggle. Later, there will be other grounds, and other books
from which the likes of you might wring wrong meaning. What
these grounds will be I cannot — even I — imagine.
BONCHOPE: Utopias? (MORE *leaves, watched by* BONCHOPE.
THE SERVANT *is clearing the table. Suddenly* BONCHOPE
seizes on the food, stuffing it into his mouth. He catches sight of
ALICE, *looking at him. He stops, smiles, then proceeds with his
feasting.*)

Scene Fifteen

MORE *is walking through the trellis ways. He is pestered at the
heels.*

THE COMMON MAN: A joke, Sir Tom!
MORE (*walking*): Not every day can jokes be manufactured. Not
every day is funny.
THE COMMON MAN: Must laugh, Sir Tom!
MORE: I see you are determined to reflect the cosmic mockery
rained down on us by our intellectual pretensions — (THE COM-
MON MAN *bursts out laughing.*) No, that's not a joke (*He
cackles.*) That is merely a reflection on the futile nature of —
(*And cackles.*) Not a joke, I say! (*He leaves* THE COMMON
MAN *behind. As he swiftly walks, he hears a voice.*)
KING HENRY: More. (*He stops. He turns.* HENRY *is seated in a
secluded rustic niche.*)
MORE: You? (*Pause*) But it's daytime! (*He smiles, bows.* HENRY
looks at him.) Much luck with the poem? (*Pause.* HENRY *merely
observes him.* MORE *is uncomfortable.*) It is a sad fact that the
loved object is more often than not more susceptible to force than
poetry. (*He grins, weakly. Long pause.*) Sometimes, when you
look at me, I know why I so loved being a priest . . .

160   *Howard Barker*

KING HENRY: **No safety in the cloisters!**

MORE: No?

KING HENRY: I look at the cloisters. And I think, what a lot of
bricks . . . ! (MORE *looks puzzled.*)

MORE: Yes, a lot of bricks, but . . .

KING HENRY: I think, there's an asset . . . (*Pause*)

MORE: An asset? The bricks? Surely, it's the thought that is the
asset, not the bricks . . . ? (*Pause*) The accumulation of philosophy . . . (*Pause.* HENRY *looks at him.*) The aggregation of
analysis and sensibility . . . (*Pause*)

KING HENRY: No, the bricks. (HENRY *drops a copy of* Utopia
onto the pavement with a definitive slap. Pause.)

MORE: Ah. Not your —

KING HENRY: Pox. (*Pause*)

MORE: You are frank today. Fortunately I am not without endorse-
ment. Today I had a letter from Erasmus of Rotterdam fulsomely
applauding its ambition and congratulating me on the maturity
of my Latin style. He welcomes me into the —

KING HENRY: Shh —

MORE: Hallowed circle of the discourses on faith and government, I —

KING HENRY: Shh! (MORE *contains himself. Pause.*) Where's
the politics?

MORE: I replaced it with goodwill. (HENRY *looks at him.*)

KING HENRY: Where's the parties?

MORE: Parties? (*He is patient.*) There are no parties because there
are no contradictions. And no contradictions because there are no
separate interests —

KING HENRY: I want to get divorced and you must fix it.
(*Pause*)

MORE: I did, I think, fix —

KING HENRY: Yes, you did, and thank you, but now I want to get
divorced again.

MORE: Again? (*Pause*) I am sure you know what you are doing,
but —

KING HENRY: I do, and everybody must agree.

MORE: Everybody?

KING HENRY: The peasant, the factory hand, the shepherd and
the sailor.

MORE: Yes, but —

KING HENRY: The roofer and the guttersnipe, the butcher, and —

MORE: Yes, but —

KING HENRY: **And all the geniuses of the cloister!** (*Pause*)

BRUTOPIA **161**

MORE: You are very modern.

KING HENRY: Modern, yes, to the buckle on my boot. (*Pause*)

MORE: You see how I prefer to prune and prattle here among the climbing and the twining —

KING HENRY: Everybody inside. Nobody outside.

MORE: What?

KING HENRY: Solidarity. (*Pause*)

MORE: Solid — arity?

KING HENRY: Good word. I found it in the dictionary. It means you must. (*Pause*)

MORE: Forgive me, but I much prefer the —

KING HENRY: **You always have to be standing on the edges.** (*Pause*) **Snob.** (*Pause*) **And now there are no edges.** (*Pause*) **Snob.** (*Pause*) Down now, in the puddle with the rest of us. (*Pause*) I'm insecure. My dad got power with an axe . . . (*Pause*) How black you are, which is the colour of self-confidence. And me, all colours, all flash. I stick my emblem in every gap, **Henry, His rose! Henry, His monogram!** Vulgar, like a yobbo bawling in the night, as if by scrawling on the fence I might keep history off . . . (*Pause*)

MORE: History? Don't you mean time?

KING HENRY: I mean whichever bastard's waiting in the alley. (*Pause. He reaches into a pocket.*) I want your signature on this. (*He draws out a paper.*) Sign and you can plant begonias until your eyes are fields of cataract . . . (*Pause. He holds it out to* MORE.)

MORE: I don't like naked documents.

KING HENRY: No envelopes.

MORE: I don't like letters pointing at my heart.

KING HENRY: My arm is suffering . . .

MORE: I don't like —

KING HENRY (*withdrawing it petulantly*): Too late! You had your chance but you preferred to stutter! Too late! (*He stares at him.*) No immunity for genius! (*And* MORE *stares.*) Genius wants to pontificate from floral havens, but reputation carries risks. You are a great-headed flower, and when the wind blows down must come the stalk. The bigger the head, the poorer the stalk, I am the wind and you damned well asked for it, you snob! (*Pause*)

CECILIA (*aside*): Brutopia, among its highest achievements, abolished the surprise. In Brutopia, nothing was surprising. To even appear surprised was certain evidence of immaturity or weak-mindedness. (*Pause*)

162   *Howard Barker*

MORE: If you killed me they'd name you barbarian from Greenland to China.

KING HENRY: If I killed you, the intellectuals would shudder
from Greenland to China too. **Oh, the wind blows on us also.**
Many monarchs would delight. Many of the second-rate would
dash for empty chairs. (*Pause, then he rises to his feet, looks
about him.*) The genius must share the garden with the yob. No
world yobfree. No world geniusfree. (*He goes away, down the
path. Instantaneously it rains.*)

MORE (*in despair*): **Meg! Oh, Meg!** (CECILIA *enters. She watches
him.*) **Oh, Meg!** (*He is weeping.* CECILIA's *face is taut with pain
and confusion. She hurries to him. He clasps her in his arms.*)
Oh, Meg!

CECILIA: I'm not Meg —

MORE: **Going to die, Meg!**

CECILIA: Die . . . ?

MORE: **Die, die!**

CECILIA: Why die?

MORE: Because I'm honest! (*He buries his head in her hair. The
rain runs down.*)

CECILIA: Be dishonest, then . . . (*Pause. His face emerges from
her hair.*)

MORE: You're not Meg . . .

CECILIA: No, I'm Cecilia . . . (*He searches her face.*) **Forgive
me, I'm Cecilia.** (*She stares at him. His hands grip her by the
shoulders. A long pause. She trembles.*)

MORE: Oh, wonderful . . . her womanly nature yields to see my
ashen mask for the last time . . . indelibly stamped on memory the visage of her doomed father, Thomas More . . . (*She
frowns.*)

CECILIA: Who is Thomas More . . . ? (*He does not relax his grip.*)
What are you — (*He stares.*) You are — (*Pause. It dawns on
her.*) Are you — instructing me — in — sham life? (*He merely
stares.*) Are you — for love — teaching me to lie — and lie —
even to myself? (*Pause*) You are . . . (*Pause*) You are trying to
save me from the world . . .

MORE (*booming*): **Meg!** (CECILIA *frees herself from her father
as* MEG *appears, running.*)

MEG: Father!

MORE: **Dead!**

MEG: What —

MORE (*grasping her in his arms*): **Dead, Meg!**

MEG: Oh, God —

MORE: Ripped from your adoration by manic power! (*As he recites, his eyes meet* CECILIA's *who is slowly drifting away from them.*)

MEG: Oh, great soul, what —

MORE: **Dead! Dead!**

164   *Howard Barker*

THE RECOVERY

Scene One

The garden.

MORE (*off stage*): **Dead! Dead!** (CECILIA *walks backwards from the spectacle. She is unaware of* BERTRAND, *and collides with him. He seizes her wrists.*)

BERTRAND: Shh.

CECILIA: Not now.

BERTRAND: Shh.

CECILIA: No, not now, I — (*He draws her back into a niche in the wall.*) No —

CECILIA (*aside*): The Brutopians suffered more than any other race from love, which was not called love, but anger. 'I am angry with you' was an expression of deepest desire. But when this anger was relieved by carnal acts, the Brutopians experienced despair. Thus men and women seemed either furious or sunk in grief, according to how far their passion had progressed.

CECILIA *emerges, adjusting her skirts.* BERTRAND *leans against the wall, staring out over a lawn on which distantly,* THE DOCTOR *is discovered staring down at a single point on the turf.* CECILIA *leans beside* BERTRAND. *Pause.*

CECILIA: You speak.
          You speak now.

BERTRAND: What?

CECILIA: Anything. Timber if you wish. (*Pause*) Or skins. (*Pause*)

BERTRAND: I —

CECILIA: Tallow. Fur.

BERTRAND: I —

CECILIA: Your voice, for God's sake. (*Pause. She puts her hand on him.*)

BRUTOPIA   165

BERTRAND: I apologize for any —

CECILIA (*in despair*): No, not that. Anything but that! (*She walks away from him, along a path. She encounters* ALICE, *distraught, but does not stop.*)

ALICE: Have you heard!

CECILIA (*striding*): Yes —

ALICE: And he says death, death all the time, what can we —

CECILIA: I heard —

ALICE: Meg is powerless!

Scene Two

The maze. A cacophony of BRUTOPIANS. CECILIA *stares, goes through the gate. They press on her. She forces her way to the centre, where* THE SERVANT *is sitting. Perfect silence prevails at the centre.* THE SERVANT *looks up.*

CECILIA: I'm pregnant. (*Pause*) Pregnant by a lout.

THE SERVANT: I'll cure it.

CECILIA: No. This is Brutopia, where nothing comes except by error, and the wanted is simply what occurs.

THE SERVANT: I'll attend you when it comes.

CECILIA (*amused*): That's to risk its life I solemnly predict!

Scene Three

MORE *is walking towards the rustic prison, with* ALICE *and* MEG *at his heels.*

ALICE: You will die of pneumonia —

MEG: You must prepare an argument on the basis of Nihil Autoritatem, the Juridicium of Aquinas —

ALICE: You have been coughing all the winter, your lungs are tissue paper as it is —

MEG: The absolution of the clergy under the Edicts of Diocletian —

166 *Howard Barker*

ALICE: What are you going to do in there? Die? Do you want to die?

MEG: Or Maximum Imperium! Yes! We invoke the clauses of the limitations!

ALICE: **It isn't fair on me!**

MEG: Be quiet! How can anybody think!

Scene Four

The centre of the maze. The BRUTOPIANS *are kneeling as a congregation.* CECILIA *passes among them with a gracious smile.*

CECILIA (*aside*): The Brutopians were never silent except when sentimental. And how sentimental they could be! They held childbearing in such high esteem, whilst frequently killing children! And funerals they loved, whilst indulging murder!

Scene Five

MORE *is in the rustic prison. He hangs his arms through the grille, staring at the ground.* ALICE *is weeping.*

ALICE: Please sleep in your bed. I will keep to my own side. Please sleep in your bed. I will not disturb you by tossing.

MORE: Your napkin of a mind . . .

ALICE: Yes, but do as I ask, I'll lie silent as a graven image . . .

MORE: Your table-cloth of a mind . . .

ALICE: It is, but —

MORE: Your ironing board and breadknife of a mind —

ALICE: **All right, but I have some rights as well as you.** (*Pause*)

MORE: Gaol is what I always wanted. Even lying beside you in a mattress plump with affection, it was gaol I ached for.

ALICE: You will have all the gaol you want, why anticipate it?

MORE: I have always been one step ahead in the imagination, and now go in, your head is wet.

ALICE: The last occupant of this place apologized, why don't you? The last occupant is smothering his children with a slobbering love, why don't you? The last occupant walks the streets intoxicated with freedom, **why don't you?**

MORE: He will be back.

ALICE: No. He is swallowing life by the lungful.

MORE: **I said he will be back.** (*He looks into her face.*) Fireside, piss on it. **No sweet like this.** (*He slaps a fistful of mud over his cheek. She winces. Pause. She withdraws.*)

ALICE (*suddenly*): **I love you.** (*She stops. Pause. She looks back. His eyes are tight shut, his face filthy.*)

MORE: In what way? (*He gives nothing. She goes. MORE hangs in this posture.*)

CECILIA (*aside*): In Brutopia everyone is sentenced to death. Without exception. The death sentence is handed out at birth and hangs above their beds, framed as a certificate. This dispenses with all the paraphernalia of courts and trials! At various times, as the need arises, these sentences are enforced. (*CECILIA approaches the rustic prison. MORE remains with his arms propped and his eyes closed. She examines him.*)

CECILIA: I have a child. (*His eyes open. Pause.*)

MORE: It's easily done.

CECILIA: Yes! Very! So easily I scarcely — (*She stops, looks at him. Pause. Suddenly she takes his face in her hands, thrusting her arms through the bars.*) **Must you die with me hating you? Must you take my contempt —**

MORE: Ow —

CECILIA: **I am so cold and —**

MORE: Ow —

CECILIA: **Dead in feeling to you —**

MORE: Ow —

CECILIA: **Dead and —**

MORE: Ow —

CECILIA: **Indifferent.** (*Pause. She releases him. ROPER is behind her, with HOLBEIN, who holds a sketchbook.*)

ROPER: Mr Holbein will begin his preparatory drawings now. (*Pause. CECILIA withdraws from the grille. She looks at HOLBEIN.*)

CECILIA: You drew me when I was a child. (*HOLBEIN inclines his head.*) Why not draw me now?

ROPER: Mr Holbein is a very busy —

168   *Howard Barker*

CECILIA: I know he is! **But what about my grief?** That needs
   catching, surely? (*Pause.* HOLBEIN *nods.*) Thank you. You see,
   a great artist does not miss an opportunity. What shall I wear?
ROPER: I don't think —
CECILIA: Black, presumably? (HOLBEIN *nods. She goes.*)
MORE: She envies me my death. She knows how well I shall die,
   and envies me. Are you drawing yet? (*He leans against the
   grille.*) Last time . . . (*The chalk works on the paper.*) How dif-
   ferent it was last time . . . ! (*He laughs.*)
HOLBEIN: Not so very.
MORE: Then I was mighty. Then I was a power. How different it
   was last time!
HOLBEIN: Not so very.
MORE: Why do you say that? I have fallen, I am dragged to the
   floor. Why do you say that?
HOLBEIN: Because last time you were swollen with power. And
   now you are swollen with the absence of power. But swollen, still
   swollen.
MORE: As you draw me I draw you, not with pencil, but I criticize,
   I am your critic and my eye is fierce as a gull's scanning your
   features as it will be on the axeman's too, he also will experience
   shame for fear he is not so good an axeman as I am a poet . . .
   (*Pause.* HOLBEIN *draws.*)
ROPER (*gaily*): I have taken down all that. I have a record of all
   that — (*He turns a page.*) Isn't it a fact that in extremity a man
   will say things possibly better composed, possibly better con-
   ceived, than he could have in the comfort of his study?
MORE: **Comfort of his study?**
ROPER: Yes —
MORE: **Comfort? It was a chamber of pain!**
ROPER: Yes. (*Pause.* MORE *smiles.*)
MORE: Have you got that?
ROPER (*writing*): Yes . . . (MORE *looks on* HOLBEIN.)
MORE: It isn't true. My study was heaven, and the best things I
   wrote were written in heaven . . . (*Pause.* ROPER *stops writing.*)

BRUTOPIA

Scene Six

A niche in the wall. THE SERVANT *is dressing* CECILIA *in funereal garments.*

THE SERVANT: I think in my unsatisfactory life my finest pleasures come from executions.

CECILIA: What does the head do on its separation from the body?

THE SERVANT: I saw a bishop's, and that was excellent, because it murmured.

CECILIA: What? What did it murmur?

THE SERVANT: Stand me up. It saw the World from upside-down, and was obviously uncomfortable.

CECILIA (*piqued*): Are you trying to —

THE SERVANT: It did not say the least thing philosophical. (*Pause.*) But your father may be different. He may mouth some wit or wisdom. Or a stream of filthy epithets. There! You are wonderful in black. (*She goes to leave.*)

CECILIA: Don't leave our employment . . . !

THE SERVANT: Leave Brutopia?

CECILIA: If you give notice, I shall follow you and beg a slave's job in your slum.

THE SERVANT: Yes, and I'll beat you, even for perfect labour. (THE DOCTOR *stands before them. She looks at him.*) He won't plead guilty to Utopia. Not now. He's arranging his funeral. (THE SERVANT *goes.* THE DOCTOR *looks at* CECILIA. *Pause.*)

CECILIA: Were you in Utopia? (*He looks, silently.*) You can't have been, there is none! (*Pause*) I see you wandering the estate, limping and intellectual, a pose I have to admire, I admit, since I adore good poses, and crippled brilliance surely is the best, but tell me, what's your trick? (*Pause*)

THE DOCTOR: You are not as shallow as you seem.

CECILIA: I am. More shallow. (*Pause*) As for your spectacles, they're false. (*She tears them off his nose, and wears them.*) Yes! Plain glass! (*She clasps his hand.*) I do admire you!

THE DOCTOR: All doctors must wear spectacles, whether their eyes are weak or not.

CECILIA: That isn't in his book!

THE DOCTOR: Not written, no. But in the book. The seeds of all our comic pains are in the book. (*She suddenly holds him in her arms.*)

CECILIA: Yes! Yes, it's true! I know it is! (*She clings to him. She rocks him in her arms.*) You're ill, and maybe dying . . . it's death, isn't it? That's smeared on you ... ? (HOLBEIN *appears.*) Draw me like this. With this man's head here, in my lap. (*She draws* THE DOCTOR's *head into her lap.*) And a little fruit ... festooning him ... (*She draws down a trailing bramble.* HOLBEIN *sits on a folding stool, and begins. Pause as he works.*)

HOLBEIN: I was talking to Meg ...

CECILIA: Meg? Oh, Meg ...

HOLBEIN: Who plans an exhaustive translation —

CECILIA: Remarkable Meg —

HOLBEIN: Of your father's correspondence with Erasmus.

CECILIA: Never throw away a letter! It will make a scholar's lunch! (*He brushes the paper with his hand.*)

HOLBEIN: This is, I think, the first time I have seen you as a woman in repose ...

CECILIA: I am not in repose ...

HOLBEIN: It will be about ten guineas, who shall I bill?

CECILIA (*gazing down at him*): Look, how his eyelids dip, like overladen coasters, get that, can you?

HOLBEIN: I assume Sir Tom's debts will be honoured — (*He blows chalk dust away.* CECILIA *has observed a book protruding from* THE DOCTOR's *pocket and is fixed by it.*) You — Your head has shifted — (*Pause. She stares.*) Miss —

CECILIA: Yes — (*She draws the book from his pocket.*) What is this? (*She extends it to* HOLBEIN.)

HOLBEIN (*wiping his hands on a rag, takes it*): It appears to be —

CECILIA: Yes —

HOLBEIN: A book. (*Pause*)

CECILIA: What book?

HOLBEIN: Handwritten. It's —

CECILIA: What? (HOLBEIN *examines the cover.*)

HOLBEIN: My English is —

CECILIA: Just read it, would you?

HOLBEIN: 'A Proposal ... for the ... Governance ... of ... Just Society ...' By ... Emmanuel Salgado ... MD ... Utopia ... (*Pause*)

CECILIA: His body is a rack of pain ... thin and hammered like old tin ... and yet no sooner does he get his paws around a pencil but he begins — he can't resist — to inscribe laws of new societies! I believe in every prison the victims of one system scratch plans for the torture of the next — on walls, in blood!

Scene Seven

BERTRAND, *restless in an orangery*. ALICE, *observing*.

BERTRAND: I am so sorry but — you have your problems, obviously — but she — Cecilia — is quite intolerable and I —
ALICE: Yes —
BERTRAND: Her moods and tempers I must confess I do not find at all endearing —
ALICE: No —
BERTRAND: On the contrary, she offends me and provokes me and I am obliged to ask myself the simple question **is this love** and I —
ALICE: Yes —
BERTRAND: Admit I am inclined to say — forgive me, you are in such turmoil but —
ALICE: No, no, you bubble —
BERTRAND: Inclined to say not love but something else and — oh, do forgive me, I am so self-regarding when you are —
ALICE: No, no, you froth —
BERTRAND: I find her quite unstable which is in its own way captivating but I have my own concerns to balance, what I require is partnership not struggle and — (ALICE *is staring over the garden at the figure of* THE COMMON MAN, *who is moving about in a massive overcoat*.)
ALICE: You! (*He stops.*) You! Yes! (*He thinks, falters, turns to run.*) Here, I said! (*He stops, and surlily approaches her, his eyes on the ground.*) That is my husband's gown you're wearing. (*He shrugs.*) No, do not shrug like that. It is his otter. **And don't shrug like that.** (BERTRAND *watches from the wall.*) Get it off this minute. (*He raises his eyes, cruelly. She meets them.*) You only stare like that because you have no power. How it hurts. You put your anger in your stare. But I stare also. Get it off. (*Pause. He does nothing.* BERTRAND *leans off the wall to threaten* THE COMMON MAN.*)
THE COMMON MAN: He gave it me! (*Pause*)
ALICE: He couldn't have . . .
THE COMMON MAN: **True.** (*Pause*)
ALICE (*thinly*): He couldn't have because I bought it for him as a wedding gift. I wrapped it in fine tissue and I laid it on our bed. He walked into the room and sunlight flashed over its collar. It is a Pope of coats, he said. It is a Tsar of garments, **get it off.**
THE COMMON MAN: Who cares, it's mine now —

172   *Howard Barker*

BERTRAND: **Get out the shafting otter coat.** (THE COMMON
MAN *smiles, cruelly. He undoes the tapes. It falls to the ground.
He is naked.* ALICE *turns her head very slightly.*)

ALICE: He has nothing underneath.

THE COMMON MAN (*triumphantly*): The Common Man.

ALICE: Yes, I know you are.

THE COMMON MAN: Steals where he can. But this wasn't stolen.

ALICE: I have my needs also. Cover yourself with your hands and
go quietly.

THE COMMON MAN: **Isn't a coat for wearing?** (*Pause*)

ALICE: No. (*He goes, naked, over the garden. They watch him.*)

BERTRAND: You are inspiring. In your ordeal. Inspiring. (*Her
eyes remain on the diminishing figure.*)

ALICE: Of course he gave it to him. It's obvious he did. (*Pause.
She looks at* BERTRAND.) He gave him my love gift. (*She
shrugs.*) So what? (*Pause*)

BERTRAND: You grow. You flourish, as if pain brought out some
hidden self. May I say this? As if Sir Thomas, in his waning,
brought out your subtler light.

ALICE: Oh?

BERTRAND: May I say this? May I? May I say that widowhood
might be your chance? May I?

ALICE: Say anything. Say what you like.

BERTRAND: I hesitate, but —

ALICE: Don't hesitate —

BERTRAND: Tremble, even —

ALICE: Tremble, yes, but speak —

BERTRAND: Weren't you a widow always? (*Pause*)

ALICE: What are you saying?

BERTRAND: I don't know.

ALICE: You do. (*Pause*) You do know. Hold my hand if that will
help. (*She stretches out a hand to him.*)

BERTRAND: I can't. (*The hand remains.*) **It is impossible, I
can't!** (*He seizes it.*)

Scene Eight

HOLBEIN *has completed the drawing. He holds it out, its back to*
CECILIA.

BRUTOPIA 173

CECILIA: I rarely look in mirrors. But this is not a mirror, is it? This is a picture of the soul? (*He goes to turn it to her.*) Don't show me yet! (*He stops.*) Have you made me terrible? (*He offers it to her, and she receives it without taking her eyes from his. Pause.*) I think, if I like it, the reasons for so doing will be false. I think I shall like only what I believe myself to be, which is not what I am, of course. (*Pause. Then she coolly tears the drawing across, first one way, then the other, her eyes remaining on his all the time. Then she swiftly departs. Pause.*)

HOLBEIN: I have never known such terrible self-consciousness. Such an agony of sensibility . . . (*The eyes of* THE DOCTOR *open.*)

THE DOCTOR: She is unloved. Do you think she could bear to see she is unloved?

Scene Nine

A part of the garden. CECILIA *is hurrying with a package. She encounters* HENRY. *She stares. She curtsies.*

KING HENRY: Cecilia More. Uncommonly sore. Bore to a bore. And cold to the core. (*Pause*) I quote the common opinion. (*Pause. On an inspiration, she holds out the package.*)

CECILIA: License my book!

KING HENRY: Refer it to the censor.

CECILIA: But you're the monarch.

KING HENRY: I don't appoint officials so I may do their work for them.

CECILIA (*smiling*): No, stuff all that, just —

KING HENRY: Authority is a pyramid, whose apex rests on functions no matter how obscure —

CECILIA: You just put H there, on the cover. (*He declines to take it.*)

KING HENRY: You are weak on constitution and what a mouth you have. It burns. It quarrels with the air. What book is it? I love brilliant women.

CECILIA: Mine.

KING HENRY: Speak some. I love learning from a woman's mouth. Men detest intelligence in skirt but I swell on it. (*Pause, then with calculation.*)

174   *Howard Barker*

CECILIA: Sum — in — caelo — magister — (*Pause*)

KING HENRY: In Heaven, are you? Why?

CECILIA: Because you're God. Why else? (*She stares at him.*) How fast I'm breathing, I — (*She closes her eyes.*)

KING HENRY: Don't come near me . . .

CECILIA: No.

KING HENRY: Because I'm savage.

CECILIA: Yes.

KING HENRY: So savage.

CECILIA: I know, yes. (*Pause*) How could I anyway, when you are murdering my father?

KING HENRY: **Trying to save him by flirtation!**

CECILIA: No —

KING HENRY: **Henry likes skirt so you have heard —**

CECILIA: No —

KING HENRY: **I hate to be used. I squirm to be used.**

CECILIA: No, I promise —

KING HENRY: **I won't have my sex wrung for nothing, death that way, see! Never!** (*She trembles, her eyes still closed.* HENRY *rests, also trembling, against a bench. Pause.*) They use me, but I can chop skirt also . . . (*Pause*)

CECILIA: I want him dead. (*Pause. He looks at her.*) I never said those words before. (*Pause*) Or thought them, either. But I want it. Do it, or I think I will become so shrunk and mad. If I'm not so already . . . (*He looks at her a long time, then turns and retires the way he came, watched by her.*)

Scene Ten

The rustic prison, where MORE *lies on a canvas bed*, THE SERVANT *beside him.*

MORE: I tell you terrible things. These things I could not tell my wife.

THE SERVANT: The servant has her uses.

MORE: Promise you're illiterate!

THE SERVANT: I swear! The whole house knows it. (*He looks at her.*)

MORE: I want to die. I passionately want it. (*Pause*)

BRUTOPIA   175

THE SERVANT: That's good, because —

MORE: I have created myself, and I am sick with my creation.

THE SERVANT: Create another. (*He looks at her.*)

MORE: How?

THE SERVANT: Pack a sandwich. Walk out the gate. Walk till you find a hag in a turf house. Live with her. Spit in the fire and kick the mangey mongrel. (*Pause*)

MORE: You see, even you, a criminal's discard, thinks life's a brimming basket! Dip! Dip! If you do not like your life, pluck out another! **There is no other.** (*Pause*) I thought I was a hermit, and I thought I was a courtier, and ached to know which was my proper self. **Both**, came the answer. I thought I was a misanthrope. I thought I was a humanist, and ached to know which one was false. **Neither**, came the answer. (*She stares at him.*) Do you understand me? You look with unfathoming eyes, I could as well address the blanket. Don't you see? I have yanked the tongues from hypocrites while writing poems on the brotherhood of man. **Both! Neither!** (*Pause*) Which road, anyway? Which hag? (*He laughs long, absurdly. The door of the prison opens, and* CECILIA *enters. His eyes find her.*)

CECILIA (*extending a hand*): Come and practise death with me. (*He stares.*) Come. Practise death with me . . .

Scene Eleven

A wide sunken lawn in winter, snow-covered. CECILIA *and* MORE *at the edge. Their breath is visible in the cold air.* MORE *seizes* CECILIA's *hands, and she leads him, staggering, over the snow.*

CECILIA (*aside*): And it was Death that governed Brutopia, His imminence was everywhere proclaimed, so the old men, by their proximity to Him, had most respect, and the young were pitied and their shallowness bewailed . . .

MORE *and* CECILIA, *unbalanced, revolve in a wide, comic and pathetic promenade,* MORE's *eyes fixed on the sky, silently. From a concealed place on the perimeter,* BERTRAND *sees.* CECILIA *leads* MORE *to the edge, and relinquishes him. She goes. He looks about him.*

176   *Howard Barker*

MORE: Meg! (*He staggers to his feet.*) Alice! (MEG *comes behind*
   ALICE, *who is watching from a different part, also concealed.*)
MEG: He's calling you.
ALICE: Yes. (*She doesn't move.* MORE *proclaims.*)
MORE: It's perfectly true the life of the genius is beset with pains,
   it is true betrayal is his destiny, and what is destined must be
   loved, and is not bitter, no, not bitter, but **did anybody want me**,
   oh, admire me, yes, lap my brains, but **want me**, copy, yes, and
   quote, but **want in nakedness? In dirty skin and bone?** (*He
   tears his shirt off, dragging it over his head.*)
ALICE: Oh, God . . .
MORE: Who did? Or called me beautiful? **Not my thoughts no,
   not my harmonies, but this!** (*Pause. His eyes search.*) **Anyone!**
BERTRAND (*catching* ALICE'*s eye*): Get him in, shall I?
ALICE: I will. (*She appears on the perimeter.*) Oh, there you are!
MORE: **Shuddup.**
ALICE: We were thinking cocoa would be —
MORE: **Shuddup.** (*Long pause.*)
ALICE: How long do you intend to —
MORE (*fixed in a position*): Hours. (*She goes to cross to him.*)
   Don't wade into my sea. (*She stops.* MEG *appears,* BERTRAND,
   SERVANTS, *like bathers on the edge of a pool.*) Oh, I soil your
   memory, oh, I soil your pity, I soil it with my dead man's mis-
   chief, **no apology!** (*Pause*)
ALICE: Oh, how you wreck the greatness of your character.
MORE: My greatness . . . how essential mankind should own the
   mould of More to jam its clumsy limbs into . . . **Be more like
   More.** He was so. He met his fate like. What a supreme example
   of. Oh, flawless, oh, immaculate — (*He detects* BERTRAND,
   moving.) **Don't enter my water!** (*He stops.*) I do this for you,
   so you may be ashamed . . . and see terrible aches in perfect
   men . . . (*As if by mute agreement, they surge over the snow and
   enclose him.*)

                          Scene Twelve

Part of the garden. BERTRAND *intercepts* CECILIA.

BERTRAND (*grinning*): There's death, and life! (*He drops to her*

BRUTOPIA   177

feet and embraces her pregnant belly.) The genius dies . . . new
genius! (*He covers her belly with kisses.*) Birth on his death day!
Can you manage it? As the axe comes, so you burst! Their souls
brush wings in passing! (*He stumbles away.*)

Scene Thirteen

*The maze, Brutopia. Snow, and a thin, cruel wind. CECILIA enters.
In the centre, HENRY, cloaked and hooded like a monk. His
LOUTS play draughts. She comes to where he is seated. He looks
at her.*

CECILIA: How beautiful you are.

KING HENRY: I've been called it often, but it was never meant.

CECILIA: Beautiful because you live the thought . . .

KING HENRY: And the thought, what is that now?

CECILIA: The thought is you would see me naked. That is the
    thought now. And later, the thought might be, she should be dead.
    (*Pause*) Shall I undress myself, or will you? (*Pause*)

KING HENRY: My fingers are too cold for buttons, I — (*She goes
    to unbutton herself.*) Wait!

CECILIA: I can't wait —

KING HENRY: No pleasure in too hasty —

CECILIA: Oh, quick, the thought's the action, quick! (*He seizes
    her hand, holds her firmly, a long time.*)

KING HENRY: There is some — unity among men — which —
    some fellowship which — and your father is not dead —

CECILIA: Fellowship?

KING HENRY: Not dead and I —

CECILIA: What fellowship? (*He falters.*) Oh, God . . . you . . . even
    you . . . are goodness-stricken . . . **what unity among men, what!**
    (HENRY *jumps to his feet and calls to the draughts players.*)

KING HENRY: Beat her!

CECILIA: Beat me —

KING HENRY: Beat, I said! (*The* LOUTS, *abandoning their game,
    pull* CECILIA *away. The sound of struggle from the maze.*
    HENRY *sits at the draught board. The* LOUTS *return without*
    CECILIA.) I could talk to More of many things. How I shall miss
    More! But not all things. (*They wait.*) Tell her husband, or her

178   *Howard Barker*

nurse. Yobs beat her, say. Say yobs climbed in. (*They go off.* THE
COMMON MAN *appears.*)
THE COMMON MAN: Sir Tom loves me. (HENRY *looks up,*
judging him at a glance.)
KING HENRY: Why?
THE COMMON MAN: I laugh at all he says.
KING HENRY: Not all he says is funny. (THE COMMON MAN
smiles. HENRY *moves a piece. He does not look up.*) Listen, I
hate the poor . . .
THE COMMON MAN: We can't be trusted, certainly . . .
KING HENRY: No, worse than that. Someone said God loves you,
and it's made you vain. (*He moves a piece.*) Behind your abject
eye lies some vanity you will inherit the earth. **Don't put your**
hand on my board. (THE COMMON MAN's *hand hovers.*)
Only the rich have humility, for they know they are con-
demned . . . (*His eyes rise to meet* THE COMMON MAN's.)

Scene Fourteen

The assembled FAMILY *and* SERVANTS *of* THOMAS MORE,
arranged on the terrace according to rank. A wind tugs their gar-
ments. At last MORE *appears, grey. They look to him, expectantly.*
He addresses them.

MORE: I was happy here. But that was a prison. I was loved here.
But that was a cell. Your kindness was a barred window, and your
respect a manacle. (*He smiles. He goes down, addressing the*
SERVANTS *individually, warmly shaking their hands.*) Thank
you. There is five pounds in the kitchen. Thank you. There is
something for you in the kitchen. Thank you. Thank you. Look
in the kitchen. Thank you. The kitchen for you, too. Thank you.
I shall miss your sponges. Thank you. (*He stops at the end of the*
row of SERVANTS. *He is level with* ALICE.) Oh, God . . . (*He*
looks into her face.) Oh, God, what am I to say to you? All I
rehearsed is rubbish . . . (*She looks at him.*)
ALICE: Look in the kitchen . . . ? (*Pause. He seizes her to himself*
with a terrible fastness.) What . . . ? What . . . ? Give me a word
. . . give me a word . . . (*He shakes his head. He moves on. He*
embraces his son. He moves on, to MEG. *Pause.*)

BRUTOPIA   179

MORE: How you will be maimed. How you will find a whole half of your being gone, like some rough butcher cleaved you down as well as me . . . (*She looks into him. He frees himself from her hands, and speaks to* ROPER, *who is next.*) Give her your little comfort . . . plug her wounds with little waddings of old husband love . . . (*He looks for* CECILIA, *who is absent.* BERTRAND, *next, speaks for her.*)

BERTRAND: She —

MORE (*silencing him with a finger*): She.

BERTRAND: She —

MORE: She. (*He smiles. He places himself at an angle to the entire company, and with supreme calculation, bows. As he does so, a familiar cry is heard.*)

BONCHOPE: Hey . . . ! (MORE *pulls his cloak around him, and walks smartly away towards the river, over the lawn. A* FIGURE *is seen hurtling towards him.*) I preach heresy! I preach! I preach the proper word of God and death so what I preach! (BONCHOPE *catches up with* MORE *and dogs his heels.*) I deny denial! I recant the recantation! God's honest arguments and death so what! (MORE *strides on.*) I speak Him, Lord, I am thy gob and death so what! I wag the Christ tongue in my mouth, His message lives so long as I, and death so what! (*He falls behind, onto his knees. The* FAMILY *are a small group in the distance.* MORE *stops. Pause. He goes back to* BONCHOPE.)

MORE: You could not resist, then? It pulled you, did it, from nest and loving marriage? **Death's tit?** (BONCHOPE *stares into* MORE.) We are so . . . We are so . . . Kiss me, enemy . . . (BONCHOPE *stares.*) My boat's waiting. Quick! (BONCHOPE *climbs to his feet, goes to* MORE. *They embrace. They go off.*)

ALICE (*to* THE SERVANT): You don't sob . . .

THE SERVANT: I shall if you require it. To keep my post I'll sob buckets . . .

ALICE: No, sob for proper or forget it. (*She turns to go to the house.*)

THE SERVANT: Nor you neither, I observe . . . (ALICE *stops. She looks over the garden.*)

ALICE: This will be a dead house, now.

THE SERVANT: Or mad, maybe . . .

ALICE: Grief-stricken and all gloom . . .

THE SERVANT: Or giggle, maybe . . .

ALICE: The garden slips . . . and old walls heave . . . moss in the unused bedrooms . . . **life without the master.** (*Pause. She looks at* THE SERVANT.) Preserve his things as if he were about to come back any minute. A clean shirt daily by his bed. And change his books around, the order of them. His inkwell, do not let it dry, and ask the postman in, whether or not he has letters. Give him brandy, as my husband did. **Life without the master.** (*She holds the eye of* THE SERVANT, *then hurries away.*)

Scene Fifteen

A quiet place in the garden. BERTRAND *sedulously attends to* CECILIA's *bruises with a bowl of balsam and a lint.*

BERTRAND: I like this . . . (*He dabs.*) I do like this . . . !
CECILIA: Why do you?
BERTRAND: Because you are in need of me. Because you're still. And for one shred of a moment — weak! (*He dabs.*) They found the louts, and they were thrashed.
CECILIA: What louts? I identified no one.
BERTRAND: No need. They confessed.
CECILIA: To what?
BERTRAND: Beating. Trespass. I forget. Is that enough?
CECILIA (*smiling at him*): Yes.
BERTRAND (*putting down the bowl*): I am so full of delight! I am childish with the thought of the child! (*He looks at her, moved.*) Hold my head. Do place an affectionate paw on my head. Though we conceived it crudely I. Aspire to your kindness.
CECILIA: Yes. I can do that. (*She puts a hand on his head.*) I can because I think so slightly of you. I can massage you like a dog . . . (ALICE *appears, smiling at them.*)
ALICE: He missed you, did Bertrand say? Or not missed. It is so hard to tell the actual feeling of a genius. Perhaps he merely registered your absence. May I sit? (*She sits on the wall.*) And now it's ours. (*She swings her ankle to and fro.*) The whole damned thing. (*She laughs lightly, bites her lip.*) I have this absurd feeling! Of course I shall be ill, of course at some stage I shall utterly disintegrate, but at this moment, I feel . . . **a rush of infantile delirium.** (*She laughs. Pause. She swings her foot.*) I can tell you. I can tell you because you aren't at all censorious. I could not tell Meg. Who could tell Meg anything? She is so censorious. I shudder at the march of Meg! Shall I go? (*She hops*

up.) I am forever interrupting, which is the function of the widow, I suspect? I'll go. (*She does not move.* CECILIA *rises, holds her close.*) How wonderful to have a baby. How I hate and envy you . . . (*She smiles, and goes.* CECILIA *watches her departure.*)

CECILIA: She loves you. You have done something with her.

BERTRAND: Me? What?

CECILIA: No, you have.

BERTRAND: Me?

CECILIA: Words, or something. You have set her on.

BERTRAND: I —

CECILIA (*briskly*): It must be time you visited the Commons, the committees will be frothing, and you have horribly neglected the Russia trade.

BERTRAND: It proceeds without —

CECILIA: It proceeds without? Then what are you for? No, you must get on, and I will harvest the baby when its hour comes, all this rurality ruins you. **You are nothing like the bastard you were once.** (*Pause. She smiles, the smile fades.*) I am certain there is goodness in me. But this goodness cannot emerge in the company of the good, who sicken me. (*Pause. He walks away, stops, turns.*)

BERTRAND: **My child also.**

CECILIA: I know that. (*He walks, stops again.*)

BERTRAND: **My tiny property.**

CECILIA: Yes. (*He goes.*)

The Caption

Sir Thomas More was executed on 6th July, 1535. His final joke was made with his executioner.

Scene Sixteen

The garden in a neglected state. CECILIA *is standing with* HENRY, *whose arms are wrapped about her.*

CECILIA: These rare visits. These expeditions in dark clothes.

And great anger in your act. I don't criticize. (*He kisses her passionately.*) These nocturnal raids. These depradations in me. I don't criticize. But the book's not printed.

KING HENRY: A king might lavish so much on a woman . . . !

CECILIA: No castles, thanks . . .

KING HENRY: Might deck her out in such — (*He nuzzles her.*)

CECILIA: The book, though . . .

KING HENRY: Shh . . . down now . . . (*He explores her.*) I suffer you . . . I squirm in aches which arch over the skies . . .

CECILIA: Me, too . . . but where's the book, I —

KING HENRY (*freezing*): **No book.** (*She stares at him.*)

CECILIA: No book?

KING HENRY: It's too much gloom.

CECILIA: Gloom?

KING HENRY: Yes. Mankind is fouled in it. (*She smiles, disbelieving him. She reaches out an exploratory, seductive finger. He slaps it away.*)

> **No.**
> **You.**
> **Grim.**
> **Hag.** (*She is horrified. He runs his hand through his hair, anxiously.*)

Can't print it though you cut me off from cunt for ever more. Can't license it though you shut me out of all your little doors. It can't be done.

CECILIA: You licensed More. *Utopia* swamps all the bookstalls, and in new editions since you murdered him. Why him, and why not me? (*He looks at her with cross irritation.*) They are sweating at the printers, fanning themselves with inky paws, everywhere *Utopia*, where is mine? (*Pause*)

KING HENRY: Literature must make us love ourselves. That is its function. And yours don't. (*She stares, bitterly.*)

CECILIA: No, that's false. (*She shuts her eyes, desperately.*) I wish I could — scoop up the arguments, but — it's false . . . !

KING HENRY: Sir Tom praised Man. Oh, good Sir Tom . . . ! (*She is speechless for some seconds, aghast.*)

CECILIA: No, listen — listen, **that's preposterous, you had him** —

KING HENRY: His democracy is luminous before our weary eyes —

CECILIA: **Listen!**

KING HENRY: Is not Utopia wonderful, for us base killers to see hovering like a mirage on the stinking draught? (*As if disinteg-*

BRUTOPIA 183

rating, CECILIA *sinks to the ground. Pause.*) No, don't splay
like that, it's not womanly. (*She is like a fallen doll.*) Up, I said,
you look a scrubber. (*She does not move.*) It's possible to cease
requiring you, it must be said, I — (*He turns to go.*)
CECILIA: Don't go! (*She struggles to recover, brushing her skirt.
He waits, his back to her.*) How could you want me so, how could
you show such greatness in wanting . . . and yet . . . hold such
mundane and shallow beliefs . . . ?
KING HENRY (*turning on her*): **Won't permit the book!** (*He
stamps and shouts.*) **You use me! Won't license the book!** (*The
sound of an alarmed hunting dog.*)
CECILIA: Now you've done it. (*It barks, it approaches. An ex-
pression of unease crosses* HENRY's *features.*) Perhaps dogs lick
your palms? I would. (*It comes nearer.*) Let me be your bitch, all
teeth in abeyance, fawning up your hip . . . (*The bark comes
nearer.* THE COMMON MAN *appears from cover.*)
KING HENRY: Call off that thing.
THE COMMON MAN: I've no authority.
KING HENRY: Then find some, quick.
THE COMMON MAN: I stoop. I wheedle, only.
KING HENRY: Then get on dog level and plead. (*The barking
becomes a low running growl.* THE COMMON MAN *and*
HENRY *regard each other tensely.*) Christ help you if it marks
me, you're for the block . . . (*A moment of recognition.* THE
COMMON MAN *plunges to all fours.*)
THE COMMON MAN: Dog! Dog! Gnaw me! Hound, rip! (*The
animal trots into sight, is placated by the spectacle of* THE
COMMON MAN *on all fours, and licks him.*)
CECILIA: So I'll be with you, when I am wild . . . (HENRY *goes
to leave.*)
THE COMMON MAN: Drink, sir! Tom did! Sandwich, sir! Tom
did! (HENRY *leans intimately to him.*)
KING HENRY: If you knew me, forget me, lout. (THE COMMON
MAN *makes a button of his lips.* HENRY *goes.* CECILIA *turns
to go to the house.*)
THE COMMON MAN: Room for another? (*She stops.*) Room for
another?

184 *Howard Barker*

Scene Seventeen

The maze in a high wind. CECILIA *enters in a shift, as if prepared for birth. A cacophony of street carnival and laughter.*

CECILIA (*aside*): The sound of Brutopia was roaring. Day and night it roared, and things were falling, things were breaking constantly, which was a sort of anthem in the unkind air . . .

CECILIA (*looking for* THE SERVANT *through a mob*): **Janet!**

THE SERVANT (*appearing beside her*): Childbirth here's a spectacle, and hundreds have to witness it, not only husbands but whole factories, whole regiments and schools!

CECILIA (*grasping her*): Support me, I'm the queen —

THE SERVANT (*leading her*): You see, what everybody hates is privacy, all acts must be seen! (*She assists her to a bench. Whistles and raucous applause.*)

CECILIA: Protect me, I'm the queen! (*An immediate silence. The* CROWD *disappears.* CECILIA *sees a* WOMAN *coming towards her. They are alone. The* WOMAN *stops, smiles.*)

BOLEYN: Everybody nowadays has a maze. I knew this one would be different, since a genius designed it. But genius abhors the arbitrary, so I found in a short time, it had its rules. It's a right turn after every three. Why three? His daughters? Or the Trinity? (*Long pause. She smiles, her eyes fixed on* CECILIA, *not unkindly.*) It is not simple for me, this. Whilst I am forever doing it, each time it burns. (*Pause*) Do you know me? I am Ann Boleyn. I made the last queen's bed, and then I simply entered it. So might you with mine, and I am here to threaten you, is that his baby you have there? I am the final queen I state categorically. Speak if you want to. (*Long pause.*) I don't accuse, I merely threaten, whilst perfectly aware endangered love affairs are the most clinging, I found it so myself we also were a risk and probably you aren't the only one, whose is the child? Do speak. (*Pause*)

CECILIA: Not his.

BOLEYN: Whose, then? You are not married I know, I investigate before these missions, and so would you. It helps to face the enemy to know their night time tricks.

CECILIA: Bert Caldwell.

BOLEYN: Him!

CECILIA: Him, yes!

BOLEYN: It is a small world!

CECILIA: Small? It's microscopic, listen, obviously you frighten me —

BRUTOPIA   185

BOLEYN: That's my intent —

CECILIA: I promise you I've no designs upon your place —

BOLEYN: They all say that —

CECILIA: No, but proof, I'm queen already, thanks —

BOLEYN: Of what, his heart?

CECILIA: Brutopia. (*Pause*)

BOLEYN: Where's that? (*Pause. CECILIA smiles.*) You're not sane.

CECILIA: I'm certain that is my whole attraction. (*Pause*)

BOLEYN: Try to be sensible, your father was. I immensely liked him, and though he was a snob he never leered.

CECILIA: He did leer. It was himself he leered at.

BOLEYN: He paid me many compliments, and sweetly put —

CECILIA: He did so many things with a straight face — (BO-LEYN *lashes a slap. CECILIA reels. Pause.*)

BOLEYN: The times I've done this and always said on setting out, Ann Boleyn, no violence! And yet no sooner do I set foot on the property I see red swimming in the bottom of my eyes! Do let's be sensible I hate to strike the pregnant.

CECILIA: Oh, don't be kind for — (BOLEYN *lashes her again. CECILIA holds her face. Pause.*) Don't hit me again, I will give up your husband. (*Pause*)

BOLEYN: Poor love, that repudiates for two little slaps . . . and he is mad for you . . . (*She gets up.*) That's simple, then. Write him a letter.

CECILIA: Dictate, and I'll put my signature.

BOLEYN: No. You are the scholar. I'm from the scullery. You do it.

CECILIA: Me? A scholar?

BOLEYN: Yes, you're Meg, aren't you? Who has your parent's cranium? (CECILIA *laughs with resignation, disbelief, shame and bitterness.*) You are not Meg . . . You are another of . . .

CECILIA: I'm another, yes . . .

BOLEYN: Of his . . .

CECILIA: Another of his, yes . . . (*Her eyes meet BOLEYN's. Her nose is bleeding. BOLEYN turns to go.*) Wait . . . (*She stops.*) You have the body of the King and may it give you pleasure, but give me something for my sacrifice.

BOLEYN: I'm not buying my own husband, dear.

CECILIA: No, but I think it will be hard to keep him off me, and for all the slaps I'm still susceptible, so bribe me, will you? Help me desist?

BOLEYN: How?

CECILIA: By balancing a greater thing against desire.

BOLEYN: And what is greater?

CECILIA: A book.

BOLEYN: Book? But you're not Meg —

CECILIA: **I'm not Meg but still I'm literate.**
I'm not Meg but still I'm perfect.
Certainly I am not Meg. (*Pause. She grins.*)
I have this work, you see, which your husband calls inhuman.
Get it licensed. You know the bishops. Get them to pass it for the printer. Do it for me.

BOLEYN (*measuring her*): I could not do what you have done.
When I loved I'd tear my gums against flint walls to reach my wanted one. (*Pause*)

CECILIA: Yes ... I am not passionate ... (BOLEYN *inclines her head, formally, and departs.* THE SERVANT *appears beside* CECILIA.) A queen's been here ... smell the air ... a queen ...

THE SERVANT: To plead?

CECILIA: To prostrate herself. To bow before the powers of my belly where her unruly husband knocks like tree trunks in high seas butt the harbour wall ... (*She laughs.*) **I am a terrible liar and I mean to have both.** (*She turns desperately to* THE SER-VANT.) **Man and book! Body and book!** (*She stops, alarmed.*) Is this a birth pain? (*She feels herself.*) I think the effort's brought me on. What's a birth pain? Call Meg! I awfully wish Meg to do my drudgery — (THE SERVANT *turns.*) Oh, listen — (*She stops.*) Was that — what I just did — was that politics?

Scene Eighteen

A child crying. THE SERVANT *walks up and down with the swaddled infant.* CECILIA *is draped in a wooden lounge chair, convalescent. She wears spectacles, and attempts to read.*

CECILIA: Oh, do stop bouncing it ...! Did you bounce me like that? No wonder I'm so. No wonder. (*She opens her arms for the baby.* THE SERVANT *gives it to her. She looks at it.*) I shan't name the child, because I am not keeping her. (*Pause.* THE SERVANT *stares in disbelief.*)

BRUTOPIA   187

THE SERVANT: Not keeping her . . . ?

CECILIA: That's what I said. (*She looks at* THE SERVANT.) Oh,
my tutor in malevolence, you are outbid. And your expression
tells me all your wickedness is shallow. You are appalled. You
are no further use to me. (*She smiles.*) Which is correct! The
student must surpass the teacher, or what's the use of knowledge?

THE SERVANT: I'll bring her up.

CECILIA: Silly.

THE SERVANT: No, let me bring her up, I'll —

CECILIA: You! (*She stares.*) With your Utopian ideas? Do you
think I'd give my loved one into you? You would load her back
with such — **convictions!** No, I have a better parent. (*She lifts
the child, now silent, in the air, and smiles.*)

THE SERVANT: She needs you . . .

CECILIA: No, she exaggerates, we all do . . .

THE SERVANT (*unable to contain herself*): I think you are a
wicked and ill woman and I should have strangled you at birth!

Scene Nineteen

THE COMMON MAN, *waiting in a place.* CECILIA *approaches
with the child. He waits. She gives it him.*

CECILIA: Make her imperfect. Make her ache for the impossible.
Teach her to detect the liar but never contradict him. Forbid her
wisdom. Teach her to draw her consolation from the stars. And
say her mother talked too much to make a decent whore. (THE
COMMON MAN *takes the child, wraps it like at item of
shopping, and bounds off.* HENRY *appears, interrupting her
thoughtfulness. He removes her spectacles.*)

KING HENRY: I hate the spectacles. They shout **scrutiny** at me.
I am not to be looked into. The long look's critical. (*She looks
down.*) The child thrives, then?

CECILIA: It lives, and yet I've lost it.

KING HENRY: Lost it? To whom?

CECILIA: Nature. (*He looks at her, puzzled.*) You see how spoiled
I am, how arid in the very heart of feeling. You drink her nour-
ishment. (*She unbuttons her dress.*)

188   *Howard Barker*

KING HENRY (*putting his hand on her wrist*): What have you done?

CECILIA: Drink me, murderer . . . (*He is uncomfortable.*)

KING HENRY: Cecilia, you will be arrested . . .

CECILIA: In my arms she lay, thinking, **this is the life!** She chuckled with a sickening complacency. But I saved her. (*Pause. She pulls his mouth to her breast.*) Rob! Plunder, then! (*They engage, passionately. Then they are still. A voice, over the gardens.*)

THE PRINTER: Miss More! (*She opens her eyes. A FIGURE in an apron is seen coming towards them.*)

KING HENRY: Hide me!

THE PRINTER: Miss More! (CECILIA *bundles* HENRY *beneath her skirts.*)

KING HENRY: Hide me!

CECILIA (*to* THE PRINTER, *who is waving a bill*): You must want Meg. She gets all the letters.

THE PRINTER: No, it says Cecilia.

CECILIA: There are Cecilias all over Chelsea.

THE PRINTER: Yes, but here?

CECILIA: Not if here means here, but there is Cecilia who makes the pastry in —

THE PRINTER: No, it's you, Miss —

CECILIA: Or the hag who lives in the beer barrel —

THE PRINTER: Look — (*He holds out a calf-bound book, slipping off its wrapping. She sees the legend* 'Brutopia' *on the spine.* HENRY, *concealed by her skirt, remains in a posture which excludes him from the conversation. A pause of depth and confusion.* CECILIA *makes a move of her head to indicate* THE PRINTER *should go. He fails to perceive its meaning.*) I have a cart outside with seven hundred —

CECILIA: Loaves! I don't want seven hundred loaves — (*She jerks her head again.*) You see, you must mean —

THE PRINTER (*confused*): I —

CECILIA: Cecily! Not Cecilia! You see, there's your error! Cecily, the baker, she has a place beside the gate and you've misjudged the turning — (*She thrusts the book back at him.*) She is the loaf enthusiast — this is not the first time she's — so off you go — (*She waves him away.*) Turn right, and right again — **take your loaves away!** (*He withdraws, faltering. She looks keenly into his eyes. He recedes.* HENRY *lifts his head, sits contemplatively.*)

KING HENRY: When More lived this place was all seclusion . . .

CECILIA: The walls are falling down and dogs jump in . . . as well

BRUTOPIA   189

as monarchs ... (*She is in a state of passionate excitement at the appearance of the book. She kisses* HENRY *spontaneously.*) I'm so — look at me — I am delighted! (*She kisses him again.*)

KING HENRY: You are. With what, though?

CECILIA: With you!

KING HENRY: Me? Solely?

CECILIA: Solely? Now, that's ambitious! No, the sun shines and the blossom blows and I — (*Pause*)

KING HENRY: I only love you because I do not know you, Cecilia.

CECILIA: Yes.

KING HENRY: And when I know you —

CECILIA: Then we're done. (*Pause*) And that's good. (*Pause*) That's proper. (*Pause. Then* HENRY *gets up.*)

KING HENRY: Down the river, now, to Hampton. Diplomacy and tennis. And as I bash, it's you. And as I smash, it's you.

CECILIA: Call my name, but half-obscured, like a curse.

KING HENRY: Bash. Smash. I carve your body on the yew hedge. Henry. His thing. (*He smiles, kisses her tenderly, withdraws through the garden.*)

Scene Twenty

TWO PRINTERS *gazing at* CECILIA. *Seven hundred copies of the book* Brutopia *stacked in a neglected greenhouse.* CECILIA, *the object of their amazement and contempt, runs her hands over the bindings. She takes a copy. She inhales it. She is without shame. She nurses and fondles the book. She meets their eyes over the cover's rim.*

CECILIA: Scotch leather. (*She inhales the pages.*) And the paper?

FIRST PRINTER: Dutch.

CECILIA: Dutch?

SECOND PRINTER: All we could get, we —

CECILIA: No, I love the Dutch ... (*With immaculate care she opens the book on a bench, runs her finger tips over the page.*) And what of the ink.

FIRST PRINTER: Clerkenwell. We make the ink. (*Pause. She turns the leaves.*)

190   *Howard Barker*

CECILIA: How much you print, and how little you read . . .
SECOND PRINTER: We don't do books. We are handbill printers.
FIRST PRINTER: The pages came. The licence came. And then
   the money. Anonymous, the lot.
SECOND PRINTER: Off we went.
CECILIA: How satisfied you must be. I am so happy for you. How
   gratified.
SECOND PRINTER: It was good money —
CECILIA: No, no, I mean — to have at long last found an object
   worthy of your skills. (*She looks at them for the first time. They
   shift uneasily.*) This is no poster for a sordid dance, is it? Or
   handbill for a quack? All your apprenticeship, and years of craft,
   at last discover a fit task. (*They look blank.*) Midwives! Allies in
   great birth! (*She seizes them in her arms. She hugs them, releases
   them.*) Come now, you must have read some of it as you laid the
   type, what did you think?
SECOND PRINTER: No, it's — you rarely read when setting
   the —
CECILIA: Of course not, no, but when you — read the proofs, the
   galleys, what are they? You — surely then you — (*Pause*)
SECOND PRINTER: We thought the margins were a bit broad,
   didn't we, John? (*Pause. They turn to go.*)
CECILIA: What is the use of a craft if it — of industry, if it —
   invention, if it — you are the printers! (*She follows them to the
   door.*) The page is also you! (*They step into the garden. She
   follows them. They retreat.*)
CECILIA: Your craft is not immune! (*They ignore her.*) **The
   printers will be killed and rightly, too!** (*They disappear
   through the hedges.* ALICE *appears beside* CECILIA.)
ALICE: Sir Tom would give them liquor.
CECILIA: Yes.
ALICE: He knew the fence that runs between labour and imagina-
   tion. He knew better than you.
CECILIA: Yes.
ALICE: May I read the book?
CECILIA (*turning to her*): I don't know. There are so few.
ALICE: And you are saving them?
CECILIA: Yes.
ALICE: For better readers?
CECILIA (*holding* ALICE *tenderly by the arm*): Obviously it must
   be read by those already predisposed to understand it. Otherwise
   it might as well be thrown up in the air, to drift down in obscure
   places where — (*She stops.*) Yes, I think that is perhaps what I

BRUTOPIA 191

should do! I should not sell them, since then the rich will know everything as well as owning everything. It would not be good for them. (*She smiles, thinks.*) On the other hand, to give them to the poor would be to have them wrongly employed, as jambs for windows, draught excluders, and the like, no, that would demean my labour, obviously the books should reach their readers arbitrarily, rather. Only then can I be assured one copy, and only one perhaps, might reach its loved one and enrich his life. I will fling them over the wall.

ALICE: Over the wall?

CECILIA: Yes. Bookshops are prisons, after all. The books are gaoled. And there's a highway over there, beyond the gate.

ALICE: Yes ...

CECILIA: So many people pass, of all descriptions, to and from the city. Of these, the vast majority are shallow and incapable of dream, but one! One might, a single soldier in a platoon, a merchant bored with wealth, who knows, but one! (*She smiles.*) I am an optimist, you see ... (ALICE *looks at her.*)

ALICE: Cecilia, you are not well, the birth —

CECILIA: The birth? I had forgotten the birth! (*She looks distantly for a moment.*) Why do you call me ill when what I say is true? Why do you? Surely the ill are the liars? Hold my arm ... (ALICE *takes her arm. They walk in silence.*)

ALICE: I have so much to tell you ... so much to talk about ... (*They walk.*) It's strange how, because you are so single-minded, I feel — I — who am not single-minded — feel I have to — odd, isn't it — confess to you ... (*They walk. Silence, they walk.*) I want you to know things and yet I am certain in my heart these things you know already! (*She stops suddenly.*) I want to confess. (*Pause*) And yet I know, when I do confess, you will say — oh, so typically of you — you will say, oh, that! I knew that! I already knew that! (*She laughs. Pause.*) So —

BERTRAND'S VOICE (*enraged over the lawns*): **Where — is — she!**

ALICE: Oh, God —

BERTRAND'S VOICE: **I said where —**

ALICE: Oh, hell — (BERTRAND *enters furiously.*)

BERTRAND: **I go to the cot and —**

ALICE: Shh, you —

BERTRAND: **I go to the cot — I run to the cot of my — and she's — the sheets cold — where —**

ALICE: You have chosen the worst possible —

BERTRAND: **I ask the nurse and she says —**

192   *Howard Barker*

ALICE: I also am enquiring and you —
BERTRAND: **My bastard daughter where is she the little love!**
   (*He stares at* CECILIA.)
ALICE: Enquiring, but more subtly . . .
BERTRAND (*not looking at her*): Shut up.
ALICE: You are so horse-like, but that's to malign the horse.
BERTRAND: Shut up.
ALICE: You are so bull-like, but that's to malign the bull.
BERTRAND (*not removing his eyes from* CECILIA): Shut up, I
   said . . . ! (*Pause. There is a moment of recognition in* CECILIA's
   eyes. She smiles.)
CECILIA: You two are lovers! It's obvious! (*She laughs. He slaps
   her violently.*)
ALICE: **Don't do that.**
CECILIA (*recovering*): How wonderful . . . your fingers touch on
   landings . . . oh, the ecstasy of the lingering, illicit touch . . . (*He
   stares.*) Marry my step-mother. Marry her and grow together like
   hard woods, gnarl like yews. She is a brilliant woman whom my
   father crushed . . . (*He stares.*)
BERTRAND: I want the child . . .
CECILIA: *Utopia* was false, and yet its falseness did not impede
   its progress. And your feelings for our bastard, perhaps they're
   false, too . . . (*She walks away from them.* BERTRAND *looks at
   her. Pause.*)
BERTRAND: Shall you send for the constable, or shall I? (ALICE
   does not reply. Night falls.)

Scene Twenty-One

A pile of books. CECILIA *seated by them, under a wall. It is night.*
MEG *comes, joins her, pulling a gown closer for the cold.*

CECILIA (*in a whisper*): I toss them over the wall. Like this. (*She
   chucks one, blindly.*) At intervals. Irregular, or some dealer will
   stand there with a net and so prevent the **legitimate reader**
   gaining access to the text. (*She smiles.*) Who this reader is, God
   knows. But that must be the point of printing, surely? The an-
   onymity? (*Pause. Without taking her eyes off* MEG, *she spontaneously chucks another.*) Three hundred and sixty-six to go.

BRUTOPIA   193

(*Pause*) I know what kindness is. It is something done to the self.
But when this self is made, give it to others. (*She chucks again.*)
Shh! (*She cranes her head to the wall.*) Footsteps! Someone
collects! Someone scampers off, amazed . . . (ALICE *comes
through the darkness, and sits with them. Pause. A distant sound.*)
MEG: Look, a comet! (*They all look.* CECILIA *suddenly throws a
book. The sound is repeated.*)
ALICE: The last wolf in England . . . shh . . . (*They listen. The
sound of oars in water.* ALICE *puts a hand on* CECILIA's
knee.)
CECILIA: Oars.
          Oars in the water.
          I think the boat's for me. (*She stands up.*)
          The agents of Utopia . . . have come for me . . .

Scene Twenty-Two

CECILIA *waits in moonlight on the sunken lawn. Some figures
appear on the perimeter. They are* NUNS. *One approaches her,
circumspectly, kindly.*

CECILIA: Be careful, I am the king's mistress. (*The* NUN *nods,
slowly.*) So one false move and — (*She nods, patiently.*) Lay a
finger on me and — (CECILIA *draws a finger gruesomely across
her neck. The* NUN *nods again.* CECILIA *whispers.*) Got *Brutopia*? (*The* NUN *looks uncertain.*) Not got one yet? It's passed
around, you see, in brown paper covers, hand to hand, in alleys
or upstairs in pubs . . .
NUN (*smiling*): We have such a nice room for you . . .
CECILIA: They said that to my dad! (*She grins.*)
NUN: Oh?
CECILIA: Same words exactly, and listen, do stop smiling, I can't
be good in the company of the good and that smile is only
violence, I'll get you a copy — (*She turns to go.*)
NUN: Not now.
CECILIA: Not now? Why not now?
NUN: It's late.
CECILIA: It's late, but you came late, so don't complain about the
lateness!

194 *Howard Barker*

NUN: You are full of wit, I do like you.

CECILIA: Good. So does everyone. For different reasons, obviously. Only my father failed to like me, and I arranged his death, which was what he wanted. I say I arranged it, no, I exaggerate, I blocked his pardon. (*The* NUN *takes a step.*) Be careful, the King does tend to — (*She makes the gruesome gesture again.*)

NUN: Shall we go? (*Pause, then suddenly* CECILIA *slaps her across the face. The* NUN *reels. From the perimeter, other* NUNS *hurry to her aid. The* NUN *gestures for them to stay back.*)

CECILIA: I'm sorry, I really cannot stand that smile. (*Pause*) Go where?

NUN: This room.

CECILIA: I have a room.

NUN: We want to care for you.

CECILIA: You mean, I am to be loved whether I want it or not?

NUN: We will love you, yes.

CECILIA: When it's soldiers, isn't that called rape? (*Pause*)

NUN: I think you are much too clever for your own good —

CECILIA: **Yes! Much too clever! Yes!** And everything I know, I thought. From the bottom to the top. From the cellar to the attic. I did not borrow. I did not quote.

NUN: How lonely, how lonely you — (CECILIA's *eyes fill with tears. The* NUN *makes a subtle signal. The other* NUNS *hurry forward and pinion* CECILIA *with ropes, spinning her round to bewilder her.* CECILIA *is gagged, and held still. The moon shines down.* CECILIA's *eyes turn from side to side. A* FIGURE *comes into her eyeline.*)

KING HENRY: Yer boat's stuck in my mooring. (*The* NUNS *look alarmed as* HENRY *walks onto the lawn.* FACTOR *and* LLOYD *hang back.* HENRY *looks at* CECILIA.) And you've trussed my tart.

NUN: We are the Collectors of the Convent of —

KING HENRY: Yes, well, I am running out of patience with the convents, aren't we all? (*The* NUNS *bow to him. He sings.*)

Oh, she who walks upon the night
Shall see such things as stop the heart — (*He ceases abruptly.*)

You are not to handle lunatics in future. I am putting lunacy out to tender. Good night. (*The* NUNS *turn to go. One stays to unloosen* CECILIA.) No, leave her trussed. (*They depart. He sings.*)

We'll slice the moon into two parts,
And lick her blood from the wet grass, (*They look back.*)
My love and I we will be wild
Unashamed and undefiled, (FACTOR *and* LLOYD *clap the rhythm.*)
I can keep going!

Off the grey corpse of charity
We'll take our dinner and our tea —

Not good —

Who dares impede our wet embrace
Let him go wary of his face,
Into her skirts my hand will be
The silent pilgrim of the faith . . .

KING HENRY *looks after the departing* NUNS. *A long pause.*

I came to kill you. Or to fuck you. I did not know which. And I find others. Killing or fucking you. I did not know which. (*Pause*) How beautiful to find you silent. (*The sound of oars in the water.*) Boleyn's been here I know, and done a deal with you. I know everything. I have to. (*Pause*) How wonderful you cannot speak. Already you are diminishing, you are evaporating in the heat of my indifference, like a puddle in the sun. How small you are! How mild you are! How did I ever? Nothing so absurd as spent passion . . . (*He goes close to her.*) Speak, then. I saved you from the madhouse. (LLOYD *and* FACTOR *laugh loudly.*) Oh! They laugh the contrary! They say I am the madhouse! (*He looks into her eyes.*) Speak . . .

CECILIA's *eyes look into his, and as if she had spoken, he nods, kindly, and turns away. The moon goes behind a cloud.*

ROME

On Being Divine

CHARACTERS

BEATRICE	The Lover of a Pope
SMITH	Her Daughter, a Widow
PIUS	A Pontiff
LASCAR	A High Official of the Church
ABRAHAM	An Old Testament Figure
ISAAC	His Son
BENZ	A Vagrant
OFFICER	Of Rome
SOLDIERS	Of Rome
DOREEN	A Cultured Woman of Rome
BEKNOWN	Her Housemaid
CARDINALS	Of Rome
SLIPMAN	A Cardinal
PARK	A Cardinal, A Pope, A Martyr
GLOY	A Soldier of Rome
DEAD SOLDIER	A Woman of Rome
HOLLO	A Lout
GENERAL	Of Roman Artillery
BARBARIAN	Enemy of Rome
SECOND BARBARIAN	Enemy of Rome
THE MARQUIS OF DREUX-BREZE	An Aristocrat of France
MIRABEAU	A Radical
TORTURER	Of the Barbarian Conquest
LE NOUVEAU	A Philosophe
OLD WOMAN	Character of the Interlude
MAN	Character of the Interlude
FIRST YOUNG WOMAN	Character of the Interlude
SECOND YOUNG WOMAN	Character of the Interlude
SOLDIER	Character of the Interlude
THE REGIMENT	
THE CROWD	
THE DEVOTS	
YOUTH	

MAN
BOY
THREE WOMEN
VOICES, ETC.

PART ONE

Scene One

A hall of culture. A door booms. A WOMAN *enters. She studies. The door booms again. A* MAN *enters. They study, they revolve. A dying* POPE *is revealed, descending.*

BEATRICE: If you are educated, but not otherwise. (*She revolves.*) Forgive me, but I am so tired of the uneducated, who for some reason, flock to me. So tired of generosity. (*They revolve, studying.*) Saying, for example, your ignorance moves me. Saying, how lithe is your intelligence! How you would benefit from education! Saying, you are as unpolished as granites against which my cultivated character seems false and frail as porcelain. Etcetera. (*They revolve.*) No, let us fuck with some deep equality, if that is what you want. I am here with my daughter but she is taking photographs. (*The* POPE *inches lower.*) I am terribly alone with my inflexible and intolerant personality, so terribly alone and yet I have a perfect arse. (*The* MAN *stops moving, and begins to undress.*) Oh, someone speaks my tongue! Oh, someone fathoms me! Reach into me! Let us live at the extremes! (*The door booms. A young* WOMAN *enters and walks to the dying* POPE.)

SMITH: I went to the shops. Hopeless! Looking for a present. Hopeless! This present was meant to comfort you. Absurd! (*She kisses his hands.*) When I knew only my self could comfort you. So I bring that. But smartly clad. Elegant, as if your funeral was already. Am I wet? It's raining. I always used to wonder, does he know when it rains? Does the fall of the rain impinge upon his consciousness? After all, the ceilings are so. And the windows, very, very. So who could blame you for never knowing what the weather was or povery for that matter. I never did. Never blamed

202   *Howard Barker*

you for anything! (*She kisses his hands again.*) Oh, you are a
modern man. Such a modern man! (*A* REGIMENT OF SOL-
DIERS *enters, with* WOMEN. *They sing as they pass, raggedly.
They ignore the spectacle of* BEATRICE *making love.*)

FIRST PASSAGE

THE REGIMENT: Forbid us
                    Deny us
                    Don't let us get our hands on

                    Spare us
                    Deprive us
                    Don't lend us the power of language

                    Or we shall sing the ecstasy of murder!
                    (*The* WOMEN *laugh staccato.*)

                    Obscure us
                    Conceal us
                    Don't let us be examined

                    Interpret us
                    Substitute for us
                    Don't let us be revealed

                    As the condition of your laughter!

The WOMEN *laugh staccato. The* PROCESSION *passes out.* BEA-
TRICE *withdraws from the* MAN, *straightening her clothes.*

BEATRICE: I'm not rich, if that's what you aspire to. And I don't
    decry riches. No, I don't scorn money, which liberates. It does,
    it does liberate and I. **How much I talk.** I am inclined to talk
    much more than necessary, revealing too much of myself at one
    go, which offends, don't say you're offended, you're not of-
    fended, are you, but certainly it is an error on my part to show
    whole elements of my character which would be better exposed
    by slow degrees as the sea washes sand from an item of wreck-

ROME
203

age, better but impossible, I shall try to be more disciplined with you where I was not disciplined at all with others, if you like me describe me in any words that come to mind, I mean make a judgement, rash as you wish! When we judge we are surely being intimate! (*Silence. The* MAN *goes out, dressed.* BEATRICE *laughs, shuddering, shaking her head. She walks to to her* DAUGHTER *and kisses her.* SMITH *goes to leave, stops.*)

SMITH (*to the* POPE): My husband — should I tell you this — my little husband is dead in an accident — and I felt such a rush of satisfaction it was as if I had myself concocted the accident — but no — it was pure luck — the sort of luck which almost but not quite — instills guilt in the recipient. (*She goes out.* BEATRICE *looks at the dying* POPE. *His eyes open at last.*)

PIUS: My Own Bitch . . .

BEATRICE: Yes.

PIUS: My odorous and fluid vixen . . .

BEATRICE: Yes, but I have to find another man.

PIUS: Futile and humiliating enterprise . . .

BEATRICE: No doubt, but I have to try.

PIUS: Degenerate and absurd ambition.

BEATRICE: I know that but.

PIUS: **Who could** —

BEATRICE: I don't know —

PIUS: **Who for more than half an hour's** —

BEATRICE: God knows but —

PIUS: **Suffocating copulation** —

BEATRICE: The odds are certainly against it —

PIUS: **Satisfy your** —

BEATRICE: Quite. (*He recovers. She walks a little. She shrugs.*) I don't pretend, I don't console myself with vistas of new life, I can assure you, I have always clung despite a certain madness, always adhered, preferring the crevice to the open floor, I am that kind of insect and at fifty —

PIUS: Show me your arse . . .

BEATRICE: Hardly expect to stumble over excellence, no, all you say is true and always was, perfect and immaculate **I am exhausted by the accuracy of every single one of your perceptions**. (*Pause*) However, I am in full health and in a strange way thriving, who knows, your death may have the unpredictible effect of generating freedom, just as an ancient house demolished liberates the vermin, we'll see, many rats are killed in falling mansions but some find other houses **all right I'll show you**. (*She goes close to him. She exposes herself to him. A long*

204 *Howard Barker*

silence). Oh, I did not want to live beyond you, loved one, but I cannot kill myself . . .

PIUS: Join me. (*She shakes her head.*) Take poison. How quick it is! Pain, and then the dark!

BEATRICE: Dark . . . ?

Dark . . . ? (*She lets fall her clothing, a gesture of spoiled hope.*)

Sometimes, even, you are derivative. Death is not dark. It blazes with the cruellest light. And rings to petulant music.

PIUS: Didn't I deliver you from all that's comic and contemptible? Didn't I snatch you as a girl from somnolence and domesticity? From futile wickedness and hours of, oh, endless hours of, compatibility? **We lived a roaring life of love**. If you know gratitude, die with me . . . (*She stares at him, half-horrified.*)

BEATRICE: I haven't the courage. Forgive me, I haven't the courage . . . !

PIUS: Beatrice . . .

BEATRICE: I have to go. You fill me with shame. Never have I felt shame with you. I cannot have our last looks soddened with remorse!

PIUS: Beatrice . . .

BEATRICE: **You inflict your death on me**.

PIUS: Your arse . . .

BEATRICE: I have shown you my arse and I must get some air.

PIUS: Your arse . . .

BEATRICE: **What of my arse**.

PIUS: It prevents my dying. (*Pause*)

BEATRICE: What? (*He looks at her.*) What?

PIUS: When I first saw your arse, I yielded you my life. One look, and I was altered. Its poise, its pride, its plenitude, its pity and its vigour, I saw God in its motion!

BEATRICE: So you said, often.

PIUS: And I can't be parted. (*Pause*)

BEATRICE: You must be.

PIUS: **I cannot die no matter that I want to**. (*Pause*) Sickness. Pain. Delirium. Nothing. (*Pause*) And my heart has stopped. (*She looks at him with horror. A* DIGNITARY *enters.*)

LASCAR: He must rest now!

He absolutely must stop talking! (*He attends to the blankets.*)

When he was young he could not speak, did you know this?

BEATRICE: Yes.

ROME

LASCAR: The words so crowded in his mouth even simple sentences were impossible for him. To communicate by speech required whole years of discipline.

BEATRICE: Twenty.

LASCAR: Twenty, yes! This delayed his progress through the church, where sentences must be uttered consecutively! (*He smiles, he plumps the pillows.*)

BEATRICE: Listen, Lascar . . .

LASCAR: He was furthermore, obsessed with death from the moment of his conception.

BEATRICE: I know that, too.

LASCAR: This moment he remembers vividly, the details of the room even, in which it occurred, the condition of his parents, their poverty, even the view from the window!

BEATRICE: I know everything about him.

LASCAR: You do, of course you do! (*He sits with a book and pen near* PIUS.) But I think it more than possible that this concentration upon death, which arguably has dominated his entire existence, has made him less prepared for it than the most unreflective peasant, for whom it arrives without warning, like a wolf from the wood. He has been dying for eight weeks and we are of the opinion there is some obstacle to his departure. Clearly he possesses resources which were concealed not only from us but from death itself. I have witnessed many partings, and it is obvious to me death waits upon consent, even from him crushed beneath the lorry wheels, from the assassinated, even. (*He looks at* BEATRICE. *The sound of battle, near and distant.*) The barbarians are getting closer. I think we must admit it, mustn't we? They are closer? And we have no pope. (*He fixes her with his stare.* BEATRICE *stares defiantly back, turns on her heel, goes out*)

FIRST ABRAHAM

ABRAHAM *with the child* ISAAC. *He unbuckles his belt.*

ABRAHAM: To love is this. To love is to inflict impossible pain. On self, and others. That's love. (*He suddenly erupts into a song of madness.*)

> Oh, the sunset is an insane bull
> Which bellows as it mounts the clouds!

                    Oh, see the blood run down the sky
                    I am God's waterfall . . . ! (*He laughs.*)

                    Come here for a kiss.
ISAAC: No.
ABRAHAM: Come on, give your dad a kiss.
ISAAC: No, because you're in a funny mood. (ABRAHAM *smiles,
   then erupts again in song.*)
ABRAHAM: The bull is kicking up my heart
                    Its hooves are splashing in my bowel
                    Oh, animal of innocence
                    Slip in my lung, sprawl in my brain! (*He laughs,
                    horribly.*)

                    No, I'm merely playful, can't a father be playful!
ISAAC: I never saw you like this before . . .
ABRAHAM: **I never was like it before so what**
                    Yesterday I was different
                    Today I'm different from yesterday so what
ISAAC (*turning*): No, I want to see my mum —
ABRAHAM: **Come here you bastard!** (ISAAC *freezes.*)
ISAAC: You see, you are different . . .
ABRAHAM: No, I just wanted to — (*He goes towards* ISAAC
   who steps back.)
                    Don't shrink I hate children who shrink
                    Did I bring you up to shrink or fear the hand of your
   own parent, no, I didn't, and I do resent my own child turning in
   that way as if — (*He grabs* ISAAC *violently.*)
                    Ha! Ha! Ha! (*He binds him with the belt.*)
                    Ha! Ha! Ha!
ISAAC: Mother! Oh, mother, father has gone mad!
ABRAHAM: No, you are the mad one! You are if you think that feeble
   cry will carry! **Silence, piece of, tissue of, scrap of human detri-
   tus!** (ISAAC *goes still. Pause.* ABRAHAM *moves round him.*)
ISAAC: I love you, what's the matter? (*Pause.* ABRAHAM *stops.*)
ABRAHAM: Clever. Very clever indeed you repulsive bit of bone
   and mucus, mobile but utterly insignificant parcel of shit etcetera, to say you love me **so did many tarts whores virgins
   women of mature sensibility boys youths of grace all over me
   my seed swallowed it with adoration so what if you love me
   thank you thank you thank you for what!** (ABRAHAM *sways,
   closing his eyes.*) Be timorous . . .
ISAAC (*calling*): Mo — ther!

ROME 207

ABRAHAM: She is in the kitchen. And the kitchen is — never to be seen again, by you. She is at the table. And the table is — never to be touched again by you. **Whimpering object of my hatred!** (*He draws a knife from his clothes.*) Kneel or stand it's all the same to me.

ISAAC: I cannot understand why you are doing this to me.

ABRAHAM: He cannot understand! He does not understand! **No reason.** All right, stand.

ISAAC: You love me!

ABRAHAM: No fond recollections of our bed-times, thank you, or descriptions of our holidays, thank you, the scrapbook of idiotic intimacies!

ISAAC: Say why you are doing this and I can tolerate it. Whatever the reason. But give me the reason. Out of love . . . (*Pause*)

ABRAHAM: Yes, well, that is it.

ISAAC: What?

ABRAHAM: Love.

ISAAC: Love?

ABRAHAM: **Love, yes, the fucking thing, the bull that rides the sky, love, yes!** (*Pause*) No, you are not making headway, Isaac . . . Isaac . . . not diverting me from my intention, Isaac . . . not one jot, Isaac . . . Isaac . . .

ISAAC: Isaac . . .

ABRAHAM (*putting the knife to* ISAAC's *throat*): Pity you wish to . . . pity you hope to . . . but what has pity to do with what I **most passionately wish to do**. (*Pause*) Thing . . . (*He goes to cut,* BENZ *enters.*)

BENZ: There is a ram over there . . . (*A terrible pause.*)

ABRAHAM: Is there . . .

BENZ: Yes. Caught by its horns. Kill it instead. (*Pause*)

ABRAHAM: It's not the same.

BENZ: Yes, kill the ram, you have shown your —

ABRAHAM: **It is not the same.** (*A brief hiatus, then* ABRAHAM *launches into the song of insanity.*)

> Oh, the sunset is boiling, boiling!
> The dying bull is stamping, stamping
> In the vat of ribs and buttocks! (*Pause*)

> Let me . . . ! Let me . . . !

BENZ (*turning to go*): No, the ram will do, thank you . . . (AB-RAHAM *flings the knife far away in utter fury.* BENZ *looks at him.*)

ABRAHAM: You ask for everything. And I want to give you everything. (*Pause*) And now you say, not everything, after all . . .

Scene Two

Part of the city. BEATRICE *and* SMITH *walk. The spasmodic effect of distant fighting.*

BEATRICE: I am forty-seven
I am in need of a change. (*A* SOLDIER *rushes on, strips off his uniform, rushes away.*)
This change cannot come from an encounter with a man. I am convinced of it . . . (*Two more fleeing* SOLDIERS *rush in, flinging off their clothes, and rush out.*)

SMITH: Possibly you require a sickness.

BEATRICE: A sickness?

SMITH: Yes. Possibly you require to walk the very perimeters of mortality . . .

BEATRICE: You have the strangest ideas. (*They stop.* BEATRICE *looks at her daughter. A* SOLDIER *runs by, flinging his clothing away.*) Don't feel you have to love me, will you? The obligation? No need for it. The imitation? No necessity. I can quite coldly march without. I can haunt empty places without weeping.

SMITH: Yes.

BEATRICE: You know that! (*An* OFFICER *rushes in. He proceeds to strip.*)

OFFICER: Scum of the Earth!

BEATRICE: Yes . . .

OFFICER: Thank God we lost because I now know what I might have laid down my life for, **scum of the earth!** In victory, oh, marvellous, but in defeat! (*He spits.*) You're attractive enough to be my mistress.

BEATRICE: Am I?

OFFICER: I dream of rich women.

BEATRICE: Do you? I am rich.

OFFICER: I dream of seducing them in warm, upholstered rooms. Stores. Carriages. Restaurants.

BEATRICE: Do you?

OFFICER: The war has really wrecked my dreams . . . ! (*He shakes his head, smiling.*) May I hold your hand?

BEATRICE: I have a lover.

OFFICER: Ah . . .

SMITH: But he's dying.

BEATRICE: He's dying, yes . . . (*Pause.* BEATRICE *takes his hand impulsively.*) We'll go to restaurants!

OFFICER: Shall we?

ROME 209

BEATRICE: Yes, why not?

OFFICER: You buy me things!

BEATRICE: I will!

OFFICER: And if I'm not precisely what you want, I'll alter! (*Two* SOLDIERS *enter, armed.*)

SOLDIERS: Oi! (*The* OFFICER *turns.*) Deserter.

BEATRICE: No. (*The* SOLDIERS *walk towards the* OFFICER.) On the contrary, he was in the very act of apprehending —

SOLDIERS: Shut up —

BEATRICE: Deserters when —

SOLDIERS: Shut up —

BEATRICE: I apprehended him. I enticed him from his duty. But for me he would be wearing trousers I assure you.

SOLDIERS: Rich bitch, shut up. (*The* OFFICER *makes a gesture of resignation. Swiftly, the* SOLDIERS *cut his throat.* SMITH *turns away in disgust. The* SOLDIERS *go to leave but stop.*) Oh, supreme arse, Mrs. (BEATRICE *looks at them witheringly.*) An arse which if inscribed upon our banner, might make zealots of us all . . . (*They go out. Pause. She looks at the corpse.*)

BEATRICE: We should have quarrelled. Or if not quarrelled, seethed. His juvenile and shallow aspirations. His comic need to satisfy. No, it would have come to violence and his plaintive voice! I couldn't have. (*A wind blows litter over the stage.* SMITH *with infinite slowness removes her clothes.*)

Scene Three

The rising sound of a large gathering, glasses etc. When she is naked, SMITH *kneels. She draws a black veil over her face.* BEATRICE *stands against her, her hand on her. The wind ceases as a substantial* WOMAN *enters among a crowd of* GUESTS.

DOREEN: I've longed for you! Hold me! I've ached for you! (*She embraces* BEATRICE.)

BEATRICE: How firm you are! How wide you are! You have not starved!

DOREEN: I've put on weight!

BEATRICE: You shallow and trivial-minded creature, you are thriving in the siege!

DOREEN: I am!

BEATRICE: The great souls die. The decent die. The honest and the dutiful, but you!

DOREEN: My cellars are replete!

BEATRICE: They laughed at you, but those who laughed the loudest starved the first.

DOREEN: Kiss me and kiss me again, I am incandescent with the joy of seeing you! And no more talk of suffering! What use is it? What pain does it relieve? (*She sees another beyond* BEATRICE *and plunges towards him.*) Oh, all my smiles are kept for you! My grins and blandishments, contemptible and artificial as I am, I thrust on you! (*She embraces a* GUEST. OTHERS *revolve. A* MAN *addresses* BEATRICE.)

BENZ: When I look at you I know that love is not to do with pleasure.

BEATRICE: No, what is it, then?

BENZ: **You aren't being real**. (*Pause. He stares in his drink.*) When I look at you I know how hard it is to mark a woman.

BEATRICE: Do you?

BENZ: **Speak properly for God's sake**. (*Pause. He swirls his drink in the glass.*) I see this sealed and polished object.

BEATRICE: I have my methods and you presumably have yours.

BENZ: **Don't waggle your absurd and haggard language**. (*Pause. She goes to walk away.*)
　　　No, the tragedy is mine, of course. (*She continues.*)
　　　Oi (*She stops.*)
　　　The tragedy is mine, I said. (*She stares at him. The dead* OFFICER *sings.*)

OFFICER: 　She has this hunger to communicate
　　　　　She splashes the shallow pools
　　　　　Come down through rotting wedding veils
　　　　　And linens worn by the oligarchs of states
　　　　　Come down, you village teacher!

BEATRICE: I have been the lover of a man for thirty years and he is dying. (BENZ *shrugs*.) God help a girl who meets a clever man.

BENZ: Come with me. I have a place.

BEATRICE: It warps. It cripples.

BENZ: Not a palace. Not a bungalow.

BEATRICE: It bends your bones.

BENZ: A box. (DOREEN *swoops on* BENZ.)

DOREEN: Benz, you are so miserable! You are so stricken! I adore Benz but he is implacable, he makes such a thing of his brutality,

ROME **211**

his honesty, his freedom from conventional etceteras, but who cares, who respects him, nobody but me, and how grim his manner is, his monosyllables and savage sentences, all meant to impress us and of course it certainly impresses me but I am shallow, and that awful face, I really could smack it, that face of concentration as if the entire atmosphere was intolerable to his sensitivity, all meant to persuade us what a roaring and oceanic soul he has, and I am persuaded, I am, on the other hand it is quite impossible to care for Benz unless you are, as I am, susceptible to silent men, don't go to his box it is a squalid thing of cardboard.

BENZ: She dislikes me.

DOREEN: Of course she does.

BENZ: Down her long nose she looks as if I were a rat.

DOREEN: Who could blame her?

BENZ: **Is poverty criminal?** (DOREEN *sees a guest.*)

DOREEN: The siege! The siege has done so much for us! And so many live, so many creep from corners! (*She sails towards him, patting* SMITH *as she passes.*) Do put some clothes on, you will freeze like that! (DOREEN *passes.*)

BENZ: You must be broken, obviously. Broken and remade.

BEATRICE: In what order?

BENZ: Unstitched. Dishevelled. And replaced.

BEATRICE: Eyes in the belly? Tongue in the knee?

BENZ (*shaking his head*): Oh, you do so need me . . .

BEATRICE: Mouth in the ankle, what about —

BENZ: **The pathetic refuge of your wit.** (*She stares at him.*)

BEATRICE: Yes . . . (*Her head falls.*)

BENZ: I adore you and I have never been denied. (*A sound off. She recovers.*)

BEATRICE: Listen! Someone is being executed!

BENZ: **I said**

I said. (*A* WAITRESS *appears beside them, smartly. She extends a tray.*)

BEATRICE: Who is dying?

BEKNOWN: Looters. This is water. This is water also.

BEATRICE: What wonderful hands you have! What treasures! And you oil them!

BEKNOWN: This one sparkles. This one is still.

BEATRICE (*holding her hand limply*): But they have been looted, too, I expect . . .

BEKNOWN: Looters get what they deserve.

BEATRICE: Yes.

212 *Howard Barker*

BEKNOWN: And all who spoil. All who can't resist. The ones who scale the wall. The wall is good.

BEATRICE: Yes...

BEKNOWN (*turning to others*): Water? This one sparkles. This one is still. (BENZ *takes* BEATRICE *impulsively in his arms. He smothers her with a violent kiss. She drops her glass, which shatters.*)

Scene Four

PIUS *lies dying. A* REGIMENT *and its* WOMEN *enters, singing.*

THE REGIMENT: We were the so-despised
               We drank from cans and forced the old off
                                    pavements!
               We were the so-reviled
               We broke the noses of the students!
               We
               Even
               Failed
               To
               Wear
               The
               Collar of your kindness!
               We were the over-understood
               We were explained by experts and by princes!
               We were the ever-pitied
               All our excesses were permitted!
               They
               Must
               Have
               Known
               We
               Were
               The wall of Christianity! (THE REGIMENT
is still.)

SMITH (*rising and dressing*): At first I thought how interesting this war will cleanse us. This siege will wipe away the dirty encrustation of a life of plenitude, of infinite consumption and spiritual banality. I thought **war will liberate the fineness in us all**. For fineness lies, fineness sits, whatever fineness does, burns probably, a tiny flame which flickers in the toxic cave of sodden consciousness, **off with the fetid garments of the social world its sham its banter etcetera**. But no. For one thing many have no fineness and sieges merely liberate their savagery. You knew that. You knew everything and I stand corrected, not by teachers but by life **I think kill off the teachers they are so poor** for which you must be partially responsible, yes, although I love you why pretend I think you blameless, that would be a silly condescension **this horror is to do with your incessant kindness** how I don't know how I can only. (*She kisses* PIUS's *hands, gets up, straightens her skirt.*) What will become of me? (*She goes to leave, walking smartly but then stopping abruptly. She smothers her head in her hands. The sound of religious rites.* CARDINALS *descend.* LASCAR *enters. A silence, a stillness.*)

LASCAR: The heart has stopped.

      I call this death.

      Given our troops are

      And the situation is so.

      I would appreciate your authority to. (*The* CARDINALS *assent by murmur.*)

      Thank you. (*A* CARDINAL *sings.*)

SINGING CARDINAL: How quiet our life appeared

      And in our sleeps the smallest irritations

      Dogs barked

      Women screamed beneath the bridge

      And wagons slowly danced in yards

      How tender things appeared

      As if we controlled the situation

      Ice creams stood on the table

      The length of skirts fell

      We talked of poverty and taxation

ALL CARDINALS: **Oh, what rode our blindness like a car!** (*Pause*)

SMITH: Confess me, somebody

LASCAR: Not now, we are involved in an election.

SMITH: I want to be confessed.

LASCAR: Find a priest.

SMITH: No, one of these.

LASCAR: Outside and turn left.

SMITH: No

LASCAR: Please.

SMITH: Never.

LASCAR: You are worse than your mother.

SMITH: **Much worse but different**. (*Pause. A distant effect of street battle. A* CARDINAL *comes forward.*)

CONFESSOR: I am listening.

SMITH: Oh, good, somebody cares!

CONFESSOR: Yes.

SMITH: Somebody knows the meaning of the verb 'to love.'

CONFESSOR: Yes.

SMITH: Battles! Murders! But my soul commands attention. That is right, isn't it? That is only proper?

CONFESSOR: Yes, but what —

SMITH: **Don't hurry me**. (*Pause*)

Father, I allowed myself to be educated by shallow men and foolish women. This education fixed in my throat like a snake and spoke through my mouth but I was only repeating.

CONFESSOR: Isn't that the nature of an education?

SMITH: It doesn't matter I was guilty.

CONFESSOR: Very well, I absolve you, I —

SMITH: **You are in such a tearing hurry**. (*Pause*)

I must get the snake out my throat . . . (*She laughs, throwing back her head.* LASCAR *steps forward.*)

LASCAR: I move we proceed to the election.

Things being somewhat.

And time is very — (*He sees a* SOLDIER *dragging another over the floor.*)

This is the college of.

GLOY: Short cut.

My oppo at the three-inch mortar.

Bollocked. (*A* CARDINAL *goes towards the dead* WOMAN SOLDIER.)

Oh, fragrant man, I seen you at my auntie's house, saying her pension was a scandal. (*Pause*)

PARK: Not me . . .

LASCAR: I'm very sorry but we must get on . . . !

GLOY: Spouting inequality was an outrage in a prosperous state. (*Pause*)

PARK: You have mistaken me for another.

GLOY: Shaking. Shaking hands with all and.

PARK: Not me, I think . . . (*Pause*)

I read in rooms so silent the whimpering of destitution could not touch me.

ROME   215

And my hands, you see — (*He shows them.*)
So washed.
So tender to proximity.
Soap.
And
Closed
Windows. (GLOY *looks into him. Pause.* LASCAR *insists.*)

LASCAR: I think we must ignore all further interruptions or —
(SMITH *laughs, throwing back her head.*)

GLOY (*to* PARK): This room. What did you learn in it?

PARK: Your pain is insignificant.

I, who never suffered, say.

Your squalor is not relevant.

I, who never went without a clean sheet, say.

Your coldness is contemptible.

I, who never went without fire, say.

Do not show me your scars unless they came for Christ.

Pause. GLOY *wavers, then strikes* PARK, *who reels, recovers.*
SMITH *climbs to her feet in exhilaration.*

SMITH: He lives!

And I searched everywhere! In sun and squares! At concerts and in filthy basements where they argued till the bottles toppled from the tables! He lives! (*She laughs, shaking her head.*) No, it's funny, though . . . all the time . . . he was sitting in a library . . . promise we will burn the bad books . . . promise me . . .

PARK: I promise.

GLOY: Choose him . . . !

LASCAR: We do not require the exhortations of —

GLOY: **Choose him or the filth will know**.

LASCAR (*at breaking point*): The Holy Convocation is not in the habit of submitting to instructions or to threats! I am the Senior Official of the Church of Rome and I am conducting an election! This election —

SMITH: All right, Nigel —

LASCAR: Will proceed according to the practices and precedents of —

SMITH: Nigel —

LASCAR: The College of Elections for which I am responsible **exceptional circumstances notwithstanding!** (*Pause*)

216   *Howard Barker*

GLOY: Whatever you say, but choose him. (*Pause. A* CARDINAL *steps forward.*)

SLIPMAN: I am the candidate for continuity. I was under the impression I was not opposed. (*The* CARDINALS *murmur in unison.*)

CARDINALS: **On the one hand/on the other**.

SLIPMAN: I represent those currents of opinion of which I fervently believe a modern papacy must be composed.

CARDINALS: **On the one hand/on the other**.

SLIPMAN: Neither radical nor cautious I anticipate an age of reconciliation which.

CARDINALS: **On the one hand**.

SLIPMAN: I flatter myself I am neither rigid nor a compromiser but.

CARDINALS: **And again**. (*A stillness. The sound of firing nearer.*)

LASCAR: I move we vote.
　　　　For Cardinal Slipman? (*Half the* COLLEGE *indicates.*)
　　　　For Cardinal Park? (*An equal vote is registered.*)
　　　　The votes are equal, in which case I will exercise my —

GLOY: Oi! (*They look at him.*)
　　　　She ain't voted yet. (*He indicates the dead* WOMAN SOLDIER.)

LASCAR: I don't think —

GLOY: **A corpse for Christianity**. (*He lifts the dead* WOMAN's *hand and points to* PARK *with the other.*)
　　　　For you.
　　　　She says. (PARK *hesitates for one second, then goes to* GLOY *and kisses the hem of his dirty tunic.*)
　　　　And no charity.
　　　　And no pity.
　　　　And no tolerance.

PARK: Go back to the trenches now. I am the Pontiff. (GLOY *leaves the body and walks out the way he entered. As he does so, a* CHILD *enters playing a tune on a tin whistle. He finishes, looking at* PARK.)

SMITH: How perfect you are. And you know nothing of the common life. How intolerably and exquisitely ignorant of things we call our needs. (*She turns to the* CARDINALS.) Off now! To your chambers and await the torrent of encyclicals! (*The* CHILD *ushers the* CARDINALS *away.* SLIPMAN *stays behind. The* CHILD *sits on the corpse and pipes.*)

SLIPMAN (*going to* PARK): The election was so close may I

ROME   217

suggest it gives no mandate to ignore those who might be seen
to be opponents of your policies?

PARK: I have just come from the library.

SLIPMAN: Precisely! Might I suggest therefore you heed the practical and seasoned advice of the administrators, on whom even
the most fervent idealist must lean for advice?

PARK (*grimly*): The library is hell also.

SLIPMAN: Be steady, then . . .

PARK: Steady? (*Pause, then* SLIPMAN *turns to go, but stops,
exasperated.*)

SLIPMAN: Nobody knows who you are! Always you walked and
thought alone! Until today I never got a sentence out of you!
(*Pause. He turns.*) Magnanimity would be such a dawn to your
— (*The* CHILD *flutes insanely and stops.*) Where did you meet
your God? I do not recognize him.

PARK: In the library, where you had chained him to a desk. (SLIP-
MAN *leaves.*) **How hard it is to speak with others! How
hard!**

SMITH: Yes, and I was wrecked by the articulate! Do words stick
in your mouth? Do they tear your tongue like thorns?

PARK (*blessing her*): Come every day, and I will hear you. You I
will not ever give idle opinion to. (SMITH *kisses his hands and
goes out with the* CHILD. *Pause.* LASCAR *steps forward.*)

LASCAR: The problem is —

PARK: I know the problem.

LASCAR (*indicating* PIUS): No breath. No pulse. And yet . . .

PARK: Words . . .

LASCAR: Yes! Words! (*Pause.* PARK *walks to where* PIUS *lies in
his throne. He lifts the hem of his robe, and to* LASCAR's *horror,
pulls it.*)

Hey!
Hey!

Metre after metre of crimson cloth reels out from the dead POPE,
as PARK *drags its inordinate length over the stage.* LASCAR
cringes, cries out in horror. The dead WOMAN SOLDIER *sits up
and sings.*

SOLDIER: I sing you the song of the fanatic!
I sing you her mad song!
I sing you the testament of butchers who
Delivered you!
I sing you the song of the bigot!

I sing you her mad song!
I sing you the slogans of the murderers who
Kept you innocent!
I sing you the song of the sorry!
I sing you her sad song!
I sing you the tragedy of the doers of deeds
That can't command your sympathy . . .

PIUS *is a pathetic and naked figure slumped in the chair.* LASCAR *sobs.* PARK *steps out of the rolls of cloth.*

Your understanding.
Your compassion.
Your reluctant approval.
Your unwilling acquiescence.
Your secret collusion.
Your.
Your.
Your.

The distant fighting drifts in. PARK *lifts the naked body of* PIUS *onto his shoulders and goes out.*

SECOND PASSAGE

DOREEN *supervising a* PROCESSION OF PEOPLE *carrying paintings and objects of art. They curse and jostle.*

DOREEEN: Art!
It's Art!
By Art I mean
Not junk or jumble
And if you bash that frame again I'll
Art is you bastard all that makes us
Including you pox eyes
Divine
Self-conscious and
You two-arsed goat you've chipped that
Twice you've chipped it

ROME   219

Twice
The hope of poverty
The confirmation of humanity
I can't carry obviously I have a back
The very essence of experience
Or else I would
The mirror of our pains
You are magnificent
You are
You are
Magnificent
And under sniper fire
I clap you
Yes
I clap
Listen my clap goes
Clap!

The PROCESSION OF PEOPLE *staggers off with its burdens.*

Scene Five

BENZ *is discovered, observing.*

DOREEN: You see, I have my passions, too. (*A shot passes. She ignores it.*)
    The barbarians will burn the lot. So what, you say, so what? (*Another shot ricochets.*)
    I will not be silenced by a vandal with a gun. (*She seizes a chair and stands on it, unwieldy. A ricochet.*)
    It's not his fault, you say, he is not educated, he is not socially advantaged and as a consequence — (*Another*) has neither morals nor compassion — **if you looked at a painting you would cease to kill** — (BENZ *laughs, another shot rings out.*)
    I do say that
    I do insist
    Laughter notwithstanding
    And contempt
    Looking is an act of love. (*Pause. Silence*)
    I've won the argument. (*She climbs off the chair.*)

220   *Howard Barker*

BENZ: His magazine is empty.

DOREEN: Always, you make me feel my life's absurd. A worm of feeling. A maggot of sense! (BEATRICE *enters*.)

BENZ (*turning to her*): How much do you love me.

BEATRICE: Less than I thought but —

BENZ: **How much I said**.

BEATRICE: I don't know ... (*Pause*) A fraction more than previously but still less than —

BENZ: **You are not trying hard enough**. (*Pause*)

BEATRICE: Trying ... ?

BENZ: I mustn't shout. Always I shout. I must attend to that. But you are not a girl, you are not a wife of twenty-two hanging out sheets on the balcony, you know how much is accident and how much pure will, so why are you —

BEATRICE: **Don't bully me**.

DOREEN: **Don't bully her**. (*They laugh*.)

BENZ: You know desire is invention. (*Pause*)

BEATRICE: Yes, I do know that.

BENZ: Then desire me.

BEATRICE: I will. Only — (*She looks offstage*.) I must be allowed to mourn. (*A* FIGURE *is pushing a wheelbarrow. The body of* PIUS *lies in it, naked, ungainly. The* YOUTH *pushing the wheelbarrow looks*.)

PIUS: She's here!. (*Pause. A distant firing of guns*.)

DOREEN: Is that —

PIUS: Stop! Here, I said!

DOREEN: Is that —

PIUS: If she won't come to me, then I.

DOREEN: It is, it's —

PIUS: Through the city weather shrapnel notwithstanding.

DOREEN: My dear.

PIUS: Troops louts and firing squads.

DOREEN: Oh, my dear.

PIUS: Notwithstanding.

DOREEN: I shan't look! If I look I shall cry and if you cry it's the end, isn't it, the absolute end to cry so rather than cry I will laugh, not a very lovely laugh but all the laughter's funny now, all the laughter's peculiar since the siege don't you think?

PIUS: Touch me I'm cold. (*Pause.* DOREEN *goes very reluctantly to the wheelbarrow and puts out a hand*.)

DOREEN: He's cold! (*She lets out a laugh, which stops suddenly. She walks away*.) This is why I cling to art, thank God for art with art at least you know, you do know where you, and he was

ROME

so handsome once. (*She stalks off, commanding passing* ART BEARERS.) The frames are just as lovely as the pictures, do remember that! (*She goes out.*)

BEATRICE: I have no more to say to you and this is Mr Benz.

PIUS: We've met.

BEATRICE: Every last word.
Every sentiment.
Spewed out.
Dug out.
Spat.

PIUS: Never.

BEATRICE: I know my own brain and it's empty.

PIUS: Who wants your brain? (*Another shot from the sniper. The* YOUTH *ducks. He smokes.*)

BEATRICE: What we had, let it be perfect in recollection and not —

PIUS: Who cares what we had
Who cares for perfect recollections
Keep your recollections
I must see your arse.

BEATRICE: Never.
Never again.

PIUS (*singing raucously, tunelessly*): Oh, how she acts gen — tility! How she apes sen — sitivity! **I am the par — ent of her soul!**

BEATRICE: Oh, what you were, and what you've become . . .

PIUS: What does it matter what I was?
What does it matter what I've become?

BEATRICE: **I can't mourn that**. (*Another shot. The* YOUTH *ducks again.*)

BENZ: Come with me now.

BEATRICE: No.

BENZ: Do as I say.

BEATRICE (*stamping her foot*): You are all as bad as each other! (*Pause*)
No.
No, that's silly, that's pure — utter — (*A shot rings out. The* YOUTH *ducks.*) It's true, there is much of me in my arse. Much of what I am. Much of what I might be. Much to ache for. Much to adore . . .

PIUS (*to the* YOUTH): Move now!
I can't endure her when she is free
When she is ventilated like this

222   *Howard Barker*

            Perceptive etcetera

            Move I said! (*The* YOUTH *goes to the handles of the wheelbarrow.*)

BEATRICE: You must learn death. (PIUS *stops the* YOUTH *with a hand.*) And I've ceased mourning. Believe me, I have closed the book.

PIUS: It can't be closed. You want it, but it can't be closed. (PIUS *looks at her with contempt. He nods for the* YOUTH *to take him out.* BENZ *is staring at* BEATRICE.)

BEATRICE: I wish you'd wash.

            Your male smell your self-neglect I often — (BENZ *slaps her. She is silent, still. She hangs her head.*)

AN INTERLUDE

Some benches in a park. An OLD WOMAN *enters clutching a bag. She feels her way to a seat.*

OLD WOMAN: I was born blind.

            Don't feel sorry for me! Don't tip your pity over me!

            I was the third child of an industrialist.

            Don't hold me in contempt!

            Don't shake your class anger over me!

            I married a bully and he fouled me in the bed-room.

            Don't bellow indignation!

            Don't intervene for me!

            I hated foreigners of all types.

            Don't sigh like that!

            Don't shrug your shoulders with disbelief!

            And sheltered murderers in my enormous home.

            Don't say she is confused!

            Don't try to fathom me!

            Hello I'm first again why is that always first and I make no special effort. (*She pokes in her bag and takes out a sandwich. A* MAN *enters, also with a bag. He sits and waits.*)

MAN: Are we sufficiently caring I ask myself for one another do you think are we taking adequate responsibility for. (*He pokes in*

ROME 223

his bag.) Oh, we are so separate and so cold let's gather round let's pull together and (*Two* YOUNG WOMEN *enter. They sit.*) You are too late as if on purpose were you nursing were you in attendance on the sick perhaps you found another orphan oh you said an orphan grab that orphan.

OLD WOMAN: My life so far has been a failure. So far. But things are changing.

FIRST YOUNG WOMAN: Looking back what a terrible world it was and all this is perhaps a necessary bloodbath from which we shall emerge cleansed often I feel a new world is looming and — (*The* OLD WOMAN *hits the* YOUNG WOMAN *with the sandwich. Pause.*) Not everyone will be welcome in this new world obviously.

MAN: Widows, why don't you specialize in them?

SECOND YOUNG WOMAN: Those who will not love deserve to die does that sound callous I say that with all love you bastards I say love with all sincerity.

MAN: I do so agree with all you say you insane bitch now he really is late normally he but justifiably I do love his paleness don't you love his paleness girls paler than poets used to be seen much action seen much pain I do love stories though with exaggeration the bare facts leave me cold. (*A* SOLDIER *enters and sits.*)

SOLDIER: Beautiful thank you.

FIRST YOUNG WOMAN: The enemy are right.

SOLDIER: Unfortunately I forgot my bag.

FIRST YOUNG WOMAN: No that's putting it too

BOTH YOUNG WOMEN: **However vile the enemy you are no better**

FIRST YOUNG WOMAN: Better

MAN: What was in the bag, then?

BOTH YOUNG WOMEN: **Whoever wins it will not be the poor etcetera!** (*They giggle.*)

SOLDIER: I get what I deserve.

MAN: And we so need we are a howling need in emptiness oh fuck he's here surround me put your bodies up like a stockade! (BENZ *enters. He looks at them. They stare ahead.*)

BENZ: You know you ^an't take anything and yet you bring these bags. (*Pause*) The pitiful contents of the bags! All calculated to make me think inoffensive lives!

SOLDIER: Give us a ...inute.

BENZ: Why?

SOLDIER: All right, don't.

224   *Howard Barker*

BOTH YOUNG WOMEN: **The future will be born out of our
sacrifice
Our statues will smile down
On an harmonious and integrated
world
Equality will**
OLD WOMAN: Shuddup!
BOTH YOUNG WOMEN: **And kindness will**
OLD WOMAN: Shuddup!
MAN: You cannot live and let live, can you?
OLD WOMAN: **Nor die and let die either!** They do so screech
and this man has a lovely voice the voice is the garden of the
soul I know I had elocution.
MAN: Everything she says is like an echo in a room.
OLD WOMAN: It is so what?
MAN: Not a very nice room.
OLD WOMAN: A nice room a nice room what's nice you are so
even your vocabulary is mundane
MAN: Listen to her
SOLDIER: **Lend me a silence!** (*Pause*)
OLD WOMAN: Decorum yes does anyone remember it it's what
priests used to have before they learned to jive
BENZ: Shh
OLD WOMAN: Yes
BENZ: Shh
OLD WOMAN: I know I just
BENZ: Shh
OLD WOMAN: My last abuse goodbye (BENZ *takes a penny
whistle from his pocket and begins to play.*)
BOTH YOUNG WOMEN: **If you think we're dancing you've got
another**
   Oh fuck (*They are irresistibly drawn off the bench and linking
hands they raise the* MAN *also.*)
MAN: Together we are different together we are not what we were
on our own!
OLD WOMAN: Hand!
MAN: Bags!
BOTH YOUNG WOMEN: **We are unanimous at last but is it
what**
OLD WOMAN (*reaching impatiently*): Hand!
MAN: Bags! (*The* YOUNG WOMEN *dance in a line, the* OLD
WOMAN *picked up on the end.* BENZ *plays to the* SOLDIER,
who is unmoved. The others are piped offstage. BENZ *stops.*)

ROME

BENZ: Not today, then?

Never mind

No rush (*He slips the pipe into his pocket, and goes to collect up the bags, peering into them.*)

The things they!

Of such paltry significance

That's not without its charm . . . (*He looks at an item, pops it back in.*)

I think Rome has to fall. The columns and the architraves. The botanic gardens and the balconies of flourishing plastic. The excellent and the insouciant. And the school children at the traffic lights, up in shreds of badges and impeccable vests, oh, the rain of flasks and sandwiches am I interrupting you? I think you are needed at the three point five. (*The* SOLDIER *gets up.*)

SOLDIER: Do you like pain?

BENZ: Oh, yes, get along now . . . (*The* SOLDIER *goes to leave.*)

And so do you. And so do you with your mute indictments. (*The* SOLDIER *stops. Pause.*)

You know the inadequacy of love . . . (*The* SOLDIER *goes out.*)

Scene Six

PARK *enters, contemplative. From the opposite end, a* YOUTH, *delinquent.*

HOLLO: I beat men! I beat them on the head or arse!

Beat I went! The perfect stranger dared to meet my eyes **beat therefore** the proud trod on my pavement **beat** or at a distance moved in such a way to draw my glance **oh beat!** I ran to beat! (*He lets out a wail which stops abruptly.*) My mother said my mother in her filth flat said **do better son than beat** proudly however proudly undeniable this pride **but what** nothing presents itself to my nothing appears to please me like or satisfy the (*The wail again.*)

Until

This

Solitary

Man (*He kneels before* PARK.)

226   *Howard Barker*

Who made all thumping liquor cunt and bollocking
A prelude (*Pause. He enunciates with dedication.*)
Prelude.
His.
Word. (*He kisses* PARK's *hem.*)
Eleven years of schooling, and they never said the word . . .
(PARK *touches his head.*)

PARK: Stand between me and the enemies of my silence. (HOLLO
nods.) Now, bring the pictures in.

PARK *goes to a chair and sits.* HOLLO *carries in a massively
enlarged photograph of a traumatically damaged face, an arch-
ival item from a war hospital. He hangs it on a wire. He goes out
again.* PARK *covers his eyes.* HOLLO *returns with another, and
hangs it beside the first.* PARK *remains with his head in his
hands. When* HOLLO *has hung a row, he stands with his arms
folded, waiting.* PARK *removes his hands from his eyes and looks.
Pause.*

HOLLO: Often, I do not understand him! Often, I cannot grasp a
single word! **Words all over the shop! Words like birds!** (*He
grabs one out the air.*) And yet I trust him. I trust him even
though I do not know the words. (*Pause.* PARK *stands, reeling.
He walks up and down in a paroxysm of pain. Then he sits
cross-legged in front of the exhibition.*)
        I cleared my mind.
        To make way for his mind. (PARK *recovers. He holds*
HOLLO *close to him, putting his hands on* HOLLO's *face. He
frees him, and at the same moment, a* GENERAL *enters.*)

GENERAL: I cannot shell the hospital! For what I call Christ I
cannot.

PARK: I am Christ's mouth and you are an artillerist.

GENERAL: So I believed until this order came. Then Christ appeared to me.

PARK: Did He? And in what form?

GENERAL: In the form of pity.

PARK: The Barbarians are in the hospital and use it as an observation post.

GENERAL: That may be so.

PARK: It is so. You must or die, and the captain will replace you.

GENERAL: He shares my abhorrence.

PARK: The sergeant, then.

GENERAL: And him.

ROME

PARK: Well, after him the corporal and so on down to the regimental spaniel. (*Pause*)

GENERAL: The last pope never stooped to tactics . . .

PARK: I am responsible. (*Pause*) Now order the bombardment, for if the Barbarians are not dislodged, they will ambush the quarter, you know perfectly well, and furthermore they must not use the sick as their protection **or they will walk behind our children**, you know this, you know it all . . . (*Pause. The* GENERAL *goes to leave.*) You do not understand the place of pity, where it finds its hold. What happens happens, and what follows is the ground for it. I order the destruction of the hospital, and I shall weep over the consequences —

GENERAL: **I do not understand a Christ who —**

PARK: **You think Christ is not also in the doing!** (*Pause*)

He is in it.

And after it. (*Pause. The* GENERAL *looks up at the gallery.*)

I said bring me the worst. And into the silence of my library they dragged men with no jaws who squealed like pets through bone all gnawed by iron whose eyes had gone whole inches into mouths and whose protuberances were pits and pits protuberances I stared into dumb messes once adored and felt my spine go muck with horror! (*Pause*) I, who never left my room . . . (*Pause. The* GENERAL *goes to him.*)

GENERAL: Give me your blessing, then . . . (*With intense pain,* PARK *dispenses a blessing. The* GENERAL *goes out.* PARK *watches him, almost with disbelief, then turns.*)

PARK: I made a speech!

HOLLO: I heard it. (*He indicates the photographs.*) Shall I take these out now? (LASCAR *enters, with papers under his arm.*)

PARK: I made a speech!

LASCAR: Excellent, I'm sorry I was not here to record it —

PARK: I so distrust good speakers, God forbid I should become one, God forbid me the facility! (*He holds* LASCAR *by the arm. The thunder of guns disturbs the air. They listen, fixedly.* SMITH *enters. She kneels to* PARK. PARK *finishes listening, releases* LASCAR.) You come here like an alcoholic.

SMITH: Yes.

PARK: Like an addict.

SMITH: Yes.

All the years I fucked and shook and danced and read the books that all read, no more dancing and no more books unless you write them.

228   *Howard Barker*

PARK: I shall write nothing as long as I live.
SMITH: Do you find me unendurable, it is your own fault if you
   do, yours surely, because you are magnificent, it is the price of
   magnificence that the poor will drink your very fluids I mean the
   poor in spirit, am I tiring you, it is devotion, which is tiring, I
   admit, and even your face I find beautiful, but enough said on
   that score, listen, we are like beggars who have seen a banquet,
   preserve yourself because when you fail we shall be so wild with
   anger, I fear what we may do to you in our frustration, and yes,
   I am a drunkard. (*She kisses his feet.*)
PARK: I should forbid you that.
SMITH: Why, it is my need . . .

SECOND ABRAHAM

ABRAHAM *holding a knife.* ISAAC *enters, stops.*

ABRAHAM: I love you. And because I love you, I should not hurt
   you. It is, after all, a definition of love. (*Pause*) But not the only
   one. (*Pause*)
ISAAC: Why is there a fire burning?
ABRAHAM: Another definition might be this. That love conceals
   nothing. That love is absolute in truthfulness.
ISAAC: And the knife, what's that for?
ABRAHAM: This truthfulness would include the fact of the
   wholly random nature of existence, which neither pities nor con-
   soles. It is not love to conceal this. It is not love to plaster
   madness with the fiction of justice or rewards.
ISAAC: I can't stay long because my friend and I —
ABRAHAM: **A new love I have wrung from the very bottom of
   my life.** (ISAAC *stares.*)
ISAAC: Are going to the city for a . . . (*Pause*) But never mind . . .
   (*Pause*)
ABRAHAM: I felt, once I felt, oh, so shallowly, Isaac, that you
   would live, and marry, and inherit, and enjoy, and see, and own,
   and exercise good judgement — judgement partly learned from
   me — measure, criticise, and sometimes, complain. (*Pause*) A
   fallacy permitted to all parents **but I honour you with deeper
   truths my son**. (*Pause*) I tell you, rather, the savage and relent-

less nature of all life. (*Pause*) What other parent would? What other parent cast aside the consoling lies of parenthood? **None I promise you.** Kiss me! (ISAAC *goes to him, and kisses him.*) To share in this, to wade in this, absurdity, demeans the very soul.

ISAAC: I never heard you speak like this before and why the fire, it's hot today?

ABRAHAM: Always I smothered the evidence. In song-singing. In dance-dancing. In love-acting. And why? **That you likewise should be deceived?** No, this chain of deception must be snapped. And you — you are the link. (*Pause* BENZ *enters, watches casually.* ISAAC *perceives the drift and makes to escape, but* ABRAHAM *has him by the waist.*) **This also is a love!** (He floors ISAAC *and holds the knife prepared.* BENZ *speaks.*)

BENZ: A ram is caught by its horns. (*Pause*)

ABRAHAM: What . . . ?

BENZ: Just there. Sacrifice the ram instead. (*A terrible pause.* ABRAHAM *releases his grip on* ISAAC, *who rises to his feet.*)

ISAAC: Are you ill? Come to the house. You're ill. (ABRAHAM *sways,* ISAAC *looks at* BENZ, *and runs away. Pause.*)

ABRAHAM: Why?

BENZ: No reason.

ABRAHAM: Why?

BENZ: No reason at all.

ABRAHAM: **I have unpicked my brain for this!** (*He looks at* BENZ, *painfully.*) How else could I assent?

BENZ: You cheated me.

ABRAHAM: Cheated . . .?

BENZ: What sacrifice was it, when you convinced yourself that life was vile? It was a liberation you were threatening your loved boy with . . . (*Pause*)

ABRAHAM: Forgive me, I do not understand what —

BENZ: Oh, they all say that! (ABRAHAM *stares at the ground.*) You were to submit, in all clarity, in the fullness of understanding, to the wholly irrational act. You were to kill your son without the benefit of philosophy. You were to make no sense of the deed, but to endure the purest pain. For my sake.

ABRAHAM: Why . . . (*Pause*)

BENZ: No reason. No reason at all . . . (*Pause. Suddenly* ABRAHAM *launches himself at* BENZ *and tries to strangle him. They stagger in an embrace. There is a cry off, from* ISAAC. *He*

230   *Howard Barker*

rushes in, seizes the knife, and plunges it into BENZ, *who falls.*
ABRAHAM *looks at the dead figure on the floor.*)
ABRAHAM: Oh, now things will be hard ... Now we will have
    only ourselves to blame ... (ISAAC *runs away, ignoring*
    ABRAHAM's *call. He runs into a street in Rome.*)

Scene Seven

ISAAC *runs into* BEKNOWN, *who is gazing upwards.*

ISAAC: Marry me!
        I know nothing about women!
        Marry me!
BEKNOWN: Look, they are hanging a spy ...
ISAAC: I'll call you darling, shall I? Do you like that word?
BEKNOWN: He isn't guilty.
ISAAC: I have read books about the female parts. Womb, for
    example. And ovaries.
BEKNOWN: But what does that matter? The point is to create an
    atmosphere.
ISAAC: Other boys had creased the pages and covered the womb
    in fingermarks. So I cleaned the drawings with a rubber.
BEKNOWN: An atmosphere of fear is necessary to concentrate the
    energies of all the citizens. Oh, look!
ISAAC: As for people who have fucked with you, I need to know,
    but not at once. Their names, and so on, all that can wait.
BEKNOWN: He's gone! He swings! And he did nothing. I know!
    The chair goes — tip! (*She puts her fingers to her mouth. Pause.*
    She turns.) Now I'm late for work!
ISAAC (*as she makes to go*): I'm nine but so what? (*She looks at*
    him, for the first time.) Child's a word. (*Long pause.*)
BEKNOWN: I am inordinately clean.
                Fastidious.
                And volatile.
ISAAC: Yes.
BEKNOWN: I sleep alone. And never laugh. That is not a prin-
    ciple, I simply find nothing to amuse.
ISAAC: I already love you.
BEKNOWN: If we have a child I shall abort it. And if you find me

ROME   231

with another man, I shall not apologise. (ISAAC *nods*. BE-
KNOWN *smiles*.) Well, then! (*Pause. She looks at him, curious-
ly*.) I live there! (ISAAC *nods. Pause, then she walks away*.)
ISAAC: See you for tea! (*She ignores his parting remark*.) Darling! (*A distant rumble of guns*. LASCAR *enters with a handcart*.)

Scene Eight

PARK *at his desk*. LASCAR *enters, pushing an empty handcart.
He stops and stares*. PARK *is engrossed in paperwork*.

LASCAR: **I.**

     I. (*Pause*. LASCAR *drops a Bible on the floor. The echo
disturbs* PARK. *He looks up*.)

     Must be honest, Holy Father. (*Pause*)

     I have a cart. (*Pause*)

     Forgive my weak and pusillanimous. (*Pause*)

     I think it possible I shall become a refugee and on this
cart I'll place my suit — this suit and my most loved items of
cutlery, the picture of my mother and the stuffed bird I have in
my bedroom, you see I think I am these things, I think in them I
discover my identity **I know you have forbidden all preparation for flight but**

     Truly you are a great pope and need nothing but air and
water whereas I a pathetic mortal — of course I'll take the
crucifix as well — require material and manifest

     I'll park it by the dustbins if I may. (*Pause*. PARK
looks at him.)

     The enemy is pressing in despite our efforts don't you
think sometimes quite simply nothing can be done? I do think
there are times when all the courage in the world —

     Which I don't have myself —

     can't —

     stop —

     what — (*He leans over the handcart like a dead thing*.
PARK *gets up and goes to him, touches him*.)
PARK: We are so cruel, we products of the library. So blind to pain.
So immune to feeling. If you resort to flight I'll have you

232   *Howard Barker*

executed. (LASCAR *nods weakly.*) There is no culture in the rooms of exile. Your little crucifix in the window of an unkind land? Your murmured Latin in the cackle of Arabia? (LASCAR *nods weakly.*) Our deaths will outlive occupation, and all deface-ment of our monuments will lodge in unborn minds, whereas your portable items will end up comic on a foreign market stall . . . (LASCAR *nods weakly. He pushes his handcart away, going out as* SMITH *enters, wearily, stained.*)

SMITH: They are evacuating the Gardens of the Martyrs! I said no. I used your authority. They want to take the mortars out to site them better, I said no, but they pushed past me, you must go down and stop them, **Are we the sole inheritors, are we?** I know you hate hyperbole, I know you think it is the solitary sin but they are faltering, the words will come **don't say we are the sole inheritors . . . !** (THE REGIMENT *enters, singing.* HOLLO *among them. They fall on their knees before* PARK.)

THE REGIMENT: Sometimes
There is a limit to the graves
Sometimes
You say your body is your only property
Give us back our stack of beers
My brother with his stupid haircut
And my mother bawling down the stairwell
Sometimes
There is a rim to punishment
Sometimes
A little cry from the heart's corners
For another day (*Pause*)

PARK: I list the lies.

SOLDIER: Swiftly, father, they are chopping off the bollocks of the stragglers . . .

PARK: **I list the lies**. (*Some shots, near and far.*)
We can make other life.
We can live in a crack.
We don't mind being another man's slave.

SOLDIER: Yes, father, but my arm is hanging by a string . . .

PARK: Humility is virtue.
Christ pities the weak.
You rags of louts you are the wall of culture and never were
more beautiful than now
Yes tell me that I ask too much
Yes shout I ask the ultimate
Yes it is death to go back

ROME   233

Death is what I ask of you
Unquestionably Death
To stand between Christ and his desecrators (*Pause.*
HOLLO *climbs to his feet.*)

HOLLO: They maim the corpses, do you know, so please collect
our bits together . . .

SOLDIER: Don't go! (HOLLO *stops.*)
Let him go. (*He indicates* PARK *with his head.*)
And chuck at them his language.
Pour on them the words.

SMITH: Oh, you very bottom of the mud thing, I hope your child
bites your hand to the bone . . .

SOLDIER (*turning to her with contempt*): Lovely, but I have this
itch to live under any bastard's rule. Look, there's my contribution — (*He lifts a shattered arm.* SMITH *swiftly stabs him.*) Oh,
fuck . . . ! Oh, fuck . . . ! (*For a second, indecision seizes them
all, but* HOLLO *recovers first, and pulling the knife from the
dying man's back with a yell of madness, runs back to the battle,
drawing* THE REGIMENT *with him.* SMITH *shudders from her
exertion. Pause.*)

PARK: That was the perfect action. The perfect action of your life.
Oh, we breach barriers! (SMITH *kisses his garment, and
goes out. A wind blows the sound of gunnery away.* BENZ *ap-
pears, pushing a baby carriage lovingly.* PARK *knows him.*)
I am saving Rome. (*Pause.* BENZ *gurgles at the* BABY.)
How hard that is. When they no longer want Rome saved
. . . (BENZ *seems to ignore him.*)
When what is gone, is the desire to be Romans . . . (*Almost
as a gesture,* PARK *flings himself before* BENZ.)
Father, I have never sinned. (BENZ *looks at him.*)
And what is more, not sinning I found easy. (*Still* BENZ *is
silent, rocking the pram.*)
It occurs to me, the ease with which I can conform to your
commandments renders me suspisciously inhuman but.
Father I am talking. (*Pause*)
Furthermore, I cannot help the feeling
All thoughts are known to God
The feeling that
So why pretend
When you examine me you experience
The shame of God
Because I am not ashamed, and when the unashamed

234 *Howard Barker*

encounter you, the shame reverts to Him who in the beginning, invented it.

There

I dare to address you as an equal

So I've sinned (*He lowers his head to the ground.*)

BENZ: I do not like you, it must be said.

PARK: Oh . . . ?

BENZ: For there are those who worship you —

PARK: I try to discourage it —

BENZ: **Do you I wonder**

PARK: Try, yes, but —

BENZ: **I do wonder**. (*Pause*) And I am jealous, as you know. (PARK *nods*.) I think you may cease to find me wonderful. If not now, then later —

PARK: I doubt that —

BENZ: I think you may discover me to be imperfect and conclude He is not better than me this God —

PARK: Impossible —

BENZ: But I am not moral, so the comparison is, I must advise you, quite irrelevant —

PARK: Of course —

BENZ: I am devoid of all morality —

PARK: Yes —

BENZ: Morality was made for you, and I am will. Will only.

PARK: Yes. (*Pause,* BENZ *removes the* BABY *from the pram and holds it up, chuckling in the air.*) I think without you, Rome will fall . . . (*Pause*) Father, have you ceased to love the Romans . . . ? (BENZ *replaces the* BABY, *moves away idly like a parent in a park.*) **I have not!** (*He looks up.* FOUR DARK FIGURES *have appeared. He senses them.*) I cannot hear your sins today . . . (*He gets up.*) Clear a way for me, I'm so far from the Palace. (*One of them blocks his route. He senses their purpose.*)

It is impossible I'll die. You know I cannot die now. (*One of the* FIGURES *carries a small box.*) Who sent you? Go back and murder them instead. In the moment of their pleasure, return the deed to them. That's humour, surely? (*The* FIGURES *close in.*) Am I not the most original man? Am I not the most perfect you ever encountered? I stepped out of a darkened room to save our culture from extinction, and you serve such dirty and stained characters, look at my hands, my hands are washed and white . . . (*He extends them.*) Kiss them, and repudiate your life . . . (*The* FIGURES *jam the box over his head, and taking knives from their clothes, plunge them through slits in its sides.* PARK *emits*

ROME   235

a torrent of sounds. The FIGURES *run off.* BENZ, *who has witnessed this, idly departs.* PARK *sways, remaining on his knees. A song is heard*)

HOLLO: I stood in my mates
My mates were clothing
I hung in my mates
My mates were wardrobes to my body
I swum my mates
As you swim in a river
And their guts were warm as the kiss of a lover!

I kept my humour
In this I was exemplary
My jokes were flocks of birds
Flying the skies of misery
I kept my humour
As a child clings to its mother
But my jokes were cold as the spite of a lover!

HOLLO *stares at* PARK. *He puts down the weapon he is carrying. He sees the blood which has oozed from the box and stained* PARK's *clothing. He lifts off the box. Pause*

HOLLO: All right, he's blind.
Blind all right so what!
I knew a bloke was blind could juggle with four sauce-pans and a sieve
So what cunt! (*Pause*)
And I did like his eyes they never left you so sometimes you felt stop boring in my skull you pervert you are peeping in my windows! I did! I did! But he. (*He laughs, stops.*)
The tongue, however. . . . ? (*A shock passes over him.*)
Master, the tongue! (*He grabs* PARK *and forces open his mouth, looking for the tongue.*)
Intact!
Intact!
The tongue intact!
Oh, wag the fucking thing my master!
PARK: **Spe — ech!**
HOLLO: Yes!
PARK: **Spe — ech!**
HOLLO: Put it between a woman's legs, you bastard! (*He hugs him.*) No, no, you wouldn't, ever want to, no, but, only a suggestion,

only a — (*He dissolves into tears, and laughter clutching* PARK *to him and swaying with him on his knees.*)

Scene Nine

A washing line. BEATRICE *is holding a basket of wet things.* BENZ *enters, pushing the pram. He stops, watching her as she pegs. Some random shots.*

BENZ: I just witnessed a tragedy. (BEATRICE *continues to peg.*) For all the blood here, there's rather little of what you could call tragedy. (*She continues.*) A man was made to suffer . . . not for his crimes . . . but for his perfection . . . (*Pause*) which Nature abhors, I find. This man was blinded. (*Pause*) Of course, this may only serve to enhance —

BEATRICE: **I do hate this.** (*Pause*)

BENZ: His already perfect character . . . (*Pause*) Hate it, why?

BEATRICE: I did not want a child. I could not have a child. My womb was barren. Alive for love, but fruitless. **And then came this appalling miracle**.

BENZ: Appalling . . .

BEATRICE: This **staggering and unwelcome** treasure . . . this **precious catastrophe!**

BENZ: It is a gift why don't you love the gift. (*She looks at him, he at her, with antagonism. Pause.*) I don't think you have — I am convinced you lack — were born without — or lost through so much copulation —

BEATRICE: **Ha!**

BENZ: The range of feeling which characterizes the nature of woman —

BEATRICE: **Ha!**

BENZ: I think there are vast spaces in your character, spaces of howling winds where there should be feeling —

BEATRICE: **Ha!**

BENZ: Yes, there are these deserts of emotion which should be filled by love —

BEATRICE: **And ha again!**

BENZ: **I will complete my diatribe —**

BEATRICE: I will not hear it — (*She covers her ears.*)

BENZ: **You are quite without belief. Political. Moral. Social. Theological. Teleological. Philosophical. Anything! And it is unforgivable!** (*Pause. She uncovers her ears, looks at him.*) Please have a belief. Let it be wrong, let it be foolish, reprehensible, misguided or malicious, but **do have one please.** (*Pause*)

BEATRICE: Why? So you can punish me? So you can pulp my little hope? (*She looks at him.*) If I had a belief, you would use it as a stirrup. Up on my back! Whip! Spurs! (*She laughs.*)

You look so pained . . . (*Pause*)

How you desire me . . . (*Pause*)

And why, Benz? Why do you desire me? (*He simmers.*)

The struggle in your eyes . . . the war in your eyes . . . (*Pause*)

You want to submit . . .

You even . . .

Ache to submit . . . (*Pause, then he kneels at her feet, hanging his head.*)

Oh, Benz, how long it took to know that what I couldn't help was also my privilege . . .

BENZ (*enraged*): **Emp — ty! Emp — ty!**

BEATRICE (*holding him to her hip*): Yes . . . Yes . . .

BENZ: **Emp — ty!** (ISAAC *runs on, pursued by* BARBARIANS.)

BARBARIAN: **Oi! Boy with a bag!**

Scene Ten

BENZ *makes love to* BEATRICE. ISAAC *is trapped by* BARBARIAN SOLDIERS.

FIRST BARBARIAN: Roman bastard with a valuable! (ISAAC *concedes.*)

ISAAC: Welcome! Rome must fall, or we cannot know the ecstasy of building it again.

FIRST BARBARIAN: Open the bag you Christian whore and suck my cock.

ISAAC: Oh, not now, surely?

FIRST BARBARIAN: Do it, filth!

238 *Howard Barker*

ISAAC: This is the right of conquest, and it would be churlish to desist, on the other hand, if I failed to show reluctance, what pleasure would there be in it for you? But how much reluctance? (*He moves back.*) It's a matter of degree . . .

FIRST BARBARIAN: Blow his brains out or I will.

ISAAC (*swiftly*): I kneel! (*The* FIRST BARBARIAN *unbuttons himself.*)

SECOND BARBARIAN: Who is the new pope? Another old man in women's clothes?

ISAAC: No, youthful, and he invents new weapons of unforgivable ferocity.

SECOND BARBARIAN: What weapons?

FIRST BARBARIAN (*about to abuse the boy*): John . . .

ISAAC: For example, the exploding whore.

SECOND BARBARIAN: Exploding whore . . . ?

FIRST BARBARIAN: John . . .

ISAAC: This is scarcely Christian but all morals are suspended for the duration. Water particularly is a trick.

FIRST BARBARIAN: John . . .

SECOND BARBARIAN: Hang about, will you?

ISAAC: If you just filled your water-bottles, empty them. They contain a substance which decays the brain in fifteen minutes.

SECOND BARBARIAN (*handing his bottle*): Drink mine, then . . .

FIRST BARBARIAN (*deflated*): Oh, fucking hell . . . !

ISAAC (*drinking the water*): Incredible, you'd never know the difference!

SECOND BARBARIAN (*taking out a gun*): Adieu, Knowall — (BEKNOWN *enters.*)

BEKNOWN: Don't kill my husband. (*They look at her.*) If you have anger, spend it on me. (*Pause. The* BARBARIANS *look at one another, grin.*)

SECOND BARBARIAN: Hus — band? (*He shakes his head.*) Take your clothes off.

BEKNOWN: If you free him.

SECOND BARBARIAN: **If**

If

What is this

If

You have nothing to bargain. (*The* SECOND BARBARIAN *goes to embrace* BEKNOWN. *Suddenly* ISAAC *rolls on the floor.*)

ISAAC: The water! The water! Aghhhh! (*With intuitive speed, the* FIRST BARBARIAN *shouts a warning to his comrade.*)

ROME 239

FIRST BARBARIAN: **Exploding whore!**
SECOND BARBARIAN (*poised*): What?
FIRST BARBARIAN: Possibly! (*A moment of reflection seizes them. The* FIRST BARBARIAN *throws his water bottle away, kicks* ISAAC, *and runs off.*)
SECOND BARBARIAN: You are the most worthless of humans and what I am about to do to you will not cost me a moment of reflection or touch my conscience so much as a breeze stirs leaves . . . (*He draws the bolt of his gun.*) Naked now, out in the sunlight with your sacred place, I have almost run out of ideas for cruelty but things somehow suggest themselves, the spectacle of nakedness is such a stimulant to flagging brains.

                              Do it (BEKNOWN *doesn't move,*
pause.)

                              If I freed you you would only laugh
BEKNOWN: We wouldn't laugh, I promise you —
SECOND BARBARIAN: **You'd laugh and clasp each other saying we mocked the barbarian undress I say**
BEKNOWN: I promise you . . .

A stillness comes over the SECOND BARBARIAN, *who closes his eyes. Slowly, he sits on the floor, cross-legged, the gun on his knees. With care,* ISAAC *and* BEKNOWN *reach out and hold hands. Laughter slowly convulses them. They run out, peeling with relief, as* HOLLO, *armed, the pope* PARK, *a cloth around his eyes, and* SMITH *enter, in retreat.* HOLLO *strikes a random blow at the* SECOND BARBARIAN, *who collapses.* HOLLO *sings.*

HOLLO: Mother!

                    I was born in your blood

                    And I grew in your temper

                    Dead woman of fury

                    I

                              Praise

                                        Your

                                                  Prejudice

                    Who says we lost!

                    Sister!

                    I laugh at your drunkenness

                    And your five husbands

                    Woman of error

                    I

                              Kiss

Howard Barker

> Your
> Callousness
> **Not lost yet!** (*He bawls to the balconies.*)

PARK: I had certainty, and with this certainty came arrogance. **A little arrogance I suppose there was** and so God punished me, for He hates certainty, it offends him, but am I changed? **I am more myself than previously** and I don't crow and I don't posture **but did He think blindness would silence me** I don't criticize I don't rebuke His ways are deep, but I yield nothing for isn't Rome greater than my character?

HOLLO: **Who says we've lost come here!**

PARK: My pain?
Or
Even
My
Disintegration?

HOLLO (*looking around with satisfaction*): Nobody . . .

PARK: I shall be Rome.
When there's no Rome.
I'll be it.

HOLLO: **And me!**

PARK: And you. And guard inside our skulls all that we are. For brain's elastic —

HOLLO: Seen it!

PARK: And can be pulled into such cloisters and cellars of accumulation that they might burn all Rome and still we might say **Rome persists!**

SMITH: Hide.

PARK: Yes.

SMITH (*to HOLLO*): And you — chuck out your weapons —

HOLLO: Chuck out my —

PARK: Do it, yes.

HOLLO (*in despair*): **No one says boo to us!** (*He sobs. PARK stretches a hand to his face.*)

PARK: I do so hate I cannot see your common face . . . it was a tablet of my rightness, so what I said I knew was true from your expression . . . (*Pause. Distant firing.*) In all my years of silence and of contemplation I kept this hope I'd one day find my equal, and pour over his open hands the pure distillation of my thought . . . and I find it is a brute requires me . . .

HOLLO: Only a brute . . . sorry . . .

PARK: A brute requires me, and a bitter woman . . . (*He surges with fury.*) **I am all that is correct and history it is that's error!**

ROME   **241**

SMITH: Shh . . .

PARK: Don't make that noise, don't mutter that hiss of consolation . . .

SMITH: Forgive me . . .

PARK: To hiss suggests you do not credit me —

SMITH: Yes —

PARK: What are you, clockwork? What are you, dynamos? You think history is a river and only fools protest at rivers? **The river is wrong.** Dare to say it. **River, you are wrong,** and if you drown me, is that evidence of your correctness?

HOLLO: Fuck the river!

       Knee to the river's balls! (*A* CHILD *has entered and watches them, distantly.*)

PARK: How absurd I must appear . . . but that is policy. How posturing and insane I look . . . but that is choice. I pass through the absurd to acres of beyond. The absurd being no more than a narrow gate, to pass through which one is required to stoop . . .

CHILD (*pointing*): Mad Pope!

PARK (*turning to the direction of the cry*): That is how it seems to you, is it?

CHILD: Mad Pope!

PARK: That is your considered opinion, is it? (*The* CHILD *runs off with a cry.* PARK *laughs.*)

HOLLO (*plucking the mitre from* PARK's *head and tossing it offstage*): Time to scarper, and all the tools of losers down in the earth, stamp, stamp! (*He pulls the cope off* PARK's *back.*) I say losers . . . (*He kicks it into a corner.*) I employ the ironic mode . . . (*He shouts and runs off.* PARK *is kneeling in a dirty, open shirt. Pause.*)

SMITH: You are a magnificent man. And nothing in you should be unrealised . . . (*Pause*) What a day! The sky is full of smoke, and yet the light is like a lick! Feel the kind light licking you . . . (*She takes his hand.*)

       Listen, do not think I am exaggerating or hysterical, but I must be with you. (*Pause*)

       I mean by that you must occupy me. (*She unbuttons her blouse.*)

       You have made a cavity of me and I must have relief. (*She places his hand on her breast.*)

       Everything is to be gained from this! (*He does nothing.*)

       If you refuse me I have made up my mind to be blind. (*He is still.*)

       Are you refusing me . . . ?

242   *Howard Barker*

PARK: Blind yourself? With what? (*Pause. She laughs a short laugh.*)

SMITH: You are afraid! You even, are afraid! I do understand your fears! You are horrified I shall think less of you! It is your secret and you think it better it remains a possibility. I was the same with my own flesh! I was the same! **Preserving flesh! Oh, I was so perfectly preserved from love!** Kiss me! (*She puts her mouth to his, ceases.*) No, that's wrong! That was **appalling judgement** on my part, that was **comic ineptitude!** (*She shakes her head briefly.*) Listen, I will be blind . . . ! (*Pause*)

PARK: Very well. Be blind if you must. (*Pause*)

SMITH: You think me insincere. How that injures me, to be thought insincere. (*She gets up. She goes to the* BARBARIAN *and takes out his unused bayonet.*)

PARK: If I am coerced, what am I? If I am pliable, what possible use? (*She kneels over the uptilted blade.*)

SMITH: You think I wanted to be gratified. When what I wanted was to be with you. (*She sways one way and another.*)

　　　　If not in ecstasy . . .
　　　　In pain . . . (*She butts her head twice, savagely.*)
　　　　Darkness!
　　　　Colours and darkness!

PARK (*grasping her action*): Hey . . . ! Oh, hey . . . ! (*He feels his way about the floor.*)

THE FIRST PERCEPTION OF THE MARQUIS OF DREUX-BREZE

A radical assembly of the revolution. Between tiers of animated DEPUTIES, *an aisle. The distant and ineffective beating of a staff. Both the sea of speech and the punctuation of the staff continue. At last, the* FIGURE *holding the staff, absurd in manner and costume, appears walking backwards. The speech sinks in disbelief, then turns to derision. The* YOUTH, *with immaculate effort, advances between the tiers.*

D-BREZE: I come from I (*They roar.*)
　　　　I command your I (*They jeer.*)
　　　　Am the bearer of this (*And whistle.*)

ROME 243

Order which (*Etc*)

His Majesty the King of All — (*They drown him out.*)

That you do cease this gathering herewith — (*They stamp.*)

Which is illegal and (*Boo*)

Shut up

I'm telling you

Shut up (*He begins to sob in the uproar.* MIRABEAU *stops the noise with a hand.*)

MIRABEAU: Tell him who sent you we are the new world and like a river can't be turned the river of the people may be guided by the wisdom of the representatives but silenced never nor deflected from its course of reason which (*A dog barks. A note. A massive carcass falls between the tiers. In the silence,* DREUX-BREZE *takes a tentative step backwards. The* DEPUTIES *are seized in a stillness. He takes another step.*)

D-BREZE: I lived! And they! I the comic and archaic manifestation of all! And clad in things that once seemed honourable I lived and they! I am the mannequin of all defunct and objectively redundant badges and trappings of! I lived and they! (*He withdraws from the tableau, breaking into a run.* DOREEN *appears at one side of the stage,* BEKNOWN *at the other.*)

Scene Eleven

BEKNOWN *is holding a tray with a teapot on it.* DOREEN *enters.*

DOREEN: Please don't go. I do so need you. Please don't go you are the only person I know who believes anything and I who believe nothing do so need you what do you want more wages why there's nothing to spend them on take money if it's money you want but it isn't is it in some ways what you believe is neither here nor there at least you believe **Is that the last drink you will ever bring me?** (*The dislocation of* LOOTERS *from the Barbarian armies.*) It is not fair because I need you more than whoever you are abandoning me for needs have rights don't they needs have authority and in any case I was more your servant than you were mine deny it if you dare you carry things but I'm the one who does the serving **Go if you must but the umbrella's**

mine (*She intercedes with* LOOTERS *who are lumbering a massive crucifix away.*) Do you want that? What possible use can you have for such a big and silly old thing when you aren't even — (*They take no notice of her.*) Are you replacing it? With what, exactly? Something of your own? (*Some* OTHERS *appear lugging a massive frame of gilt.*) Now, that is such a terribly, terribly old thing, all worm-eaten and horrible, don't say you want to — (*She is shoved aside.*) Good riddance to it! You can have too much antiquity, I say — (*More* LOOTERS *enter with sculpture or mirrors.*) Now, where did you unscrew that from! If you like old stuff — and personally I don't — that really isn't very fine and such an awkward shape you'll never get it in your bags — what do you want it for, to show your kids? I wouldn't touch it but everyone to his own — (BEKNOWN *pours a cup of tea and walks to* DOREEN.) Those busts are rubbish! Rubbish! Yes! I wouldn't give a thank you for those — **Agghhhh!** (*She sees a fine object passing.*)

Take no notice of me!

Agghhh! (*She points in despair as it passes.*)

Take no notice of me!

BEKNOWN: I am going to be married.

DOREEN: **Get out and leave your apron then**. (BEKNOWN *turns to go.*)

Moralist!

Resist the moralists! (DOREEN *turns back to the* LOOTERS.)

Do you really need that? Sorry but wouldn't something smaller do as well, I just — (*They beat her. She totters.* BEKNOWN *is suddenly anxious, hesitant.*) Go on, get out and take your education with you! (*Back to the* LOOTERS.) That isn't in the least bit valuable, only my father —

My people are in it you (*The* LOOTER *stops, looks at her.*)

Repulsive

Scrap

Of

Animal

Disorder (*The* LOOTER *strikes her. She goes down. As she does so, she sings madly.*)

Oh, let the rubbish go down
Down goes the rubbish!
Oh, let the stupid go down
What's flesh in history?

ROME   245

> Shall I go down or you go down,
> If I'm staying up you've got to go down,
> Goodbye to the up!
> Hello to the down!
> Down goes the rubbish! (*More objects are looted.* BE-
KNOWN *watches, holding the tea cup.*)

BEKNOWN: I walk away.

DOREEN: Down goes the rubbish!

BEKNOWN: I walk away. (*She does not do so.*) Go on, then, walk!
(*Still she does not leave. The last* LOOTERS *depart, dragging
an altar piece. Some distant cries of ridicule and madness.*) I
think, when I look at you, I see all that is ridiculous in us — and
all that is powerful in us — and weak in us — in one incomprehensible, unfathomable ball of flesh and mischief! (DOREEN
sits up.)

DOREEN: I've wet myself. . . . (*She shakes her head.*)
> Never forgive. . . .
> Our enemies. . . .
> **Never forgive.** . . .
> And all who taught us weakness. . . .
> **Never forgive.** . . . (*Pause. She looks at* BEKNOWN.)
As if it matters, you might say, whether an old woman
forgives or not. But my unforgiving will be **stone as arches,** will
be **iron as bridges.** (*Pause*)
> How?
> Oh, I don't know yet.

Pause. With a calculated action, BEKNOWN *drinks the tea. She
tosses away the cup and saucer, which shatter.* ISAAC *enters. He
sees* DOREEN's *pitiful condition and goes to help.* BEKNOWN's
words stop him.

BEKNOWN: Don't pick her up.

ISAAC: Don't.

BEKNOWN: If you pick her up, how will you ever put her down
again?

ISAAC: Just move her to the —

BEKNOWN: **Don't or else.** (*Pause*)

ISAAC: Else . . . ?

BEKNOWN: My body. My red and teeming under-the-clothing
thing. Can't strip for kind men. (*Pause. He acquiesces, turns to*
DOREEN.)

ISAAC: I read history and history says —

246 *Howard Barker*

DOREEN: Don't. (*Pause*) Comfort me with history. (*He shrugs. He extends a hand to* BEKNOWN, *who takes it. They turn to leave.*) The first slave was not captured. But knelt of his own free will.

ISAAC: Really? That's not in the history books.

DOREEN: The first slave was a master, who grew tired of mastery and put the torque on his own neck.

ISAAC: That isn't in the books!

DOREEN: **All right it's not in the books.** (*She smiles weakly.*) Off you go and be happy! **I don't know where.** Off you go and all the best! (*She laughs cruelly as* ISAAC *and* BEKNOWN *leave. The stage fills with* HOLIDAY-MAKERS *carrying deck-chairs. They erect them, sit, chatter, sleep, whoop.*)

Scene Twelve

HOLLO *enters holding a crude cross on his shoulder, made from scrap timber. Attached to him,* PARK *and* SMITH, *blind.* HOLLO *talks out loud to anyone who will listen. The* LEISURED *ignore him, uneasily, in their deck chairs.*

HOLLO: I like the new government. It shows the same films as the old. (*He addresses another.*) I like the new government. It encourages gambling. **And they said they would abolish horse-racing, never!**

PARK: Where is this?

HOLLO: Can't you smell?

SMITH: It's near the sea!

HOLLO: Can't you hear? (*He waves the cross above his head.*)
    I wave the ban — ner of my hope!
    Look, they think I'm insane! (*He threatens one of the* LEISURED.)
        Whaddyer wanna be brown for?
        Whaddyer wanna shake yer hips for?
        Do you know the gospels?
        Do you know the Greeks?
    I will say this for you. I will say this. You have got character, yes, real character, you stand out like a tulip on a coffin

ROME   247

Switch the fucking music off (*He throws down the cross, and squats.*)

No, I'm trying to improve, I am trying to learn manners, which my master says is first ditch against this **int — im — acy!** (LASCAR *is discovered pushing his handcart through the* LEISURED. *He sees the pope* PARK, *stops.*) Do I offend you? I killed three hundred, yes, I did keep count, **three hundred of your enemies!** Well, that was last week, admittedly, but I am improving, do you find me offensive? I humbly submit, you are more offensive, yes, I dare suggest, you are supremely —

LASCAR: Psst!

HOLLO (*to the* INDIVIDUAL *moving his deckchair*): Supremely damaging to **human dignity!** What's that?

LASCAR: Psst!

HOLLO: Human dignity, oi! What is it? Seen some?

LASCAR (*crouching by* PARK): They are looking for you. I am a well-wisher. (*He coughs.*) There is a preposterous reward. Dead or alive I am a well-wisher.

PARK: Lascar, you don't have to say you are a well-wisher —

LASCAR: Ah, you recognize me . . . ! And I thought I'd changed my voice! I so admire you, nothing escapes you and I haven't got the handcart with me, I live from hand to mouth, I scuttle over —

> **Yes I have**
> **I have got it**
> **It's over there**
> **Ha ha**
> **Yes**

PARK: Shh . . .

LASCAR: **Laden with bits**

PARK: Shh . . .

LASCAR: **Who cares for your instructions your encyclicals and ordinances who**

> You must go to another country

PARK: I am Rome now. Rome is me.

LASCAR: They are not extinguishing the faith, on the contrary they are promoting whoever denounces you to Supreme Pontiff **even a shopkeeper even a lout** they are not stupid are they on the contrary they (*Pause. The thin sound of popular music.* LASCAR *gets up from the crouching position to his feet.* SMITH *intuitively interprets his silence.*)

SMITH (*pulling* PARK): Get up!

248   *Howard Barker*

      Hollo! (HOLLO *is wandering about a distant part of the*
  beach.)
      Get up!
LASCAR *(unstoppered)*: **Hey! This man is the blind pope!**
SMITH: Quick!
LASCAR: **This man is him!** (*The* LEISURED *rise to their feet as*
  one.)
THE LEISURED: **We might hide him in our numbers**
                We might swallow him in our crop of heads
                                    and our
                Legs might make a forest of obscurity
                No
                Hunter
                Could
                Penetrate
HOLLO *(too far away)*: **Oi!**
THE LEISURED: **Yet**
HOLLO: **Oi!**
THE LEISURED: **We found him rather too intense** (*The stage*
  freezes.)

Scene Thirteen

A FIGURE *enters from a long distance, holding a small bag. He*
comes to PARK.

TORTURER: What made you blind?
PARK: God, it was, I think.
TORTURER: Pity. But there is much of you left.
PARK: I have read so much about torture. And when last I was
  tortured I blasphemed. I doubt now will be any different.
LASCAR: Is that my throne? (*He looks around him.*) I have a
  throne, I believe, with lights. . . . (*The* LEISURED *depart silent-*
  ly, taking their buckets and spades.) A modern one?
PARK: I was never ashamed to be human, even whilst I wanted to
  be more than human. **This is human.** (*He lets out a terrible*
  cry.)
LASCAR *(in horror)*: I did this because how much better it is that
  (PARK *cries again.*)

ROME   249

A true believer occupies the throne than one who might (*And again.*)

This is a calculation historians will assess not at face value but as

Don't hurt him will you
There is no need for
I pray
I pray
I pray for you

TORTURER (*to* PARK): I have instructions to make an idiot of you.

PARK: And you can do that, can you?

TORTURER: I think so, yes. I think as you feel your reason going from you you will experience the most terrible despair. You will hate yourself, which I daresay will be novel.

PARK: Yes. I have never hated myself. On the contrary, I have held myself in the highest regard, which a man must do if he intends — (*A cry from his depths. Items of papal regalia fall from the sky about* LASCAR.)

TORTURER: I imagine, were the boot upon the other foot, similar skills to mine would be employed against your enemies.

PARK: Yes. How can I conceal from you — above all people — how can I conceal — some equally degrading spectacle would occur, given how little charity I have — (*He cries out.* LASCAR, *kneeling, tries on the regalia.*)

TORTURER: I must admit — to you —

PARK: Thank you —

TORTURER: There have been those — I am not vain, as you are not either —

PARK: Not vain —

TORTURER: I knew that at once! He is not vain, this one! Who — by some chemical impurity — I cannot express it any other way — failed to respond to the most complex colourings of pain.

PARK: They died . . .

TORTURER: Died yes, indeed, but I have never seen this as evidence of heroism, though it is considered so, rather it is in my experience, an implacable, molecular rigidity — (LASCAR *sits in the costume of a modern pope*) — and these broke me — yes — I have been broken I do not mind telling you — I bear the scars of mutual struggle, for it is struggle we are engaged upon, a struggle with matter, which even you can witness, as a man might watch his transplant on a little screen . . . (*An* OLD WOMAN *enters with a bun on a plate.*)

250   *Howard Barker*

          Mother, I am very busy, put it over there . . . (*She*
puts it down.)
          She makes me buns.
          She says it is elevenses, give the boy his bun.
          She calls me boy.
          I never eat the buns. (*He calls out to her.*)
          This was the Pope!
          Yes! (*She shuffles out.*)
          Now you think I am odd! But I have children also!
(*He looks at* PARK, *puts a hand on his shoulder.*) I think you
must say goodbye to yourself now. One self, anyway.
          And welcome another . . .

Scene Fourteen

*The sound of an engine and trucks labouring on an incline. A
massive dining-table descends, obscuring* PARK *and the* TOR-
TURER. BENZ *enters.*

SMITH: Why is it people of utter truthfulness inspire hatred in the
   rest? I think nobody loves the blind pope, only me . . .
BENZ: Isn't that how you would want it? You wouldn't want to
   share him, surely, with a pack of devotees? The common adula-
   tion of the herd? **What do you want a pop star?** (*He shakes his
   head.*) You must find the flaw in him. Dig, and pick, until the
   flaw is seen. **That's the cure for love.** (*He comforts her, nursing
   her head as she kneels.*) **I so want to hurt things. I do so long
   to spoil.** (*A sack rolls down a slope. The train labours. The*
   TORTURER, *in a coat, emerges with a bag.*)
TORTURER: The eloquence I found somewhat corrupting, even of
   my toxic nature. He gave a running commentary on his own
   decline, which distracted me. (*He goes to walk, stops.*) What is
   torture but theft? And yet the thieves have all the glamour! Sometimes this piques me. Women so love thieves! Yet the attraction
   of the thief I daresay is only this — he seems to render privilege
   a little less oppressive **isn't intelligence privilege isn't beauty
   privilege** I take those things I steal those items am I not the most
   incredible of thieves **where are my admirers my doting mis-
   tresses!** (*A* CHILD *enters, crying out a greeting.*) I was so nearly

ROME 251

late! My little one! Today I was so nearly late at the school gate my loved and loving! (*He extends his arms.*) Lunch box! And I'll take yours! (*The* CHILD *extends a lunch box. The* TORTURER *gives his in exchange, a loving routine. The* CHILD *jumps into his arms. They go off.* SMITH, *acute to the sack, scrambles crab-like towards it, stops. She moves around it, her ears cocked. At last she finds the tie-string and undoes it. The cry of a baby comes from within. She lets out a wail of despair. It is* PARK.)

BENZ: Why must I discredit everyone? Why must I? I slander saints and disparage innocence. I smear the perfect hermit with ambition, and call fasting vain. As for charity, what's that hut vulgar liberality? (*Pause. Another cry from the sack. He looks at it. It weakens him. He writhes. Covering his head with his arms. He hurries out. The new pope* LASCAR *enters. He watches for a moment as* SMITH *rolls down the sack and exposes a disastrous* PARK.)

LASCAR: Oh, my dear fellow.

Oh, my dear man how utterly.

Much going on in there I wonder?

Noisy in there I wonder or silent underwater sort of thing? (SMITH *assists the crippled* PARK *to a seat at the table, where he lolls.* SERVANTS *bring in food and drink. Spoons and plates are musical in the silence. It stops.*)

What did he mean by Rome?

I think you have to ask that question really I do it can't be simply taken for granted we must examine the appalling inequalities and lack of flexibility that he during his short Rome yes but whose Rome Rome for whom etcetera and (*Silence but for the same music of spoons and plates.*) Many people had no Latin therefore what was being said was simply sound where was the sense in my view people need to draw their own conclusions not to be **what did he mean by Rome I ask perhaps only** (BEATRICE *enters, goes to the table, sits.*)

BEATRICE: Since Rome fell I am not followed so much. Not pestered which surely is a good thing. It is as if a terrible contentment had appeared which renders all ambition quite superfluous. Or am I ugly? I am post-sexual perhaps? Post-everything? (*Pause*) I don't think so, do you? (*Pause*) No . . . (HOLLO *enters, in a suit, and sits.* SMITH *sobs suddenly, briefly.*) No . . . (*Pause. She drops her spoon.*) **I could not go on being. I could not go on.**

SMITH: Of course not, no.

BEATRICE: **This.**

This.

SMITH: You don't have to say these things to me or find words for it, even . . .

BEATRICE: I adore you

SMITH: I know

BEATRICE: **Adore** (*Pause*) And you are hard as floors. (*Pause*) Give him to me, now. (*She unbuttons her elegant jacket and blouse. She exposes her breast and feeds* PARK.)

PART TWO

Scene One

A place in the ruins of Rome. PIUS *draped over the handcart. His* YOUTH *smokes.*

PIUS: I'm all absence. Is that death? (*Pause*)

I'm nothingness wanting. Is that death? (*Pause*)

Come on, you're a moron, aren't you, speculate! (*Pause*)

Oh, I was sensitive once. So sensitive! I trembled like a leaf at all experience. And dumb with fear. Where did that go? I was beautiful with delicacy, I flushed to meet a stranger's eyes, that's how tender I was, the slightest rebuke lodged in me like a spear **death has made me coarse, oh, so very coarse,** who has her arse now, who sees it, who sits in its light, who marvels at its tensions **you sit there you perch there caring not a jot, what poverty of life is slopping in your skull?** (*Pause*) To think it moves, and independently of me! To think it passes clothed or unclothed in another's gaze **or several possibly** she was ambitious, she could dream high numbers when it came to love (*The* YOUTH *steps on his cigarette and goes to the cart handles.*) **Don't go till I say so** you think one arse is like another **don't move until I give the signal** you think flesh is flesh and love is born of character **oh, you bag of sticks and ignorance** perfection's not accountable and every pain was smothered in the vision of her arse! (*The* YOUTH *drops the handles and sobs. Pause.*)

I do inflict.

I do unforgivably encroach.

Say you understand how hard it is for someone of my powers to apologise. (*The* YOUTH *nods.*) Take apology for granted, will you? Assume it lies beside the insult? Stamped on

254   *Howard Barker*

the bottom of each curse? (*The* YOUTH *picks up the handles and propels* PIUS *offstage.*)

Scene Two

A mass of dark FIGURES. *From a distance the faint lights of* LASCAR's *illuminated mitre, as he approaches through them.*

LASCAR: Peace! Wonderful peace! Peace! Oh, perfect lotion and emollient! (*He trips, and falls.*)

CHORUS: I fell.
               And lay.
               I overcame the shame of falling.
               I was still.
               I smothered the compulsion to scramble up again.

LASCAR: And lying, thought, there is another. There is a different. And commanded myself, when I rose I would be this other. Or not get up again. (*A long pause. At last he rises to his feet, and brushes his soutane with his hand.*)

CHORUS: What was absurd last week. (*A wind blows down the city.*)
               And what was revered. (*A can rolls in a gutter.*)
               Change places.
               The routine and the eccentric.
               Switch.

The CHORUS *burst into song, of a popular and festive kind.* HOLLO *enters. The* CHORUS *disperses. Pause.* LASCAR *and* HOLLO *observe one another intently.*

LASCAR: What seemed a betrayal . . .
HOLLO: Was not.
LASCAR: What seemed expedient . . .
HOLLO: Was not.
LASCAR: Not dirty . . .
HOLLO: No . . .
LASCAR: Not opportune.
HOLLO/LASCAR: **Not. Not.** (*Pause. They stare.* LASCAR *disburdens himself of the mitre with a flourish.*)

ROME   255

LASCAR: Oh, you had nothing but contempt for me!

HOLLO: Well . . .

LASCAR: Nothing, nothing, but contempt!

HOLLO (*laughing*): I wished you dead!

LASCAR: Dead was only the beginning! You were wringing with revulsion!

HOLLO: Well . . .

LASCAR: Revulsion poured from your mouth, and yet . . . !

HOLLO: That changed.

LASCAR: You asked yourself, what use was this revulsion? What possible use?

HOLLO (*thoughtfully*): I'm in decay. Or I have overcome myself. **Which do you think!** (LASCAR *smiles*.) I'm a poor thing. Or a great thing. **Which! I like you in all the chambers of my heart**.

LASCAR: You have used thought as a rope. And up the rope you scramble. You were in the pit but now.

HOLLO: Daylight!

LASCAR: And looking back, peering back into the dark think who was this youth of anger?

HOLLO: Hollo? Who's he?

LASCAR: Lascar, him? Don't know the man. Kiss me. Or not, do you think?

HOLLO: Not now.

LASCAR: Not now, no.

HOLLO: Not this minute.

LASCAR: **We must go through, mustn't we?** Say you agree.

HOLLO: Through, yes.

LASCAR: Everything, I mean. Through everything. Say you agree.

HOLLO: You know I do.

LASCAR: Oh, I feel so mobile! Oh, I feel so fit! I sleep hardly at all — are you like this — for fear during my sleep **old self might smother me**, no, I need to concentrate all hours, even in the dim poor hours of the madman's shrieks and thinking of you helps, kiss now, surely? And what was Roman about Rome in any case, I am expiring for a kiss from you, I am suffoc — (HOLLO *thrusts himself on* LASCAR, *driving him backwards with the force of his kiss. He stops, suddenly, and leaves* LASCAR *staggering*.) Come again, soon . . . ! (BEATRICE *enters, as* LASCAR *recovers. Pause*.) There is nothing wrong with the Barbarians.

Nothing.

It was prejudice. (*He picks up his mitre*.)

What do these words mean? Barbarian? Or Roman?

What? The words must go. The words are like thorns in the brow of Christ. They scratch and irritate.

      Inferior. Superior.

      No.

      No.

      Variety, surely?

BEATRICE: And Rome?

LASCAR: I think we must forget Rome now. No! Not forget it, no, be positive, **abolish** it. I am not afraid to talk about the future or to face a fact, **who cares for this archaic notion?** There, I say it, and having said it, say it again. Rome indeed. Do you want a drink, I have some sherry. I understand the Blind Pope said a word, though tongueless, articulated it, and the word was — yes — don't laugh — **Rome** — fancy that — what else would he have said — **All right I am in bad taste so what** — hardly likely he would have uttered **reconciliation!**

BEATRICE: Too many syllables —

LASCAR: Did you say yes to sherry — listen I have excellent relations with the people sometimes called formerly called absurdly called Barbarians and they are not at all what you. (*Pause*) I do open my arms to change. (*Pause*) Whereas he. In the dark and howling corridors of devastated mind. Can only. Heave one.

BEATRICE: He is going on a pillar.

LASCAR: Word. (*Pause*)

      Pillar? Why? (ABRAHAM *appears, hoeing*.)

      Pillar! Why!

BEATRICE: He wants to hang his pain on a hook. (*Pause*) I say he wants. I am not sure if he wants at all. But he is wanted. So it hardly matters what he wants.

LASCAR: **I am not ashamed of my life**.

      Or any thing.

      Or act.

      Or thought.

      No.

      None.

      Did you say yes to the sherry?

ROME   257

THIRD ABRAHAM

BENZ *enters as* ABRAHAM *hoes.* ABRAHAM *resolutely refuses to meet his gaze. At last, finding the tension unbearable, he throws down the hoe.*

ABRAHAM: I am not the same! (*Pause*)
             The same man how could I be. (*He drags up his eyes to* BENZ.)
             How you misunderstood. How you who knows the heart of man misunderstood.
BENZ: Perhaps I owe you an apology.
ABRAHAM: An apology? A God who apologises? **A sorry God?** Please, let a man do his garden, let a man.
BENZ: **I also have some needs I also and apology might be one.** Don't pick up the hoe. Don't pick it up. Or else, I nearly said. Or else what, however? Leave it. (ABRAHAM *relents.*)
ABRAHAM: Listen, you sorry God, I so wished to kill my son. I so required to do the thing for you. The unforgivable. The limit and beyond. So needed to, but you said no, the demonstration was enough. It was not enough. **You killed faith in its apotheosis.** (*Pause*) I had mastered pity. I had crossed the frontiers of humanity for thee. I broke down the gates of Heaven for thee. **Thee, yes Thee, I called you Thee.** (*He shakes his head in resignation.*) 'Sacrifice the ram instead . . .' **Oh, Deity without imagination.** A graven image knows better than you do how we long for our subordination. 'Sacrifice the ram instead . . .'
             God's human! (*He stares at* BENZ *with contempt.*)
             Give us the hoe.
             Go on.
             Give us the hoe. (BENZ *picks it up, and gives it to* ABRAHAM, *who hoes slowly off.*)
BENZ: I wanted to be loved, but they only wanted to fear me. (*He laughs, he goes swiftly to* BEATRICE, *sits beside her, joins his finger tips, stares away.*) You are not tender, did you know that? (*She sips sherry.*) Much as I admire you, tenderness is not among your attributes. (*Pause*) And I want tenderness. Obviously I require it. (*He taps his foot.*) We never seem to talk. Now, that is tenderness of some description.
BEATRICE: We often talk.
BENZ: We talk but it is soddened with impatience on your part. Tenderness is unhurried, surely, it has all the time in the world. You feed the blind and dumb pope suppose I wanted it.

BEATRICE: What?

BENZ: The milk.

BEATRICE: What do you want milk for?

BENZ: **You see that is what I mean by tenderness.** (*Pause*) It is not a matter of wanting but of intimacy which I do want and which you deny me.

BEATRICE: I deny you nothing.

BENZ: You take your clothes off, certainly.

BEATRICE: I call that intimacy.

BENZ: You murmur and you cry out in the act of love.

BEATRICE: That's intimacy.

BENZ: You are magnificently unashamed, but that is the product of experience, surely, and not a compliment to me —

BEATRICE: **You want a compliment?**
          You?
          After all you
          And everything you
          Ask for a (*Pause. She walks, stops, turns.*)
          Compliment . . . .

BENZ: You're so right.
      You are so.
      Absolutely right and I. (*He gets up, refreshed.*)
      Some couples make rugs. Rugs! They do! They work from either end . . . ! (*He turns to go.*)

BEATRICE: I do adore you. (*He stops.*)
          I mean I do so want to
          I do try. (*Pause*)

BENZ: Yes.

BEATRICE: The fault is mine. (*Pause. The murmuring of an active* CROWD. *Darkness falls. She goes out.*)

Scene Three

FIGURES *with ropes and tackle, commanded by* SMITH. *The flash of torches.* PARK, *on a small platform, is raised to the top of a Corinthian pillar.*

DEVOTS: He does not speak
        And therefore can't be wrong

ROME

He has no words
And therefore is no liar
SMITH: Careful not to tilt the platform the platform must be —
DEVOTS: No slogan ever fell from him
Or ejaculation
SMITH: Level —
DEVOTS: Vituperation or
SMITH: And the ropes pulled evenly not jerked —
DEVOTS: The creaking gramaphone of pity
SMITH: Hand over hand —
DEVOTS: He does not stare
And therefore can't humiliate
He cannot weep
And therefore can't manipulate
Our
SMITH: Lift him now —
DEVOTS: Sympathy
SMITH: Still now! Still now! (*Silence. Dawn. SMITH is alone but for BENZ. PARK is perched on the pillar. SMITH attends to a tray and a pulley. Pause.*)
BENZ: **Graven fuck — ing image!** (*She ignores him. She attaches the breakfast tray to the rope and draws it* up.)
Graven fuck — ing —
SMITH: Please don't abuse what is incomprehensible to you. (*Pause*)
BENZ: They'll have him down of course, you know that, don't you? The Barbarians? Down in no time. (*She ignores him.*) They won't allow that, will they? **Thing on a pole.**
SMITH: Please, you are creating an unpleasant atmosphere.
BENZ: They will, though, won't they? Ask yourself.
SMITH: Then we will erect it again.
BENZ: **And then they'll have it down again, won't they, daft git?** (*She works on.*)
Sorry I'm a yob.
I am.
Can't help it.
Sorry. (*Pause*)
You haven't any eyes.
Not that it seems a handicap.
SMITH: I did not want my eyes.
BENZ: Nice! Nice when God gives you eyes you say no thank you!
SMITH: He has no eyes.
BENZ (*pretending to examine PARK*): Oh, no, he hasn't . . .

SMITH: So I wanted none. (*She pours water into a tin flask and winds it up to* PARK.)

BENZ: So if some genius of medicine or surgery put back your eyes —

SMITH: I'd tear them out again.

BENZ (*pointing in triumph*): Knew you'd say that! Ha ha! Ha ha! (TWO MEN *enter*.)

DEVOTS: Be quiet.

BENZ: Be quiet, why?

DEVOTS: Be quiet we said.

BENZ: Everyone tells you to be quiet. I don't wanna be quiet. (*One of the* DEVOTS *threatens with a move*.)

All right! (*They bow to the pillar.*)

Just a lout you see . . .

A lout . . . (*They leave. Pause.* BENZ *watches* SMITH *at work. He changes.*) Perhaps you haven't yet suffered enough? Has that thought occurred to you? (*She resolutely attends to her duties.*) You are so diligent — and your body moves — so cleanly — blind or not — a body which — God gave you and which you perhaps — ignore the rhythms of? (*She ignores him.*)

He gave it to you for a function, obviously. The body.

SMITH: It is functioning.

BENZ: What? All of it? (*Pause. She goes to continue.*)

Don't move like that. (*Pause*)

SMITH: Like what?

BENZ: So sedulous. And passionate. So humble and —

SMITH: I cannot help the way I move —

BENZ: Adoring —

SMITH: My gestures are my feelings —

BENZ: Such chastity and such piety **take your clothes off blind girl I have to see you naked.** (*Pause. She is still for some seconds, then proceeds to her task.*)

I said. (*She stops again. A bottomless silence opens between them, broken at last by* PARK's *cry.*)

PARK: **Ro — me!** (BENZ *gets to his feet.*)

BENZ: Rome? What does he mean by Rome? (*He walks towards her.*) He says that as if we should know what he meant by it. (*Pause*)

Be naked I said.

SMITH: You heap more misery on a place already —

BENZ: Your pain is my pleasure, don't you see —

SMITH: Suffocated with humiliation —

ROME 261

BENZ: Your cry is my ecstasy —

SMITH: And offence —

BENZ: And your despair my satisfaction, don't you see. (*Pause*) I am wholly worthless but I walk upon the earth and the perfect such as you must occasionally encounter us less perfect.

Naked I said

The nightmare of variety

Naked

Naked (*Suddenly* SMITH *makes to dodge him, but he is swifter.*)

Blind women shouldn't run! (*He holds her tightly from behind.*)

Perhaps you blinded yourself only in order to be caught more easily by me. (*Pause. They are still.*)

Have you considered that? (*Pause*)

Perhaps the reason you thought you blinded yourself was not the real reason at all?

PARK: **Ro — me!**

SMITH: That is a consideration of truly lethal proportions . . .

BENZ *takes* SMITH *against the pillar, as* PARK *in despair rains down an assortment of tin plates and bowls, which clatter in the silence.* HOLLO *enters, casually, and watches this. It ends.* BENZ *goes out, contemplatively.* SMITH *sinks to the foot of the pillar, is still.* HOLLO *walks slowly to the front, looks up at* PARK's *kneeling, listening figure.*

HOLLO: My manifesto

Can you hear or not?

My powers of articulation are greatly improved but words can't go through concrete, can they, they're not armour-piercing, are they?

Raise an arm

All right, don't

Do you like the suit it was a gift from someone who respects me yes respects a funny thing it must be what I always wanted

Can he hear? (*Pause*)

It changes, you see. The world. It cannot help itself and we —

SMITH: **The moon**. (*Pause*)

HOLLO: Come again? (*Pause*) Can't stand still, either, so I'm sorry but —

262   *Howard Barker*

SMITH: **Goes round the earth.** (*He looks at her, puzzled.*)
HOLLO: We either welcome change or we —
SMITH: **The earth** (*Pause*)
HOLLO: We shrivel in these crippling prejudices which —
SMITH: **Goes round the sun.** (*She turns to* HOLLO *for the first time.*)
       Is that a prejudice? They do not go in a straight line, do they? (*Pause.* HOLLO *senses her meaning.*)
HOLLO: **I done enough of that rib cracking and blood drinking when inside me was another of**
       moderate
       and
       social
       inclinations. (*Pause*)
SMITH: You have been seduced.
HOLLO: I found another living underneath my skin. Also me. I found a different sheltering inside my bones. Also me.
SMITH: Someone has got you on a bed.
HOLLO: This sweeter me ached to express itself **don't bring my old animal to birth again.** (*Pause. He looks up to* PARK.) Shouldn't he have a raincoat or something? A sunhat? Gloves? (SMITH *is adamantly silent.* HOLLO *goes out.* SMITH *collects herself, goes to pick up the tin plates, staggers and holds herself. Pause.*)
SMITH: I have a feeling
       What occurred just now
       Will reoccur
       Will be perhaps a terrible routine
       And in the end I will be killed
       Some lunatic with throbbing veins
       Will do me an appalling hurt
       Does that matter at all
       I don't mean cosmically
       I don't mean theologically
       To you?
       In your deep store of feeling?
       I must know you esteem me
       It is my dirty little spasm of self-regard
       Give us a sign of love! (*Pause*)
       Nothing! (*Pause*)
       No, well, it would be incongruous. (*She tidies up again, she stops.*)

ROME   263

The fact is we are held by the impossible.
The impossible it is that keeps me here and were you
to capitulate to my nagging desire for affirmation
I've no doubt I'd scarper
like a bottled bee
into the stagnant world

Scene Four

A small light. ISAAC *enters.*

ISAAC: My wedding. (*A cacophony of abuse.*)
　　　　She. (*Again*)
　　　　Wanted the light off (*Again*)
　　　　And in the dark spoke things with no impediment. Words
I had seen. Words I had cleansed from atlases of the female
form. From her perfect mouth all these words off walls and these
words caused her to shake. In the darkness I felt her shake with
words.
　　　　Why do you need these words I said
　　　　Do these words not
　　　　The commonness and
　　　　Violence of them (*Pause*)
　　　　I forgot to say she was across the room we weren't in bed,
you see. (*The light spreads to show a room where* BEKNOWN
is seated in an armchair.) We are married so you say but in what
way, exactly, I am your husband which is wonderful but we
haven't yet, you must decide of course the time, what sort of
marriage, could you say? (*She smiles lovingly.*) At school I shut
my eyes to words on lavatory walls thinking what power must
reside in **clean language** or **silence even** I did I shut my eyes.
(*Pause*) They hate, you see. The words are hate. Therefore how
could those words live in your **and you heaved you heaved!**
(BEKNOWN *jumps up.*)
BEKNOWN: Look! Our doves! Our fantails! I have got one to eat
out of my hand . . . (*She extends a hand.*) Not today, though. Your
questions will kill the birds!
ISAAC: I don't see how —

Howard Barker

BEKNOWN: They will! Your questions will! They are like a cloud, a miasma of exhaust in which their perfect natures will be suffocated!

ISAAC: I am so

BEKNOWN: Shh!

ISAAC: I am so

BEKNOWN: Shh! The birds! (DOREEN, *decayed and poor, enters*.)

DOREEN: Give us a cup! On your own china! Give us a sip! I've nothing but gratitude, would that be of any interest, and of course the animal admiration we all feel in the presence of success! (*She drops her bags.*) You are even taller I believe than when you were the statuesque attribute of my drawing-room, give us a cup . . .

BEKNOWN: God, you are a squashed orange of a hag now, I could laugh.

DOREEN: Laugh, then.

BEKNOWN: You are a vegetable scrap and something's running out your leg. Laugh or weep I don't know which.

DOREEN: Laugh for Christ's sake, look and laugh. The fall of Rome suits many, laugh away, nothing you do can be wrong, does it offend you to be adored by me? It's your own fault, look, I salvaged something and if you licked my sores I would not give it you **some independence left**. (*She explores in her clothing and pulls out a china cup.*)

> Rome.
>
> In every contour. In every spasm of the brush. (*She sings.*)
>
> The half-blind decorator splashed this red
> Where your mouth goes
> And let the blue run like a vein of age
>
> Gold he squandered to corrupt a soul
> And in the bowl the glaze is milkwhite
> As your belly
>
> My china cup is so self-satisfied
> I share its falseness and its pride
> Also its power to survive
> The passage of contempt
>
> It rings to terrible conclusions
> And chimes with idiotic fables
> Finding itself promoted when the pain
> Is past

To

Other

Tables (ISAAC *brings a tea pot, kindly. He fills her cup.*)

BEKNOWN: I think you should be dead.

DOREEN: I will be dead.

BEKNOWN: When, though? (*She walks.* DOREEN *sips.*) I think to linger far beyond your time shows such a disregard for others I think dragging yourself about like that is a mute criticism.

DOREEN: Mute criticism . . . ?

BEKNOWN: Silent reproach, then.

DOREEN: Silent reproach . . . ?

BEKNOWN: I think we must look into vagrants and rebutt their charges.

DOREEN: Charges?

BEKNOWN: Yes, charges, your looks are charges and I am unashamed. (*Pause*)

DOREEN: Yes, and that is why I love you

Mistress.

Deity.

ISAAC: You are so cruel!

DOREEN (*picking up one of her bags*): Shh!

ISAAC: So cruel to her!

DOREEN: Shh!

Carry my bag instead.

BEKNOWN: No. (*Pause.* DOREEN *shrugs, goes to pick up the other.*)

ISAAC: Must help her —

BEKNOWN: Don't —

ISAAC: Must! Must!

DOREEN: **Don't help she says.** (*She glares at* ISAAC, *who is repulsed.* DOREEN *leaves.* HOLLO *in a gaudy beach shirt is discovered.*)

266   *Howard Barker*

Scene Five

The POPE's *study.*

LASCAR: Come in. (HOLLO *doesn't move.*) Come in, do you
   want to borrow a book? Oh, your entire body is heaven and you
   will not last, you are so temporary, you are a moment of perfection, no more than a raindrop in time which I catch with my lip
   — (*He extends it.* HOLLO *goes to kiss him.* LASCAR *squirms
   aside.*) Can't! Mustn't! Stay there, Heaven! (*He dances.*) You
   make me ridiculous! You make me farcical! **Hold my foot!** (*He
   extends a foot.* HOLLO *takes it.*) Now, turn me. Twist me! I am
   a top! I creak, I hum like a top a schoolboy found in an abandoned
   attic! (HOLLO *turns him round.*) Stop! Stop! (HOLLO *stops,
   holding him tightly.*) Tell me I have given you something, too.
HOLLO: Yes . . .
LASCAR: Yes, he says. Monosyllabic male. I mean, flood me with
   words. Of such — egregious complexity and wealth. Such as.
   You copy, I'll say. Such as — (*He invents.*) 'I was a thing of
   insignificance blowing in the mundane winds of urban squalor,
   and you crafted me.' Your own words, however paltry, however
   mundane . . . (*Pause.* HOLLO *releases him, cogitates.*)
HOLLO: I was a —
LASCAR: Yes —
HOLLO: A slender whiteness marching beneath the maternal
   moon —
LASCAR: Good —
HOLLO: As unprincipled as a flower —
LASCAR: Excellent, excellent!
HOLLO: Which a worthless servant plucked, and buttonholed,
   sniffing, giggling, and staining with saliva my immaculate leaves
   . . . (*Pause*)
LASCAR: Petals.
            The leaves of a flower are petals. (*With decision.*)
            Let's look at a book! (*He grabs one.*)
            De rerum theologicum. (HOLLO *stands beside him.*)
            I can see down your shirt the buttons of which are
            Dancing open
            Oh, you are going to decay, you are going to spoil . . .
HOLLO: I suppose I am . . . (LASCAR *is still with grief.*)
            I saw him on a pillar. On three boards. (*Pause.* LASCAR
   nuzzles HOLLO's *neck.*)

Absurd.

Why had he made himself absurd? (LASCAR *proceeds.*)

And the woman . . .

Man after man . . .

Boy after boy . . .

They park their bicycles and —

LASCAR: **I do not wish to know**. (*Pause*)

You spoil my

You wreck my

Fragile concentration with your (*He withdraws from*

HOLLO. *He suddenly and passionately recites.*)

The poor

The sick

The recipients of stray bullets

The occupants of wheelchairs

The sufferers from viruses

And those who fell under the tram

Yes

To

Them

And

No

To

Saints

on

Poles (*He laughs, slapping his thighs.*)

I do get

I do so throb with temper

Scene Six

Some books fall from the sky. PIUS *is rushed across the stage. A* CROWD *materialises led by a* BOY.)

BOY: **Life under the Barbarians**

VOICE 1: They allowed us to continue

VOICE 2: **There were no camps**
VOICE 1: They banned nothing that we noticed
VOICE 3: **No executions or exterminations**
VOICE 4: They let me open my shop on Sundays
VOICE 5: And fishing in the reservoir was not banned
VOICE 2: **A few did**
VOICE 6: My girlfriend was still beautiful
VOICE 2: **A few**
VOICE 6: Her hairstyle was if anything improved
VOICE 2: **Individuals**
VOICE 7: And new music with a hypnotic beat
VOICE 2: **Disappeared so what they were such snobs**

Silence but for a wind. BENZ *strolls in holding his* BABY. PIUS *lies in his cart. As the* CROWD *dissolves,* BEATRICE *is revealed naked.* BENZ *walks to and fro.* BEATRICE *is resolute.*

BEATRICE: All right, worship me.
Don't laugh it's hard to be naked
Don't laugh it's only a sheet to handle yourself
under laughter
Look
I shan't resist a moment longer your determination to
adore me
Look I said
Isn't every part immaculate the flaws even the essence
of perfection and marks of decline sites of my perfect history
I am incapable of love
A thing I now confess
A thing I hid even from myself
A thing I felt shame for
I am impervious
So worship
I have turned all that caused me pain into
A catalogue of qualities
Worship then (PIUS *reaches out a hand to touch*
her belly.)
PIUS: The hot blood pumping in her belly . . . the hiss of the uretha
. . . the womb turning in its blood . . . the thud of arteries . . . even
in the bus queue . . .
BEATRICE: You ceased to love God when you met me . . . (*She*
looks at BENZ, *who is staring at her.*) And you, when you did,
ceased to be Him . . . (*She suddenly covers herself.*)

Cover me!

Cover me! (BENZ *drapes her with his coat.*)

I was naked and it was possible

I was their idol (*She laughs, still on the spot.* BENZ *walks away.*)

PIUS: Do be careful he has a look. God's look. I know God's look, it's pained and spiteful.

BEATRICE: I know his look.

PIUS: Be careful!

BEATRICE: I said I know his look! (*She pulls on a skirt, a jumper.*) I have ceased to apologise. I have ceased to apologise even to myself. Can you imagine the freedom of that? (*She steps into her shoes.*) I am divine, therefore. Divine! (*She drags a brush through her hair, then ceases suddenly, fixed. The sound of a soul divided, excruciating, which stops.* BENZ *walks in with a* BABY's *shawl. He throws the shawl to her feet.* BEATRICE *knows the child is dead.*)

PIUS (*in an access of recollection*): Oh, she rode me so well, she rode me so skilfully, the hours were running beside us like lurchers at the carriage wheels, and her breasts hung, oh, hung, with the slightest motion like tapestries stirred so lightly by a breeze . . . !

BEATRICE *controls every emotion in her stillness, under* BENZ's *gaze.* BEKNOWN *walks in with a chair. She places the chair behind* BEATRICE, *who sits, crossing one leg over the other.* BEKNOWN *withdraws.* BEATRICE *takes out a cigarette, and lights it. Papers blow over the stage.* BENZ *cannot tolerate the power of* BEATRICE's *silence.*

BENZ (*pointing in the direction of his crime*): I —

I —

I — (*He is speechless.*)

BEATRICE: I am greater than you.

Lonelier and greater than you. (BENZ *falls at her feet, rocking to and fro on his knees.*)

THE SECOND PERCEPTION OF THE MARQUIS OF DREUX-BREZE

The distinguished philosophe LE NOUVEAU *is seated at a desk. Outside the window, drums and public excitement.* DREUX-BREZE *enters.*

D-BREZE: Save me!

LE NOUVEAU: I am writing a constitution.

D-BREZE: Save me, I said!

LE NOUVEAU: Why should I? How can I? Who are you?

D-BREZE: A man born into the wrong era.

LE NOUVEAU: The era is right. It is you who is wrong. Take a seat.

D-BREZE: I can't, I can't sit I am too excited.

LE NOUVEAU: The world is casting its skin. The world is washing its body.

D-BREZE: Yes —

LE NOUVEAU: With blood. What else could it be washed in?

D-BREZE: Yes to all you say. Now give me a passport.

LE NOUVEAU: Blood, and yet more blood. What do you want a passport for?

D-BREZE: I don't know. I am a marquis. I have never needed one. **The mob was this close to my neck ...!** (*For the first time, the* PHILOSOPHE *looks up.*)

LE NOUVEAU: The **mob**?

D-BREZE (*conceding*): The people in a state of moral excitement. (LE NOUVEAU *examines the young man.*)

LE NOUVEAU: What is your life to me?

D-BREZE: I am a landowner, an heir to fifty thousand acres and a Gentleman of the Royal Bedchamber. I have no call upon your pity. But I must have the piece of paper you call a passport. I am twenty-one. Look at me. I am perfect. It would be an offence to nature if a man as beautiful as me were killed through your indifference or antipathy.

LE NOUVEAU: You are a manifestation of arrogance and decrepitude —

D-BREZE: Yes —

LE NOUVEAU: Social reaction and mental rigidity —

D-BREZE: Yes —

LE NOUVEAU: And your death will weigh in history no more than a dead moth tips a scale! (*He goes to ring a bell on his desk.*)

ROME   271

D-BREZE: Ring the bell and you die. (*He takes out a pistol and points it at* LE NOUVEAU. *Pause.*)

LE NOUVEAU: I am too vital to the future to allow myself to die at the hands of a degenerate like you. The people would never forgive my pride.

D-BREZE: Quite so. (LE NOUVEAU *reaches into a drawer. He takes out a paper, dips his pen. He writes.*)

LE NOUVEAU: This may extend your life. It cannot save it.

D-BREZE: The extension will suffice.

LE NOUVEAU: This revolution is only the first. As cogs in wheels turn other wheels so freedom works engines in places you mistakenly regard as refuges **my ideas are machinery**. (*He flings down the paper.*) You will die in exile in a dirty room, and your death will be a misery to you, knowing your life contributed precisely nothing to the progress of human society **absurd man I will contact the frontier guards by telegraph**. (*Pause*)

D-BREZE: Telegraph?
              What's telegraph I hunt all day. (LE NOUVEAU *smiles.*)
              I said I hunt all day.

LE NOUVEAU: Oh, paradox . . .

D-BREZE: **Paradox, what's that?** (LE NOUVEAU *shakes his head with contempt. Pause.*) How you hate to be enforced. Get down on your knees.

LE NOUVEAU: Certainly not.

D-BREZE: Yes, you must, and ask God for forgiveness.

LE NOUVEAU: **God
              Me
              Ask
              God**

D-BREZE: You will because the people need your brain (*He cocks the pistol.*) You will because the progress of — what did you say — human what?
              Society requires it
              Don't hang about I'm impatient. (D-BREZE *thrusts the barrel at* LE NOUVEAU's *head.* LE NOUVEAU *collapses to the floor, kneeling.*)
              I have no arguments, and I am hated. I am not modern and I am absurd. I will die in a squalid room while the cogs of progress grind around me and the telegraph goes hiss hiss what is telegraph, is it steam? (*Pause, he snatches the paper off the table.*) Say sorry God.

LE NOUVEAU: There is no such thing.

272 *Howard Barker*

D-BREZE: He's not a thing He's a person, say it.

LE NOUVEAU: This is cruelty for its own sake and I —

D-BREZE: **What about my execution is that cruelty or not?**

LE NOUVEAU: No. How can justice be construed as cruel?

D-BREZE: To Nature, look at me! Cruelty to Nature to destroy the perfect body, look at me! (*Pause. LE NOUVEAU looks up.*)

LE NOUVEAU: Your body is not modern, either. The new body will be developed more about the thigh, and deeper-chested, obviously. (*Pause*)

D-BREZE: Deeper-chested?

LE NOUVEAU: To work the telegraph. (*A profound silence falls between them.* D-BREZE *lays down his gun on the desk. He leans against it, wearily.* LE NOUVEAU *is still. At last he climbs to his feet, and in a businesslike way, returns to his chair and continues writing.*) Hurry along, then. (*Pause*) Hurry along. (D-BREZE *leaves the room.*)

Scene Seven

The pillar of PARK. *Sounds of laughter and cruelty.* BEATRICE *enters. A* MAN *walks by, adjusting his clothing. He looks at* BEATRICE.

MAN: Some can take twenty.
  I've seen it.
  Or more.
  Which never fails to make me — (*He is lost for a word.*)

BEATRICE: Passionate . . . ? (*Pause. The* MAN *goes out.* SMITH *emerges, dishevelled, bruised. She leans against the pillar.* BEATRICE *looks at her.*) Is it bad luck, my lovely daughter? Is it luck merely? (*Pause*) Luck, or something else? (*Pause*) I put this exquisite garment on to walk the rubble in **I report it merely as a fact**

> **There is the fact**
> **And there is the emotion** (*She demonstrates.*)
> They come apart and in the gap's divinity.
> **I don't believe it's luck and nor do you**.
> Kiss me. (*They embrace.* PARK *gurgles from the top of the pillar.*)

SMITH (*ending the embrace*): The Interpretation of The Blind
Pope Also Dumb!

His words

My mouth

Rome he says is cleanliness not only of the

Body also of the eye

The clean eye seeks only horizons (PARK *gurgles louder,*
strangely.)

He sings! He sings!

I sing the Blind Pope Also Dumb! (*She sings.*)

Rome is to touch when touching is necessity

Rome is to sing when singing cannot be denied

Rome is to keep your heart in chastity

The refusal of apology

The proper place for pride!

SMITH *is exhausted by the effort of her song.* HOLLO *has entered*
and watches, with LASCAR.

SMITH: He sang that!

He sang that! (*They walk, like visitors to a shrine.* PARK
is beating a tin plate with a spoon. Hearing this, SMITH *goes to*
the pulleys and sends up a chamber pot.)

LASCAR: I must confess to some extent I do find you — both of
you — inspiring, but clinically it has been certified he has a
mental age of two —

SMITH: He says what he has always said —

LASCAR: And is incapable of formulating concepts, let alone dis-
tinguishing between —

SMITH: He is wholly and utterly consistent —

LASCAR (*betraying his temper*): **What's so wonderful about**
consistency! The oak tree bends to the prevailing wind, the
headland is shaped by the weather, all right? I've other meta-
phors, if you want some, why don't you leave him as a monument!

SMITH: A speaking monument.

LASCAR: He's not speaking, you are! (*The* DEVOTS, *a group of*
youths, enter, stooping.) Who are these? (*They bow to the pillar.*
Some kneel and pray.)

God help us, it's the young . . .

Oh, spare us the rubber enthusiasms of the adoles-
cent . . .

Their elasticity

Oh, dieu nous sauve les horreurs de jeunesse
I thought youth was full of sarcasm
Think it through, boys, think it through!

SMITH (*to the* DEVOTS): Under the earth, Rome! And they think they can bury it! Under the floorboards, Rome! And they think they can obliterate it! Under the disco music, Rome! And they think they can smother it!

HOLLO (*to* SMITH): I don't think you care one little bit for human happiness . . . I mean, ordinary loving love . . .

SMITH: They don't require love. And as for happiness, they do not know the word . . .

HOLLO (*bitterly, indicating* LASCAR): This man . . . this man is . . .

LASCAR: Don't, please —

HOLLO: This man — for all his —

LASCAR: No, no . . .

HOLLO: Yes! For all his — prevarication and his — compromises is — **a moral edifice.** (*He turns to* LASCAR.) I say you are. Stop trembling. (HOLLO *boldly extends a hand to* LASCAR, *who takes it. They go out hand in hand. The* DEVOTS *bow, and leave.* SMITH *calls to* PARK.)

SMITH: They bowed!
Oh, my master, they adored!
Their eyes were like a flight of steps to you!

A torrent of flowers and petals fall on PARK *and* SMITH. *BENZ enters, seeking* BEATRICE. *He sees her, bides his time.*

BENZ: I'm surprised to see you here. I thought you were **immune to the irrational.** Let me touch you ever so lightly, let me brush your hand with mine. I thought she won't go where the herd goes, no, I shan't stop pestering you, my body is a rack of pain to see you standing there and rubbing your ankle with your heel
Is that to torture me? It does. It does! (*She looks at him at last.*)

BEATRICE: So what it was a child so what
Forgive
What is there to forgive
One child among the teeming millions
One among the mountain of new flesh that every second heaves itself into the sultry air (*She clicks her fingers.*)
Another baby mountain!
Do you think I'll fold for that

ROME   275

Do you think I'll collapse like a stool?
Another one! (*Pause.* BENZ *looks deeply into her.*)
BENZ: Beatrice, you are greater than me. You are colder than me.
And even I am tired of giving pain, let us marry and — (*He
stops.*) Ha! You know my every move and can run rings around
my petty conspiracies. I love you, Beatrice, there is no tenderness
in you that I can injure . . . (*He goes close to her.*) How wonderful to suffer the indifference of a woman, there is no pain like it,
the ecstasy of her patronising smile and the knowledge when you
are gone she thinks nothing of you, **no fraction of her soul is
stained by your existence**, that's Heaven, surely? (BEATRICE
turns to go.) You really make me cruel and someone will have to
suffer! (*He shrugs. She goes out, passing* DOREEN, *who comes
in, poor.*) Old friend of melancholy memory, I am in a state, have
you a minute!
DOREEN: Given me a flat!
BENZ: I am uncommonly distraut, I don't mind telling you . . .
DOREEN: A flat with music that comes through gratings in the
floor.
BENZ: Who has?
DOREEN: The Barbarians! The flats they have erected!
Forests of flats!
BENZ: She lies to my face! How can she be what she pretends to
be? She is ill, surely, Beatrice? (DOREEN *removes a teacup from
her clothes and cleans it.*) What's in the cup?
DOREEN: My people.
BENZ: Your people? What people is that?
DOREEN: The Romans.
BENZ: Romans? In a cup? How's that? It's for putting tea in.
DOREEN: When the music starts, I look into the cup. You cannot
have the flat without the music. I gaze into the shape, I gaze into
the pattern, and I suffocate it. **I drown the music in the cup**.
(*Pause*)
BENZ: Show it to me. (*She shakes her head.*) Oh, come on, show
me. (*Again she refuses.*) Why on earth won't you —
DOREEN: I —
BENZ: Allow me to —
DOREEN: For one reason or another —
BENZ: Examine the thing? (*Pause*)
DOREEN: You would have to tear my arm out of its socket, Benz
. . . (*Pause. She smiles.*) And some people don't even have a cup!
No cup! Poor things, how do they know who they are? (*She goes
to the pillar and kneels along with others. A sound of ritual*

276   *Howard Barker*

*murmuring, which rises in volume and passion. It stops suddenly,
As* HOLLO *cries out from a bed).*

HOLLO: **Shut up, will yer?** (SMITH *addresses* PARK, *who
squeals faintly in the deep silence.*)

SMITH: Your picture hangs in the kitchens of appalling slums and
your words are scratched on walls by the illiterate.
   It must be time to descend therefore.
   They chant you in the midst of riots
   And in the infants' class they practise painting blind
   Time to descend surely?
   Some model you in wax and mount the effigies on poles,
whole buses quote you at the traffic lights and the police cover
their ears
   No question it's time to descend (*She laughs like a girl.*)
And we cleaned our teeth at night, passing the brush up, and
passing the brush down again . . . (*She shakes her head. At last*
PARK *stands, with difficulty. A rope ladder falls from his platform. He begins his descent, agonizingly. A wind blows. He
reaches the bottom. He stands, blindly peering one way and
another. Nothing moves.*) I speak the Blind Pope Also Dumb!
(*His hand flaps irritatedly.* SMITH *ceases. With an effort of
terrible will,* PARK *articulates.*)

PARK: **Kiss — me!** (*Pause.* SMITH *is frozen in disbelief.*)

SMITH: The Interpretation of His Thoughts! I speak the Blind
Pope also — (*Pause*)
   Kiss you?
   Where?
   The hand?
   The cheek?
   The immaculate blessing of supreme intelligence . . .

SMITH *walks to* PARK, *who seizes her in his arms and smothers
her mouth with his own. She falls. He covers her. The* DEVOTS
enter chanting their adoration.

DEVOTS: We seize his things
               Guard his clothes we know their worth
               His sandals
               And his vest
               We praise the hour of his birth
               And turn our faces to his mother's garden
               Where he lay ill in childhood!

ROME   277

SMITH *tears free of* PARK *and runs. A cope of stained and sordid ugliness descends on* PARK, *from which only his head emerges.*

Scene Eight

PIUS *lying on his cart, alone.*

PIUS: Death's endless. First blow to the optimists. Death's an ante-room, tell the tired old lady who aches for peace. Anterooms all the way! **I was the most perfect man of my time** and that's not difficult the competition was negligible **I boast I boast** the proof however yes the proof exists the proof is that I ceased to please when I ceased pleasing **I flourished I put forth leaves**
    True
    True
    Your scepticism is a passing shower
    And I fucked deeply
    Deeply yes
    Jeer on
    Howl on (SMITH *enters, immaculately clothed.*)
    I do not argue with the living
    Who are they?
    I am in the ante room (*She sits on a single chair. Pause.*)
SMITH: He put his tongue into my mouth. (*Pause*)
    I rinsed.
    I gargled. (*Pause*)
    And clambered me. (*Pause*)
    I bathed.
    I soaped every pore. (*Pause*)
    Perhaps his mind, like Rome, was open to the sky?
    And ugliness collected there like litter? (*She puts out an arm to* PIUS, *who takes her hand. Pause.*)
    So this leaves only me . . . !
    One only.
    Against Barbarity.

Pause. The giggling of THREE WOMEN *is heard. The* MARQUIS OF DREUX-BREZE *enters with female companions.*

THE THIRD PERCEPTION OF THE MARQUIS OF DREUX-BREZE

D-BREZE: My land!
Careful where you tread!
My land! (*Thunder rumbles.*)
Oh, and it rains! On my land! It rains when I have so recklessly drawn you to this point where the temple is as yet unbuilt! I have lured you to where shelter is no more than the whim of my architect! (*The* WOMEN *giggle.*) You daughters of modernity! You sprigs of the rising classes, I am hardly thirty but steeped in sexual invention! (*They squeal.*) Which is the solitary product of breeding! (*And squeal again.*) Breeding, yes! Forbidden word in the democracy! It's in the veins, my daughters of servility! The peasant does not know how to love and revolution made him **yet more incompetent!** You should know! (*They kiss him.*) And I assure you all, I promise you, I was never once **not once I shout it to the clouds** The victim of an idea, never! (*They kiss him again.*) Other than the idea I must **live**. Why live?
To give you pleasure! (*They laugh.*)
Sufficient reason surely. (*They cease laughing, suddenly afraid of him.*)
How hard you are, and they say I'm hard.
How callous and uncontemplative.
And they call me shallow.
When you touch a man it is
A bargain (*Pause. He shoots a laugh at them.*)
I must shut the gates and have the locks warped with blow torches, obviously. Because whilst it is true my nimbleness spared me the consequences of **enlightenment justice progress and equality** I find the process has seeped into such is its subtlety it has transfigured **love** (*He peels with laughter, the* WOMEN *also, less convinced.*) No, even the organ is disturbed and I shall never find my equal, yes, never find her, but for the moment you will do, you so soon to be married to **aspiring men** you sensibly despise. Undress or are you undressed already? (*They giggle.*) I have so much to teach you you can never learn, so much to impart you are impervious to, and yet you think me handsome, insane, provocative and handsome, take off your clothes or are they off already, the rain has made them cling as wet rose petals adhere to paving stones, and you are so coarse! Far from improving yourselves by scaling the social wall, you wore away whatever kindness possibly remained. I long for a

ROME 279

breast which has known pain! I shall be an inmate soon, I have all the characteristics of the inmate, such as surviving revolution, restoration and women of new classes such as you, I shall be the inmate of my own asylum and beat the windows while you walk your repulsive children to their school! (*They laugh*.) How terrible, nothing bewilders you, how sickening, you ask for nothing, I could tell you the key to the universe and it would not crack a single filament in the cabinet of your satisfactions, **if you cannot find your equal you must lie with less**, shh! Your bridegrooms are drunk with ardour, you all deserve each other, you are a mash of shallowness with your athletic bodies and gymnastic minds **why do you come to a lunatic for love?** (*The* WOMEN *roll him onto the ground, laughing, tumbling. His roars and their shrieks. A* SERVANT *enters with a tray and four glasses of Malmsey. He attends. They recover, finding their breath. The* MARQUIS, *first to his feet, gently embraces the* SERVANT.) They think your wig is comical. They think your livery is slavery. What do they know? (*They take the glasses, sip, staring in different directions*.) You will want me again. I shan't however require you. You will leave notes by the lodge gates. I shan't however, reply. (*He replaces his empty glass and starts to leave. Suddenly, he seems to collapse. He turns to them*.)

> My loved one!
> Hoi!
> My loved one!

Scene Nine

A dim light. PARK, *his head protruding from the great cope, is surrounded by sleeping* DEVOTS. BENZ *enters, looks at him.*

BENZ: I've been unlucky, falling for a woman who (*Pause*)
No, not unlucky. (*Pause*)
I sought her. And she is almost devoid of humanity. (*Pause. He walks*.)
By effort. By will. She is not unlike you in her single-mindedness and I must admit I do admire it, I — (PARK *emits terrible sounds*.) You're not listening. (*And again*.) No, you are more interested in your own pain than mine, and **so it always**

280   *Howard Barker*

**is with those who stagger to the altar what of my pain what
of the agony of God**. (*Pause*) All right, speak. (*Pause. PARK's
eyes swivel to BENZ, in disbelief.*) Speak! (*His mouth forms words.*)
PARK: I'm different . . . (*Pause*)
BENZ: Different? How different? And I came for a spot of consolation

> **How different
> I want to be different myself**.

PARK: Tell them . . .

> Disabuse them . . .

> **I love . . . !** (*Pause. BENZ looks at PARK with contempt.*)
BENZ: Oh, the fall of Rome . . .

> You are besotted with the blind and filthy servant of your
dynasty . . . (*He laughs.*)
PARK: **She's Rome!**
BENZ: In what way is she Rome? I had her up against the pillar
you may recollect yes me it was and not entirely contrary to her
instinct I suggest

> **Rome
> How
> Is
> She
> Rome?**

> No, this is preposterous, your brain is swimming in a soup
of adolescence, unspent desire running like a tide through the
dusty arches of a celibacy you now regret

> **Rome
> Her
> How?** (*He sits. Pause.*)

> I'm cruel. (*Pause*)

> It's expected of me.

> I am cruel and anyway she finds you repellent. (*Pause*)
PARK: Put love in her heart. (*Pause*) They transport me like a relic
and quote things from another age my words are out of context
and half the clauses are removed she has no pity for my solitude
put love in her heart, father . . . (BENZ *looks at* PARK, *pitifully.*
HOLLO *enters with a gun in his hand.*)
HOLLO: The dalmatians. And the lobelia. (*Pause*)

> Every morning, down the park with the dalmatians.

> Every evening, water the lobelia. (*Pause*)

> His pants and mine, dance on the line . . . (*Pause*)

> Happy for the first time since I was born and won't have
it buggered . . . (HOLLO *aims the gun at the head of* PARK.*)

ROME 281

BENZ (*to* PARK): Give you a voice, and you can plead. How's that? (BENZ *goes out.*)

HOLLO (*to* PARK): Goodbye, then. (HOLLO *pulls the trigger. It clicks impotently. He tries again.*)

      And forgive (*And again.*)

      A simple (*And again.* SMITH *comes in, elegant, in dark glasses. She holds out her hand. He yields to her.*)

SMITH: The safety catch is on

      You the killer who smothered your tunic with death badges has left the safety catch on (HOLLO *hangs his head.*)

      Oh, why are we so headlong propelled to throw off all things that lent us greatness? (*He shakes his head.*)

      You great and angry youth now stoop and crouch in corners of soiled intimacy . . .

HOLLO: We must let the past lie down . . . we must let the uniforms go to the moth and the Bibles to the worms, surely? (*The sleeping* DEVOTS *become upright as tulips around* HOLLO *and* PARK.) You use the dead to kill the living!

PARK (*in a voice of falsetto bathos*): My boy is — (*The* DEVOTS *laugh in staccato rhythm.*)

      My boy is — (*And again.*)

      Listen to my angry boy —

A noose swings idly over their heads. A silence falls. It glides to and fro. The light goes. SMITH *walks away.*

Scene Ten

SMITH: I put on this exquisite suit

      Old-fashioned but exquisite

      And all compliments I know to be sincere

      I tell by the tone

      The blind rely on this (*The boy* ISAAC *enters, stares at her.*)

ISAAC: I have a wife but she will not let me touch her.

SMITH (*stopping*): Is that so? She prefers to imagine, perhaps.

ISAAC: She does! But I must touch! Look how clean and spare my body is and I am wise beyond my years! May I touch you instead?

282   *Howard Barker*

SMITH: I am a cold and bitter woman.

ISAAC: Really? You can't tell that by looking . . .

SMITH: I shall grow old and sit in cafes. People will say, 'Look, there goes the last Roman, and her stockings are falling down!'

ISAAC: You might, but on the other hand —

SMITH: All right, undress me. (*Pause* ISAAC *walks to her, touches her.*)

ISAAC: I so love women.

SMITH: I can tell. (*He begins to unbutton her tight clothing.*)

ISAAC: It's true, I follow them.

SMITH: Do you? I'm often followed.

ISAAC: I'm not surprised! I should certainly want to follow you! And sometimes I steal their clothes.

SMITH: Why not?

ISAAC: You don't mind that?

SMITH: No, I admire that!

ISAAC: Really, you are so appreciative, and my fingers are all —

SMITH: Thumbs?

ISAAC: Yes, and I'm so excited I have hardly got the first —

SMITH: Am I not still enough?

ISAAC: Oh, yes, still as a —

SMITH: A tethered mare?

ISAAC: A tethered mare! Yes! Oh, I can't seem to —

SMITH: You are obviously impatient!

ISAAC: Impatient, yes!

SMITH: Me too. Perhaps I am too warm and sticky in my garments.

ISAAC: Possibly, but really it's the buttons that —

SMITH: Buttons?

ISAAC: So many buttons! I never saw a skirt that had so many buttons!

SMITH: It's true, these suits of the Roman era were not designed for —

ISAAC (*in a spasm of exasperation*): **I can't get you out of your clothes!** (*He hangs his hands. Pause.*)

SMITH: No . . . But perhaps I am not meant to come out of my clothes? (*He looks profoundly wretched.*) Oh, and you are such a beautiful boy! (*She holds out her arms.* ISAAC, *ashamed, walks away.* SMITH *refuses to lower her arms, defying the weariness of her limbs. She sobs with the effort.* BEATRICE *enters, looks at her daughter, whose arms at last fall to her sides. Pause. There is a chanting off stage.*)

ROME
283

DEVOTS (*off stage*): We sing the Blind Pope Also Dumb
We sing his words
Little
Bald
Geezer
On
A
Stick
His piss His snot His turds
Are
Holy! (*They repeat this as they enter.*)

FIRST DEVOT: The Four Principles of Rome!

SECOND DEVOT: Please, and in proper order

THIRD DEVOT: Lovely evening for a walk

DEVOTS (*in unison*): **Are Holy!** (*They wait.*)

SMITH: Tell them.

THIRD DEVOT: Tell them or

SECOND DEVOT: Lovely evening for a walk

SECOND DEVOT: **Little bald geezer on a stick!** (*Pause.* BEATRICE *denies them.*)

SMITH: Do tell because

FIRST DEVOT: Yes do

THIRD DEVOT: A walk

SECOND DEVOT: **Little bald geezer!** (*Pause*)

SMITH: She knows them obviously. (*Pause*)

Mother. (*Pause. In the silence, the body of* PIUS *passes, drifting through the scene on its handcart. The wind rises.*)

I want to be a girl again! I want my clean socks and my satchel! Put the slides in to my hair and say **learn everything!** (*Pause*)

While you went to the park and met your lovers . . .

Music of a Viennese waltz, rising in volume. Silence and darkness. A sudden light on the MARQUIS OF DREUX-BREZE.

D-BREZE: I do
I do detest
The inspirers of the young
They are so thin in the heart
The walls of their hearts
The floors of their hearts
So thin
You can hear your heels on the floors of their

Hearts
And the jokes
Drip from their mouths as a stabbed dog's blood gouts
on the paving (*The figure of* DOREEN *waddles onto the stage.*)

Scene Eleven

DOREEN *appears to have marched a long distance, and is under bundles. She stops.*

DOREEN: I was so flexible once. And now! I loathe it.
        I was so adaptable once. And now! I squirm.
        'Hullo,' I said, 'are you angry? So am I!'
        'Hullo,' I said, 'are you happy? So am I!'
        Thus I scuttled through a world. But now.
D-BREZE: No, well, that mutability must end. That accommodation, fuck it.
DOREEN: Warps the soul.
D-BREZE: Erodes it.
DOREEN: And I have such very dry bones.
D-BREZE: What do you keep in your drawers? (*Pause*)
        I ask
        Knowing full well
        This hiding place
        This nest of
DOREEN (*wails*): **Don't take my last and solitary** (*Stops*)
        It's beautiful and it belongs to everyone
        Unfortunately only I can be trusted with it
        I would rather show you my naked arse which
        I have never shown to another.
D-BREZE: I don't require your arse . . .
DOREEN: All right, you don't require it.
D-BREZE: Please, I hate to quarrel and I have killed in places much more populous than this my calmness is illusory.
DOREEN: All right — (*Pause*)
        A cup (*Pause*)
D-BREZE: Yes . . .
DOREEN: A cup and saucer . . .
D-BREZE: Thank you

ROME   285

Exactly as I expected!

DOREEN: **Rome had to be destroyed only then did they know what had been lost**

Too late obviously
Damn everybody
Damn you
And everybody
I'm not going any further do what you will

D-BREZE: And you thought there was a safe place
There you thought, no one will stoop to look
What do you know about life (BENZ *strolls in.*)
I said what does she —

DOREEN: Benz!

D-BREZE: Know about the —

DOREEN: This man is a murderer!

D-BREZE: Poverty of manners?
After all
They exist to be infringed . . . (*He bows to* BENZ.
Pause.)

DOREEN: Oh, God, you two are allies and I'm miles from any-where . . . (*She sits in a heap.*)

BENZ: My love is dead and did it to spite me. (*Pause*)

DOREEN: Oh . . . ?

BENZ: Beatrice whose arse was Heaven to the Pope is dead and without telling me. (*Pause*) Ungracious . . .

DOREEN: Oh . . .

BENZ: **Oh, yes, oh.**
Beatrice who stifled every hope and smothered indignation
Oh, yes, oh.
Who lived a life of prayer strange prayer **oh, yes, oh.**
(*Pause*)
I don't know if I'm sad or angry. If I am offended or distraut. **She could have saved herself with four words.** She knew the words, why didn't she **to injure me to make me stagger?**
I shan't find another
Shall I
Find another
Four little words of trifling significance
No
It isn't
Is it (*Pause*)
Human . . . ?

286   *Howard Barker*

D-BREZE: Do cry I often do my sobbing can be heard in the most
  unexpected places usually in the mornings or can't you?
DOREEN: He never has. To my knowledge. (BENZ *looks at them,*
  bewildered.)
BENZ: That's what you'd all like, isn't it . . . ?
       That would really be a
       Victory (D-BREZE *goes to* BENZ, *and puts his arms*
  around him. BENZ *weeps.*)
D-BREZE: It's you, isn't it, who longs to be human? (BENZ *tor-*
  rents in tears.)
             Oh, be careful!
             Be careful, God! (*He laughs loud and cruelly.* DOREEN
  reaches down into her clothes and extracts the tea cup. It rains.
  She flings the cup high in the air. Darkness. Gulls wheel and
  screech. Sea.)

Scene Twelve

A dawn light. ISAAC *hurries over the stage, gazing up, his hands*
extended. BEKNOWN *follows, a cape over her head against the*
rain, which ceases. He catches the cup in its descent. He examines
it. SMITH, *walking with a stick, enters, beneath an umbrella held*
by a GUARD. PARK *is wheeled behind by* DEVOTS.

SMITH: My mother, who believed nothing, fell among those who
  believed a few things. And she was so tired of pretending. I
  admire her.
ISAAC: A cup . . . a tea cup . . .
SMITH: I could have saved her, obviously. But I loved her.
ISAAC: A tea cup!
BEKNOWN (*going to* ISAAC): So it is. A tea cup.
SMITH: Everybody understands that in the severest test of love —
BEKNOWN: I carried this . . .
SMITH: To love is to allow.
BEKNOWN: On a tray. And it's chipped, look . . .
SMITH: Everybody go now! Scatter! Play! (ISAAC *goes out with*
  the DEVOTS.) How little pleasure we require. How little
  laughter. And they tell us, laugh and laugh. I am the most desir-
  able woman in the world and I have had no pleasure. As for

laughter, not once. **Not once.** (*She goes to* BEKNOWN.) You see,
the Barbarians cannot last . . .
BEKNOWN: He never abuses me.

He never ridicules our sex.

Or strikes me in a temper.

And when I have a child he will lift it from my womb
so skilfully (*Pause. She smiles.*)
SMITH/BEKNOWN: **Unbearable**

Or

Not?

BEKNOWN *hurries away.* SMITH *and* PARK *are alone. Sounds
of distant laughter. A cloud passes.* PARK *speaks, in a high-
pitched, falsetto voice.*

PARK: He lent me a voice.

Oh, listen

He lent me a voice . . . (SMITH *looks at him, at last. Slowly,
she begins to laugh. She shakes with laughter.* PARK *shakes his
head in despair.*)
SMITH: Oh, the malevolence . . . !

And I thought — for him — what can remain but death?
but no, malevolence breeds such imagination. (*Pause*)
PARK: Hear me.
SMITH: You have the voice of a child . . .
PARK: Hear me. And the words will wash away the mockery of
accents . . .
SMITH: **The voice of a child**

Great

Pontiff (*She goes close to him.*)

What? They mustn't hear you. Say what you must, but
swiftly.
PARK: Swiftly?
SMITH: Swiftly yes abbreviate your message and then return to
silence. (*The sounds of laughter and games. She waves to
others.*)
PARK: There is no culture without love . . . (SMITH *smiles, waves
again.*)
SMITH: You want me to take my clothes off . . . (*She waves. She
kneels.*) Oh, listen, I adored you. I ached for you in the marrow
of my bones, you scraped the crust of education off me, you
washed enlightenment away, I could not sleep for adoration,
I could not breathe so powerful were you and so superb so

288   *Howard Barker*

excellent with life he could plunge both his hands into a corpse
and lift the heart — (*Pause*)
                    I said he . . . (*Pause*)
                    He, I said . . . I called you he . . . ! (*Pause.*
PARK *extends a hand.*)
                    A boy loves me (*The hand remains extended.*)
                    This boy has loved me since he could think
                    His first thought was of love
                    Saw pictures of me on his father's roof
                    And in the atlas of anatomy
                    The ovaries
                    The kidneys
                    Were mine
                    By staring at the drawings he could make them
                                                         flush
                    With blood
                    My blood.
PARK: Rome
SMITH: What a love that is! Of course he's innocent in many ways
but innocence is — (*She takes his hand, smothers it with kisses.*)
PARK: Rome is wanting . . . (*She sobs, shudders.*)
          Wanting (LASCAR *enters, in an ill-fitting bronze-col-
oured suit.*)
          Wanting
LASCAR: You can't see this but I am wearing such an awful suit,
such a travesty and a mockery of a suit which he had tailored . . .
(*They are still.*)
          Love's a little bottle of fragrance rolling off a table top
Oi! My bottle's bust! (*He weeps*)
          Ridiculous suit he was so tasteless
          Love's the little corner of a drawer in which you poke
your treasures **Oi! My drawer's been plundered!** (*He shudders.*)
                    Two-toned indeed if only you could see it
                    It's worth having eyesight for the humour
                    And vest
                    Never washed it
                    Obviously (SMITH *climbs off her knees. Pause.*)
                    I can't forgive.
                    Nobody can I forgive. (*He smiles.*)
SMITH: Go away, now. The Barbarians will give you a caravan
with curtains in a field. And a little pension. Every morning, over
the stiles with your blue-veined legs, and your testicles will go

ROME

flop-flop, how smart he was in his papal suit the locals will recall
. . . Goodbye. Goodbye. (*She stares blindly at* LASCAR, *who
does not move. The sounds of laughter and games float over the
field.* PARK *sings in his strange voice.*)

PARK'S ANNIHILATION OF ABSURDITY

PARK: If I am infantile educate me
If I am impossible to love
Instruct me in the necessary qualities
Teach me the words

You are a modern woman
But I am now an ancient man
All I believed has lost significance
And time has left me
A rock
Of
Screaming
Birds

SMITH: Goodbye I said! (*She laughs, she draws aside her blouse.*)
This bra! Oh, isn't it pretty, this bra? Embroidered with flowers!
(LASCAR *goes to leave.* SMITH *locates him, detains him.*)
Look!
My body is a ruin. And people walk into it as if it were a
house!
Goodbye! (*He starts to leave.*)
Listen! (*She stops him.*)
Isn't it painful? The genius who masturbates? The gifted
who envy? The martyr who is vain? (*She releases him.*) Good-
bye! (LASCAR *goes at last.*) How grey my hair is. My hair-
dresser lies to my face. (*Pause. She is still. A parcel of pain. At
last she goes to move to* PARK, *but her stick strikes the cup, left
on the ground by* ISAAC. *She stops. She taps it again. It rings.
Suddenly the* DEVOTS, *with* ISAAC *and* BEKNOWN, *enter,
animatedly. Her stillness silences them.*)
I speak the Blind Pope Also Dumb
Take me to the water's edge
Abandon me to the incoming tide

> I fear nothing
> But my own divinity . . .

The sound of water on a beach. They do not move. Far away, BENZ is discovered, rolling up his trousers to paddle. The DEVOTS with ISAAC and BEKNOWN, wheel PARK towards the sea, and leave him at the water's edge. They play. BENZ paddles towards the abandoned figure of PARK, and pushes him slowly into the depths. ISAAC, bearing BEKNOWN on his shoulders, runs along the beach. They giggle and shriek. Silence returns. The water slops on the shingle. SMITH turns, feeling the fall of sunlight. She is perfectly alone.

UNCLE VANYA

Notes on the Necessity for a Version of Chekhov's *Uncle Vanya*

Chekhov's *Uncle Vanya* is a *danse macabre*. Its charm lies in its appeal to the death wish in ourselves. In its melancholy celebration of paralysis and spiritual vacuity it makes theatre an art of consolation, a funerary chant for unlived life.

By the power of his pity Chekhov subdues our innate sense of other life and innoculates us against the desire to become ourselves. Vanya, the greatest of his characterizations, is the apotheosis of self-denial. In this broken soul the audience is enabled to pity itself. It is necessary for our own spiritual health to know Vanya need not be Vanya.

We love Vanya, but it is a love born of contempt. It is Chekhov's bad faith to induce in his audience an adoration of the broken will. In this he invites us to collude in our own despair.

When we approach a great writer, we come naked, with a certain innocence and fear. We fear what subtle damage might be done to a carefully-constructed life. In Chekhov, this painful exposure is not satisfied by what might be experienced as an act of love. Rather he sends us away more than ever bound in our own clothes. And we are gratified, with the sick gratification that attends on a seduction which is abandoned. Is it not too much trouble to seduce?

It is necessary therefore to demonstrate the existence of will in a world where will is relegated to the comic or inept.

Chekhov's apologists argue his contempt is concentrated on a class, but we know that in diminishing the lives of a class he bleeds the will of his entire audience, making them collaborators in a cult of futility and impotence. Can the individual not burst the barriers of class and repudiate decay?

I remade Vanya because I loved his anger, which Chekhov allows to dissipate in toxic resentment. In doing this I denied the misery of the Chekhovian world, where love falters in self-loathing and desire is petulance.

In rescuing Vanya from resentment I lent him no solution, since there is no solution to a life. My Vanya is however, cleansed of bad blood, his actions liberated from the sterile calculations of the plea-sure-principle, and his will to self-creation triumphant over guilt. In making him anew, I seized on the single instrument Chekhov had, as it were, left lying idly in his own text. Vanya's quitting of the Chekhovian madhouse became a metaphor for the potential of art to point heroically, if blindly, to the open door . . .

CHARACTERS

SEREBRYAKOV   A Genius in Decay
HELENA   A Woman in Search of Experience
SONYA   A Spinster with Powerful Arms
VANYA   An Undefeated Man
MARYIA   A Widow Inclined to Forgive
ASTROV   A Conscience Without Power
TELYEGHIN   An Apologist for Himself
MARINA   A Discriminating Servant
CHEKHOVA Loved Dramatist

ACT ONE

Scene One

A MAN *appears.*

VANYA: Unc — le
   Van — ya (*Pause*)
   Unc — le
   Unc — le (*Pause*)
   Van — ya (*Pause. A guitar is strummed.*)
   Stop strumming stop that idle futile strumming you
   stop it.
   (*It ceases, then continues.*)
   I'll kill you
   I'll (*It ceases.* ASTROV *enters.*)
ASTROV: Man is endowed with reason and creative power so that
   he can enhance what he has been endowed with but up till now
   he has been destroying and not creating there are fewer and fewer
   forests the rivers are drying up the wild creatures are almost
   exterminated the climate is being ruined the land is becoming
   poorer and more hideous every day when I hear the rustling of
   the young saplings I planted with my own hands I (*Pause*)
VANYA: Unc — le
   Unc — le (*Pause*)
   Van — ya
ASTROV: I'm conscious of the fact that the climate is to some
   extent in my own power too and that if mankind is happy in a
   thousand years I will be responsible when I plant a little birch
   tree I. (*Pause. The guitar begins again.*)
VANYA: **Kill you I said** (*An old* SERVANT *crosses the stage.*)
MARINA: Shh . . .
VANYA: **Absolutely kill**
MARINA: Shh . . . (*She goes out. The guitar stops.*)
VANYA: I detest your futile and transparent attempts to suffocate

my hatred in what you call love what you call compassion what you call what you call your absurd maternal and anodyne endearments what you call what you call (*The music begins.*) **Who is that guitarist stop him**

ASTROV: Stop him yourself

VANYA: The very sound of life-loathing

Shuddup (*It ceases. A wind blows.*)

I have a gun. For so long now I have had a gun. This gun I clean most nights. I clean it with oil in the light of the moon. This is certainly the habit of an assasin.

ASTROV: Vanya

VANYA: Unc — le

Unc — le

Unc — le

Unc — le

Van — ya (*Pause*)

ASTROV: I think you should give me the gun.

VANYA: Never. But do go on. I detest your views but do go on. The trees and so on. I detest your selflessness your abnegation your love of unborn generations which is simply an excuse to avoid living yourself **I know all that's wrong the whole of it but** knowing is insufficient hence the uselessness of all criticism but but but **you hide in criticism like a little boy** whom murderers are seeking your caring your concern your (*The guitar begins.*)

All right

Telyeghin

You asked for it (*It ceases.*) is impotence admit it admit it why don't you

ASTROV: It is you who is impotent.

VANYA: It is me who is impotent and that is how I am able to recognize the condition in you.

ASTROV: So what if I were? If women loved men for the dimensions of their

VANYA: They do

ASTROV: The dimensions and mechanical reactions of

VANYA: They do

ASTROV: Their phallic

VANYA: **Precisely they do** (*Pause*)

ASTROV: I can't talk to you, Vanya, I really cannot talk

VANYA: You are so modern

So

Very

UNCLE VANYA   297

Painfully
And
Miserably
Modern (HELENA *enters.* VANYA *intercepts her.*)
It's true, confirm it, please.
HELENA: What?
VANYA: The phallus.
ASTROV: Oh . . . !
VANYA: Its energy is
ASTROV: Stop trying to exercise power by — (VANYA *lets out a long cry.*)
VANYA: I was
      I was
ASTROV: Bullying young women
VANYA: **Trying to take power I was I was** (MARINA *crosses the stage.*)
MARINA: Shh . . .
VANYA: I was
MARINA: Shh . . . (*She goes out.*)
VANYA: Because I love you.
HELENA: Love . . . !
VANYA: Yes, love. Love, yes. Love. Love. Why not love? That is the thing I mean, the word is certainly adequate, and though I dislike you I most cogently affirm love is what I mean and love is what I intend and no other synonym will suffice neither lust nor desire **Don't go out of the room I'm talking** (HELENA *stops.*)
HELENA: You are most exasperating and I must tell you I am not interested in you in that regard, so please
VANYA: **In this regard**
      In that regard
      In this regard
      In that regard
ASTROV: Vanya . . .
HELENA: On the other hand — (*She stops. The guitar is plucked.*) I don't know who I am interested in.
VANYA (*going to* HELENA): You will be interested in the man who forces you to be interested in him. (*Pause. The guitar stops.*)
HELENA: Yes.
      Obviously. (*Pause*)
ASTROV: You see the forests are diminishing at such a rate that
HELENA: My husband look.
      I

Young woman of perfect fecundity
My husband look.
Naked he is
Comes into my room at night and (*Pause*)
Into my room and (*An old* MAN *appears.*)

SEREBRYAKOV: I ache today.

HELENA: Yes.

SEREBRYAKOV: So much of me is aching.

HELENA: Yes.

SEREBRYAKOV: That only a little part of consciousness is left to me. Pain invades the little territory of self. The shrinking territory of self. Is anyone interested in pain?

VANYA: No. (*Pause*)
Well, are we? (*Pause*)
No! (MARYIA *enters, kisses* SEREBRYAKOV's *hand.*)
Oh God
My mother
Oh God
My utterly and incurably

HELENA: **Fucks me hard**

VANYA: Radical and progressive mother so full of life so full of vigour demonstrating with the workers paying the fines of anarchists and sewing banners her convictions are so (*He lets out a howl.*) She loves the primitive and disappearing tribesmen of the outer territories and thinks the weak are wonderful and on her blouse she wears the badges of the badges of so many badges (*And howls again.*)

MARYIA: Forgive me for saying so, Jean, but you have changed so much in the last year I positively don't recognize you —

VANYA: **I have a gun**

MARYIA: You were a man of positive convictions, an inspiring personality and now —

VANYA: **This gun**

ASTROV: Oh, shut up about your silly gun —

VANYA: **Was given me by Chekhov.** (*Pause*) And having given it to me, he was profoundly sorry . . . (*He sobs.* SONYA *enters.*)

SONYA: Why are you weeping? Uncle? (*She goes to him.*)
Uncle . . .
Uncle . . .
Vanya . . . (VANYA *spontaneously recovers.*)

Scene Two

VANYA: You love me.

You love to love me.

You love me more than anyone.

I am the so-loved.

I am your alibi.

I am your pretext for.

Pity runs from you like snot from the nose of a sick child

Or vagrant thawing over soup (SEREBRYAKOV *moans.*)

SEREBRYAKOV: Pain — is — invasion

VANYA: Do you agree the professor is vile or do I slander him am I correct or extreme **He goes to bed with such a young woman** am I poisoned by sexual jealousy or **He puts his flesh inside her body** or or or **And this success with women he enjoyed from infancy** yes **Infancy** my sister his first wife a beautiful woman of sky-blue innocence had more admirers than she could count and loved him with such **absolute** as for my mother she dotes on him and spent her perfect years in writing envelopes for his campaigns **These absurd campaigns** what happens in their bedroom and naked he must be naked imagine the collision of her white skin and the

SEREBRYAKOV: I dozed off just now and imagined my left leg didn't belong to me

HELENA: Shh . . .

SEREBRYAKOV: I am disgusting even to myself.

HELENA: Shh . . . (*The* SERVANT *crosses the stage.*)

MARINA: Shh . . . (*She goes out.*)

SEREBRYAKOV: You find me repulsive, admit it.

HELENA: If you wish me to.

SEREBRYAKOV: I wish you to.

HELENA: All right, I admit it.

SEREBRYAKOV: I am a monster of egotism and self-regard I am a savage of acquisitiveness and gratification but I deserve it aren't I talented aren't I rare?

MARYIA: You are talented. You are rare.

VANYA (*to* HELENA): You are in the room next to me. I can hear you breathe at night.

HELENA: Shh.

VANYA: **All this shhhing!**

Your empty thighs. I adore you. But are they empty? I am only forty-four and not dead yet

Not dead
Not dead
Yet.

MARYIA: Shh.

VANYA: These thighs I think of day and night.

HELENA: Really.

VANYA: Yes. And if I talk ridiculously it is the fault of your thighs. You make me talk gibberish but if I talked sensibly nothing would change either. Give me your underwear I will treasure it.

HELENA: Shh.

VANYA: **I am not a dog**.

HELENA: Everyone is so stupid, so utterly stupid.

VANYA: It is not stupid to want — no — to **crave** — your underwear, on the contrary is is you who are stupid to describe it so. It is yet another sign of your shallowness.

SONYA: I love the doctor. But could he love me?

VANYA: No. He also is too shallow to reciprocate your love. He has the appalling shallowness of the idealist whereas Helena at least is shallow in a thoroughly introspective way. Astrov's shallowness is that of the idealist with whom it is impossible to disagree. In your case it is better to pine than suffer the appalling bathos of fulfilment, believe me.

SONYA: Why should I believe you?

VANYA: No reason! I have spent a lifetime translating the professor's shallow books and consequently I know nothing but I do have these darts, these arrows of intuitive perception one of which is sticking in the doctor's heart and there is no blood, just ideas you cannot disagree with, trickling, trickling out (*He suddenly gasps.*) **I know Chekhov's fear! I know his terrible fear!**

SEREBRYAKOV: You are insane.

VANYA: Yes.

SEREBRYAKOV: I am ill and you are insane.

VANYA: Possibly.

ASTROV: The ignorant are dull and the educated are boring. That is my conclusion. Nanny, bring me a drink!

SONYA: Don't drink.

ASTROV: Don't drink? Why not?

SONYA: Because you are beautiful.

ASTROV: Am I? Am I beautiful? I think I could never love a human being. Though what does still affect me is beauty. I think if Helena wanted to, for example, she might turn my head . . .

UNCLE VANYA

VANYA: Fancy! Fancy, for all his terrible decline which is our fault, for all his tragic loss of hope, which is our fault, he could just — he might just manage —
To fuck Helena!
SONYA: Stop it, Uncle!
VANYA: Unc — le
Unc — le
Unc — le
Van — ya
I'm going in the garden I'm going in the garden the garden the garden fewer liars in the garden . . . (*He goes out.*)
SEREBRYAKOV: Mad.
HELENA: He asked me for my underwear!
ASTROV: Come to the plantation tomorrow. About two o'clock.
HELENA: I can't possibly.
ASTROV: I will wait for you.
HELENA: Out of the question.
ASTROV: Two o'clock.
HELENA: No.
Yes.
No.
SEREBRYAKOV: Meet him. See what he can do for you. And then tell me. (HELENA *looks at* SEREBRYAKOV.) Maryia, I must hold a meeting here tonight.
MARYIA: Whatever you say.
SEREBRYAKOV: I am not a practical man.
MARYIA: No.
SEREBRYAKOV: I am a man of the mind.
MARYIA: I have studied your mind. I have scoured your mind. I have stood in teeming rain beneath platforms in parks and squares listening to the treasures of your mind — spill . . . spill . . . fragile with concentration, the audience was like an egg, a single egg in your hand, and you made this egg vibrate with truth! What a truth teller! His shock of white hair fell across his brow, **Peace**, he said, **Peace is your**
ASTROV: Naked
Naked
Naked
VANYA (*entering with the gun loosely in his hand*): Oh, metal thing which moonlight clings to, which starlight occupies . . .
ASTROV: Put it away, Uncle . . .
VANYA: Listen, it is the lever of my life. **And Chekhov hated it!** (*Pause*)

302   *Howard Barker*

SONYA: Uncle . . . you are not . . . you are absolutely never to take
  your own life with that thing . . .
VANYA: Sonya, I haven't the courage to commit suicide.
ASTROV: Then what do you want it for?
VANYA: To coerce others with. What else? (*He examines it.*) It has
  a number on . . . (*He drifts out again.*)
SEREBRYAKOV: This meeting is to discuss the property and the
  management of my remaining years.
VANYA (*coming back in*): Let me be clear about one thing. The
  professor is not worse than other men. Not actually worse than
  others similarly endowed with greatness. It is true he has access to the body of a young woman to which he has no natural
  right, but what is a natural right? It's true this offends me, but so
  what? No, my offence is neither here nor there, what disgusts one
  about the great is the **and we will call him great I am happy to
  apply the term to him** is their **knowledge** of their greatness
  which is inescapable which is endemic to greatness itself, what
  use would modesty be to greatness, it would be absurd, offensive
  in itself, no it is the self-awareness that is unforgivable, whilst
  being simultaneously, inevitable. (*Pause*) The serial number is
  7786955797. (*Pause*) What meeting is this, anyway? **I don't
  think Chekhov is clean. Not clean.** (*He shoves the gun in his
  pocket.*) I'll put it away because whilst I want to coerce I cannot
  coerce and that is surely the worst condition that surely is the
  death of my soul, what meeting?
MARINA (*passing*): No one cares for the old!
SEREBRYAKOV: How true . . .
MARINA (*leaving*): No one pities the old!
VANYA: And how correct they are you would bend our backs if
  you could, no, this meeting, what is it? (*He pulls the gun out
  again.*) I haven't lived! Oh, I have not lived, I have annihilated
  the best years of my life!
ASTROV: Do stop waving that gun about!
HELENA: You should stop grumbling and reconcile people to one
  another, that's what you should do, there is so much petty emnity
  about and all you do is —
VANYA: Be quiet, you are idle and shallow.
HELENA: Yes, I am idle and I hate it. (*Pause*)
VANYA: No! No, you should be idle!
MARYIA: Oh, do stop offending everyone, it is so pitiful and —
SEREBRYAKOV: He can't help himself —
VANYA: She should be idle. Her terrible power is the product of
  her idleness. You know it as well as I do. Stay idle, for God's

UNCLE VANYA   303

sake. An idle woman has the ripe smell of unplucked fruit, please
be idle, refuse all labour, I beg you.

ASTROV: That is ridiculous — (*He moves the barrel of* VANYA's
gun, which is held loosely in his direction.) She could do such —

VANYA: Who is interested in what she could do? We are interested
in what she is. Let her be. Essence.

ASTROV: Rubbish.

VANYA: You would not want her if she were a whit less idle than
she is. Hypocrite. (*He looks at the gun.*) The handle is ivory, why
is that?

MARYIA: To beautify an evil purpose.

VANYA: It must be that!

ASTROV: Think of the elephants that die in order to —

HELENA: Yes!

ASTROV: Conceal with arabesques a monstrous design of human
barbarity. The weapon pretends not to be a weapon. Vile.

VANYA: Vile? It's human greatness, surely?

HELENA: It is sin.

VANYA: **It is not sin it's human. Humans sin. It is the essence
of their beauty**. I'm going out.

SONYA: Uncle Vanya will be happy one day, won't you Uncle,
happy one day?

VANYA: Unc — le
       Unc — le
       Unc — le
       Van — ya (*He stands, swaying for an inordinate length
of time, then goes out.*)

SEREBRYAKOV: I am an academic, bookish man and have never
had to do with practical life, and it is impossible for me to remain
living here, we are not made for the country life. On the other
hand —

SONYA: Papa, Uncle Vanya is not here —

SEREBRYAKOV: To live in town on the income we are receiving
from this estate is out of the question, therefore I propose —

SONYA: Papa, Uncle is not here —

MARYIA: Shh —

HELENA: Shh —

SEREBRYAKOV: We sell the estate and invest the capital in suitable securities, thereby raising four or five per cent, which will
enable us to buy a villa, say in Finland —

VANYA (*entering*): What was that?

SEREBRYAKOV: Finland —

VANYA: Finland? What about Finland?

304   *Howard Barker*

SONYA: Papa is selling the estate. (*A pause. A wind.*)
HELENA: The madman wants my underwear! (*A pause.*)
VANYA: Now wait a
          Wait a
          Wait
MARYIA: Shh —
VANYA: Wait because —
MARYIA: Don't contradict the professor —
VANYA: Because —
SONYA: Shh —
VANYA: **I have been running this estate for twenty-five years**
MARYIA: Don't shout.
VANYA: **Twenty-five** —
MARYIA: Don't —
VANYA: Mummy I am not shouting —
          Years
          Sending him money
          Reading his articles
HELENA (*rising to her feet*): I am not sitting here —
VANYA: **Quoting his pamphlets and**
HELENA: Listening to this —
VANYA: I could have been an architect, Helena! (*Pause. She looks at him.*) I have such a such a such a clever brain . . .
SEREBRYAKOV: You are a nonentity. (*Pause*) I have no wish to be offensive, but you are. (*Pause*) Isn't he?
SONYA (*through tears*): Please, Papa, Uncle Vanya and I are so unhappy . . .
MARINA: Shh!
SONYA (*opening her arms*): Nanny! (VANYA *drifts out. Pause.*)
SEREBRYAKOV: I was unkind.
MARYIA: He does provoke the most —
SEREBRYAKOV: I was unkind. (*Pause*) When you are famous, when you are in demand, how little you observe the pains of those who cluster at your feet . . .
MARYIA: You need not justify a single action. You have articulated the hope of all good people who —
SEREBRYAKOV: I'll talk to him. (*He gets up.*)
MARYIA: No need! No need! (*He goes out.*)
ASTROV (*to* HELENA): Come to my room.
HELENA: Which room is that?
ASTROV: You know perfectly well which room is — (*A shot. They are silent. Suddenly* SONYA *gets to her feet.*)
SONYA: Our paralysis is nothing more than the reflection of our

UNCLE VANYA

economic crisis the decline of rents and the aggressive style of capitalism in a backward economy we — (*Another shot. Pause.*) The rise of the proletariat and the exploitation of rural labour by — (*And another.*) Interest rates which — (*And another.*) **Stop! Stop!** (*Pause. At last* VANYA *enters, with the gun.*)

MARYIA: Who gave you that gun . . . ?

VANYA: Chekhov. Chekhov did. (*They stare at him.*)

SONYA: Uncle Vanya, what have you —

VANYA (*quietly*): Ivan.

SONYA: Have you hurt anyone, have you —

VANYA: Ivan. (*Pause*)

    Hatred.

    Hatred.

    How perfectly it guided me. (*Pause*) ASTROV *goes to move.*)

ASTROV: Oh, God, he's —

VANYA (*levelling the gun at* ASTROV): Don't go. (*He stops.*)

SONYA: Uncle, have you —

VANYA: Ivan. (*Pause*) The word uncle castrated me. I forbid the word.

SONYA (*defiantly*): You are my uncle and I'll — (VANYA *slaps* SONYA's *face. She reels.*)

MARYIA: Jean!

VANYA: No, that's French. And Vanya is diminutive.

    No more diminutives, or endearments, abbreviations or

    Things to hang yourself on

    Ivan is the name.

MARYIA: Oh, pathetic man, who thinks the act of violence will —

VANYA: Yes, violence is the door **Oh beautiful ivory gun of ivory my doorway my birthplace** (*To* HELENA.) Get undressed.

MARYIA/SONYA: Certainly not!

ASTROV: She will do no such thing you are out of your —

VANYA: It was not enough to kill him. I disfigured him as well. (HELENA *lets out a cry.*) See for yourself! (*Pause.* HELENA *starts to unbutton her dress.*)

ASTROV: No need for that —

MARYIA: Helena, no need to —

HELENA: No, I —

ASTROV: Please don't concede to his —

MARYIA: Quite unnecessary —

HELENA: What's nakedness anyway? It's only nakedness —

ASTROV: Please, I love you and —

306 *Howard Barker*

VANYA: Stop there. (*Pause*)

HELENA: Stop, but I've only just — (VANYA *silences her by a look*.)

VANYA: I am surrounded by such poor minds, such educated and poor minds. My mother and her causes, my sister and her modesty, the doctor and his forests, and this immaculate object whose very nothingness is her potential to inflame our minds, such thin dreams, and such an ache for pain **not too much pain however not tragedy** just an odour of deep-seated harmlessness, you all smell bad and **yet** . . . (*Pause*)

MARYIA: I hate you. You have murdered the greatest man of our time.

VANYA: Exuberance!

MARYIA: The hope of generations . . .

VANYA: Ebullience!

MARYIA: The voice of sanity . . .

VANYA: Ecstasy! And I am so calm. Have I, the eternal apologizer, ever been so calm? I am a lake among crags, dark, deep, and not toxic. Not toxic any more. Drink me. I'm sweet. (*Pause*)

HELENA: Serebryakov was . . . (*Pause*)

ASTROV: Shh . . .

HELENA: **I want to speak**. (*Pause*)

VANYA (*taking his own pulse*): My pulse is —

HELENA: **Want to speak**.

VANYA: Normal.

HELENA: A liar in some way. In his handling of my body.

ASTROV: Yes. Yes . . .

HELENA: A liar, yes. The hands lied. (ASTROV *nods seriously*.) They were skilful but —

ASTROV: I know what you're saying —

HELENA: **You don't know**. I must talk about his way of fucking —

MARYIA: Don't please, he's lying out there in a —

HELENA: They moved, his hands, like those of a priest at mass — that practised and swift covering of ground — so expert and —

MARYIA: Please,
　　　　 Please,
　　　　 Helena

HELENA: **And he was potent God he was for all his sixty-seven** (*She stops*.) Did you shoot him in the face?

VANYA: Yes.

UNCLE VANYA

HELENA: And I wanted him, am I lucid enough? I did. It made me shudder when he walked into my room naked and vaguely ugly yet he — (ASTROV *impetuously kisses* HELENA *on the mouth*.)

VANYA: The face yes, I obliterated it, I think because it was in his face the genius lay, I also had a face from which my character peered, this way and that, as if from curtained windows and afraid to walk the street, whereas he **walked out of his face like an industrialist, an emperor, a bridegroom!** No, not a bridegroom, they're afraid, no, **a pamphleteer on the morning of the revolution.** (ASTROV *parts from* HELENA's *mouth*.)

MARYIA: We must have geniuses, Jean, and swallow all their truths, Jean, and you want to substitute your temper for their truth, your envy for their —

VANYA: **Not envy.**
No
Not
Envy

The sound of the guitar is heard. Then it stops. There is a scream offstage. TELYEGHIN *enters, aghast.*

TELYEGHIN: I —
I —
I —

VANYA: Yes, I did it, shut up and sit down —

TELYEGHIN: I —
I — (*He points offstage.* VANYA *pushes him in the chest so he falls into a chair.* HELENA *bursts out laughing.*)

VANYA: My name is Ivan. That is how my father christened me. In that christening was hope, which every abbreviation chewed to dust . . . (*He turns to* TELYEGHIN.) Chekhov supplied the gun. I only used it.

HELENA (*to* ASTROV): I can't desire you. You want me to go into the homes of the poor and sacrifice my body in kind labour. Then you could say, how kind Helena is! How useful is her life! But would you want me? No. You suffocate your manliness in pity, I think you are dirty in some way and it comes off. (*She spits in her hands and rubs them together. She turns to* VANYA.) How long before you turn yourself in?

VANYA: Turn myself in?

HELENA: Yes. Saying God knows what came over me I was.
We drove each other to the brink etcetera.

308   *Howard Barker*

> How long?

ASTROV: Helena —

HELENA: Helena? You don't say it properly. (*She looks at* VANYA.) You must command me with your voice . . .

ASTROV (*defiantly*): I am going to the police — (VANYA *stops him with the gun. Pause.*) Nevertheless I am going to the police —

HELENA: Mikhail, you are ridiculous and he will shoot you.

ASTROV: He will not shoot me because —

VANYA: I will —

ASTROV: You will not because —

VANYA: **All right you asked for it** —

MARYIA: **Sit down, Mikhail!** (ASTROV *stops in his tracks. Pause. The figure of* SEREBRYAKOV *enters, with a hood, or bandaged face. He sits in a chair. He lights a cigarette.*)

SEREBRYAKOV: Chekhov says put the gun away before it leads to

VANYA: No

SEREBRYAKOV: More trouble and

VANYA: No

SEREBRYAKOV: Disturbs the fragile

VANYA: No
            No
            No

SEREBRYAKOV: Balance of characters and

VANYA: **He gave me the gun he supplied me with the means**

SEREBRYAKOV: He knows this perfectly well

VANYA: **He provided me**

SEREBRYAKOV: He profoundly regrets this

VANYA: **Does he now**

SEREBRYAKOV: Melodramatic interlude

VANYA: **Too bad too late too everything** (*Pause*)

HELENA: I loved old men. Old men excited me. I wanted them to handle me intimately in public places. Doorways, for example, in wet weather. Train corridors on sunny afternoons. Department stores among the furnishings. Say you understand me.

MARYIA: No one understands you!

HELENA: No one?
            No one?
            No one understands me?

SONYA: You see we are a dying class who cannot actually control our destiny because of the high level of inflation

VANYA: **Shut up**

UNCLE VANYA   309

SONYA: The marginalisation of the intelligentsia is
VANYA: **Sonya shut up**
ASTROV: Helena —
HELENA: No one says my name properly —
ASTROV (*bitterly*): **How do you want it said!** (*Pause*) You do not
   want to be respected, do you? Quite simply, you do not want to
   be respected, you are —
HELENA: **It is respect to be commanded**. (*Pause*) But you can't.
   (*Pause*)
SEREBRYAKOV: The problem with an action Chekhov says is
   that it leads to others
VANYA: I do not wish to know what he says
SEREBRYAKOV: Each action more ridiculous than the last
VANYA: So be it
SEREBRYAKOV: Ramifications of such outlandish character the
   perpitrator forfeits every sympathy
VANYA: **I don't require sympathy tell him**. (*Pause*) It is possible
   I am not human. I was comic and now I am inhuman. The comic,
   the pathetic, the impotence, made me lovable, but underneath I
   was not human. And nor is anyone. Underneath. Human. **Tell
   Chekhov!**
SEREBRYAKOV: He knows.
VANYA: Does he? He knows everything, then! (*He turns away.*)
   It is me Helena loves. I murdered her husband in pursuance of a
   theft. The theft was her. We have nothing in common but a certain
   brutality. But that is sufficient for love. Helena, I must see you
   naked. Here or elsewhere.
HELENA: If you insist.
ASTROV (*horrified*): **If he insists! If he insists!**
MARYIA: Poor Helena . . . Oh, poor Helena . . .
HELENA: It is you who is pitiful, Maryia Vassilievna.
MARYIA: Is it, why, my dear?
HELENA: Smothering all your aches in works, works, and more
   works. I anaesthetize nothing. The ache cries out.
MARYIA: What ache is this?
HELENA: My need cries out.
MARYIA: What need? What need? Aches and needs, what does
   she mean? Look for the truth in a man.
HELENA: The truth? **The truth in a man?** Oh, God spare me the
   truth in him, the terrible transparency that shows him thin and
   stooping, lying and banal. (*She turns to* VANYA.) I do under-
   stand! **I do so clearly understand!**
VANYA: What?

310   *Howard Barker*

HELENA: Why you required my underwear. (*Pause*) Worship it.
VANYA: I will.
HELENA: My relic. Treasure it.
VANYA: I will. Obviously, I will. (*She laughs, with delight, staring at* VANYA, *then stops, breathless. Pause.*)
ASTROV: We must protect ourselves from this. We really must protect ourselves — (*He goes to move.*)
SONYA: **You all adore her**
          Oh you all
          Crazed for her every one (*Pause. She indicates* VANYA.)
          I want this man
          My uncle
          Down the police station
          In the cells
          The prisoner transport
          All of it
          Rotting in a pit
          Chains and frostbite
          Cossacks' whips etcetera
       We could have lived at such a low, slow pulse like toads in winter waiting for God to lift us off the landscape (*Pause*) I do want you to suffer. Telyeghin, get down to the police post, my uncle yearns for his first interrogation. (*Pause*) I haven't been so animated for years! (*Pause*) It's hatred, isn't it? Animates me so? Telyeghin.
TELYEGHIN: I'm sorry, no.
SONYA: Do as you're told.
TELYEGHIN (*looking at* HELENA): She'll hit me.
SONYA: All right, I will. (*She gets up.*)
VANYA: Sonya, I will put a bullet in your back. (*She stops.*)
SONYA: Yes, I think you might. (*Pause*) This is a long way from knitting! (*Pause. She turns on* VANYA *and hugs him, laughing.*)
SEREBRYAKOV: Chekhov says — (SONYA *and* VANYA *turn and hug, round and round.*) Chekhov says —
SONYA: Iv — an!
          Iv — an Voi — nit — sky!
ASTROV: Don't call him Ivan, that's what he wants!
SEREBRYAKOV: Art is similar to medecine . . . (VANYA *turns on* ASTROV. *Pause. Then he tosses him the gun.* ASTROV *catches it. A void.*) But what sort of medecine?
VANYA: Mikhail, you drape your sensitivity like a dying cat hauls

UNCLE VANYA   311

its entrails over the floor. (ASTROV *holds the gun. Suddenly he sits, as if broken.*)

SEREBRYAKOV: We reverence him because
We reverence Chekhov
Because in such a confined space the melan-
choly of
Not tragedy
The melancholy of
Our unlived life is exquisitely redeemed
We are forgiven
We are forgiven
We
Do
So
Need
To
Be
Forgiven
Why
Is
That?

Pause. Suddenly, TELYEGHIN *begins to stamp his guitar into fragments, with the routine thoroughness of a farm-hand treading grapes. When it is reduced to splinters, he stops, a smile on his face.*

VANYA: I've saved you from dying.
Congratulate me, then!
Express your gratitude!

The sound of splintering wood and breaking glass. Part of the verandah slips. They freeze in terror. A wind is heard. Pause.

SONYA: It's Chekhov.
VANYA: Shut up.
SONYA: **It's Chekhov, Ivan, Chekhov wants to**
VANYA: Shut up, Sonya
SONYA: **Punish us** . . . ! (*Pause.* SEREBRYAKOV *laughs. Pause.*)
VANYA: Thirty minutes since the murder. Thirty minutes and no regrets . . . (*Pause*)
HELENA: I'll go upstairs. I'll lie down and you.
VANYA: No, don't lie down. (*Pause*)

312   *Howard Barker*

HELENA: Not lie down . . .? What, then?
VANYA: Stand up —
HELENA: Stand up, yes, and then —
VANYA: Wait —
HELENA: Wait, yes —
VANYA: Impatiently —
HELENA: Impatiently, yes, I adore you, Ivan Petrovich —
VANYA: I know you do —
HELENA: Not love — not love, but —
VANYA: Who cares what you call it?
HELENA: Who cares, yes!
VANYA: First, I am burying your husband —
HELENA: If you wish —
VANYA: Not deep, however —
HELENA: Not deep, no —
VANYA: Deep graves take time —
HELENA: And we —
VANYA: Lack time —
HELENA: Yes —
VANYA: So little time I cannot hope to wash my hands —
HELENA: No —
VANYA: But must come dirty-handed —
HELENA: Yes —
VANYA: Helena —
HELENA: Yes —
VANYA: Helena . . . (*The wind blows through the broken windows.*)
SONYA: And I
        And I (*She gets up as if inspired.*)
        You see, the world is sad! Sad, oh, very sad and this sadness is the precondition of all action not the end of it. This sadness is the climate of and not the prison of, the world. Sadness is not a shroud. It is not the end, but the beginning. (*She laughs.*) I lecture! I lecture you! (*She turns to* ASTROV.) I want a child and you must give it to me.
ASTROV: I —
SONYA: Now, yes. I love you, I always have loved you, and I insist.
ASTROV (*bewildered*): Give you a —
SONYA: Yes. I'm fertile. Give me one. (HELENA *bursts out laughing.*)
VANYA: Where are the shovels? (*He turns to go.*)
SONYA: I know you can do it, Mikhail Lvovich, you are poten-

UNCLE VANYA 313

tially magnificent, you possess all the ingredients of masculinity but in the wrong order, I will help you, it's only a matter of **Why shouldn't I have what I want?** (*Pause.* HELENA *goes to leave.*)

HELENA: Not deep ... Ivan ... (*She goes out.*)

SEREBRYAKOV: This is precisely the degeneration of the inevitable corruption of

VANYA (*to* MARYIA): Where are the shovels?

MARYIA: How should I know?

SEREBRYAKOV: Human decency that Chekhov anticipated once melancholy was usurped

VANYA: Telyeghin, get up and find a shovel!

TELYEGHIN: Yes! Yes, of course, Ivan Petrovich! (*He jumps up, goes out.*)

MARYIA (*to* VANYA): You've never dug a hole in your life.

VANYA: How you hate me ...

MARYIA: Hate you? You're my son!

VANYA: Hate me, yes. And always did. Hated me for being nothing, and hated me for being something. Hated and hated even while words of charity cascaded from your mouth. (*Pause*)

MARYIA: I don't know.
    I don't know, Ivan, I'll think about that

SONYA: These arms are very strong. I was born with strong arms. I did not know until today the reason for these strong arms, which often I have felt ashamed of, felt to be unwomanly or mishapen. I denied myself a proper love of my anatomy. But now it's clear! These arms were granted me — yes — I was **favoured** with these arms — to seize Mikhail Lvovich in a terrible embrace! (*She laughs.*)

ASTROV: For God's sake, Sonya —

SONYA: **Don't prevaricate**. (ASTROV *shakes his head at* MARYIA, *who shrugs, wearily.*)

MARYIA: You will make him hate you, Sonya, which can't be what you —

SONYA: **It is what I intend**. (*Pause*)

MARYIA: I don't understand ... I don't understand! (TELYEGHIN *enters with a shovel.*)

TELYEGHIN: I'll dig! (*Pause*)

VANYA: All right, dig. (TELYEGHIN *goes out and begins on the ground outside the windows.*)

SONYA: You see, what is terrible, what is unforgiveable, what is **pure toxin** is — resentment, isn't it? And we all — oh, we all **resented everything!** (*Pause*) Which was comic. Which was

314 *Howard Barker*

pitiful. Which was utterly demeaning and hateful of mankind **Get your clothes off, Mikhail**.

ASTROV: Certainly not.

TELYEGHIN (*calling*): This ground is hard as iron, Ivan . . . !

SONYA: Or I will take them off.

ASTROV: This is so outrageous . . . !

SONYA: Isn't it?

ASTROV: And you are a bully! One day you are a Christian and the next day a bully, **stay away from me, Sonya!** (*He aims the pistol clumsily, then, seeing himself, tosses it away, stands up in frustration.*) **This is so —**

TELYEGHIN: Ivan — (VANYA *is watching* SONYA *and* ASTROV *with fascination.*)
　　　　Ivan — (*Pause*)

ASTROV: You — (*Pause*)
　　　　There is — (*Pause*
　　　　I must admit something in you —

SONYA: Quick, then, before Chekhov comes —

ASTROV: That I — had never — (*Pause*)
　　　　A child . . . (*Pause*)
　　　　Yes!

A sudden sound of further collapse, both masonry and splintering wood. TELYEGHIN *ducks. This shock is followed by a surge of sound as waves break and flow with the appearance of the sea.* TELYEGHIN *points, in dumb astonishment, to the spectacle.*

MARYIA: Oh, look, a view!

SONYA: The sea!

VANYA: **The sea! The sea!** (*They gawp, rejoice.*) Chekhov won't come now . . .

MARINA (*entering*): The tea urn's gone! Look, the tea urn's in the sea! (*They laugh.* MARINA *picks up random small objects and pelts the urn.* SONYA *joins her.*)

SONYA: Got it!

MARINA: No, that was me!

SONYA: Sorry!

MARINA (*throwing again*): Got it!

SEREBRYAKOV: Chekhov knows the brevity of pleasure
　　　　　　　　The insubstantiality of

MARYIA: **I'm paddling!**
　　　　Anyone?
　　　　I'm paddling! (*She rolls up her skirts. She sees*

UNCLE VANYA   315

VANYA *throw off his jacket and go upstairs to* HELENA. *She hesitates.*) My son is going upstairs. To fuck. With a woman whose husband he has killed. Naked him And naked her. (*She turns, inspired.*)

Look at the waves! (*She skips out to bathe in the sea.*)

SEREBRYAKOV: All euphoria he knows to be merely the prelude
All ecstasy the mere preparation for
Inevitable

MARINA (*throwing an ash tray*): Got it!

SONYA: It's sinking! The tea urn's sinking, nanny!

MARINA: I am not your nanny. (SONYA *looks at her.*)

SONYA: No. (*She laughs.*) No, you're not!

SEREBRYAKOV: Inevitable

Solitude

SONYA: You were. And now. You're not. (*She laughs.* TELYEGHIN *comes in, throwing down his spade. He goes to* ASTROV.)

TELYEGHIN: Mikhail Lvovich, we are not within a thousand miles of sea . . . (ASTROV *ignores him. He turns to* MARINA.) Marina, can you explain —

MARINA: Be quiet, you are a bore — (SONYA *laughs.*) He is! He is a bore! (*She goes out.*)

SONYA: If you don't believe it, stand in it.

TELYEGHIN: It isn't that I don't believe it, it's that — no, I don't believe it, I — I'm sorry, Sonya Alexandrovna, I —

SONYA: **Listen, you will let Chekhov in.** (*Pause*)

TELYEGHIN: I wasn't intending to —

SONYA: If you let Chekhov in it's silence and the ticking of the clock — do you understand me — it's your guitar, it's emptiness and infertility, **do you want that!**

TELYEGHIN: No —

SONYA: I am fertile and I will not be robbed! You are not to abort me, do you understand, Telyeghin . . . ! (*He stares at her, appalled.*)

TELYEGHIN: Abort? I wouldn't abort a — abort? All I want is —

SONYA (*to* VANYA, *who enters*): Ivan —

TELYEGHIN (*seeing* VANYA, *going to him*): Excuse me, Ivan Petrovich, the sea is not there, is it? Not really there?

SONYA: Ivan, I want you to tie up Telyeghin.

TELYEGHIN: **Tie me up, what for!**

SONYA: Please, it is crucial Telyeghin is tied up and gagged.

TELYEGHIN: **Gagged!**

SONYA: Yes.

MARINA: I'll do it.

316   *Howard Barker*

TELYEGHIN: **Please, I am only asking for a** — (*He appeals to* VANYA, *who goes to a chair and sits.*)

VANYA: Let us talk about impotence. (*Pause. The sea washes.* SEREBRYAKOV *chuckles.*)

Yes.

Let us talk about this thing. (SEREBRYAKOV *chuckles more.*)

Yes

We mustn't be afraid of it because (SEREBRYAKOV *stops.*)

It is a god. I declare it to be. A god. (*Pause*)

A god who brings you to the very rim of the world and shows you — for those with eyes to see — such an expanse of clear, translucent light. It is transfiguration. (*He gets up.*) Listen, he who refuses shame becomes a master **I did not let Chekhov kill my pride I did not let his fingers throttle my desire** (*A sound of a new born child is heard.*) Tie him up if you want to, listen, listen I never wanted a single thing, one thing, more in my life than the nakedness of Helena and she also had me in her arteries, **I inhabited Helena** I was the skin under her skin I was the tenant of her brain and backbone and she undid her clothes not me she Astrov would have burned whole forests to have witnessed it —

ASTROV: Yes —

VANYA: Wonderful, he confesses —

ASTROV: Yes —

VANYA: Whole wards of patients could expire of neglect —

ASTROV: Oh, yes!

VANYA: Wonderful, he admits it — undid her clothes and I — (*A pause.* HELENA *enters. She takes* VANYA's *hand in hers, squeezes it powerfully, then wanders out towards the sea. Pause.*) It's true, I experienced the beginnings of a profound horror. A howling night which came down on my eyes and she was by no means charitable **thank God Helena is not charitable**

not
one
word
of
comfort

And in the wilderness I came to myself. I met myself. Between such wanting and such failing was — (*Pause*) Truth . . . (*Suddenly, with passion.*) I don't like the word, either! I scorn it

UNCLE VANYA 317

I assure you! (*He laughs.*) Truth! What's that? And I left the room.

ASTROV: I must talk with Helena . . .

SONYA: Why?

ASTROV: Where is she? (*He calls.*) Helena!

SONYA: Why must you?

VANYA: He thinks he is my rival. He thinks to compensate her with his ever-ready flesh, **I have no rival**. He thinks she aches for his prosthesis, **it's me she wants**. (ASTROV *goes out.*) I will kill Astrov. His superficiality enrages me.

SONYA (*looking after* ASTROV): Yes . . .

VANYA (*going to* SONYA): Sonya, I triumphed. I did not submit. I turned shame inside out and silenced his contempt. The laughter died in Chekhov's mouth . . .

SONYA: Yes . . .

VANYA: **I smothered him**.

SONYA: Yes . . . (*She kisses him.*)

TELYEGHIN: Don't tie me up. Ivan Petrovich. Please. If you say the sea's outside the door, then I'll . . .

VANYA (*taking him by the shoulders*): Walk in it. Go on, walk in it . . . (*He propels* TELYEGHIN *out of the room and returns.* MARYIA *comes in, her clothes wet from the waves. She looks at* SONYA, *then at* VANYA.)

MARYIA: If the sea is there . . . we can . . .

VANYA: Sail on it?

MARYIA: Yes.

SEREBRYAKOV: This
                       Pathos
                       Of

VANYA: Sail where, however?

SEREBRYAKOV: This
                       Formless
                       Urgency

MARYIA: I don't know where but

VANYA: Exactly

SEREBRYAKOV: Undirected
                       Aspiration
                       For

VANYA: **Here**

SEREBRYAKOV: Meaningless
                       Mobility

VANYA: **And only here can we be free** (*Pause*) You must look without wanting. You must see without trying.

MARYIA: But it exists, therefore . . .

VANYA: It is a mirror on which you will discover only more of yourself. Self and more self. This self you must attend to and not attempt to evade by flight. There! I have advised you. Look at the sea by all means, but you will achieve precisely nothing by trying to cross it. You have so little time. You are old and Chekhov lies in wait for you. You more than anyone, perhaps . . . (ASTROV *enters. He hesitates in the doorway.*) Mikhail! You have the appearance of a man who thinks he might have sinned! (ASTROV *ignores* VANYA. *He sits.*) And this would haunt you. This would certainly make you tremble in your reed-bed of a soul . . . (*Pause. He looks at* ASTROV.) A breeze is blowing through the reed-bed of Mikhail's soul . . . I hear it . . . listen . . . flutter, rustle, crackle **what have you done to Helena you bigot?** (ASTROV *leans forward on his knees, weeping.*) You see? One act leads to another, everything is a consequence of everything else, like puppies pouring from the belly of a bitch, the room is filled with births — (MARYIA *goes to assist* ASTROV.) **Don't comfort him!** (*Pause*)

MARYIA: Ivan
      I think you are
      Ivan
      As you call yourself
      I think you are

VANYA: Yes —

MARYIA: The most —

SONYA (*to* ASTROV): Get up.

VANYA: Yes, I am —

SONYA: Get up, I said —

VANYA: Implacably unkind and heartless man . . .

MARYIA (*holding* VANYA): Save yourself! Save yourself dear Jean, it is not too late! (HELENA *enters. She stands in the doorway.* MARYIA *abandons* VANYA. *Pause.*) What do you expect? All this. What do you expect? This. Nakedness and so on. No, I don't mean nakedness I also love nakedness I always have the wind the air **I mean the throwing down of things** to go to bed with a man yes but **freedom is a place somewhere between desire and** I was the first to be naked believe me the first but **every impulse cannot be every urge just licensed** oh yes very very naked and to look at me you might not think it why shouldn't I reveal since everyone is yes **with all sorts** but never painful never hurtful never did I trespass on the rights of others freedom is the point of balance surely **nights of passion yes but**

UNCLE VANYA

violation I . . . (*She dries.*) I have not been happy . . . (*She closes her eyes.*) Why? Why? (ASTROV *stands up, and turns to go, as if with a decision. Spontaneously,* SONYA *takes him round the neck, forcing him back on his heels.*)

HELENA: The worst thing in a man . . .
No . . .
The only bad thing . . .
Is apology . . . (*She turns defiantly to* MARYIA.)
Did you find that?

TELYEGHIN (*entering*): It's true, Ivan Petrovich, the water is — (*He sees* SONYA *is asphyxiating* ASTROV.) Maryia —

MARYIA: Shh.

TELYEGHIN: Maryia Vassilievna —

MARYIA: Shh I said —

TELYEGHIN: Vanya — Vanya — she —

VANYA: I'm not Vanya —

TELYEGHIN: Ivan, then — (SONYA *is lowering the dying* ASTROV *to the floor.*) **Someone!** (*He is fixed.* SONYA *stands upright.*)

SONYA: There will be some who will say this act — this deed — was motivated by a spinsterish frustration. But I saw Chekhov there. Hovering. Always, he hovers. Of course I shall be misjudged. One lives always in the horror of misjudgement, but so what? Chekhov was looming. We are like boats on the pleasure pond, rather poorly steered and sometimes we must take the boat hook and prod! Prod! Chekhov was near and I prodded him away! (*She smiles.*) These arms! These arms are made for prodding obviously, and I thought they were made for love!

MARYIA: What arms! I never knew a woman with such arms . . . !

SONYA: We are all given what we require, Maryia Vassilievna. It is merely a matter of locating the requirement, isn't it? (*She looks down.*) Poor Mikhail. And he did want to die! Oh, he so wanted to die! And when death came he did not resist me. He would have preferred Helena to —

HELENA: No — no —

SONYA: Much preferred it, yes! But frankly — (*She smiles.*)

HELENA: I haven't the arms . . .

SONYA: You haven't the arms, no. (*Pause, then with childish glee.*) I shall talk about Mikhail all the time now! I shall be such a bore! Mikhail this and Mikhail that! Oh, on and on until I die! I pity all of you! There will be this person Astrov and he will be a saint, a myth, a martyr! He will be a marrow, a balloon pumped up at a fair, pumped and pumped into extravagance! The inflation of the dead! That was my finest moment and it's all downhill from now!

VANYA: And now there is no doctor. Now, the community must endure all its pains. No wheedling, no whimpering, 'Doctor, doctor, prolong my melancholy life, lend me another summer!' How they pleaded, and how he hated them. But also, how ashamed he felt. Ashamed for hating them. No wonder he wished to die . . . (SONYA *suddenly cries*.) Yes, weep! Do weep!

SONYA: I don't know why I'm —

VANYA: You must weep! Weep, and look him in the eyes!

MARYIA: No, that is —

VANYA: Look at your deed, Sonya —

MARYIA: That is morbid and obscene —

VANYA (*turning on her*): Is it morbid to stare death in the face? How tiring you are with your celebrations, your festivals and your street affairs! No, we must stand alone with Death, look at it and say — say — (*He hesitates.*)

SEREBRYAKOV: Pain
    And
       Civility

VANYA (*moving away from* SONYA): I don't know, I don't know, but that's because —

SEREBRYAKOV: Pain because we do not act . . .

VANYA: Because we are — still at the beginning!

MARYIA: The beginning! Two deaths and that's the beginning?

SEREBRYAKOV: And Civility because we do not act . . .

SONYA (*recovering*): Who knows! Perhaps you should die!

MARYIA: Me!

SONYA: You sit there and you — perch there and —

MARYIA: Me?

SEREBRYAKOV: Pain
    And
       Civility

SONYA: Yes! Why not you? Do you think age lends you immunity? If you knew how I detested your maturity and sense, your experience and your sound conclusions —

MARYIA: I was not happy! I have said how unhappy I have been, Sonya!

SONYA: **Much deserved unhappiness I say**

MARYIA: That is so — so very — (MARINA *enters*.) Marina! Mikhail is dead! (MARINA *looks at the dead man*.)

UNCLE VANYA   321

MARINA: Now, that's peculiar because only this morning he said to me, 'Nanny,' — he called me nanny —

TELYEGHIN: Everybody did —

MARINA: Everybody did at one time, yes — 'Nanny, how long have we known one another?' Eleven years I said. He must have known he was about to die . . . (*She goes out.*)

MARYIA: He — he — (*Pause*) What? (*She looks to* VANYA.) Was there an accident?

TELYEGHIN (*getting up*): **Acci — dent?**

MARYIA: A fall, was it . . . ? (*She drifts out.*)

TELYEGHIN: **Acci — dent** . . . ! (*Pause*)

SONYA: Telyeghin, what is the matter with you?

TELYEGHIN: With me? The matter with me? First there is is a sea which is not there and now there is a murder which is called an — (*Pause*) Where is my guitar? (*Pause. His shoulders heave.*) Oh, where is my guitar . . . ?

VANYA: You trod on it. (*Pause. He looks around, red-eyed.*)

SONYA: Telyeghin . . .

TELYEGHIN: Yes . . . ?

SONYA: The gag. Remember the gag. (*Pause.*)

TELYEGHIN: I wish to say.

        Come what may.

        I have to state. (*Pause*)

        How profoundly I regret

        My spontaneity . . . (*Pause, he sits.*)

        Now, do what you will. (SONYA *laughs loudly.*)

        Yes . . .

SONYA: You have all the arrogance of the incurably feeble, Telyeghin. **Who wants to do anything to you?**

HELENA: Do you not think we should bury him? I am all for looking Death in the face but not for days on end and there are shovels there.

SONYA: Yes! Wonderful Helena! Yes! But not you! No, you —

HELENA: I want to dig.

SONYA: Ivan, she is not to dig, is she? I am the digger. I have the arms. Marina, help me carry Mikhail Lvovich to the beach —

HELENA: Why can't I dig?

SONYA: **Because he's mine**. (*Pause.* HELENA *looks at her.*)

HELENA: Yes.

        And digging would —

SONYA: Spoil your hands. (*Pause*) It would. And I believe in your hands. I believe your hands should not be soiled. No sarcasm. No wit. They should be perfect. They should be the merest —

suggestion — of your body, lying like pale flowers, yes, I do mean this. (*Pause*) Marina! (MARYIA, MARINA *and* SONYA *remove the body of* ASTROV.)

SEREBRYAKOV: Civility he thought hung between desire and the act, but culture —

TELYEGHIN (*standing*): You've forgotten the gun — (*They ignore him.*) Ivan Petrovich — The gun . . . (*He points to the gun lying on the floor which has slipped from* ASTROV's *pocket.*)

VANYA: You have the gun, Telyeghin. (*Pause*)

TELYEGHIN: Me? Don't you want the gun?

VANYA: I've used the gun. I no longer require the gun. Whereas perhaps you do? (*Pause.* TELYEGHIN *goes gingerly to the weapon and picks it up. It weighs heavy. He looks at it. Slowly. He walks out.*)

SEREBRYAKOV: Culture

       Culture (ASTROV *returns as a corpse, like* SEREBRYAKOV, *and takes a position.*)

       He had no theory of

HELENA: You are so beautiful, I would not care if I died. (*Pause*) You are so perfect to me I am afraid to know you better. (*Pause*) I am fixed between wanting you and dreading you. (*Pause, then with despair.*) I am artificial, Ivan! Are you?

VANYA: Yes. (*Pause*)

HELENA: Thank God.

VANYA: I am the creation of my own will, Helena. And possibly entirely false. And yet this falseness is —

ASTROV: Give us Chekhov

      Give us

      Give us

      Chekhov

      Who helps us to die

VANYA: **Quite unashamed, Helena** (*He smiles.*) What do I care if he violated you! Did he? It's nothing to me, on the contrary, it is another aspect of your intangible perfection yes, it is a further — did he do it — element of your distinction and even — yes — a peculiar contribution to your innocence —

      How

      Where

      Naked or not

      Standing or

      And a testimony to your

      Obviously it failed

      Describe it to me

UNCLE VANYA

HELENA: No

VANYA: Yes

HELENA: I can't

VANYA: Who knows what detail might unlock the gates of your appalling history to me

HELENA: **How can I describe it**

VANYA: What insignificant gesture will

HELENA: **I can't I said** (*Pause*)

VANYA: Lodge in my imagination and shake my doors all hours of the night? (*Pause*) All that befalls you, Helena, is enhancement. **You know that and so do I.** (*Pause*)

HELENA: Am I clean?

VANYA: Yes.

HELENA: Infinitely clean?

VANYA: Yes. (*Pause. Distant cries on the beach.*)

HELENA: He abused me —

VANYA: Obviously —

HELENA: And this abuse was —

VANYA: Mundane —

HELENA: Mundane, yes, but —

VANYA: Vehement —

HELENA: Vehement, yes, and his face!

VANYA: A mask of anger —

HELENA: Anger, yes, and I said —

VANYA: Pleaded —

HELENA: I think so — pleading — yes, I suppose it was a plea but —

VANYA: Shh! (*He walks a little, sits, and putting his hands to his face, appears to think. The sea. The cries. After a long time, HELENA begins to laugh. VANYA also, before standing and confronting her.*) **And pregnant!**

HELENA: Yes!

VANYA: Obviously, yes! (*They stare at one another.*) I will be merciless to you.

HELENA: And I

       Merciless to you, Ivan (MARYIA *hurries in, windswept.*)

MARYIA: Come and see this boat! (*They are oblivious to her.*) This boat is (*And still.*) Don't you want to see this boat? (VANYA *turns to her.*) A man is drowning . . .

SONYA (*hurrying in*): It tacks one way, then the other, but it can't possibly survive, do witness this, Ivan!

MARYIA: We think the man can't swim, but even if he could —

324   *Howard Barker*

SONYA: The sea is so —

MARYIA: Even the swimmers drown . . . (VANYA *looks at her.*)

VANYA: We must guard our lives. Having made our lives, we must
be on guard for them. We must stand guard over our creations.

MARYIA: Yes . . .

VANYA: Let him drown, therefore.
Mother.
Can you do that?
Watch?
Just watch? (*Pause*)

MARYIA: My instinct — my whole instinct is to —

VANYA: No, that is not your instinct. (*Pause*)

MARYIA: Isn't it?

VANYA: No. You no longer know the difference between your
instinct and your culture. It is your culture that impels you to
rescue someone who might perhaps, who knows, be your worst
enemy. (*Pause*)

SONYA: Ivan is correct but (*Pause*) I need a man. (*Pause*) Perhaps
this is a man whom I might love. A poet. Or a fisherman. **No not
a poet who wants a poet** no, it is a fisherman who as he staggers
up the beach I shall embrace, I shall crush him in a consuming
love! (*She looks at her arms.*) These arms have killed but they
might also shield . . . in them a child might hide as a city hides
inside a wall. I already love him!

MARYIA (*decisively*): I have to save him! I have to and you are
wrong! (SONYA *hurries out.*)

VANYA: Wrong?

MARYIA: Wrong, yes. (*She shrugs her shoulders.*) Wrong (*She
goes out.*)

HELENA (*watching her depart*): Your mother will drown, won't
she?

VANYA: It would be entirely appropriate, a fit ending to her life.
(*He goes to the doorway, watching her.*) Goodness excited her.
It's true. Serebryakov made her throb with his politics. His utopias.
She trembled in her bowels. (*Pause. Cries of the* WOMEN *on
the beach.*) She can perhaps conceive of no better death than
perishing for a stranger. Who this stranger is, his complete worth-
lessness, perhaps, is irrelevant to her . . . (*He is seized by a
thought. He turns.*)
I know who it is!
I know
I know who it is! (*He rushes about.*)
The gun! Who has the gun! Look for the gun!

UNCLE VANYA

HELENA: Telyeghin had the —
VANYA: **Telyeghin!**
HELENA: Ivan — who is it —
VANYA: **Telyeghin!**
HELENA: **Who is it I said.** (VANYA *stares at her.*)
ASTROV: Man is beautiful but under what conditions the play
    asks under what circumstances can we let our whole hearts flow
    only in despair the play says and I agree (*Pause.* TELYEGHIN
    *sits up from behind the furniture. An unpleasant smile crosses his
    face.*)
TELYEGHIN: Hidden it. (*He laughs.*)
                 Hidden it and not telling!
                 (*He covers his face in terror.*)
                 Not telling even if you
                 Torture me
                 Castrate me
                 Hang me from a tree
MARYIA (*off*): He's alive!
SONYA: Alive! (*Joyous laughter.* MARYIA *appears in the door
    way, sodden, flushed.* MARINA *enters, looks.*)
MARYIA: Marina! He's alive! (*She opens her arms to* MARINA.
    MARINA *slaps her brutally across the face.*)

ACT TWO

All the characters are standing in a row. Their heads hang like penitents. They are motionless. CHEKHOV, a figure in a crumpled, stained suit, is walking up and down towelling his hair vigorously. He stops, stares at VANYA.

CHEKHOV: Uncle

Uncle *(Pause)*

Uncle Vanya! *(He laughs, towels again, tosses the towel aside, reaches for a packet of cigarettes, extracts it from his soddened pocket, looks at it.)*

I must stop smoking.

I must stop and as if to influence me in this wisdom the sea has spoiled the packet

The compensations of severe exposure *(He tosses the packet to MARINA.)*

Dry them out I may smoke them later *(He laughs at himself.)*

MARINA: I won't.

CHEKHOV: You're a servant, aren't you? Do as you're told.

MARINA: No. *(She is rigid. CHEKHOV walks around, stops.)*

CHEKHOV: Uncle

Uncle

Uncle Vanya

TELYEGHIN: I nearly died! They nearly killed me! She especially, wanted to castrate me and tread on my eyes!

CHEKHOV: Shh . . .

TELYEGHIN: Sonya, little Sonya Alexandrovna, who would have believed?

CHEKHOV: Shh . . .

SEREBRYAKOV: We know what a play is but what is an author?

UNCLE VANYA   327

                    The author also sins
                    The author is not very clean
                    Is he clean
                    I often wonder
ASTROV: His impeccable authority I must say I
SEREBRYAKOV: His infallibility sometimes strikes me as
CHEKHOV: The sea!
                    Certainly it was rough!
                    And certainly I was in danger of my life! The foam,
    as it were, reached out for me! This impatient foam required my
    body for its satisfaction! I enraged it by continuing to exist! (*He
    laughs.*) But I am inextinguishable, it seems. I am beyond the
    reach of temper or of climate, and like a cork still bobs in quiet
    bays long after ships have foundered, I endure, why, what is it
    gives me this — (VANYA *lets out a profound sob. His shoulders
    heave.*) this — perpetuity? Clearly, I am necessary. In me, there
    lies a terrible significance. Don't think I exaggerate or indulge!
    I am the least indulgent of men but.
HELENA (*to* VANYA): Don't. Don't sob.
CHEKHOV: But it is as well to know these things about yourself.
    It is pitiful to shelter behind disavowals and pandering hu-
    milities, no, it is obvious even to those who do not care to heed
    me, even they must admit my — religiosity (*His hands goes to
    his pocket, stops.*) Look, reaching for cigarettes again! That is
    how poor my discipline is! That is the extent of my convictions!
    But I have been ill. I, the doctor, have been ill . . .
HELENA: Voinitsky is my lover
                    Ivan Voinitsky is my lover
                    Stop sobbing
                    Him and I
MARINA: Good girl!
HELENA: Naked
MARINA: Tell him!
HELENA: Half naked
MARINA: Yes!
HELENA: In the street and out of it
MARINA: I love you, you bitch!
HELENA: His hand in the very heart of me
                    His hand
                    In
                    My
                    Heart!
MARINA: Yes

328   *Howard Barker*

> My
> Mistress
> I
> Long to serve a
> **Bitch like you!** (*She laughs. Pause.* CHEKHOV *walks*
up and down.*)
CHEKHOV: Uncle,
> Uncle,
> You are in luck.
TELYEGHIN: They go on like that all the time it sickens you they
can't keep their fingers out of one another's clothes —
CHEKHOV: Shh . . .
TELYEGHIN: It's true —
MARINA: Shut up —
TELYEGHIN: You know it's true —
MARINA: **You couldn't keep your own wife, Waffles!** (*Pause*)
TELYEGHIN: So what? I loved her. Even when she abandoned
me, I loved her. I still love her. **That is love**. Love, and no returns
. . . (*He smiles, shrugs.*)
CHEKHOV: You see, I don't know which of you is the more
comic
> **And I love to laugh**
> **Oh, to laugh delights me**
> The strenuous or the spineless both of whom in the
last resort appear equally absurd both of whom are smitten with
self-adulation, both of whom are posturing and yet so frail I
could
> I almost could
> **Embrace you**
> Vanya of you I am particularly fond
VANYA: I am not fond of you
CHEKHOV: You fill me with laughter
VANYA: Do I.
CHEKHOV: A laughter which is without malice or contempt, a
laughter such as the moon might laugh at the homeward journey
of a drunken man . . .
VANYA: I would rather kill myself than —
CHEKHOV: Shh . . .
VANYA: Live one hour as —
CHEKHOV: Shh . . .
MARINA: **Don't shush him you — you** — (CHEKHOV *laughs*
at MARINA's *vehemence.*)
VANYA: This self-defiling man —

UNCLE VANYA

MARINA: **You** — (*She shakes her head in frustration.*) **creeping priest!**

VANYA: Called Vanya!

CHEKHOV: I do love a mutiny!

MARINA: **And I like priests, but not the creeping sort!**

CHEKHOV: A mutiny is merely the affirmation of things after all, isn't it, Helena? Helena knows a mutiny is only a despairing love . . .

HELENA: I want to say

Without temper

If possible without the least sense of the heroic

Without even that measured ambition to speak the truth

which is only another vulgarity

To say

I am not what I was

Indeed

I was nothing and now I am at least a possibility of

something

And this

I will defend (MARINA *claps.* MARYIA *follows suit, even* TELYEGHIN.) No, you see, you have — you've spoiled it — you have encrusted it with virtue . . . (*She shakes her head bitterly.*) You will drive the sea away . . . !

SONYA (*to* CHEKHOV): Go away, now, you have seen what hope she has, you can see the frail and precious hope she — (*Pause*) You're smiling . . . (*She turns to the others.*) He's smiling . . . !

ASTROV: The theatre is a contract

SEREBRYAKOV: Between the living and the dead

ASTROV: The dead inform the living of their fate

SEREBRYAKOV: A requirement

ASTROV: A necessity

ASTROV/SEREBRYAKOV: **Chekhov**

How

Tolerant

You

Are

SEREBRYAKOV: He makes it possible for us to forgive ourselves the crime (*Silence*)

CHEKHOV: I have a disease . . .

SEREBRYAKOV: Of self-murder

CHEKHOV: Listen . . .

SEREBRYAKOV: Self-betrayal

CHEKHOV: I have a disease . . .

ASTROV: And self-disgust . . .

VANYA (*as if clinging to a rock*): **I am a murderer**.

CHEKHOV (*standing*): Yes, so you are . . .

VANYA: **Serebryakov has no face**

CHEKHOV: Yes . . .

VANYA: **No face and I**

CHEKHOV: You did it, yes —

VANYA: **Do you know how hard it is to be a murderer?** (*Pause. CHEKHOV looks at him with contempt.*)

CHEKHOV: Vanya, I have such a withering knowledge of your soul. Its poverty. Its pitiful dimensions. It is smaller than an aspirin which fizzes in a glass . . .

VANYA: I don't give in . . .

CHEKHOV: An innocuous fizz audible only to those who place their ears against the rim . . . (*Pause*)

VANYA: I don't give in . . .

CHEKHOV: **Oh, Ivan, Ivan, your resilience, your adamantine naughtiness!** (*He laughs at his own wit.*)

VANYA: What do you think murder is, a hobby!

HELENA: Shh!

VANYA: He thinks it is a hobby!

HELENA: Ivan —

VANYA: It is an act of profound psychological and philosophical significance! (*Pause. CHEKHOV smiles.*)

HELENA: Ivan, he is making you infantile. Please don't go on.

VANYA: I lost my temper.

HELENA: I know. And that is his aperture. It is the open skylight to your soul. It is the hole in your perfection by which he enters in.

VANYA: Yes —

HELENA: And burgles you. And makes a shambles of your self — your hard won self —

VANYA: Yes —

HELENA: You are magnificent and you can't be spoiled. (*She turns to* CHEKHOV.) **We are not spoiled**.

MARYIA (*bitterly*): Bravo, Helena! Everybody loves Helena! Helena is the epitome etcetera the pinnacle etcetera and the apotheosis of! What a wonderful girl! What a magnificently fecund female and her depths are pure red so hot and red and she never lifted her voice for the oppressed not one syllable or lost a second's sleep for another's pain. Magnificence! And yet she has a soul, she does, she has a soul you cannot diminish Helena, can you? Obviously I hate her but you cannot — (*Pause*) **I want to die I cannot tolerate another hour of myself this self squatting**

UNCLE VANYA   331

like a bear on my brain . . . (CHEKHOV *goes to her, and un-buttons her dress at the breast. He exposes her breasts. Others watch* . . .)

CHEKHOV: Her breasts . . . are not without their power . . . like birds in an abandoned nest . . . they shan't be — and that's the beauty of it — shan't ever be touched . . . and if they were . . . how swiftly they would rise and fill like — they shan't however, **shan't be, shan't be** . . . ! (MARYIA *nods, weeping*.)

SONYA: You are — vile . . .

CHEKHOV (*turning on her*): Do you want to lose your beauty? Do you want to forfeit your perfect neglect — for that? (*He indicates* VANYA, *then* MARYIA *again*.) Look at her, she is in such immaculate **solitude** . . .

VANYA: Please cover my mother's breasts . . .

CHEKHOV: She does not want to be covered.

VANYA: Mother, will you —

MARYIA: **I do not wish to be covered**.

HELENA (*to* CHEKHOV): You are evil. Not vile. Not common vileness, evil!

MARYIA: You would say that to a god!

CHEKHOV: She calls me a god!

MARYIA: You are! You are a god!

CHEKHOV (*shrugging*): How can I refuse a compliment of such — oh, look, and I reached for a cigarette! There! Even I responded to a compliment with modesty! The cigarette was intended to cloak my embarassment! I am human, after all! (VANYA *goes towards* MARYIA.) **Don't touch her, you imposter!** (*He laughs, then proceeds to button* MARYIA.) I sometimes bully. I sometimes throw my weight about. And Helena's right. I'm evil. I don't like the word, it is too theological for my — (*Pause*) No. It is the word. My crimes are, after all much worse than Ivan's, Ivan who thinks murder is serious, who sports his murder as a badge, who hangs his life from a hook, **Ivan who is fundamentally inert.** (*He turns to* HELENA.) It is preposterous you love this man, a woman with such thudding veins should cling to **Ivan** such flooding such pulsing in her belly **Ivan of all people** isn't he a fumbler in women's wardrobes?

HELENA: Yes

CHEKHOV: There are things even I do not understand **and impotent at that** really it is so unclean I could laugh, I do laugh, I resort to laughter when I am deepest in offence, listen I am dying I have come here to die . . . (*Pause*)

ASTROV: Chekhov, how he draws a line across the world.

332　　　　　　　　　　*Howard Barker*

> How kneeling to the earth with chalk
> He comforts our horror of distances
> **Stop**
> **Stop** (*A flood of music.* MARINA *sings.*)

MARINA: The pain of ambition is the proof of my existence give me the impossible to do . . . ! (*The music stops. She laughs in the silence, shaking her head. Pause*)

CHEKHOV: Will someone sit with me? (*Pause*) Ivan . . . (*Pause*) Preferably . . .

VANYA: Me? But you hate me.

CHEKHOV: Yes. (*Pause*)

VANYA: How can I refuse, I —

HELENA: Of course you can refuse. (*Pause*)

VANYA: Yes.

> I can refuse.
> **I can refuse**
> However, I —

HELENA: **I don't advise it.**

CHEKHOV: Helena, you are the best thing ever made. How wonderfully you deny the little traps of charity! To be loved by you! Oh, to be loved by you! To be your child! How hard your hawk-eye scans the land for treachery!

HELENA: Yes.

> I want this man.
> Undamaged.

CHEKHOV: I promise him. How's that? (*Pause.* HELENA *leaves swiftly.* MARINA, SONYA, MARYIA *follow.* TELYEGHIN, *hangs back.* ASTROV *and* SEREBRYAKOV *laugh, suddenly, voraciously, and are silent.*)

TELYEGHIN: I put the gun — (CHEKHOV *waves a hand dismissively.*) I mention it because it's possible he may — by accident — (CHEKHOV *dismisses him again*) stumble on it and —

CHEKHOV: The gun was always an error. The gun was always false . . . (TELYEGHIN *bows and withdraws. Pause.*) As Vanya knows.

VANYA: I disagree —

CHEKHOV: You disagree but —

VANYA: I merely state — my differing opinion —

CHEKHOV: Yes —

VANYA: On the subject of the gun —

CHEKHOV: Yes —

VANYA (*suddenly and defiantly*): 7786955797! (CHEKHOV *looks at him.*) The serial number. (*Pause*)

UNCLE VANYA   333

CHEKHOV: It's odd — and this was itself the certain proof of the
extent of my disease — its fatal dimensions — that I have lost
the will to argue, and even, dear though it was to me, to castigate.
Even as I began those cruel sentences I felt — more is required,
you are not sufficiently — enraged. It was as if I knew that what
I said, whilst being true, whilst being impeccably and incon-
trovertibly true, was still not fit to be articulated, as if it was an
effort greater than life itself could justify . . . do you know this
state, Ivan . . . ? (*Pause*)

VANYA: Yes.
No.
Well, sometimes we all —

CHEKHOV: You are trying to protect yourself against me! (*He
laughs.*) Understandably, you are anxious to be on guard
against infection, for as I have explained, I am dying of a disease, and no man willingly exposes himself to a disease. I am
talking of a truth so absolute, so ponderous, that even to enun-
ciate its laws would command more energy than we possess. It would, I honestly believe, kill us with the exhaustion
of articulating it, and though it is proximate enough, though it
is manifest enough — like some meteoric relic protruding
from the soil — it is far better left undisturbed. I am tired. I am
tired even thinking of the labour, and in any case, who hears?
Who hears, Ivan? (VANYA *shrugs.*) To grapple with this truth
is fatal, obviously, so why do I persist? Why should I attempt to
lift this inert mass upon my fragile shoulders? It's fatal, as
you say.

VANYA: Did I say . . . ?

CHEKHOV: Fatal, and whilst there is a certain heroism in it, heroism for whom? I am not moved by the common man, I do not
love everywhere. That commandment I ruptured early on. I have
no faith, Ivan, which perhaps enables me to die, don't flinch from
me — you flinched like a child who cannot read the intentions
of a stranger —

VANYA: Did I flinch?

CHEKHOV: You flinched to be loved — you flinched to be drawn
into the agony of another man, I do understand that! I do sym-
pathize with that, I also never trusted the extended hand, you are
on guard against me all the time —

VANYA: I am, yes! I admit it!

CHEKHOV: One day I hoped I would reach out and tell myself,
pour myself like a liquid from a jug into the void of another, all,
entire, to the last drop, how I struggled with this dream to pour

334 *Howard Barker*

myself into another man! A woman! To be drained . . . ! (*Pause. There are sounds on the beach of voices.*) And in abandoning that dream, I found something like freedom. In discarding all that was arguably, the best in me, I found a peace of sorts. We are entirely untransferable. So hold my hand . . . Ivan . . . (VANYA *extends a hand to* CHEKHOV, *who holds it.* CHEKHOV *dies.* TELYEGHIN *hurries in.*)

TELYEGHIN: The sea's gone!

             The sea's gone or to put it another way —

VANYA: Shut up —

TELYEGHIN: It was never there! (MARINA, TELYEGHIN *and* HELENA *enter, distraut.*)

HELENA: The sea —

MARINA: The sea's not there!

VANYA: All right, it's no longer there! (TELYEGHIN *squeals with laughter.* HELENA *stares at* VANYA. SONYA *enters, looks about her, goes to a chair, sits.*)

SONYA: You see, the rural gentry . . .

           In its imagination, even . . .

           Was constrained by economic impotence . . .

           It could not even dream. (*Pause*)

HELENA: Ivan, you are holding his hand . . .

SONYA: They talk of liberty but what is this word?

           Is this word not devoid of meaning if.

HELENA: Ivan . . .

SONYA: If consciousness itself is not crushed by the weight of social failure? It is a paste jewel surely?

HELENA: Shut up.

SONYA: A **paste jewel** . . . !

VANYA: Chekhov's dead . . .

MARYIA (*entering*): Marina, I think we all need a cup of tea . . . (*Without demurring,* MARINA *turns to go.*)

VANYA: **Chekhov's dead!** (*They all look at him. Suddenly, in a gesture of profound ugliness, he lets go* CHEKHOV's *hand, which falls.* MARINA *turns.*)

MARINA: Where's the samovar?

MARYIA: The samovar?

SONYA: You see, only with social transformation can imagination be — can life be — and until then all we can do is — work for this — postponing all and —

MARINA/MARYIA (*laughing*): **It's on the beach!** (MARINA *points at the damaged tea urn.*)

MARYIA (*springing up*): Help me pull it in, Marina! (*They go to*

UNCLE VANYA 335

it.) It's full of sand . . . ! (MARYIA *and* MARINA *begin beating it to loosen the sand, giggling all the while.*)

HELENA: Ivan . . .

Ivan . . . (*The sound of a guitar is heard, badly played.*) **We are not the same as we were.** (TELYEGHIN *holds up the guitar, which is undamaged.*)

TELYEGHIN: Look! (*He shows it, sits, begins a tune. The guitar, the beating of the urn.*)

HELENA: I said we are not the same as we were . . . (VANYA *does not look at her.*) If you betray me, I will kill you. I have the right to kill you. You don't dispute that right, do you?

VANYA: Not in the least . . .

TELYEGHIN (*seeing her expose the gun*): There it is! Where did I leave it, Helena Lienochka?

HELENA: You are making me, who was so malleable, coercive! You are making me, who willed nothing, adamantine and imperative! **So be it. So be it.** (*Pause. She sways.*) And not desirable. No longer desirable. **So be it.** I must admit I'm spoiled for some. Are you Ivan, or are you not? Oh, are you Ivan or — (*An effect of light and sound. A monstrous mirror descends, in which HELENA sees herself. She giggles.*)

336   *Howard Barker*

ACT THREE

In the darkness, HELENA's *laughter, different in tone. The light
shows her sitting on a chair in front of the mirror watching herself.
The other characters are sprawled lifelessly around the stage like
the remnants of a party.* HELENA *is dressed in underthings. A few
notes trickle from* TELYEGHIN's *guitar. A silence.*

HELENA: I'm thinner. (*Pause*) I'm thinner or is it only the glass?
   Some glass does that some glass has the propensity to narrow or
   to broaden the **how good is this glass Ivan how** you can be
   starved in one and bloated in another **where's it from I mean**
   the Venetians they make lovely glass but small chance this is
   from Venice surely I have lost weight but so what so what I prefer
   it I like to be a kite a basket of thin but pliant bones on which
   my skin translucently stretches etcetera you are pretty thin yourself thin and white the wonderful whiteness of your flesh it is a
   sign of your religion your skin is the white cope of an archbishop
   walk in my palace stride through my aisles an energetic archbishop obviously. (*She laughs. A silence. The guitar's three
   notes.*) I am talking about beauty. **Does anybody mind I know
   how uncomfortable you get** beauty does upset you beauty does
   irritate your nerves it is so very **undemocratic beauty** it is an
   unforgivable thing **I have it however so** and all things lead to
   my body what else is there but my body **all things lead to it**
   including physics mathematics linguistics **where else could they
   lead** psychology hygiene and weapons training **ask the student
   on the train who seems consumed by numbers** where his efforts lead my body is the end of thought the terminus of ration-
   ality and instinct both my husband thought that but he couldn't
   say it it depressed him it humiliated him but not you surely **I am
   the point and purpose of the world** which dared to announce

UNCLE VANYA 337

itself and that surely is **sin** is it, is it sin? (*She turns to look at* VANYA, *who is standing watching her with his hands in his coat pockets.*) It's sin, I think, to state the obvious . . . (VANYA *makes a move towards her.*) **Don't touch.** (*He stops.*) This thinness of mine. I am a rack of bones from which swords might be made. Did you know the body was a resource for instruments, the ribs for needles and the shoulder blades, what are they for, axes probably **I am a lethal object** careful you might cut your fingers and bleed from a caress. How is your sickness today? (*Pause.* VANYA *walks a few paces, stops, is about to speak.*) I do hate that attitude. (*Pause.* VANYA *looks up, querying her.*) I mean that gesture. Those few steps, the shoulders the half-turn and so on it is the preamble to some it is a minuet to some and false as if the thing you want to say could not be relied upon to speak for itself but needed decoration I despise it. (*Pause.* VANYA *laughs. So does she.*)

VANYA: Yes . . . !
　　　Yes! How closely you observe me . . . !

HELENA: Yes. I love you and that permits me to see both more and less than others. I love you, Ivan, and you are deteriorating, I must say so or that makes me a liar, too. Do you want me to collude in your lies?

VANYA (*with a gesture*): No, no, that would be —

HELENA: There it goes again!

VANYA: What?

HELENA (*laughing*): That — I know what it is! **It is the remnant of charm!** (*They laugh.*) Stop it. Say what you want to say and keep still. (*A profound silence. A faint giggle from* SONYA, *who is making a ball of wool from a skein held by* MARYIA.)

VANYA: I've forgotten the number. (*Pause. A strum of four notes.*)

HELENA: The number . . .

VANYA: The number of the gun, I've forgotten it. (*Pause.* HELENA *gets up, pulls on a skirt. He stares at her.*) **What does it mean!**

MARYIA: Shh . . .

VANYA: I have been walking up and down out there, I've racked my brain and thrashed my memory
　　　　but
　　　What
　　　What is it
　　　　Perhaps I'm happy, is that it? Is this happiness? It doesn't feel like happiness, unless happiness is fog, perhaps it's fog, yes it must be

338 *Howard Barker*

778 —
It was a pair of sevens
77 what, though?

HELENA: Ivan —

VANYA: **Who wants fog, not me!** May I touch you? Let me touch you . . . (*She does not concede herself.*) **I'm sorry I cannot remember the number I have tried.** (*A wind blows through the ruins of the house* HELENA *covers her face with her hands.*)

HELENA: Ivan . . . are you afraid . . . ?

VANYA: Only of you. I am afraid of you. **I always was afraid of you**

MARYIA (*irritably*): Shh . . .

VANYA: **Always**
      Always
      Afraid of you (*Pause*)

Which was correct. Which is the way it should have been. Which is the perfect condition of pure love. **Of course I am afraid of you** this fear made me a murderer this fear drove me this fear whipped me it is a servitude a magnificence an abject and triumphant thing which is (*Pause. He shrugs.*)

HELENA: Make love now.

VANYA: Rinsing the life out of me . . .

HELENA: Make love. (*He shakes his head.*)

VANYA: 7786955797 . . . (*They laugh.*)

He hated the gun.

Oh, how he hated the gun.

It was as if he knew it was the enemy of all his melancholy compromise . . . (*Pause. They look at one another.* TELYEGHIN *moves a chess piece in a game he is playing with himself.* HELENA *takes the gun from her clothes. She sits across the chair, facing* VANYA. *A short giggle from* SONYA *and* MARYIA, *who are winding wool, oblivious.*)

HELENA: Four bullets you fired into my husband's face.

VANYA: And two —

HELENA: Remain. (*Pause. She tosses the weapon to* VANYA, *who catches it. He pulls a chair to him, and sits in it, opposite* HELENA. *Pause. They laugh, infectiously.*)

HELENA: I'm afraid of you, too.

VANYA: Excellent. (*They laugh again.* MARINA *shuffles across the stage.*)

MARINA: Tea, anyone . . . ?

HELENA: Am I magnificent, Ivan? Am I?

VANYA: Yes.

UNCLE VANYA   339

HELENA: I knew I was. Always I knew I was. I overcame him, didn't I?

VANYA: Yes. (HELENA *laughs*.)

MARINA (*off*): Or vodka?

HELENA: I'm so sorry not to be your executioner, Ivan so sorry you must do it all alone . . .

VANYA: I'll manage it.

HELENA: Yes!

VANYA: I have a steady hand.

HELENA: I have observed that!

VANYA: You have?

HELENA: So very steady, which surprised me, which I took as a sign of your supreme self-confidence, whereas if I were to do it, if it were assigned to me, then the possibility of —

VANYA: Ugliness —

HELENA: Ugliness, yes — would be — (*She shuts her eyes.*) Will you say or just —

MARINA (*returning*): Doesn't anyone like vodka any more? (*She passes through with a tray.*)

VANYA (*cocking the pistol*): I think — just do.

HELENA: Yes. Without announcing.

VANYA: I'm aiming it. (*He lifts the pistol.*)

HELENA: And so much unsaid!

VANYA: Inevitably, yes —

HELENA: Inevitably but so many of the things one said perhaps ought not to have been said whereas —

VANYA: The things one should say —

HELENA: Are forever secret! Yes! How hideous that is!

VANYA: Hideous? I don't know about hideous . . .

HELENA: Hideous, yes!

VANYA: But if one waited, if one postponed, until all things that needed to be said were said then —

HELENA: God, yes —

VANYA: Impossible —

HELENA: Ridiculous, oh, yes —

VANYA: Helena, my arm is aching —

HELENA: Those things must be imagined, I suppose —

VANYA: Helena —

HELENA: Or taken for granted, perhaps —

VANYA: I'm talking —

HELENA: Yes —

VANYA: We did succeed —

HELENA: I'm shaking —

340   *Howard Barker*

VANYA: Listen to me, I am talking —
HELENA: I can't —
VANYA: **Keep still I'm talking** —
HELENA: **I can't** — **I can't** — (*He shoots. The other characters
   instantaneously chant in unison.*)
ALL: **Unc — le**
        Unc — le
        Unc — le
        Van — ya (VANYA, *kicking over his chair, walks frantically
   up and down the stage.*)
        The murderer is never satisfied

VANYA *stops. He holds the gun at arm's length and cocks it again.
Wind and a thin sound. He raises the gun to his temple. He sways
in a tempest of emotion. He becomes still. He points the gun at the
floor and fires the shot. Pause.*

VANYA: Missed. (*Pause*)
        Damnation. (*Pause, then he laughs. He calls.*)
        Nanny! I can't look at her. You must do it. I apologize,
   these things are more than a servant is required in normal circumstances to perform however I and no one liked Helena no one
   liked such power admiration she aroused and plenty of respect
   but — (*He chokes in sobs.*)
ALL: Shh . . . (VANYA *wails.*) **Shhh!**
VANYA: Na — nny! (MARINA *enters. Some giggles or routine
   sounds from the others. She looks. She pokes among the fallen
   chairs.*) It is better to kill another than to kill yourself. (*Pause*)
   Better for whom, however? (*Pause*) And I'm out of ammunition
   . . . (*He throws the gun down.*) Coat!
MARINA: It's cold out, Ivan Petrovich . . .
VANYA: **Coat I said.** (*She waddles out. Pause.*) Better for the soul
   of man, of course . . . (MARINA *comes in with a heavy over-
   coat.*) Nanny, I should be dead. I failed, presumably because —
MARINA: I'll hold it for you —
VANYA: I sensed — presumably I sensed —
MARINA: Falling apart, this thing —
VANYA: Some necessity attached to my continued existence, it
   was not pure fear, I promise you, but this entails —
MARINA: It's heavy, Ivan Petrovich . . . !
VANYA: This — (*he extends his arms*) is — a contract with —
   partly with Helena — partly with myself — the clauses of which
   demand of me the highest —

UNCLE VANYA

MARINA (*brushing the shoulders*): What a state it's in!

VANYA: The highest responsibility towards — me — my own potential obviously — but also —

MARINA (*shaking her head*): And the belt . . . !

VANYA: Also — (*He stops suddenly.*)

Where am I going (*A catastrophic silence.*)

Where am I

VANYA *closes his eyes, and with an effort of will, strides out of the room. Pause.* TELYEGHIN *lets out a small cry of satisfaction at a chess move.* SONYA *murmurs to* MARYIA. *Time passes.*

SONYA: He'll be back . . . (*Insignificant moves. Time passes.*)

MARYIA: He'll be back . . .

They proceed with their lives. The lights diminish. VANYA *does not return.*

*TEN DILEMMAS
IN THE LIFE OF A GOD*

The Incarceration Text

CHARACTERS

DRAPER	A Landowner, A Criminal
BECKER	A Woman, His Equal
LILAH	
SUSANNAH	Sisters to Draper
VIVIAN	
SHARP	A Decent Man, Formerly a Soldier
SERVANT	To Draper, To Becker
PLAYDEN	A Musicologist
ORBITER	A Musicologist
A GAOLER	

MEN AND WOMEN OF THE VILLAGE

ONE

A MAN *enters, boldly. He stops. He laughs, breathlessly. Silence.*

DRAPER: Not dead.

And my suit like razors from the tailor
Pristine me
I shine with a peculiar health
And my shirt like a prayer
I glow with a strange light
Welcome me
Welcome me
All right don't (*Pause. A* WOMAN *enters. He keeps his back turned.*)

And you

Oh, how wonderfully decayed you are I could not have asked for better signs of your deterioration
Still supposed to love you am I
Love that
Madam you are humorous today
Obviously I can destroy your photograph because quite simply quite truthfully quite factually etcetera **it is no longer who was this?** (*He holds out a worn snapshot.*)

Who

Who

Indeed (*Pause. He turns to her. He looks profoundly into her face.*)

I carried this for years and when a lout they were all louts for what he called his humour robbed me of it fought a ghastly fight in stinking latrines and I fight nobody you know I hate to fight kill yes at a distance but knee to groin stuff never **fought the most vile fight** when all the time it was all the time shrinking the truth was draining out of it absurd absurd whereas the opposite is true of me I think you must admit

I am more myself than ever (*He laughs, ceases. Pause.*)

I say louts
I mean they lacked my vision
Who doesn't lack it
Have you met another man I only ask and who is he what's his fascination you are the victim of someone's gaze that's obvious who cares and do take the photograph he might cherish it

Who cares
So what
My arm is aching take it please (*Pause. She makes no move. Pause.*)

BECKER: Yes. (THREE WOMEN *enter, speaking as a chorus.*)
CHORUS: **Gaol has not injured him**
How many years
And governments and hemlines all risen and declined
How many years
And slogans gone down gutters with the rain
LILAH: Dear love we prayed every hour
DRAPER: I know! I felt it!
LILAH: And looked towards the city like mad religionists . . .
BECKER: They did. They really did. . . .
CHORUS: **How splendidly preserved your lips which are the first to shrink are**
DRAPER: Yes, in perfect order . . . ! (*He passes intimately by them.*) It's going to be hard with Paula. How terribly hard . . .
VIVIAN: We lived a life. Some illnesses. Some bitterness.
DRAPER: Illness? I had none.
CHORUS: **And still that way of standing nothing has eroded him**
LILAH: Whereas we are round-shouldered now
VIVIAN: Speak for yourself
LILAH: I am and I had the best deportment arguably
BECKER: They imagined your pain. They sat round tables and evoked it
VIVIAN: We rehearsed your awful days . . .
DRAPER: Awful?
Awful days?
All my life I wanted to be locked up

Not in this form, of course, not precisely in this manner, I mean the utter the absolute the unrelenting stagnation and depravity not perhaps in those proportions **I was under the roof** which some envied not knowing life under the roof as I at times envied the dungeon not knowing the dungeon and there I boiled all summer through

Not worse than Paula however
Not a worse boiling

How is the estate vanished I assume I got no politics I got no history and never wanted it but so many ideas were loose like dogs I recall like urban animals something must have happened when they bit much blood much alteration I shut my eyes in the carriage to spare myself what must be seen but later later I detest the habit of looking things directly in the eye later will do **under the roof I lay and slowed my heartbeat down pitch black they had no windows**

Not malice
Not premeditated
Just no windows
Not every cruelty is planned
Paula's man is what exactly
A violinist
A photographer
Oh, not an actor surely not an actor
I am not glad to be home . . . (*Pause.* SUSANNAH *hurries to him and encloses him in her arms.*)
Not glad . . . (*He nearly concedes, then removes* SUSANNAH *from him.*)
But
But

CHORUS: **We want to smother you**
We want to suffocate you in our arms
Our odours
Our unwashed shoulders will recall a childhood of
continuous

DRAPER: I still love
CHORUS: **Summer**
DRAPER: I regret to say
CHORUS: **Knickers socks and statues** (*They laugh infectiously, and cease.*)
DRAPER: A love of unrelenting and juvenile intensity
Paula I did not die as you predicted
Was I not in gaol

Oh so rehearsed
In separation
From the first look? (*He utters a savagery.*)
Paula! (*A MAN appears, as if appealed for. He stands, looking at DRAPER. DRAPER begins to laugh, stops.*)
Oh
He
Oh
The temporary proprietor of your soul . . .

BECKER: He —

DRAPER: **Don't list his qualities**
Don't describe his attributes
My favourite day was Tuesday don't ask me why
Nothing distinguished it
Nothing characterized it

CHORUS: **Tuesday!**

DRAPER: For no reason I embraced it for no reason prison is the absence of all reason after all the thing is arbitrary so

CHORUS: **Tuesday!**

DRAPER: Yes
I think I always was a random man . . . (*He goes to* SHARP.)
And idle
Hours hung off me like anchors
Whereas you your face suggests find life too brief for
your intentions
Oh God he shimmers with goodwill
Paula the poverty of your choice does not dismay me
No
I'm not dismayed

CHORUS: **Our brother is**
Our beloved brother
Reclaims his estate

SHARP: I will defend myself if necessary I am not a saint but on the other hand I recognize —

DRAPER: Shh

SHARP: The situation is a complex one —

DRAPER: Shh (*Silence.* DRAPER *walks a little, stops as if to listen.*)

BECKER: I had this terrible requirement —

DRAPER: I sense a certain desolation in the fields oddly the sound of fallowness is quite distinct and where the ornamental stream ran is audible stagnation but so what

TEN DILEMMAS

BECKER: For

DRAPER: **Who cares for your requirements**
What happened then was there a war
Don't tell me
Reasons who wants reasons any more I never did

SUSANNAH: Lunch!

VIVIAN: Lunch!

LILAH: For God's sake lunch!

CHORUS: **If we appear conciliatory it's only the effect of guilt**

SUSANNAH: We were not nice to Paula . . .

LILAH: It must be said . . .

SUSANNAH: What will come out at some point . . .

VIVIAN: Might just as well be quickly and honestly confessed . . .
(They smile and hasten to fetch a lunch table, a cloth, the plates of food. As they move swiftly about, SHARP *addresses* BECKER.)

SHARP: I cleave to you.

BECKER: Thank you for your reassurance.

SHARP: Stand guard over what we so carefully and patiently —

BECKER: I am full of gratitude.

SHARP: Paula —

BECKER: **What**
Paula
What
No
No
You are nice
You are everything I ever wanted
You personify my needs
What
Paula
What
No
I do reciprocate all you
All of it
Honestly
Don't abandon me *(She smiles at once, and goes to the* table, *clapping her hands.)*
I never smile
Do I
Never smile
But these animal laughs well interpret as you will my
noises

And sniffing
Forever sniffing

They think I am about to cry no it is something from my past I don't understand it I least of all understand it did I sniff when you were here? (*She looks at* DRAPER *a long time.*)

DRAPER: Sniff?

BECKER: Arbitrarily? (*A pause. They stare. The* WOMEN *sit on the chairs. A clash of crockery and activity. At last* DRAPER *joins them, served by* SUSANNAH.)

DRAPER (*to* SHARP): Do you feel lost? She does somehow contrive to make the most secure bonds practically liquid **oh we never ate like this** I say we the rest were louts by louts I do not mean to denigrate quite simply they were louts I use the word lout freely and often thoughtlessly by louts I mean they lacked my vision
Who doesn't lack it
I did not see them for four years but heard them
That was adequate
What are we celebrating by the way? (*To* SHARP.)
And do you feel lost?
This is not a relationship
It is the detonation of two brains
Don't be alarmed (*He smiles at* SHARP.)
I feel sure you will make indelible impressions on this
                                                          woman's
Soul
I nearly said
Soul

SUSANNAH: We dug

DRAPER: Did you?

SUSANNAH: And dug

DRAPER: I think I heard you I think I heard the shovel striking flints

VIVIAN: Until my hands were —

DRAPER: They were not good, your hands, it must be said —

VIVIAN: Not perfect but —

DRAPER: No, don't bewail the damage to hands that never were a subject for the eye Lilah's one might regret but yours

LILAH: He recollects my hands!

DRAPER: Yes

LILAH: My long and languid

DRAPER: Yes

TEN DILEMMAS

351

VIVIAN: How impeccable his memory is

DRAPER: **They trod on mine**

Oh, accidentally

I did not protest

My hands were wrongly placed I left them rather carelessly on floors and naturally they became entangled with the boots of officers

How could it have been otherwise I am not offensive

I was a model

Oh, a model of accommodation to the rules

We must have rules

And I was a killer

Paula was a witness not to say I won't say of course accomplice (*To* SHARP.)

You knew all this she whispered it on your first pillow I daresay (*To the rest.*)

How did I keep sane do you ask

How did I keep sane

I did not

I did not

Keep sane

Well, you can see I didn't

This is scarcely

CHORUS: **He is in such appalling need we will exert ourselves**
to humour him

LILAH: These vegetables we grew ourselves

CHORUS: **And stroke his cold brain**

Oh, look he has lost hair around the temples

LILAH: Not Paula

She disdained to crop. Cropping was never Paula's —

BECKER: I'd rather starve —

LILAH: Not her vocation —

BECKER: Than get dirt in my fingernails —

SHARP: Shh . . .

BECKER (*icily to* SHARP): No —

LILAH: Or even water lettuces —

BECKER: Lie and die because I hate to labour even to preserve my life —

SHARP: Shh . . .

BECKER: No, you think I am exaggerating, I am not exaggerating I am speaking with perfect and —

SHARP: Shh . . .

BECKER: **Absolute lucidity I detest all effort it offends me** (*To*

352   *Howard Barker*

DRAPER, *who is smiling*.) Where did you find that smile that is
a new smile you never had a smile like that —
DRAPER: God knows I was in darkness —
BECKER: I don't dislike it I don't criticize —
DRAPER: Not permanently in darkness, obviously —
BECKER: I smile myself sometimes but not in front of mirrors —
DRAPER: How intimate we are —
BECKER: Already?
DRAPER: Intimate, yes —
SHARP (*standing*): I do think —
DRAPER: When were we not intimate? Intimacy I took for granted
—
SHARP: I wish to say —
DRAPER: Even in the darkest moments I presumed this intimacy
was undiminished, was I wrong?
SHARP: **I have assumed responsibilities.** (*Pause*)
        These responsibilities I — (*Pause*)
        Can't be —
DRAPER: The word's peculiar, of course —
SHARP: **Shouldered out of** —
DRAPER: Intimacy . . . (DRAPER *covers his face with his hands.*
SUSANNAH *goes to him.*)
SUSANNAH: We have prepared a room, and this room is so clean!
So light! With little furniture and windows crystal clear! I was
polishing as the car came up the drive, still polishing!
VIVIAN: His passion for clean windows —
LILAH: We forget nothing —
SUSANNAH: Polishing! Polishing!
SHARP: Change occurred. I have to emphasize. To all who hope
for continuity. To all who —
BECKER: Sit down —
SHARP: Ache for sterility —
BECKER: Sit down, you bore me —
SHARP: Because it is sterility to hanker after —
BECKER: **Oh, fuck the mundane nature of your consciousness!**
(*She seizes his hand.*)
        It's all right —
        It's all right — (*He stares bitterly at her.*)
        I love you —
        It's all right —
        The love is safe —
        Intact I promise —
SHARP: You promise . . .

TEN DILEMMAS 353

BECKER: I do, I do —

SHARP (*shaking his head*): Always she . . . Always . . . (*He sits.*)

CHORUS: **She never wrote a single letter not one or sent a token of her sympathy**

DRAPER (*recovering*): I was with such a pleasant murderer and he murdered without malice it was a craft with him. The details of this craft he communicated to me so I am technically as lethal as (*To* SHARP.) **I don't threaten you.**

SHARP: You are vain and authoritarian and I will not let you spoil her she had achieved a rather common happiness with me —

BECKER: You embarass me —

SHARP: Who cares a common happiness by love and kindness —

BECKER: Your words are —

SHARP: Who cares about the words a good and honest —

BECKER: **I hate your words** —

SHARP: **I renounce nothing I yield nothing everything before I came was artificial** —

DRAPER: Where did you come from exactly —

SHARP: **And macabre** —

DRAPER: When I left I shut the gate —

SHARP: **And diseased** —

DRAPER: Who opened it again?

SHARP: **And I came like a wind of health** —

BECKER: For God's sake —

SHARP: **And hygiene to this woman** —

BECKER: **Shut up** —

SHARP: **And fucked her yes**. (*A bottomless silence, swiftly covered by* DRAPER's *laugh.*)

Yes

Well

Yes (SHARP *gets up, pushes in his chair.*)

I vacate nothing. (*He goes out. A silence. A dog barks.* BECKER *goes to* DRAPER *and drapes her wrists over his shoulders.*)

BECKER: He won't go. You'll have to kill him. (*Pause*)

DRAPER: At one time I thought the whole world lied in unison to hurt me but all the gaoled think that we are so tender we are so bruised and gradually the louts received their letters me however never me never this was certainly a distinction this adamantine silence they pitied me and yet I was not diminished and wore this smile because I knew you loved me or not loved no the louts talked love no I lived in you with or without permission I inhabited your arteries and stalked your brain love no the very word a lout's word surely I thought I had abolished it but I lack consistency in all things but one and that's (*He stops abruptly. Silence. The dog barks.*)

My (*Pause*)

Don't let me out I said

I was not sincere

Don't let me out

Not entirely sincere

Obviously I yearned the fields the meadows the trams etcetera obviously the faces of my sisters and the racing clouds yes those obviously but

Paula to resume with Paula

And they offered me a ticket to another place they do that they name five towns and I did hesitate I thought of their cathedrals yes cathedral towns they were some in the South some in the frontier district I might be sitting on the train now scouring the horizon for the spires to come into view but no I'm here as if I'm here notwithstanding and you know I love cathedrals

Back

Back

As if choices were

Back

A fiction of the inverately political (*He gets up, goes to each of his sisters and kisses them on the head.*)

Forgive me

I could have been so much

Oh, what a life I might have

But I exist only to make love to this woman which (*Pause. A distant train climbs an incline.*)

I never have yet and . . . (*Pause*)

May never . . .

TWO

The whinnying laughter of young MEN. *The* SERVANT *extends a tray of glasses as* two PROFESSORS OF MUSICOLOGY *enter behind* BECKER, *holding small cases.*

TEN DILEMMAS

BECKER: Silly, isn't it? (*She gestures to the room, the character of things.*) Oh, so silly, isn't it, and I so utterly swollen with **contempt** (*She takes a glass.*) I cannot tell you the **depths of comedy** you will swim here you will plunge in **bottomless archaisms!** (*She giggles. The* MEN *take glasses from the tray.*) It is the world, however! It is incredibly **still the world** yes you are not dreaming. Alongside the real world **the real world**. (*She bites her lip, gazing at the* MUSICOLOGISTS. *Pause. They look about them. She addresses the* SERVANT.) Or is it? Or is it? I am giggling today! He hates me giggling but it is rightly or wrongly an authentic aspect of my character! Why should I change it? Why should I do surgery to what is in most men's eyes **perfection** no I giggle unapologetically **I assert my right to common and undistinguished things** these men are professors yes so young and yet professors might I have been a professor do you think I have the brain God knows oh yes a brain of he says **a continent of a brain**

ORBITER: Obviously!

BECKER: Obviously, he says, and these professors will overturn the world **oh, not again** yes overturn it, they are musicologists **what he says**, ignorance in a wig, yes, they have no manners I'm afraid, musical and mannerless! (*She laughs.* DRAPER *enters. She ceases laughing, reluctantly.*)

DRAPER: I'm so delighted you could make it, Paula has such interesting friends, gifted all of them, utterly, utterly gifted or she would not stoop to —

BECKER: Shut up, I love you —

DRAPER: Stoop to garner them —

PLAYDEN: Garner? (*He looks at* ORBITER, *who giggles.*) Garner?

DRAPER: Garner, yes, she is a proper horticulturalist when it comes to friends **and don't laugh at the servant he has his dignity as well as you**

BECKER: I love you, I said —

DRAPER: Have you enjoyed the views?

PLAYDEN (*to* ORBITER): Did we, I don't know that we saw a lot of views —

DRAPER: Oh, do submerse yourself in landscape, it is after all, a diminishing asset —

BECKER: Love, I said —

DRAPER: I heard —

BECKER (*to the* MUSICOLOGISTS): **We have such awful nights** I won't go into detail these nights you could not imagine the pain the nakedness the pain dare I say it even the **absurdity**

356   *Howard Barker*

DRAPER: What is the subject of your study? Paula said music but
        music is a mystery to me —
BECKER: Don't be self-deprecating, will you —
DRAPER: Music I confess to sheer —
BECKER: He is about to say something so —
DRAPER: Ignorance of —
BECKER: Egregiously untrue **he has a mind like an axe no not
        an axe a razor an-axe-and-a-razor** don't be lulled don't be
        lured by his modesty he is a liar in his soul (*She kisses* DRAPER
        passionately, and separates from him.)
ORBITER: We encountered Paula in the street . . .
DRAPER: She is often in the street. I never am.
ORBITER: Not in the street exactly. At a table and her hands were
        folded like —
DRAPER: I know how Paula folds her hands —
ORBITER: Like this and we thought simultaneously —
PLAYDEN: We can't be certain it was simultaneous —
ORBITER: Michael is pedantic —
PLAYDEN/ORBITER: **She is the visual counterpart of progress
        in all fields**
ORBITER: We hate
                Oh, how we hate
PLAYDEN: The current state of music is a gaol
ORBITER: A gaol of the emotions we know whole classes of
        mankind are suffocating on bad music what an absurd room our
        latest book has sold eight thousand copies and we lecture in the
        capitals of the world no sooner has our plane touched down than —
BECKER: They are celebrities I knew at once these are celeb-
        rities —
PLAYDEN: We are off again —
ORBITER: How nice to rest a while —
BECKER: They possess the faintly angry smiles of the celebrity
        who never can accumulate enough acclaim —
ORBITER: Fatuous room . . . ! (*Pause. The* MUSICOLOGISTS
        walk about, gazing. BECKER *watches them, sipping from her
        glass.*)
DRAPER: She sits in public places yes just as you encountered her
        she makes mistakes in dress sometimes perched in the torrent of
        male gaze their glances rinse her like a waterfall dirty glances
        sordid glances obviously but a goddess cannot discriminate be-
        tween her devotees can she and she is rather ugly in the morning
        who would know but me her ugliness . . . ? (*The* MUSICOLO-
        GISTS *meet one another's eyes. They stifle their laughter. Pause.*)

TEN DILEMMAS

Take their bags now and put them side by side. (*The* SERVANT *goes to collect the bags.* ORBITER *steps in front of him.*)

ORBITER: I don't allow another man to wait on me. (*The* SERVANT *stands back.*)

DRAPER: You've injured him.

ORBITER: We carry our own bags.

DRAPER: You have horribly offended him. (ORBITER *shrugs.*) What does it matter! Who cares if he is wounded in his soul! His soul perhaps is rather small . . . some are . . . so small . . . (*Pause*) I'll carry your bags!

ORBITER: No —

DRAPER: I want to. (*Pause*)

PLAYDEN: Let him transport the bags, Michael . . . (*Pause*)

ORBITER: He is doing it for the wrong reasons . . . (BECKER *squeals with laughter.*)

BECKER: The wrong reasons! **The wrong reasons!** I am so glad you came! (*She half-embraces them.* DRAPER *picks up the bags.*) I was terrified you wouldn't come! I sat in the car thinking these celebrities have better things to do! (*She stops.*) Why do I throw my arms round people all the time? Why do I? (*To* DRAPER.) You detest it, I know how profoundly you detest it . . . (DRAPER *leaves with the bags.*) So much of my behaviour, so much of my instinct, injures his sensibility . . .

ORBITER: Too bad . . .

BECKER: No, he is right to be offended . . .

PLAYDEN: How can he be? What you do spontaneously is —

BECKER: **Spontaneous what's that!** (*She laughs.*) Forgive me, oh, my manners! Forgive me! No, he loves me and he hates me to be demeaned, I understand that —

PLAYDEN: Demeaned?

BECKER: Yes. Because it attracts you, you do not care to notice that I am demeaned. I am, however, and he is right. Nearly always, he is right **don't pull faces at one another it is true!** (*Pause. They look at her.*)

ORBITER: Paula, you don't have to —

BECKER: No —

ORBITER: Live like this, live like —

BECKER: I love cafés! He has not yet eradicated my love of cafés, a beautiful woman must be seen in cafés, hour after hour as the world writhes in its labours, births, mutinies and silent vigils by martyrs' graves, I advertize myself at tables, half-hidden by a newspaper I do not read, it is after all, only a skirt, a newspaper . . .

358   *Howard Barker*

PLAYDEN: Come with us to America.

BECKER: Silly.

PLAYDEN: You would do wonderfully in America.

BECKER: Would I? Do what wonderfully? **Do what!** (DRAPER
   returns.)

DRAPER: Do you like fountains? Go off together any time you
   like, I know you are lovers, and if I did not know, by now it
   would have rendered itself obvious, you have the same, exactly
   the same, contemptuous giggle, and I don't criticize, how I
   should love to share a noise with Paula, even a cough, even a
   snort, no, we are apart, we have not done that thing yet **perhaps
   we will who knows one day some time this symbiotic flinch
   or twitch** I'd adore it I'd thrive I promise you, no, the fountains
   are the feature you should make an effort for, they leap above the
   treeline, startling and random, their mechanisms defy predict-
   ability I don't know how I am not an engineer and desecrate the
   summerhouse if you want to, lovers do that I am only too aware,
   scrawl your abuse and obscene drawings we can always have it
   painted when your love has died and let your laughter ring out
   on the lake that laugh of utter hatred for a declining class I ache
   to hear it **ring ring that laughter** I want to be alone with Paula
   now . . . (*Pause*)

ORBITER: The future belongs to us. And this future will be one
   of song. New song, which rushes from the mouths of common
   people —

BECKER: Shh . . .

ORBITER: No, I must state my desire here because he tries to
   make us foolish. **A world of song.** (*He goes out, followed by*
   PLAYDEN. *Pause.*)

DRAPER: Oh, listen to my horror, will you?

BECKER: Yes —

DRAPER: That man would kill —

BECKER: No, he is a sweet and passionate and slightly-deformed
   about-the-ankle-youth who —

DRAPER: **You know he'd kill.** (*Pause*) Look, they are holding hands
   as they cross the lawn, the two professors of musicology . . .

BECKER: Don't abandon me . . .

DRAPER: After me . . . another . . .

BECKER: Never . . .

DRAPER: **Never? It's the way of things**
             More beautiful of course to rot in celibacy
             The slow raking the slow hoeing the sifting
             And disintegrating bridal wear

Of old oaths and arguments more beautiful but hardly
possible
And they are luminously happy
You would submit to the first that came along
BECKER: **I would not**
DRAPER (*staring over the lawn*): Look, luminously happy . . .
BECKER: Oh, God, you have given me such terrible nights . . .
(DRAPER *covers his face with his hands, and* BECKER *weeps.
The* SERVANT *observes. Pause.*)
DRAPER: Listen, I do not expect punishment for any crime I
might commit I am in love with you and that is sufficient retribu-
tion for the most outraged parent, surely? (*The* SERVANT *walks
slowly out. In the silence the* CHORUS *enters.*)
CHORUS: **This is our brother**
Who does not read the newspapers
Do read the newspapers we say
Do hide in world affairs

This is our brother
Who forges no allegiances
Do join with others in some cause
We urge never mind if it's correct

This is our brother
Who stands still without warning
And whom the beggars curse
For never yielding them the street

DRAPER (*looking out*): Revolutionary musicologists who will certainly assasinate no that's too kind will trample in the bowels of
men whose miseries they do not care to hear and their clothes
cost a fortune let alone their hair styled on the boulevards I have
met the type before —
BECKER: Yes —
DRAPER: Always longed to kill them their little bags are wrig-
gling on the eiderdown, hear the bags
BECKER: Yes —
DRAPER: Oh, such articulate bags! (*He turns to his* SISTERS.)
Paula found these dead men in the café she habituates. They liked
her. **Everybody likes her!** Come down, she said, and I will meet
you in the car!
LILAH: How wrong you are to think she is profound. How absurd
your pursuit of a profundity that if she ever had was stamped out
in the clinic

SUSANNAH: You are like a bullock that butts and butts against the gate —

LILAH: Her gate —

SUSANNAH: A gate that never will be opened to you.

DRAPER: **Oh, the common intimacy that you wish for me**. The mundane kissing and domestic oh the routine and familiar gestures of universal marriage **do I want that?** (*Pause. He looks at them. He shrugs.*)

> Yes.
> Oh, yes, I do want that
> Perhaps I earnestly
> Perhaps I desperately
> Perhaps
> Perhaps (*The* MUSICOLOGISTS *enter, smiling.*)

PLAYDEN: Hilarious.

ORBITER: We got soaked.

PLAYDEN: The fountain we thought has the musical quality of redundancy, by which we mean it is the objective music of a leisured class.

ORBITER: Hilarious.

PLAYDEN: We got soaked. (*Pause.* DRAPER *gestures to the* CHORUS.)

DRAPER: These women are my sisters. They will wash tne blood off you.

ORBITER: Whose blood?

DRAPER: Your own.

ORBITER (*amused*): Thank you! We saw the summerhouse, we saw the lake, and we experienced the peculiar ambiguity —

PLAYDEN: Not for the first time —

ORBITER: Not for the first time, no —

PLAYDEN: Of simultaneously abhorring and enjoying privilege —

ORBITER: We quarelled —

PLAYDEN: Not exactly quarelled —

ORBITER: We did quarrel, it was a quarrel —

PLAYDEN: All right —

ORBITER: We quarelled over whether this ambiguity arose from the fact we were born in the working class and therefore —

PLAYDEN: It was residual envy or a particular anxiety produced by —

ORBITER: Biography or Ideology —

PLAYDEN: An aesthetic tremor, a transgression possibly — (*Pause*)

ORBITER: Yes. (*Pause. A dog barks distantly.* PLAYDEN *is suffused by awareness.*) We lecture in America —

TEN DILEMMAS   361

PLAYDEN: Shh —
ORBITER: In America we are held in —
PLAYDEN: Shh —
ORBITER: A tumultuous respect —
PLAYDEN: Michael —
ORBITER: They say of us **these young men will tear up thought like builders rip away linoleum** . . . (*He is silent with horror.*)
PLAYDEN: Paula . . .
BECKER: Oh, don't appeal to me . . . !
         Not that I
         Not that you
         Could find the dignity to die without dissent
         Me least of all and I am so
         He says it all the time
         So

PLAYDEN *makes a swift stride to the door but the* SERVANT *is entering and blocks his progress. The* SERVANT *has something wrapped in a sack under his arm.*

BECKER: Inchoate
DRAPER (*to the* SERVANT): Oh, is this not the perfect love
         He knows without instruction
         He anticipates
         My every need
SERVANT: My poor master . . .
DRAPER: Yes . . .
SERVANT: Oh, my poor master . . .
DRAPER: Yes, yes . . . (*To* PLAYDEN *and* ORBITER.) I have given my life to this woman and what might I not have made with it, who knows **not that the universe cares not that the galaxies care or the rivers plunging down the gorge** and anyway is not one enterprise as fine as any other? She is mad, and all my efforts to arrange her chaos are as futile as putting combs through her extraordinary hair, which cannot be combed, which shatters the teeth of combs . . . look at it . . . (*He lifts her thick hair to show it.* PLAYDEN *goes to move.*) **Don't run away what is there to run away to?**
BECKER (*to the* MUSICOLOGISTS): When you came to my table you thought **oh, she is one of us moderns, oh, she breathes such sweet opinions** how beautiful and elegant she is she must be one of us, oh, what a fatal error, what supreme arrogance, and I thought I was arrogant, no, I prefer love under the old regime,

362   *Howard Barker*

and in any case I am divine — (*The* SISTERS *laugh.*) Yes, they
laugh but I am how else is it my breath is never stale? Ask him,
never, never stale (*She lights a cigarette.*) **Not even now** (*She
exhales.*) I want to share nothing, I do not understand the verb to
share, or shake hands either even though the priest demands it,
no, this hand shaking is a blasphemy and I fuck so badly, so very
badly, unapologetically but badly I admit although I dance in
cafés so suggestive of **never mind** and will the new regime
abolish underwear? It is to me suggestive of a pleasure I can't
know . . .

ORBITER: Paula, we can save you . . .

PLAYDEN: Your unhappiness is . . . the product of . . . distortion
. . . and social . . . paralysis . . .

ORBITER: Paula . . .

BECKER: They are offering to show me the way out of the
maze . . .

ORBITER: Yes . . .

BECKER: But I like the maze . . . ! (*Pause. She erupts into a
laugh.*)

DRAPER: They don't hang for murder here. They lock you in a
fortress and lose the key . . . but obviously I require to be in
a room without a key . . .

PLAYDEN: Let us live . . . we have so much to give . . .

DRAPER (*puzzled*): Give who?

PLAYDEN: We are of such infinite utility . . .

DRAPER: To whom?

PLAYDEN: The blind. The unborn. The still unknowing . . .
(DRAPER *appears to ponder this, and then smiles.*)

DRAPER: But they . . . not knowing . . . could not know what
might have been known, and therefore, could not suffer their
ignorance . . . (*Pause.* ORBITER *suddenly plunges out the door,
leaving* PLAYDEN, *who howls.*)

PLAYDEN: **I thought you —**
              Loved me!

DRAPER: It is such a big park . . . it is quite scandalous . . . the
dimensions of it . . . (*The* SERVANT *removes his wig, and goes
off after* ORBITER.)

CHORUS: **She will live such a life in your absence**
           Intolerably vain
           And posture while you suffer

DRAPER: I anticipate that . . .

CHORUS: **Drifting from room to room**
           She will exhaust our patience

TEN DILEMMAS

    And attract a rabble of admirers
    Think

DRAPER: All poor, however, all outrageously mundane . . .

CHORUS: **Think**

DRAPER: I know her taste! I was an aberration from which she never will recover . . .

CHORUS: **And us**
    Obliged to witness her mischiefs

DRAPER: Pathetic, her mischiefs, I promise you . . .

PLAYDEN: Why me . . . ?
    Why me, when I am nothing to your life, but merely passing by?
    Why me?

DRAPER (*taking him gently in an embrace*): Why not you? By the same token, why not?

PLAYDEN: **I did no wrong to you**

DRAPER: Oh, the irrelevance of that! The pathos of such a calculation, as if murder could follow only on offence! You do offend me, but how innocently, no, nothing can attach to that, you were chosen by her beauty, as I was. Her beauty sank your life, as your death will sink mine . . .

PLAYDEN: I refuse to be an element of your degenerate life . . .

DRAPER: Yes . . .

PLAYDEN: I refuse . . . !

DRAPER: Yes, and how appalling it is nobody knows but me **I require no pity** and you are petulant to quarrel like this, isn't he, when my mind is
    I must be locked away and you're the means (*The* SERVANT *enters.*)
    Where is he?

SERVANT: In a boat . . .

DRAPER: A boat?

SERVANT: He took a boat out . . .

DRAPER: How strange . . . he must be under the impression the lake's a river . . . and leads somewhere . . .

PLAYDEN: **My lover! My life!** (*He wails, ceases.*)
    Yes, well, that's that, then, that's the end of all and what bad luck to have incredibly bad luck but oh is that it then no more to say on that subject I had such hopes such stupid now I see and any action likewise rendered idiotic by you don't prepare yourself you really don't and then (*He is utterly still. Silence.*)

BECKER: Other men, did you say? I don't know. And parties possibly I will go to though why I can't think

364 *Howard Barker*

> **I love you so terribly so**
> Your sisters will be vile to me
> **I love and I love and it leads to such a** (*Pause*)

SERVANT: My dear master I have never criticized though we are capable of criticism nor her either oh yes perfectly capable they break my heart for such a suffering you'd go beyond mere service for such pain you'd hang your judgement up a useless thing a garment full of holes **on a nail with judgement**

> **I'll inform the police, shall I?**
> Or will you flee? Think of fleeing, will you?

(DRAPER *smiles and shakes his head: he extends his hands for the gun in its wrapping.*)

> No, of course . . .
> No, that is hardly the . . .
> Forgive me . . . my insouciance . . .

CHORUS (*of* PLAYDEN): **His death remains a platitude**
> > **No matter if he is unique**

BECKER: This parting is —

CHORUS: **Such things he might have said**
> **Startling perceptions**
> **Never to be articulated**

BECKER: Obviously necessary and yet —

CHORUS: **The peculiar accents of his prose**
> **There must be a memorial perhaps a prize**

BECKER: My darling —

CHORUS: **Presented annually**
> **The two professors who fell**
> **Into the hands of intolerable love**

BECKER: I will be a thing of such terrible triviality I will be the maligned image of a futile life (*She laughs brightly, briefly.*)

> So what
> So what
> **We can't bear this nakedness another day**

THREE

Labourers are raking in a line. They are VIVIAN, LILAH, SUSANNAH. BECKER *is standing nearby.*

TEN DILEMMAS 365

VIVIAN: It is not bad without him

LILAH: Bad but less bad

VIVIAN: Than expected, yes

SUSANNAH: Our fears are entirely for Paula. She is the focus of our concern but

VIVIAN: Even she is less

SUSANNAH: Much less

VIVIAN: Much less damaged it appears than we anticipated

LILAH: Wrapping herself in something

VIVIAN: Some comfort

LILAH: Some resource she's plucked from nowhere

SUSANNAH: For which we all respect her

LILAH: Yes

SUSANNAH: Whilst also

LILAH: Yes

SUSANNAH: Resenting this resourcefulness

VIVIAN/LILAH: Unjustly

SUSANNAH: Obviously (*They cease raking and look at* BECKER.) We want you to be happy. We want you to find what loving him banished you from . . . (*Pause*)

BECKER: Oh, God, your collective gaze . . .

SUSANNAH: Yes . . . (*Pause. She looks at them.*)

BECKER: Yes!

> Thank you!
>
> Yes!
>
> The first thing I discovered was wit, the thing called wit, detestable and paltry wit, the laws of which are facile and once discovered, oh, so easily employed to fend off every creeping dissonance, every stealthy horror which comes behind you like — **off! off!** I have — (*A distant rumble of gunfire. Pause.*) He lay on me like —

SUSANNAH: Don't say —

BECKER: Don't say? But I so —

SUSANNAH: Don't say his habits to us, please. (*Pause*)

BECKER (*defiantly*): Like a bench, and all of him so hot, a bench which could not yield itself to me **and I a bench also me especially a bench oh, I was more a bench than him** and really aren't our bellies and our bowels soft for the welcoming of love? I know everything, you see and yet — (*A second rumble of gunfire. Pause.*) I am not a bowl of love, though I have hips, a bowl in which he might have bathed **I'm not weeping I shall never be happy only full of wit**

> I'm not weeping . . . (*The* SERVANT *enters, his livery*

faded. She turns at once to him.) This is the time to be consistent! This is the time to hold to what you know! **Keep to your manners, keep to your laws!** (*She gestures to the gunfire.*) This is merely the wind, merely the showers, slanting over the land . . . (*She grins at him.*)

VIVIAN (*listening*): I was expecting this. As if from birth, looking from the window through infant eyes, thought placidity, excellent though it is, cannot be anything but brief . . .

BECKER: **I have fucked with others and**
                    Yes
                    Pleasantly enough (*To all.*) Rake! Dig! Or they will think we have no faith!

LILAH (*raking*): I'm scared . . .

SUSANNAH: Me too but still we . . .

LILAH: Obviously our troops have fled . . . !

SUSANNAH: Scared but really it is an ordinary day.

LILAH (*stops hoeing*): **How is it how an ordinary day**

SERVANT: I'm sorry I cannot keep this tray still in my hands . . . (*He holds it out to* BECKER.)

BECKER: You must not drop the tray . . .

SERVANT: No, but still it's —

BECKER: **Do not drop the tray** (*The* SERVANT *shudders.*) If you drop the tray something more terrible will happen than ever might transpire from stray bullets I assure you, am I not inspiring, I am a higher type than you yes altogether higher and take your strength from me borrow from me you are not absurd . . . (*The* SERVANT *is still.* LILAH *drops her rake as a foreign* SOLDIER *enters. She senses rather than observes him. Silence.*)
                    You're on my land. (*Pause*)
                    I say my land it's theirs in actual fact but I loved their brother so I have some rights (*Pause*)
                    And still I do (*Pause*)
                    Still love because it never was made proper (*She turns.*) Whatever that might be . . .
    (*She gestures to the horizon.*)
                    From there to there . . . (*The* SOLDIER *goes to the* SERVANT *and grips him cruelly by the jacket.*)
                    Love . . .
                    We caught like a disease . . .
                    Aren't you interested in the subject? (*She turns.*)
                    Don't hurt him because your life is bare . . . (*Pause*)
                    All right, do! Rip him up and leave bits of him on trees! Do! (*Pause. The* SOLDIER *stares at* BECKER.)

My lover
He never was considerate
Nor did he thrust
Nor any expertise
Imagine! No expertise! But fucked me eye to eye, oh, we were so —

Mind you his eyes were somewhat not at all common those eyes we swam in one another's gaze that was the act of love —

Not fucked no we never did
I say fucked
No
I exaggerate
It was more than fucking could be I assert
And I should know I had some very rough men in my
Oh, my history is
Believe me (*Pause*)

Horrible . . . (*The* SOLDIER *throws down the* SERVANT, *who lies still with fear.*)

His dreams of course, were monstrous . . . (*Pause*)
As were mine . . .

CHORUS: **Take her out**

Oh, and do whatever

In the trees there is a perfect place for an atrocity
(*The* SOLDIER *jerks his head to tell* BECKER *to walk off ahead of him. Pause.*) **Small trees**

The remnants of an orchard (BECKER *goes out. The* SOLDIER *follows. The* SERVANT *rises to his feet. He stares after them. His mouth opens to emit a howl but is silent.*)

He can't

The age of service must be dead (BECKER *reappears, holding the* SOLDIER *by his hand.*)

BECKER: You see, we live . . . we do . . . live . . . which is perhaps the very worst thing and what makes us . . . unforgivable . . . this . . . ability . . . **I won't say appetite** . . . for . . . continuance . . . (*She looks at the* CHORUS.) Do you agree? It is repulsive, isn't it? He loves me. He is smitten and all his orders have been drowned somewhere in my belly . . . **I can do what I like with him** (*She lets out a laugh, half-contempt, half-satisfied. To the* SERVANT.) Get up and give him a room, not the best room, not the one with the view, four doors from mine and — (*She embraces the* SERVANT.)

I forgive you

368   *Howard Barker*

> I forgive you (*To the* CHORUS.)
>   See, I ask rather little of him, and the result is that he
> wants to give me more . . . (*The* SISTERS *take* BECKER *in their
> arms, and embrace her. The* SOLDIER *unbuttons his tunic and
> throws it aside.*)

SHARP (*to all of them*): I'll help this woman . . . and this field's
badly ploughed . . . (*He walks off behind the* SERVANT.)

FOUR

Hammering on the door of a cell. It is irregular but relentless.

DRAPER: All right!
         All right I am enraged I am dislocated and my sleep
                                pulped my sleep shattered
         Any letters
         I ask this formally
         I ask this habitually
         Any letters I say
         In this voice
         Meek
         Quavering
         Any letters
         Why not?
         Why not say it?
         Knowing the answer does not ridicule the question
         In any case the answer no brings me relief
         Did you say no?
         Oh, the pleasure in not examining the envelope
         Oh, the sheer ecstasy in being spared the stamp
         And as for slitting it
         Oh, the menace in the crack
         The message sitting there like an axeman
         And she has no style
         I mean by this the style is not her own but merely a
                                reflection of her last book
         Sometimes Goethe
         Sometimes Baudelaire
         And American

TEN DILEMMAS

Yes

Their films she dotes on

No, the fifth year without a letter and thank God

He is good to me

He is solicitous

The terms of her affection and abuse would only make
me suffer

Imagine my scrutiny of the syllables

No, a letter would be a road to sheer insanity and that
I am as yet

I say so

Disagree if you want

Unacquainted with (*Pause. A* GAOLER *enters with a
newspaper. An inordinate pause.*)

Ah . . .

Ah . . .

The newspaper . . . (*Pause*)

But it's dark . . . (*The* GAOLER *extends it. Pause.*)

Please . . .

I shall only eat it as I ate the last . . . (*In despair.*)

Is there no letter? (*Pause*)

This is most amusing this insistence on the newspaper
I appreciate it yes I who always hated wit still recognize it and
for one who aches for letters

No I exaggerate one letter only

To proffer newspapers

Yes

Is profoundly cruel

I don't criticize I merely describe

The news

The news

What a savage substitute

Anyway she is immune to politics

Who cares where the frontier runs

Some do

Some have their reasons for

Not me however nor her there was this other little
matter we called

Ah

Ah

Yes I slept well thank you anyway until you knocked

Why doesn't she write you must know

You know everything

You are divine I know you are
How like a god to hide my letters
Five years of letters
Do you masturbate do you expose yourself to her words
the ends of which flowed off the page
That was another affectation that was
Copied from a thing of Diderot
That flowing off the page thing
I could see through that
Nothing she did was hers how sad how moving to be
made of imitations but why not perhaps she knew herself to
be inferior
Know your own poverty
That's a starting point (*Pause*)
I am suggesting
Warily
There are letters
I am implying something manifestly false
That letters from her actually exist
Did I say this yesterday
Did I
Oh, I did
No, I didn't because the thought has just arrived
**Her letters have been coming with a scrupulous
monotony**
I am not making complaints
Only grappling with
**And I wouldn't want them oh believe me this is
better this world of silence oh much better than her poor
expressions of**
I can't say the word
Desire
Would be
I'll say it in French
That would really wreck my mind
So I'm grateful if my paltry suspiscions are founded in
truth and you have them in your
Bedroom is it
Kitchen or
They must take up a lot of space
By now five years' worth is a (*He stops. A long pause.*)
GAOLER: She sleeps the sleep of the beautifully fucked . . .
(*Pause*)

Now ... breathing ... in ... his ... breath ... (*Pause*)
And breathing out again ... (*Pause*)

DRAPER: The gaoler is a poet ... but only since knowing me ... (*The* GAOLER *goes to leave.*)

GAOLER: She loves you ...

DRAPER: **Oh, don't make things worse for me**

GAOLER: She loves you! It's obvious!

DRAPER: Obvious? Is it? Why obvious?

GAOLER: Because no woman could help loving you
No water today cunt

DRAPER: But it's hot in here!

GAOLER: **Today is Tuesday no water today you cunt**
No water
No water
It's Tuesday

DRAPER: Yes

GAOLER: **Tuesday you cunt** (*Pause and stillness, utter.*)
Of course she loves you. (DRAPER *goes to the* GAOLER, *on his knees.*)
Oh, such a love ... (*He rests his forehead on the* GAOLER's *feet.*)
Oh, love ...

FIVE

BECKER *in a stiff black dress which envelops her.* VIVIAN *enters, stares at her, ponders ...*

VIVIAN: Why do you put your legs in castles? (*Pause. She contemplates her.*) Your body is a poor thing in some ways I always think that body of hers belongs in a ditch I know you think it belongs in a ballroom but I see it as a few sticks by the road
Get along to confession (*She shakes with laughter.*)
It is the sort of dress they wear to plead in, isn't it, it creaks with apologies for life
Absolve me father I

VIVIAN *seizes* BECKER *fiercely and struggles with her, forcing*

372 *Howard Barker*

her backwards in a repulsive dance, releasing her as suddenly as she began, and shuddering.

VIVIAN: I don't criticize violence, I really don't, it has its —
   You dress like that as an affront (LILAH *and* SUSANNAH *enter.*)
   I rebuked her I hit her and if we don't kill her someone else will I've hurt my nose now this is what happens when four women live together like this and one of them is so utterly aloof and cold so cold detestably cold give me a handkerchief (*To* BECKER.) **Not you**
SUSANNAH: I haven't a handkerchief
VIVIAN (*taking* BECKER's *proffered handkerchief*): All right **oh, what a vile thing she has ironed it** everything about her is immaculate and **look at this it's for wiping your nose on** and she makes a treasure of it (*to* LILAH) does she enrage you **and starched it is actually starched** (*She blows her nose loudly. They watch her.*) No, this is more than I can stomach but at least I have sex I do have sex I am comfortable in my body with whom did you say with a number with a variety (*She smiles, holds out the handkerchief to* BECKER. BECKER *does not move to accept it.* VIVIAN's *arm remains outstretched.*)
   Take it
   Snot and
   Muck and
   Take it (*Pause*)
LILAH: It's bad manners to return a soiled —
VIVIAN: **I haven't any manners** (*Pause. She throws the handkerchief on the floor.*)
   I'm going to a lover
   The effect of my legs on this lover
   Imagine can you
   He witnesses my legs and
   Like a horse
   A horse
   In the hallway hardly have I entered and **Horse-like he** (*Pause. She goes to* BECKER.)
   I think you are a bully because you cannot love a man . . .
BECKER: Yes . . .
VIVIAN: Yes. That is what makes you a bully. And it appears, to others, I am the bully . . . (*Pause*)
BECKER: Nothing could be further from the truth.

TEN DILEMMAS   373

VIVIAN: She knows ... (VIVIAN *leaves smartly.* SUSANNAH *picks up the handkerchief.*)

SUSANNAH: Shall I wash it or —

BECKER: Yes, wash it.

SUSANNAH: And iron it, obviously —

BECKER: Yes. (SUSANNAH *goes out, and immediately returns.*)

SUSANNAH: **I cannot bear to see you wasted**
               I cannot bear it
               Your blood is pumping in your veins
               Your belly is
               I've seen it
               Tight with fecundity
               And you rot

BECKER: Does it anger you, that I rot? (*Pause*)
               Listen, once I thought **Oh the things I thought of such simplicity**
               I mean the torrents of fictitious
               The paintings
               I was always in the galleries
               He met me in a gallery
               It started in a gallery
               Where else I was the habituee
               Could I be met but under
               Particularly the Quattrocento
               Under frames of such relentless life
               I had my models
               Oh, so many models
               Even learned the gestures yes the very gestures (*She demonstrates them with one hand.*)
               Annunciation
               Crucifixion
               Deposition
               Grief
               Abandon
               Yes oh yes I was a girl did you not know I was a girl

SUSANNAH: Yes

BECKER: Oh, girl I was and fucked with boys but very girlishly

SUSANNAH: I don't know what that is

BECKER: **Do I speak a foreign language then?**
               And laughed a lot

SUSANNAH: I remember your laughter

BECKER: Yes and that was a bargain

374   *Howard Barker*

SUSANNAH: I liked your laughter when you laughed I thought I
do so understand my brother's adoration of her

A bargain how can laughter be a bargain you say
such things as if deliberately to and I'm not innocent to break us
down you refuse to live not that I live not that we live here much
we are not exemplary but (*Pause*)

I'll iron the handkerchief (*Pause*)
A bargain with whom!
BECKER: Men (*Pause*. SUSANNAH *turns to go.*)

I like you, Susannah (SUSANNAH *stops.*)
By which I mean
Oh, what do I mean? (*She smiles.* SUSANNAH *goes
out.*)
I mean
I've ceased to be
And yet not yet become
I bleed
I bleed

BECKER *folds, swiftly, like a stool. She sits on the floor in the
creaking dress. She closes her eyes.* SHARP *enters, watches her.*

SHARP: I'm what's called a good man. Do you hold me in con-
tempt?
BECKER: Yes. (*Pause*)
SHARP: I can endure that . . .
BECKER: Endure it why should you . . . ?
SHARP: Endure it and turn indifference into need . . . (*Pause*)
BECKER: You ask so little
I do find that touching
The littleness of your ambition
I say touching I am being kind
Uncharacteristically kind
Oh
Oh dear
Even the man I loved I was sarcastic with
And he went white
The veins stood out
SHARP: Shut up
BECKER: **He trembled and**
SHARP: Shut up I said (*Long pause.*) He will be back, of course
. . . for quite a long time I thought he will die in gaol . . . of
cholera . . . and then I heard . . . the gaol had been visited five

TEN DILEMMAS

times by cholera and he was ... he still ... he has learned to live without water ... it appears ... (*Pause. She bursts out laughing, and stops. A sound. The* SERVANT, *naked but for his wig, is discovered trembling in the doorway. The sound grows in volume, to the accompaniment of voices.*)

CHORUS (off): **We so**
We so want the reign of placidity
We so abhor this everlasting alteration
In our habits and
The redundancy of badges
The coinage
The sauce bottles
Even Christ is renovated like a house

BECKER: Oh, his pathetic loyalty ... he senses you and I are making love ... (*To the* SERVANT.)

It is not love ... ! (*The* SERVANT *shakes his head.*)
And he is sick ...
Not love I promise you ... ! (SHARP *slaps* BECKER *hard. She reels. She recovers. She goes to the* SERVANT.)
He knows ...
He knows ...
This is ... mere ... imitation ... (*She holds the* SERVANT *in her arms.*) Necessary, no doubt ... ! Necessary ... ! For my health ... ! And anyway, let us not forget love has its forms, its histories, why not! If costumes change, if empires change, the shape of love, that also must submit ... ! It stands to reason what constituted love under the Romans now we would not recognize! (*She turns brutally to* SHARP.)
I fuck badly
Really
I hardly can be said to fuck at all (*To the* SERVANT.)
But perhaps he is not interested in that!
Perhaps that is too coarse an instinct! (SHARP *moves.*)
Don't take me away from my servant (*She caresses the* SERVANT.)
Take off your wig ... (*She removes it, kissing his bald head.*)
Nothing I do is ridiculous
To this man nothing I do is ridiculous
That alone is the justification of service
He looks at me completely without opinion
Judgement?

376   *Howard Barker*

         Judgement? (*She kisses his head.*)
         What is that? (*She gets up.*)
         Don't kill him, will you? (*She starts to go.*)
SHARP: Get the skirt off and go into your room.
         Sit in your underclothes and wait. (*Pause, then* BECKER
laughs brightly.)
BECKER: But can't I rot? Why can't I rot? Everybody wants to
rescue me! (*To the* SERVANT.) Not you, of course, you under-
stand! You have the infallible insight of **take my clothes off
what do you think you'll find?** (*The* SISTERS *enter, watch.*)
What does he think I am? A dark continent? (*She looks from one
to the other.*)
             My lover is in gaol!
             I have a lover thank you but he is in gaol!
VIVIAN: Do as he says, Paula.
BECKER: I'd love to, oh, I am very very, my whole nature inclines
me to compliance but the fact remains
SUSANNAH: Paula . . .
BECKER: I'm so to speak, reserved, not even reserved but incon-
trovertibly . . . (*Pause. She looks to the* SISTERS.) Are you . . .
his . . . (*She makes a gesture of emptiness, despair and resignation.*) Not allowed to rot . . . (*She examines her own gesture,
from hand to hand.*) Garden of Gethsemene . . . (*She goes out.
Pause. Then* SUSANNAH, *cheerfully, runs after her.*)
SUSANNAH: I'll unzip!

                              SIX

The SERVANT *alone, still naked on his knees.* DRAPER *enters,
with a tunic of an imperial army. He drapes it carefully over the
naked man.*

DRAPER: So many men have worn this so many poor and grovelling minds which is perhaps why I revere it so I like the lies of
life I love the falsities and masquerades it is so pitifully abused
so rinsed in laughter no one now would be seen dead in it least
of all dead perhaps but me I was a gifted officer remember and
in battle possibly my apotheosis rather brief apotheosis admittedly even Paula was abolished **not for long however** remember I

TEN DILEMMAS   377

was decorated for my part and the medal was a thing of tin they had run out of silver or the profiteers had filched it it was **tin** but still I swelled still I thrived **tin so what** and him who pinned it on me was half an idiot **so what** the diseased nephew of an emperor **so what** I am not critical though who can deny the dynasty was poor and they had been executioners once look at their portraits . . . ! (*Pause. He goes to a chair and sits. He lights a cigarette.*) Third week . . . And all the ancient habits come like vagrants to the door . . .

    I also drink . . .

    I who was so fine in gaol submit without a protest to . . . demeaning vices of all sorts . . . (*Pause*)

    The question is how much of the truth will you reveal? (*The* SERVANT *shrugs.*)

    I shan't hesitate to torture you but even then the very phrasing of confession might mislead me . . . !

SERVANT: No need, I love you . . .

DRAPER: Yes, you love me but what has that to do with it? You might tell monstrous lies from love when honesty would be a mark of common contempt, anyway it is not honesty I require rather it's — (*Pause*) Pain. (*Pause*) Are you up to that? You had an education of considerable complexity, foreign universities and the like but I don't think of you as particularly —

SERVANT: I'll try —

DRAPER: Gifted —

SERVANT: I'll try —

DRAPER: In speech . . .

SERVANT: Master, I said I'd —

DRAPER: Yes, yes, you'll try . . . (*Pause.* BECKER *enters and sits silently on a chair.*) For example, her cry came, did it? How was that? (*Pause*) And his? Bellow, was it? (*Pause*) You look at me as if deciphering my needs, no ignore my needs, it is the truth I require, the truth will be perfectly intolerable on its own, perfectly savage on its own, already its teeth are in my bowel, yes, yes, I require this cigarette as men horribly maimed on stretchers do, I've seen it, yes —

SERVANT: **She did yes**

DRAPER: She did, what, often or —

SERVANT: **Over and over**

DRAPER: Loudly or a whimper, some women are not —

SERVANT: **Loudly**

DRAPER: Vociferous —

SERVANT: **Loudly, yes** —

DRAPER: And woke the house? How loud? And always loud, or sometimes not?

SERVANT: **Always loudly**

DRAPER: Always?

SERVANT: **Horrid like a birth** ... (*Pause.* DRAPER *gets up, and walks, contemplatively, stops.*)

DRAPER: Nightly, was this?

SERVANT: Oh, yes, and in the afternoons ... (*He walks again, stops.*) I felt ... merely in the exercise of my duties ... an embarrassment ... except ... they were not embarassed ... You could — stumble on them — anywhere ...

DRAPER: **Anywhere!** (*He looks at the* SERVANT.) What — how — him on top — or —

SERVANT: Not always —

DRAPER: Not invariably —

SERVANT: No, all sorts of —

DRAPER: **No list them do not say all sorts what use is it to me to say all sorts am I expected to imagine for seven years I have imagined**
    Forgive me
    Forgive me
    How I reward love
    How badly I reward it
    Do go on (*Pause*)

SERVANT: Sometimes she mounted him, and sometimes they were standing, and on one occasion —

DRAPER: Where —

SERVANT: Which —

DRAPER: This one occasion you are about to —

SERVANT: In the garden —

DRAPER: **The garden is enormous the garden is extravagant**
    At least it was (*Pause*)
    In its dimensions ... scandalous ... (*Pause*)

SERVANT: Against the summerhouse which is —

DRAPER: Which summerhouse?

SERVANT: Beside what was the tennis court he lifted her and —

DRAPER: Shh! (*Pause. He contemplates it.*)
    I must go there, obviously ...

SERVANT: It's fallen down since —

DRAPER: **To where the timbers lie, then!** (*Pause*)

SERVANT: Yes ... (*Pause*)

DRAPER: And like a pedant, kneel ... the archaeologist of her ... ecstasies ... (*He crumbles, wrapping himself in his hands, fold-*

TEN DILEMMAS

ing his legs, becoming a ball of pain, slowly turning on the floor. Long pause. BECKER *enters.*)

BECKER: It's nothing
Nothing
Nothing
It's nothing
Nothing
To be fucked
I

Learned more looking in your eyes I grew more in your glances and your voice oh your voice it was such a caress no I'm banal I'm ordinary God help me I am ordinary when I so require to be (*She stops.*)

Oh, believe me I am immune to pleasure... (*She laughs, bitterly. The laugh is lost in a cacophony of whispers. A* CROWD *enters and distributes itself about the stage, an audience anticipating.* DRAPER *springs to his feet.*)

DRAPER: Shh!

Your inane comments notwithstanding I

Your irritations in the bowel and skin diseases I insist you cease attending to!

Shh!

No scratching!

Yes I know the aristocracy is dead

I rely entirely on my character

Have you been in gaol

You have?

But poorly poorly

Few know the virtues of experience

That also is a gift of nature

I was your master now you must appreciate my life

instead

Isn't that democracy?

I was your landlord now you must adore me

For my poverty

Yes

And stop whispering you will miss a word

My poverty will move you

My poverty will bring tears to your eyes

You love me to be poor

But also I am (*He laughs.*)

Yes (*He laughs again.*)

Yes

380 *Howard Barker*

Don't look away this is my beauty
You will cringe of course
And wish you had refused my invitation but
Too late too late
To watch another's pain is not contemptible
To stare
No not at all
Do stare
Do lick
The long tongue of a decent curiosity
I applaud it
Impotent
And always was with her (*A long pause. The* CROWD
is very still. He sits in the chair.)
I am so tired of my secrets and have asked you here to
prod among the remnants of my character . . .
Walk through . . . as if it were a house . . . and pick up
this or that . . . examine it . . . (*The* CROWD *are still.*)
Go on then walk in me . . . (*They sway slightly, like
grass in a breeze. A dog barks distantly.*)

BECKER: I want to talk of love —
DRAPER: Not now —
BECKER: Yes —
DRAPER: **Not now they're thinking**
BECKER: I have to —
DRAPER: Shh! (*Pause. He tips back his head.*)
They're pitying me . . .
They . . . of such . . . ineradicable banality . . . are pity-
ing me . . . (ONE OF THE CROWD *comes forward and kneels
before* DRAPER, *placing a hand on him.*)
I was once . . . capable . . . but that was hatred . . . (*He
looks into the eyes of the* MAN.)
You know . . . hatred . . . do you?
In between a woman's legs . . . ? (*The* MAN *shakes his
head.*)
You do!
You do! (*He stands up, swiftly.*)
My fault is this — if I have a fault — and possibly I
have no faults — we must take seriously the possibility I have
none — **only a fool ridicules the possibility** — yes, this fault
might be — my clarity . . . which comes . . . which grows more
dazzling in the solitude of the penal cell . . . for clarity makes us
. . . **vicious!** Yes, we bite, we savage, oh, we **maim** the fondly

TEN DILEMMAS

cherished virtues of the civic life (*He turns on the kneeling* MAN.)

Hypocrite!

No, no, I deny myself the pleasures of accusation and as for indignation

None

That I

Retched out

Long ago

I killed two strangers to deny myself the sight of her

Why not kill yourself, you say

That idea I entertained but suicide is not amenable to me

Or her kill her you say

That idea I entertained but murder of a loved one?

Even I have principles (*He stops, he hangs his head. Pause.*)

Help me, I must enter her body, help . . .

You illiterate and mundane witnesses . . . help . . . (*The* CROWD *studies him. An* OLD WOMAN *goes to him. She takes his head in her arms.*)

WOMAN: Idiot . . .

DRAPER: Am I?

WOMAN: Oh, idiot . . .

DRAPER: Abuse away . . .

WOMAN: All this pain and still . . .

DRAPER: Yes . . .

WOMAN: All this misery for . . .

DRAPER: Yes . . .

WOMAN: For what dogs do . . . (*Pause. He straightens from her hands. He considers. He is patient.*)

DRAPER: No . . . oh, no . . . it is not what dogs do . . . (*Pause. In the silence,* SHARP *enters. He goes to* BECKER, *and unopposed, lifts her clothes and takes her from behind. She yields to a pleasure. Pause. The* CROWD *laughs, as if with relief, and applauds.*)

BECKER (*to* DRAPER): That was for you! (*They applaud further.*)

For you! (*They laugh with the condescending kindness of wedding guests. She turns on them.*) Shut up . . .! Or I will slit your throats! (*They laugh again, and in a plethora of frothing conversation, withdraw. Pause.*)

DRAPER: His fluid . . . travels . . . down your thigh . . . (*Pause*)

382 *Howard Barker*

BECKER: Your fluid ... (*She looks boldly at* SHARP, *then to* DRAPER) **Yours**.

DRAPER *covers his face with his hands.* SHARP *looks over the landscape. The* SERVANT *is still, gazing at the floor. They endure their positions, agonized, for an inordinate length of time.* BECKER *at last makes a gesture towards* DRAPER, *of pure longing.*

DRAPER: Yes ... (*Her hands fall.*)
BECKER: You're not alone ... you're not — **unless you wish to be unless you need to be unless you** truthfully you make this man this honest and banal and masculine object of contempt you make him necessary to me **I who match and partner every aspect of your soul** you make him **oh God help me** indispensable (*Pause*) which is sufficient for him ... which is the object of his life ... (*She laughs, pathetically.*) He says so ... (*She shakes her head.*)

SEVEN

The SERVANT *is alone in a field of light. He is watching an event offstage. He turns away.* VIVIAN *enters. She looks at him.*

VIVIAN: I'm not young any more and he was — (*Pause*) How quickly he came ...! For which he apologized ...! I said apologies were inappropriate in love, the thing is so finely balanced, after all, between — (*She seizes, as if choked. Shooting is heard, distant, staccato. The* SERVANT *watches* VIVIAN *without assisting her.* DRAPER *enters with* SUSANNAH, *carrying a picnic basket.*)
DRAPER: This is the viewpoint! From this eminence all can be witnessed at negligible risk!
VIVIAN (*recovering*): **As if willpower had anything to do with it!** (*She laughs.*) He was so young! He said the spectacle of my belly so moved him he (*Pause*) Not very perfect belly ... (*Pause*)
SUSANNAH: Our brother is so happy today ...! Why, we don't know, but his happiness is infectious. Even I am happy, and I'm rarely happy as you know ...

TEN DILEMMAS

VIVIAN (*to* DRAPER): Why are you wearing dark glasses?

DRAPER: Soon the wounded will begin to trickle in. You will experience ambiguous feelings, of pity and disgust. I advise you against pity, it will wear you out, it will leave you wringing like a rag . . .

VIVIAN (*looking at herself*): My belly is too big . . .

DRAPER: **Who cares if the world is heaving?**

VIVIAN: Too big according to whom, however? Some silly magazine?

DRAPER: **Who cares if the world is suppurating?**

VIVIAN: Do you seriously believe the prejudice of some fashion editor will suffocate my life? **I refute it!**

SUSANNAH: Yes.

VIVIAN (*to* DRAPER): You always hated people in dark glasses . . .

DRAPER: **And disease**
And malnutrition
And the collapse of cities from geological faults

(*Fusillades off. The* SERVANT *goes to* DRAPER *and holds his head.* DRAPER *sings.*)

> The separation of the limbs
> And flesh disposed about the street
> Only inspires comedy
> The train has fallen from the bridge
> And lies in turbulent water
> So
> So
> The burning hospital incinerates the sick
> Drink
> Drink
> To eyes that are smiling on me! (*He becomes calm.*)

If Christ comes, it must be me who puts his hand into his side . . . (*He turns.*) Do you agree? It must be me?

SUSANNAH: Yes.

DRAPER: Only I have the courage. (BECKER *enters.*) **Who said you could attend?**

BECKER: I thought I might be helpful.

DRAPER: To whom? Helpful to whom? Oh, let's not quarrel, **what possible help can you be?**

BECKER: Someone might appreciate my —

DRAPER: **What, your what?** (*She shakes her head. He stares at her. He indicates the battlefield with a hand.*)
Pain.

Conviction.

Pain. (*He laughs out loud, stops.*)

Let's not quarrel —

BECKER: I wasn't —

DRAPER: Let's not —

Let's not —

BECKER: Quarrelling . . . (*They look deeply into one another.*)

DRAPER: The world will force us apart . . .

BECKER: I know . . .

DRAPER: If we permit it . . .

BECKER: Yes . . .

DRAPER: **It wants to get in and**

BECKER: Yes . . .

DRAPER: **Drown our intimacy with its noise** (*He jumps up.*) What's happening over there? My eyes are so poor since I was gaoled the darkness spoiled them though I liked the darkness damage obviously was done describe please somebody narrate **with passion however I do not like the facts** no make it live in the memory the facts alone the facts without the gilded mirrors of prejudice what use are they? I walk in prejudice like a Renaissance prince down corridors of shimmering acquisition, Paula do it, you have the vocabulary to make death ring in the ears **I want to fuck with Paula but I am happier with farm women what's the explanation what mean humour of the bowel and blood does that I ask you** not however expecting an answer **our nights you could not imagine the contest or the despair** could they? This lot? Could they? The weeping in the dark, the words cascading to the floor, the sheets in revolution, **even the sheets wept to hear us** sheets can be sympathetic they do not always scratch the flesh perhaps they hate the easy lovers perhaps they are discriminating and bind us in their arms as we lie like slain children under the moon **oh, what our bed has witnessed I would not heap you with you could not bear it I promise you your soul would burst with pity**

However I

However

However

Keep your facile copulations (*Pause*) Paula, the battlefield, please . . . (*Pause*)

BECKER: They . . . (*Pause*)

They . . . (*Pause*)

Absurdly . . . (*Pause*)

No!

TEN DILEMMAS

385

No, you see always I describe things as absurd, when —

VIVIAN: That's true, Paula does —

BECKER: I do, you've noticed it —

VIVIAN: Yes —

BECKER: When so many aspects of behaviour are absurd **if not all of them** it's obvious I use the concept of absurdity as something to shelter behind **how does it help to say we are absurd** no, they are not absurdly anything, they are walking in lines towards their certain extinction and some of them are singing, no, there is nothing whatsoever absurd in that **I do similar things at night with you**, and waving flags, no, I rather approve of it, it has a certain fascination — now they are falling down, exactly as I predicted! **All of them!** Not just a few, but all! The fire is withering! And unceasing even though the dead are dead, they twitch, they bounce like puppets, possibly because the bullets stir them into a parody of life! Am I describing it well? I am inspired! And now the opposite is happening, the soldiers in the purple coats are — yes — oh, God! Doing exactly the same thing and it is not absurd, no, **I defy you to call it absurd**, marching over the bodies of the greencoats towards such a withering fire!

DRAPER: Don't repeat withering —

BECKER: Did I say withering?

DRAPER: Of the first army, you said their fire was withering —

BECKER: It was! And this is withering too, but let me find a better word —

DRAPER: Please —

BECKER: **Ferocious** —

DRAPER: Yes —

BECKER: Ferocious — that's what it is — and they are undeterred — they carry on, their weapons glinting in the sun —

DRAPER: I can see that —

BECKER: And blowing bugles —

DRAPER: And hear that also —

BECKER: Which the first lot didn't do, they had no bugles, but I cannot say this bugle blowing is any more effective than their singing was **down go the flags** they dip, they sink like masts on stricken vessels —

DRAPER: Good —

BECKER: Yes, and it's true, the standard bearers it appears are first to die — **the last one's gone!** (SHARP *enters, slowly.*) And now they — oh, dear — they are — it seems they are entertaining thoughts of — oh, dear — they lack the resolution of the first

386   *Howard Barker*

army and some are — lots are — it's infectious — running back
**but that is equally absurd because they merely are presenting
their backs!** (*She bursts out laughing.*) I don't mean absurd!
Absolutely not absurd!

SHARP: Shh, now . . .

BECKER: They are tumbling, whole rows like dolls pushed off the
nursery shelf!

DRAPER: Yes! Good!

BECKER: As if —

SHARP: Shh, now . . .

BECKER: A petulant child had swept the contents of — her cup-
board with a —

SHARP: Paula —

BECKER: A —

SHARP: Paula —

BECKER: Shut up — (*Pause*)
         I've lost my concentration now —
         A — (*Pause*)

DRAPER: Callous arm . . . (*Pause*)

BECKER: Yes . . . not bad . . . I . . . not bad . . . (*Pause*)

SHARP: It's you who is the petulant child, I think. Go back to the
house, now . . . (*Pause*) I am going down to help the wounded . . .

BECKER: **But that's absurd.** (*She laughs, shakes her head.*
SHARP *goes to her and slaps her face. Pause.*)

SHARP (*to the* SISTERS): Give me your skirts for bandages . . .

DRAPER: Do no such thing. (*He looks at* SHARP.)

SHARP: They must have bandages . . .

DRAPER: Must?

SHARP: Have bandages, yes —

DRAPER: Must? (*Pause.* SHARP *goes to* DRAPER.)

SHARP: Were you always — so unhappy — so terribly unhappy
— as this? (*Pause.* DRAPER *stares ahead.*)

BECKER: Oh, you mundane man . . . you firm-muscled and fine-
looking . . . mundane man . . . take me and fuck me somewhere . . .

SHARP: I want — (*Pause*) bandages . . .

DRAPER: **You don't want bandages you want oblivion**
(BECKER *laughs.*) Go down, bind up their wounds, carry them
on your back to the widows in the villages —

SHARP: If Christ came here —

DRAPER: He would choose me to speak to. He would pick out me
for company . . . (*Pause. Suddenly* SHARP *seizes the hem of*
BECKER's *dress and tears it violently, ripping it. She does not
resist him. He goes off.* SUSANNAH *watches.*)

TEN DILEMMAS

387

SUSANNAH: I must go, too!

SUSANNAH *runs off, after him.* DRAPER *removes his dark glasses, and cleans them with a handkerchief. Suddenly, he tosses them to the floor and rising to his feet, seizes* BECKER *in his arms and covers her face with kisses. They stagger, weeping together, clasping one another's heads in their hands. The* SERVANT *cautiously picks up the dark glasses, and restores them to a case. The lights sink.*

EIGHT

DRAPER *alone with a ragged book.* LILAH *enters. Pause.*

DRAPER: You have come to interpret Paula! My favourite sister, how you love me! How you long to compensate me for my pain! (*Pause*) I call you my favourite. Susannah is my favourite. But I'm not stable. At this moment Susannah is usurped. It could be your skirt. Or the weather. No, it's you today . . . (*Pause*)
LILAH: The man. (*Pause*)
       The other. (*Pause*)
      Fucks with his eyes closed. (*A long pause.*)
DRAPER: I kept this diary, every day, what could be more fatuous, I was not even susceptible to visions, hunger, thirst, no, nothing stimulated visions yet I wrote this book day in day out, it is the pathos of all incarceration **only her name however just the word** although the writing changes, in the summer months it is spidery and in the winter, for some reason, rather bold, look — (*He extends it.*)
LILAH: His eyes . . . are closed . . . (*Pause*)
DRAPER: And the ink . . . that is . . . never twice the same . . . (*Pause. He struggles with his curiosity.*) I did use blood! Not to dramatize myself, no not to glamorize the text, but . . . (*Pause*)
LILAH: I love you, so I tell you things. Me, the coarse and brutal —
DRAPER: Don't say that —
LILAH: Yes —
DRAPER: Don't humiliate yourself —
LILAH: The strong and frequently indelicate — (DRAPER *shrugs.*)

Someone must express the inexpressible
Someone must
The burden falls on me
Why not
Why not me, after all
My sensibilities were kept for you, it seems, but the instincts I got full measure of, dear brother she is impossible to love. (*Pause. She shrugs.*) Some are. (*Pause. He looks at her.*)

DRAPER: You cannot know how hard I wished her dead . . . wars . . . accidents . . . plagues . . .

LILAH: We had them all . . .

DRAPER: You had them, yes . . . closes his eyes does he . . . Thank you, thank you, closes them to hide from her —

LILAH: Yes —

DRAPER: I never did, not once —

LILAH: You never did —

DRAPER: He hides from her and yet . . . (*He smiles.*) Enters her . . . which I never did . . . (*He is thoughtful, silent.*) Is this to compensate me I do think you is this supposed to lend me joy these small intelligences brought to me wrapped like a toy I wrote her name four thousand times in my own blood no not to impress you no it was the ink shortage I don't criticize the prison they had difficulties with supplies and why should I have taken precedence after all my diary was monotonous not literature not art I found it hard to make a case for stationery let alone the ink (*He goes close to her.*)

How does it help me to know that . . . ? (*Pause*)

Lilah . . . how does it help . . . ? (*He clings to her.*)

LILAH: Oh, my dear . . . (*The* SERVANT *has entered and waits.* LILAH *observes him,* DRAPER *does not.*)

DRAPER: If I can't enter her . . . I can't live . . .

LILAH: Yes . . .

DRAPER: Absurd act done by animals by snails . . .

LILAH: Yes . . .

DRAPER: Let me be an animal! Let me be a snail . . .

LILAH: She prevents you . . .

DRAPER: Does she? How? It is a bridge between our pain how does she prevent me? She longs for me how?

LILAH: Shh . . .

DRAPER: You know . . . you know and you don't say . . .

LILAH: Because she hates herself too much . . . and you do not hate her . . . sufficiently . . . (*Pause. He looks into her.*) You see, he closes his eyes . . . (*He kneels, holding her about the waist.*)

TEN DILEMMAS 389

DRAPER: I saw her and it was like being wounded . . . I was wounded once . . . remember . . .

LILAH: Yes . . .

DRAPER: And it has never healed . . .

LILAH: Yes . . .

DRAPER: **She is me. I collided with myself** . . . (*He heaves with a spasm of despair, and buries his face in* LILAH's *clothes. the* SERVANT *goes to leave but he is heard.*) Who's that? (*The* SERVANT *stops.*)

SERVANT: Me, Master . . . (*Pause.* DRAPER *gets up. Pause.*)

DRAPER: I thrash you.

SERVANT: Yes . . .

DRAPER: You know why . . . ?

SERVANT: I think so, yes . . .

DRAPER (*going to him*): And you . . . so greatly cultivated . . . understand . . . ?

SERVANT: Yes . . . (DRAPER *flings down the* SERVANT, *scattering his tray and wig. The* SERVANT *falls.* DRAPER *rains kicks on him.*)

DRAPER: I thrash him! I thrash him! (*The* SERVANT *cries loudly.* DRAPER *stops. The* SERVANT *stirs.* DRAPER *picks up the tray and returns it to him.*) When you recall today, you will remember — what?

SERVANT: The thrashing . . .

DRAPER: Yes . . .

SERVANT: Only the thrashing . . . (*The* SERVANT *bows, goes out. He passes* BECKER, *entering.*)

BECKER: Why did you smack his face? (*Pause.* LILAH *leaves the room.*) I don't criticize! (*She sits.*) Let him leave if he. . . . (*Pause*) Well, of course he can't . . . because he loves you . . . and so do I . . .

BECKER *sees the diary on the floor. She picks it up. She leafs through it. She laughs. She stares at* DRAPER. *They look. The book slips off her lap onto the floor. They look. Her hands involuntarily form the gesture of the Annunciation. There is a roar of laughter off stage and animated conversation.* DRAPER *jumps to his feet as a* PARTY OF GUESTS *enters, clad for the summer outdoors.* SUSANNAH *among them.*

DRAPER: I entertain you! I entertain you! I who have not stood in daylight for seven years advertize the resilience of the human animal **not any human animal not the common kind** but was

I not sustained I was I was sustained and by the very thing that murders me **don't say it hate to say it yes** in French perhaps in Latin I concede **not love no silly not l'amour** oh, stuff l'amour and my eyes grew weak confessedly these glasses are the sole sign of deterioration but sunlight I was never fond of rain yes it washed us yes and how we needed washing some of us **who died in the war then?** Nobody? (*The* GUESTS *are still. They grin silently.*) I built a summerhouse to make love in ... was there ever greater redundancy ... **and the revolution surely that** ... ? (*Pause. He claps his hands.*)

I sing now.

I sing the absence of apologies. (*A* GUEST *produces a mandolin. Applause.*)

SUSANNAH: Please, don't ...

DRAPER: Oh, my little sister fears I shall humiliate myself ...

SUSANNAH: I love you and ...

DRAPER: I am loved. I am. It is true, the extent of this love surprises even me who spent his life abolishing surprise, the surprised ever were ridiculous, no, I draw love as a silent star pulls moons into its orbit **do the moons protest I wonder** perhaps the heavens moan, I shall sing, please permit me ...

SUSANNAH: You are greater than any man I ever knew ...

DRAPER: Yes ... so don't fear for me ... (*He puts out his hand to her. She declines it. The* MUSICIAN *strums an introduction but* DRAPER *suddenly clasps his hands to his head. The music ceases.*) It is so hard to sing. ...

MUSICIAN: Yes ...

DRAPER: Oh, God, it is so hard to sing ... (*Pause. He indicates he should continue.*)

> I am an intimate of Death
> Her insolence I cannot criticize
> I am her ally and her lover
> She is more humorous than me
> And her lips are impossible to cover
> With my own mouth ...
>
> I am the confidant of Pain
> She strides the city faster than police
> We smoke into the deepest night
> She is more infantile than me
> And her uneven teeth are white
> From gnawing my shoulder ...

TEN DILEMMAS

Kiss me where kindness was
I have a place so red and growing bigger
In your body's echoing silence
I walk whole corridors of mirrors
I shall do the stranger violence
Or my own face disfigure.... (*Pause. The* PARTY *claps vehemently.*)

You are too kind! You are excessively appreciative! And what does it mean? I don't know...! (SUSANNAH *holds him in her arms.*)

SUSANNAH: She does this to you....

DRAPER: Someone does ... someone certainly....

SUSANNAH: The waste! The appalling waste...!

DRAPER (*seizing her cruelly*): **Of what. Of what am I so wasted from**...? (*She looks fearfully. He throws down her wrist. She smarts, tearfully.*)

BECKER: And I am also a singer! (*The* PARTY *approves vociferously.*)

I really am...

I am after all, trained at the piano, and could have been — oh, what I could have been but for several accidents! I won't go into details but rest assured I had if anything **too many choices** this happens this does happen to the gifted and bewildered we stagger into the darkness, being blinded by so many lights, it's true, you must take my word for it since your own experience is so poor by comparison...! (DRAPER *laughs.*) Play something...

DRAPER: How can you not love this woman? I ask you, how could you **keep back the torrent of love** for such a frail woman...? **I weep for her**...

BECKER (*to the* MANDOLIN PLAYER): Anything...! I'll put words to it! (*The* PARTY *applauds.*) **I can do that, too!** (*The* PLAYER *begins.* DRAPER *kisses* SUSANNAH, *who hangs her head.*)

Have you thought how she suffers
The beautiful woman
Have you sensed her shame?

Have you heard her weeping
The beautiful woman
At the sound of her name?

Have you thought how she dies
The beautiful woman
In an unclean room?

Trains pass her window
Full of workers
Not one of whom

Observes her blind is down
For the third day
Impossible that they

Should look up from a magazine
Pity the beautiful woman
Who is looked upon but never seen

(*The music stops. She looks round, defiantly.*)

Not true. None of it. (*She laughs. They look at one another.*)

SUSANNAH (*to* DRAPER): You come back . . . and you are still . . . the same . . . !

DRAPER: Yes . . .

SUSANNAH: What is the use of suffering if . . . what is the use of pain if . . . ?

DRAPER: The use of it . . . ? **The use of pain?** It has no use . . . it has no use . . . it merely . . . **exists** . . . Really . . . ! The pathos of it . . . as if we needed to be raised upon the ruins of our past . . . (BECKER *laughs at him, with him.*) And yes, the world, now, that does change! That does, doesn't it? (*Pause. He goes to a* MAN.) That does?

MAN: You're not the landlord any more . . .

DRAPER: I'm not the landlord, no! There is change for you, there is a ripping of the landscape, and your shoes have rubber soles . . . ! (*Pause. He seizes him in an embrace.*) You know I killed men . . .

MAN (*horrified*): Yes —

DRAPER: I don't boast —

MAN: No —

DRAPER: Why boast of something that came easily?

MAN: No —

DRAPER: So easily I was myself surprised —

MAN: Is that so?

DRAPER: Oh, so surprised — but don't tremble —

TEN DILEMMAS 393

MAN: Am I trembling?

DRAPER: Well, yes, you are, but — (*Pause. The* MANDOLIN PLAYER *picks out a tune.* DRAPER *listens.*) It won't occur again ... next time ... I shall myself be killed ... (SUSANNAH *weeps, desperately.* BECKER *goes to her, holds her. The* CROWD *becomes instantly vociferous and laughs, released into a fête.* DRAPER *spreads his arms.*)
>   Arcadia!
>   Arcadia!

SHARP *enters, workman-like from a field. He stops. He looks.* BECKER *stiffens, and this is observed by* DRAPER. *Casting a glance at* BECKER, SHARP *starts to leave again.*

DRAPER: It's all so — out of date! (SHARP *stops.*) Don't you think? (SHARP *shrugs.*) This triviality ... (SHARP *goes.*) I do detest the way he sets examples ... I do detest the ostentatious purity of his soul ...

BECKER: It's not pure ...

DRAPER (*turning to her*): Is it not? I rather hoped it was ...

BECKER: No. It's you who's pure ...

DRAPER *looks at her. The conviviality ceases.* DRAPER *falls to his knees. The lights dim as if for a storm. A cry comes over the fields.* SUSANNAH *covers* BECKER's *head with a scarf and draws her away. The* CROWD *also scatters. Only the book and the mandolin remain on stage.* DRAPER, *lying, stretches in the rain.*

NINE

The SISTERS *are seated in a dim light. After a long pause,* SHARP *enters. He takes a fourth chair. The chairs creak.*

LILAH: How we love our brother ... (*Pause*)
>   Too much some would say ... (*Pause*)
>   **I am the spokeswoman God knows why** some people elect themselves (*Pause*)
>   Is it because my body's strong? Always I stepped forward not wanting to but unable to endure the (*Pause*)

Silence (*Pause*)

And now it is a habit. I will change the habit but not yet . . . (*Pause*)

VIVIAN: We agreed by instinct. Not by argument. We did not arrive at anything, or initiate debates. It took so little, really no more than a look, to confirm what each of us had separately (*Pause*)

I say seperately but (*Pause*)

And then it seemed there was no possible alternative (*Pause*)

It required no (*Pause*)

Did it?

LILAH: None. And this could only be because we knew this **please Susannah please be strong** was no more nor less than what he **yes you can be strong I know you can** no more nor less than what he —

VIVIAN: Requires —

LILAH: That's not the word —

VIVIAN: That's not the word, no —

LILAH: There is a better word —

VIVIAN: Aspires to —

LILAH: Aspires, yes — (*To* SHARP.) You say something now . . . (SHARP *is silent*.)

Because his life is

I mean we cannot bear to watch

VIVIAN: Stand idly by —

LILAH: And watch this man deteriorate —

VIVIAN: Say something, will you?

LILAH: The horrific spectacle of a degenerating man we all of us adore —

VIVIAN: You speak —

LILAH: While she who should be in the fullest state of woman-hood is —

VIVIAN: The mother of perfect children —

LILAH: Is —

VIVIAN: Your children —

LILAH: Is — (SUSANNAH *breaks into sobs*.)

VIVIAN: Susannah agrees with this, she finds it hard but she agrees with this —

LILAH: Not in so many words —

VIVIAN: Because words were irrelevant —

LILAH: You speak now —

TEN DILEMMAS   395

VIVIAN: We looked at one another, in this room, one evening, and we knew . . .

LILAH: **Susannah even knew** —

VIVIAN: In fact Susannah I think Susannah if I recollect precisely was the —

LILAH: And she loves him more than any of us, isn't that true? (*Pause*) **Susannah? That is why she did so perfecfly** (*Pause*) Articulate . . . the need . . . (SHARP *is still as rock . . . so are the* WOMEN.)

SHARP: Very well, I'll kill him. (*He looks at them. Distant barking of dogs.*)

SUSANNAH: Vile word . . . (*Pause. She looks at the others.*)
            Isn't it . . .
            Vile? (SHARP *gets up, as if to go, stops.*)

SHARP: It isn't him you love . . .
            It's her you hate . . . (*Pause*)
            Still, I'll kill him . . . (DRAPER *enters, smiling.*)

DRAPER: I let the dogs out. **Dogs my one salvation**. No, it's silly, when we had four thousand acres I had no dogs and now it takes five to guard the turnips (*He laughs, hysterically.*)
            I exaggerate
            I do so need to exaggerate
            Five dogs indeed
            Really it is a spaniel . . . (*He looks at* SHARP.)
            I slept all night, my mouth against her belly, and her odours drifted in the forest of her hair, like smoke out of a bonfire . . . (*Pause*)
            Oh, the silence . . . (*Pause*)
            Gaol . . . ! (*Pause. He looks at the four of them.*)
            And more gaol . . . (*He goes near to* SHARP.) A thing that is not done, yet must be done . . . How could you know, the ecstasy of that never to be satisfied compulsion . . . ? (*To the* WOMEN) Or you . . . ? (*Pause*) No, it is immaculate . . . ask Paula . . .

VIVIAN: It's madness . . .

DRAPER: Is it? (*He is suddenly enlightened.*) **We really did offend, then** . . . ?

SHARP: Keep still —

DRAPER: Yes —

SHARP: And close your eyes —

DRAPER: No, that's what you do —

SHARP: All right, leave them open —

396   *Howard Barker*

DRAPER: The prostitutes, they tell you, close your eyes, why is
    that, I wonder, are they ashamed to be examined?
SHARP: I don't know, I don't go to prostitutes —
DRAPER: I did, I did often —
SHARP: Forgive me —
DRAPER: What for?
SHARP: Forgive me, that's all —
DRAPER: Of course I forgive you —
SHARP: I am doing this for Paula — (*He goes to move. The*
    SERVANT *enters.* DRAPER *turns, at bay.*)
DRAPER: Thank God you're here! (*He holds out his arms.*) The
    servant never fails! His master's pain flies to him like a bird!
    (*Pause*) They want me to die . . .
SERVANT: Yes . . . I know they do . . . (*Long pause*)
DRAPER: And you . . .
            Your . . .
            Attitude to this . . . ? (*Pause. He anticipates.*) The mas-
    ter asks his servant for opinion no that is decadence that's sheer
    (*Pause. He howls. The* SISTERS *smother their faces in their*
    hands. Pause.)
SERVANT: She
            Her
            Barrenness
            Is because of you . . .

The sound of a procession and carnival. DRAPER *listens to it. As*
SHARP *moves on him,* DRAPER *pre-empts him by drawing a blade*
from his own clothes. The procession grows louder. DRAPER *turns*
his back and goes as if to walk away from them, but stops, and by
an act of supreme will slashes his own throat. The blade falls to the
floor. DRAPER *does not fall.*

                              TEN

BECKER *is alone on stage.* LILAH *enters, dragging a sack.*

BECKER: I don't think it has ever been more lovely here I mean
    the colours last night the sky was indigo, the colour of a passport,
    the colour of a bank book, I never thought to see it so luminous

TEN DILEMMAS

so vivid the colour of a motor car **another grey hair this morning** and the smoke from chimneys rising vertically don't tell me what's in the sack, don't, Lilah, **don't** . . . ! (*Pause. She laughs.*) Another grey hair this morning, did I say? I resort to dye as cowards turn to whisky **and whisky too**, no, I need the compliments, I need the flattery, I can absorb unlimited amounts of flattery from yes from **scum of the earth** let alone the better sort from students, waiters, vagrants, louts, **why do I require it why I wonder** he hates me sitting there cross-legged he so detests it **not from jealousy** he thinks I have another self **what self however what** all right tip it out if you want to . . . (*Pause. LILAH leaves the sack, goes to a chair, lies in it.*)

LILAH: He loves you . . .

BECKER: Yes . . .

LILAH: He so loves you the word love is an offence to use . . .

BECKER: I know . . .

LILAH: He so very much loves you the word much is a mockery of meaning . . .

BECKER: I know that, too . . .

LILAH: My poor brother . . . (*She closes her eyes.*) He could have been . . . oh . . . a minister . . . a diplomat . . . we had the connections . . . he could have been . . . oh . . . a professor of languages . . . a writer of travel books . . . oh, so many dazzling roads he might have explored . . .

BECKER: He explores me . . . he governs me . . . he speaks my language . . . **I also am the universe** . . . what's in the bag, it's obviously for me . . .

LILAH: Obviously . . . ?

BECKER: Everything's for me that happens here . . .

LILAH: You believe that, don't you?

BECKER: Yes **if you don't open it I'll open it myself**

Yes

Yes

He taught me so **I am the entire world he said** he did not worship me no never worship he was not blind because he called me perfect

I am so possibly

Grey hairs notwithstanding

I am perfect and of course detestable I do so understand why I'm detestable and why therefore the sack contains a horror . . . (*Pause. LILAH looks at her, not unkindly.*)

LILAH: And you . . . oh, could have been . . . a surgeon or a novelist . . . (*Pause. BECKER stares at her.*)

398   *Howard Barker*

BECKER: Oh, you have killed the man who fucks me and these
   are his bits . . . ! (LILAH *just looks.*) You've waylaid him and . . .
   dismembered him . . . (*Pause*) What is it, the legs? (*Pause*) **I
   never loved his legs so where's the triumph I'm not hurt or
   face either never looked at it** (*Pause*) Or head I couldn't give a
   piss for for me in all mankind there is one head one mouth one
   pair of eyes the rest, no **chop away** it must have been hard work
   for women
                He fucked me all the time so what
                You are so base
                You are so literal
                To think his seizing of me
                His bringing me to breathlessness against the wall was
   anything but
                Stale routine
                Oh, my dear
                Oh, you make me feel a mother to you for your little
   mischiefs . . . (*She smiles.*) I'll look, shall I? Is that what you
   want? BECKER *shakes her head like a patient parent, and goes
   to the sack. She kneels. She opens the mouth of the sack, and
   looks inside. She is motionless for some seconds, then allows the
   sack to close. She lifts her hands in a gesture, studied, recol-
   lected, classical, invented. A dog barks distantly.* SHARP *enters,
   stands, observes the movement of* BECKER's *soul. He speaks at
   last.*

SHARP: What I have I hold . . . (SUSANNAH *runs in, as if waiting her moment. She embraces* BECKER.)
SUSANNAH: We do love you . . . !
                This surely shows our love for you . . . ! (VIVIAN
   enters, stands watching.)
VIVIAN: We put emotion on a shelf. We left it there, for a few
   hours. And in emotion's place we put **and I am emotional** judgement and now the thing's done **emotion come back, anger flood
   our veins at the world's —**
BECKER: Not the world's —
VIVIAN: **The world's appalling**
BECKER: **Not the world's.** (*Pause*)
                Listen, I am insane
                I shan't wash again
                Or comb my hair
                So speak all the bereaved but
                Stink

Bleed
So say all the bereaved
And drag some mad religion from my past
Or sit on pillars in the rain
Shh
Shh
Why tell you my plans
He never entered me but looked
You think you look
You never look
That penetrated me
That governed me
Look
Look
The word darling
The word
Will never pass my lips again
They all say that the bereaved!
Every lie is unintended I think sometimes
Every lie (*Pause. She climbs to her feet.*)
Thank you
Thank you
Well, it couldn't go on
Ten years is more than ample

Sometimes we must put ourselves in the hands of those the visionaries the practical the simply caring the realistic and

A fictional life is what I (*She puts her fingers to her lips as if to prevent the utterance. She beckons* SHARP *with a finger. He hesitates, then comes to her. She demonstrates with her hands, and with an impeccable gesture, kisses his cheek as one might a statue. Pause.*) Darling . . . !